Sharing
Mountain Recipes

The Muffin Lady's Everyday Favorites

From the very beginning, love is shared by the giving of foods. Different foods offer a sense of comfort, of tenderness and love. As we grow we develop likes and dislikes, favorites and extra-special favorite foods that stick with us throughout a lifetime. These foods are then passed along in the form of a written recipe, for the purpose of sharing the same mouth-watering, memorable flavors with future generations. These are the recipes that we grow up on, brighten our day, bring us together, speaks of love and fill the following pages. Many of the recipes and tips have been passed on and shared for years; some are trendier. All have been prepared high up on a mountain, but found to work just as well in lower elevations, including a block from a beach. A treasure box filled with everyday homemade foods ranging from Oatmeal Bread and Muffins to Stews and Puddings with a few Salad and Dinner recipes in-between.

Please note, that it is important to read the Tips and Suggestions, beginning on page vii as well as the instructions per recipe.

This book is published by:
The Muffin Lady Inc.
1532 Yankee Creek Road
Evergreen, Colorado 80439 USA

Original Copyright 2006, The Muffin Lady Incorporated

Library of Congress Control Number: 2006906920

For any questions concerning the preparation of any of the recipes in the following, please e-mail The Muffin Lady at: muffinchic@earthlink.net

ISBN# 0974500-2-8
ISBN# 0974500-2-8-97809745008-2-9

Printed in China by Artful Dragon Press

Front Cover: Red Chili, p. 200
Cheddar Muffins, p. 48
Back Cover: Cherry Almond Muffin, p. 52

$28.95

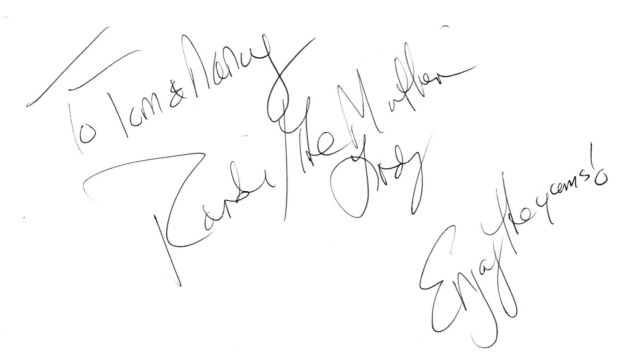

There is one extraordinary

ingredient that goes into everything that I cook

and bake. Please do not forget this ingredient,

for it is imperative to all recipes.

Whenever I am cooking or baking,

I add extra spoonfuls of Love

to all of my recipes.

Love added to all things good,

makes them just a little bit better.

The following pages

are dedicated in loving memory

to my

Grandmothers'

My Parents

and to all who enjoy the wholesome goodness

of everyday, homemade foods.

SMILE and ENJOY!

Table of Contents

Acknowledgments

All my love to: my **Great-Grandmother**, my Grandmothers, **Gert** and **Doe Levin,** and my **Mother**. Although you are not here anymore, I will never be able to thank you enough for teaching me how to cook, instilling in me the goodness of and an appreciation for homemade foods.

Arms of hugs and thank you's to the following: **Elizabeth Luciano, Rhonda Shank, Ann Kennedy, Aunt Lillian Gomberg, Aunt Gert Bohrer, Cookie Grabell, Patt Roscoe, Pat Congdon, Lizanne Holmes, Mary Littlewood, Bob Jackson, Carl Bowersox, Juanita Valdez, Kathleen Gebhardt, Corey Hiseler, Susan Doyle, Stephen Block, Brendan O'Farrell, Julie Bello, Christina Glassier, Larry Pilot, Cecil Unruh, Valerie Gleason** from Chef's Choice and **Carolyn Comandini;** for your smiles, friendship and immense generosity in sharing some of your own and your familys' recipes for publication in this cookbook.

Endless amounts of appreciation and admiration to my Editorial team: **Hassell Bradley Wright, Corey Hiseler, Rhonda Spellman** and **Cheryl Bezio-Gorham**. A special offer of thanks to **Betty Teller**, my Copy Editor, for taking this project on in such short notice. Your faith, smiles and professionalism helped make this cookbook what it is.

Kimberlee Lynch, my amazing Creative Designer; your patience, artistic ability, grace and expertise are treasures never to be forgotten.

I cannot thank **Craig Stein** and **Pamela Seaboldt** of Photo Express-It in Evergreen Colorado enough, for the time you both spent helping me pick and sort through the many photos brought to you to be processed. The two of you are shining stars and I am immensely grateful. To **Jon Sheppard**, a wonderful photographer, I thank you for your time, energy and assistance with a couple of the supplied photos.

Armfuls of respect and appreciation to **Lynne Olver**, editor The Food Timeline (www.thefoodtimeline.com). This site is invaluable for anyone who treasures the historical facts relative to foods, where they came from and how and when they were developed. A priceless site if ever there was one!

A basket of thank you flowers to **Dave, Linda** and staff at Sundance Gardens, Evergreen, Colorado for allowing me to rearrange your displays for the purpose of a photo, you guys are great!

To **Kevin Lilliheu, Chester Ridgeway, Maggie Weirman, Leonard Zemmel and Paul Wexler**. Without you and your incredible patience, skill and knowledge, I would not be here today to share. So I again, I thank you, my Doctors, with all my heart.

One last special note to **Elizabeth H. Luciano:** Girlfriend, I cannot thank you enough for the hours spent listening to these words and for being there when the times got hard. Your sisterly love, inspiration, and faith helped make this cookbook possible.

Introduction

This cookbook has been written for the purpose of sharing recipes that have been used and requested over and over again by my friends, family and customers. Some of the recipes within the following pages have been shared with me so that I may share with you. Many have been used for generations, and thus have been tested, tasted and found to be irresistible. Although written for use in high altitude, all of the recipes in these pages can and have been used in both high and low altitudes.

Many people have said or have come to believe that cooking and/or baking at high altitude is a complicated and tenacious process, when actually it is not that difficult. Within the following pages I will share basic tips illustrating just how easy it really is to cook and bake in higher elevations — anywhere else, for that matter. I am not a scientist, physicist or nutritionist, nor a certified culinary professional, I am simply one who loves to bake, cook and share my creations. My experience was not acquired in a culinary school, but rather in my grandmothers', mothers', and aunts' kitchens, as well as in an everyday kitchen located high above the ocean. With the tips and recipes in the following pages, my hope is that you will find that cooking or baking anywhere is not a stressful experience, but rather quite easy and enjoyable once you know what to do and you have a delicious variety of simple recipes to follow. You see, the ones who taught me about foods also taught me that foods, recipes and knowledge are for sharing, not for hoarding.

Have you ever noticed that when people get together, whether family, friends or both, it is usually around food? I have observed that food brings people together. Whether at the dinner table, a party, or just for an excuse of getting together with a friend. There are many kinds of scrumptious foods throughout the world today. Many of these foods, some of us may never taste, or better yet, be able to pronounce them, but they continue to be treasured in their homeland and bring comfort to those who devour them.

The enjoyment I get from playing around with recipes began as a little girl. I often went to my grandmother's, and she would pull out what appeared to be a magical metal box, full of folded up paper pieces and index cards. From this box she would pull out a page or card and then we would begin to make some of the most amazing treats one could imagine. To this day, I continue to believe that the treasures in this box have no end. I will be forever grateful to my grandmother, for she specifically instructed my father to send me this treasured metal recipe box upon her death. Once I received it, I had to figure out the means and ways of achieving the same looks and tastes in Colorado that I fondly remembered from her Philadelphia kitchen. It took a lot of trial and error, but I finally got the adjustments perfected.

I will be forever thankful to both of my grandmothers for they were some of the finest cooks I have ever known. Both not only taught me how to bake and cook, how to add an extra pinch of this and spoonful of that, they also taught me how to think about the foods I was preparing: how the dough should feel, how to dice veggies, how a roast should look, how to simmer delicious soups, etc. These were my first lessons in preparing foods and they have stuck with me and I use them daily.

I began baking professionally after being diagnosed with a rare and dreadful disease. I found it devastating because I had to discontinue my career as a Special Education Teacher and Counselor and literally had no idea what I was going to do for a living. However, while undergoing a second surgery, a small miracle occurred in my life; a good neighbor watched my babies: the dogs, the cats and a horse. Although taking care of them was relatively easy, it was time consuming and I greatly appreciated it and offered to pay her for her help. She refused any monetary payment, so I baked her up a batch of cookies. She enjoyed them so much she suggested that I market them, as well as several of my other baked goods that she had tasted and enjoyed.

So I searched my grandmother's recipe box, full of savored and cherished recipes, found a few more recipes to my liking and proceeded to make the high altitude adjustments, fill a basket up with fresh-baked treats and distribute them around my hometown of Evergreen, Colorado. The responses to this endeavor were amazing. Local people and businesses began asking for more, or if I could make this or that. An employee of the local Post Office began calling me The Muffin Lady each morning when I would arrive, so about a year later I went legal with this name and added a full commercial kitchen to my home.

Little did I know at the time that this act of sharing with a neighbor would take the shape of a small miracle and a whole new profession.

One day about a decade later, a friend called and suggested that I write a cookbook. My initial response was, *"I don't know how to write a cookbook, are you nuts?"* His response to this was that he had a client who had been editing cookbooks for almost 50 years. A few days later I met my editor, who was with a wonderful woman who would help me with the publishing aspect of my project. Both of these beautiful women have not just shared their knowledge with me, but have also become dear friends whom I feel lucky to have in my life, I thank the Lord for their patience, which has been pushed on too many occasions.

A few months went by, and lo and behold, I had written my first book, *Baking at High Altitude; The Muffin Lady's Old Fashioned Recipes*. The book responses have been much more exciting than I could have ever anticipated. The thank you and e-mails from customers and strangers have been astounding.

Amazingly, I have won two awards to date with this specific book. One was from the Colorado Independent Publishers Association; the second one was the absolute shock of my life. After receiving the CIPA Award, I searched for other cookbook contests and found one, so I entered the book with a prayer in the wind. Keep in mind that I had absolutely no idea what I was getting myself into, for I am just a mountain gal with a passion for cooking, baking and sharing foods. About a week later I received a call from a man I had yet to meet. He informed me that he liked my writing and that I should write more books. I told him that I wrote the book from my heart to share and that if everyone in the world began sharing again, the world would be a much better place! A few months went by, and then I received an e-mail message, simply but elegantly stating that, *"Baking at High Altitude* is the WINNER in the category of Best First Cookbook in English, USA,"* and would now compete at Grytthyttan Province in Orebro, Sweden in the category for Best First Cookbook in the World, 2004. Oh my, my, my!

So with many good wishes in hand and a heart full of hope, I boarded a jet to Sweden, and on February 11th, 2005 my book was announced Best First Cookbook in the World 2004 from Gourmand World Cookbook Awards.

That phone call and shocking e-mail, in alliance with the outstanding award and many customers' requests for more, were the inspiration to continue sharing treasured recipes. I find it amazing what your heart can do when you put it to work. Many of the following recipes have been shared with me to share with you. All were donated to me with laughter and friendship. I believe different people sharing a part of themselves makes for laughter, togetherness, patience, love, friendship, satisfaction, fun, and comfort! For me, that is what the tastes of memories are made of.

That small miracle that I referred to earlier was the act of sharing with a neighbor in times of need and look what came from it: more sharing.

General Cooking and Baking Tips

• For recipes that are lower in cholesterol and/or fat look for a ♥ next to the recipe title.

• For recipes that can be made with a sugar substitute, look for a **SUGAR** next to the recipe title.

• Many people have been known to add sugar, honey or molasses to **tomato** or **spicy sauces** to decrease the concurrent acidity. I myself do this. However, when one has special dietary needs, and cannot use sugar, 1 teaspoon of baking soda works just as well.

• There are several recipes in this book where a sugar-free product can be substituted for **white** or **brown sugar**. I prefer to use Twin or Splenda as my substitutes. The decision about what kind of substitute to use is up to you. Please take the time to consider that sugar substitutes have a tendency to be very sweet, so if you want to decrease the amount of your chosen substitute, do so by about 1 tablespoon per cup. Due to the fact that sugar adds moisture to baked products and decreases the acidity in some fruits and vegetables, decreasing the sugar more than suggested may create a sour sauce or a dry batter, resulting in a dry batch of treats.

• Always make sure that your **oven** is preheated to the designated temperature before cooking or baking anything unless specified otherwise.

• Although **cooking/baking times** are supplied, all ovens and ranges heat and cook differently, so the baking, cooking, simmering or roasting durations in my oven may be a few minutes different from yours. Always test a product before removing from the oven, pot or pan. You can taste, slice, or insert a clean knife or a toothpick into the center of a product and remove it carefully. For meats or poultry, make sure that the product is not raw or severely pink in the middle. For baked products, such as a cake, if there are several crumbs clinging to the knife or toothpick, or it comes out of the center very moist, this means that the product is not fully baked and needs a few more minutes in the oven.

• **To poach versus to steam:** Many times I have been asked what the difference is between poaching and steaming vegetables, eggs and fruits. The answer is simple, poaching means to cook something in a lightly simmering pot of water or liquid, whereas steaming is to cook something in a pot, bowl or pan above simmering or boiling water, such as in a double boiler.

• **To enhance the flavor when simmering sauces**, stews or soups that contain garlic, always rub down the sides of the pot/pan with garlic prior to adding ingredients.

• **When peeling the skin off an onion**, make sure to also remove the first layer of the onion. It tends to be tough, and will not be appealing in your product.

• **When handling fresh chilies like jalapeños** make sure to wear a pair of latex or plastic gloves, for the juice can burn your fingers and be very painful if it gets into any scrapes, cuts or bruises.

• Make sure that all **fresh vegetables, fruits, poultry, meats and seafood** are thoroughly washed in lukewarm water prior to using.

continued on next page

- **For all soups and stews** used in this book, you will know when your product has simmered enough when the meat/poultry begins to peel away from the bones. For example, when stew meat becomes soft, tender and simply falls apart, it has stewed sufficiently. For bean or vegetable soups and stews, you will know when it has completed simmering when the vegetables/beans become tender and easily pierced with a fork, but not mushy.

- **Soups** normally produce a layer of thickened fat on the top after cooling. To remove this layer of fat, use a slotted spoon and simply skim off the fat. However, if you are in a hurry and do not have the time for the soup to cool, remove as much fat as possible with a spoon, then use two clean paper towels to blot off the remaining fat from the top of the soup.

- **Roux:** A roux is made by mixing flour, fat and liquid and is used to thicken many soups, sauces and gravies. Usually roux is made slowly, heating of 2 tablespoons each of flour and fat, mixed to form a paste to which 1 cup of liquid is added, mixed in and heated until thickened. This is then added to the base of the desired product. For most white-toned, cream-based sauces and soups, you would want to use butter, but for most meat-based sauces and soups you will want to use the grease expressed from cooking meat (i.e., bacon or sausage fat/grease) for a browner roux. The beef fat/grease can be stored in the refrigerator or freezer for an extended period of time until used.

- Many of the following recipes call for **grated vegetables and/or cheese**. The easiest means to accomplish this is to use a food processor, with a grating wheel attached. I use this same mechanism for grinding nutmeats. If you find that there are still chunks of nutmeats remaining, pour all into a plastic baggie and using a hammer or other hard utensil, pound the nuts firmly until no more chunks remain. In many recipes, especially cookies, leaving any chunks in the nutmeats can compromise the results.

- **To julienne vegetables** means to cut them into little sticks or strips. The easiest means to do this is to first slice the vegetables lengthwise into ⅛-inch strips, and then cut these into 2–3-inch lengths.

- **Most recipes require a greased pan**. I have found that unflavored pan spray, butter or margarine work best when preparing a pan prior to adding a roast, casserole, batter or dough.

- **For all meats, poultry and seafood**, try not to allow the product to sit at room temperature for more than an hour. Allowing these foods to sit out in the open air for too long may compromise food safety and cause food poisoning. Additionally, make sure that when storing, the refrigerator temperature is between 38 and 44 degrees Fahrenheit or 7.22 degrees Celsius.

- The recipes in this book are to be prepared with an **electric mixer** unless specified otherwise.

- **When using brown sugar**, I suggest dark brown sugar, for it supplies a more seasoned flavor to fresh-cooked or baked products. If you only have light brown sugar on hand, add about 1 teaspoon of molasses per cup sugar to gain the dark brown sugar flavor. Always remember to lightly pack the brown sugar when measuring.

- **When a recipe calls for cocoa**, use Dutch or European processed cocoa. Simple store-bought processed cocoa is neither as dark nor as rich as these two types. European cocoa can be purchased in specialty and/or gourmet shops, and Dutch-processed cocoa is now available in many grocery stores.

- Whenever a recipe calls for **oats**, please use quick-cooking oats unless specified otherwise. Old-fashioned oats have a tendency to absorb more moisture in a baked product when compared to quick-cooking oats.

- **To toast nuts and seeds**, use butter or margarine to coat a cookie sheet or small pan. Sprinkle the nuts all over the sheet, leveling into them a single layer and bake at a 375° F for 1-3 minutes, not any longer. Many seeds only require about 50-60 seconds, so be careful of burning.

- Unless specified otherwise, always have **butter, margarine or cream cheese** softened and at room temperature prior to using.

- Always wash **fresh produce** with lukewarm water, not hot or cold.

- I have found that using **canola or safflower oil** in some of the recipes is best for your health. These oils help keep treats moist, and are lower in fat and cholesterol than solid shortenings. Additionally, these ingredients may be substituted for melted margarine and/or butter in most recipes and the taste does not change.

- In all recipes that call for **butter or margarine**, always scrape the excess shortening off the wrapping with a rubber/plastic spatula to ensure adding the accurate amount.

- When baking a product with **yeast** added, it is always best to grease the bowl in which you place the dough to rise, as this helps retain moisture during the proofing process. Many yeast doughs require two separate risings. The first one takes 1-1½ hours until it doubles in bulk. The second rise takes about an hour, sometimes more. You can tell when the dough has risen enough by gently sticking your little finger into the mass. When an indentation remains, the dough is ready. If the recipe calls for you to knead it again after the first rise, punch the dough down, knead it again, then shape the dough into loaves, rolls or a cake and allow it to rise to almost double. Make sure that you do not allow the dough to over-rise the last time, as it will also rise during baking.

- If you do not have time available to allow **yeast dough** to rise thoroughly, you could prepare the dough, allow time for the first rise, shape it and then place the dough in a large baggie and refrigerate over night. The next morning, allow the product a little more than an hour to double in bulk from the size it was when you put it in the refrigerator and bake accordingly. The dough may rise a little while resting in the refrigerator; be careful not to let it over-rise.

- I have found that if one wants a softer look and feel to the **top crust of a bread loaf**, you will want to brush a small amount of butter onto the top immediately upon removal from the oven. Another tip is to brush an egg wash (1 egg white mixed with 1-2 tablespoons of water) on top of the dough prior to placing in the oven. This will enhance the color and crisp the top of the baked product.

- **When rolling dough out** onto flour, keep the flour usage to a minimum. If your dough continues to stick, place a sheet of waxed paper on your surface. Sprinkle a little flour onto the paper and then roll out the dough.

- You may notice in many of my baked recipes that I usually do not use **salt**. It is not an omission; I usually do not add salt when I am baking. I honestly do not know why, I simply consider it an unnecessary ingredient that one can choose to add or not. If you prefer adding salt to the baking recipes, do so by ¼ teaspoon per 1 cup of flour. I have found that a little bit of salt added to yeast products will assist them to rise properly while in the oven.

- **There are three sizes of muffin pan sections** that I use for most of my muffin recipes. A large muffin pan section is about 3½ inches across the top, the regular size muffin pan section is about 2½ inches across the top and the mini muffin pan section is about 1-1½ inches across the top of each muffin section.

continued on next page

Some of the best tips that I can share with you are related to handling baked products once they are removed from the oven. Both bread and muffins should be removed from the baking pan within the first minute or two after removing from the oven to prevent further baking in the heated pan. I have found that retaining the moisture in most baked products is a little bit different in higher elevations than it is in lower altitudes. At higher elevations, the air is thin and very dry, while in lower altitudes the humidity level is higher, so much of the steam needs to evaporate to prevent excess moisture from being retained in the product. Please read the following tips for proper handling and maintaining the ultimate freshness of a baked product.

MUFFINS

At higher altitudes, wrap the muffins in plastic wrap within 5-10 minutes after removing from the pan; at sea level allow the product to rest about 10-12 minutes before wrapping in plastic wrap. Additionally one could also place 2-4 regular size muffins or mini muffins into a Ziploc bag to seal in the moisture at high or low altitude. If serving the muffins shortly after removing from the oven, place them upon a plate and cover the entire plate with plastic wrap until served.

COOKIES

After cookies are removed from the oven, let them cool for 5-7 minutes at higher altitudes. At sea level, allow cookies to cool on the pan for 7-10 minutes; then either wrap them in plastic wrap, place them in a tin can with a tight fitting lid or store them in a sealed Ziploc bag. If using a decorative can, layer the bottom and sides of the can with waxed paper or plastic wrap, fill with cookies, and then cover with plastic wrap, making sure that the lid fits snuggly so no air or moisture can get in. I usually wrap the larger cookies (4-5 inches) individually in plastic wrap. If serving cookies shortly after removing from the oven, place them on a plate and cover with plastic wrap.

I have found that some of the cookies will stay crunchier if wrapped in plastic wrap; if placed in a baggie, they get softer. Personal preference will determine which method to use. Several of the cookie recipes found in these pages taste best when they remain crunchy. A perfect example is Shortbread: When placed into a plastic container or a baggie they have a tendency to get too soft. By the way, I have found that Shortbread Cookies will stay fresh the longest compared to the other cookie recipes in these pages; they should not be immediately covered with plastic wrap or they will lose their crunch.

CAKES

It is usually best to let cakes cool in the pan unless specified otherwise. For best results, cover the cake completely with plastic wrap within 5-7 minutes at high altitude; 10-12 minutes at sea level after removing from the oven. Serving a coffeecake warm is fine, but let it cool for at least 10 minutes prior to cutting the cake into pieces. For a layer cake, wrap each layer in plastic wrap and let each layer cool completely until you are ready to apply the icing.

BREADS

After removing the bread from the pan, let it cool for 5-10 minutes at high altitudes; 10-15 minutes at sea level; then wrap in plastic wrap or place in a large baggie to seal in all the moisture. If serving shortly after baking, allow to cool for 10 minutes before slicing or the pieces may fall apart. When baking yeast breads, brush a little melted butter on the top immediately after removing from the oven to prevent a hard, dense crust.

BROWNIES

Allow brownies to cool for 4-5 minutes at high altitudes and 10 minutes at sea level; then cover the pan with plastic wrap. Most brownies can be cut into pieces 10 minutes after removing from the oven, unless specified otherwise. Always keep the brownies tightly covered in the pan when not serving. **_Do not_** cut brownies into individual pieces while storing in the pan; that will dry them out more quickly, only slice the number of pieces that are being served. If you are taking them somewhere without the pan, cut them, wrap them individually, place them in a plastic container with a lid or place them upon a plate and tightly cover with plastic wrap.

FRUIT BARS

Let fruit bars cool for about 7-10 minutes at high altitudes, and 10-12 minutes at sea level; then cover the pan or dish with plastic wrap or a casserole lid. If serving immediately, simply let the product cool for 5-7 minutes or you may burn some tongues. If taking fruit bars, crisps or cobblers out of your home, cover the pan/bowl completely with plastic wrap; cut into individual pieces and wrap each piece in plastic wrap; or cut and place them upon a plate that you then cover tightly with plastic wrap. Make sure that you cover any remaining product tightly with plastic wrap. If serving a cobbler or crisp shortly after removing from the oven, you do not need to cover the pan with plastic wrap. All cobblers and crisps need to be covered and refrigerated once they are completely cool; fruit bars do not need to be kept chilled, although in warm, humid areas it is suggested. To reheat a cobbler or crisp, cover the fruit-filled dish with foil and heat at the original baking temperature for 10 minutes, or dish out desired amount and reheat in the microwave.

PIES

Pies are easy; you simply need to let them cool for a bit prior to eating. When transporting a pie, please cover with plastic wrap or place in a plastic container. Cream pies should be kept refrigerated until ready to serve. Unless you have a very cold refrigerator, place the whipped cream on top of the filling just prior to serving, or the cream may lose its fluffy consistency and look as if it has melted.

Tips for Baking at High Altitude

Be prepared to hear many different versions for high altitude baking and cooking requirements. All of the recipes in this book have been tried and tested many times at sea level, at 5000 feet, as well as over 8000 feet above the ocean. Throughout the years of professionally cooking and baking for others in higher elevations, I have often been asked for my secrets and tips. Honestly, for me, it was simply a matter of trial and error, with an extra cup of love and logic mixed in.

Four basic rules of thumb for cooking and baking at higher elevations are:

1. All cooked and baked products will take longer to cook. This can be anywhere from an extra minute for scrambled eggs, 5 minutes more for muffins, to more than an hour for roasts.
2. **Flour:** Add an extra 1½ slightly rounded tablespoons per cup flour required. In addition, if a sea level recipe calls for using cake flour, substitute all purpose flour and sift twice prior to adding to other ingredients. Cake flour has been sifted many times, causing air pockets in the flour. When used at high altitude, these air pockets cause the product to rise rapidly and look fabulous, but then the product begins to deflate just as rapidly, and ends up flat and tough. When substituting all purpose flour for cake flour, add an extra rounded tablespoon of flour per cup flour. For example, if the recipe calls for 1 cup cake flour and 1 cup all purpose flour, use 2 cups plus 2 tablespoons of all purpose flour.
3. **Liquids:** Add an extra 1-2 tablespoons per cup liquid called for.
4. When using **sugar**, decrease the amount just a smidgen, or about 2 teaspoons per cup called for in recipe. I usually measure the sugar to just below the cup line, rather than to the top of the line in a measuring cup. When decreasing the amount of sugar, keep in mind that sugar adds moisture to a baked or cooked product; in drier environments you will not want to decrease the amount by much. In humid areas, I would suggest decreasing the amount of sugar by approximately 2 tablespoons per cup.

- Always keep a **cooked product** tightly covered to retain the moisture. This is especially true for casseroles and roasts as well as baked goods. Therefore, when roasting, or cooking a casserole, try to keep the product covered with foil (unless indicated otherwise) until the last few minutes when browning of the top is required. If a product is to be cooked uncovered and the topping begins to brown too quickly, simply cover with foil and continue cooking. For baked goods, always keep the product tightly sealed or covered to retain moisture.

- More than a few cookbooks state that when baking at high altitude, you should **increase the oven temperature** by approximately 25° Fahrenheit or 3.88° Celsius. I do not, nor have I ever. However, I do know a few who increase the temperature with successful results. I am sure that this will remain a controversy for many years to come; therefore, my advice is to use that which you are more comfortable with. If your product is drying out too quickly after raising the temperature, then lower the temperature back to the suggested temperature. Without the necessary adjustments to ingredients when baking in higher elevations, the product may lose its shape anyway. Additionally, you may want to experiment and make the product at the temperature suggested and then make another batch and raise the temperature by 25° and then determine which you prefer. I simply give products a few extra minutes to bake. For those who live in high altitudes where there is much moisture, you may want to raise the temperature by 10-15° degrees. F. or -12, -9° C. to compensate for the excess moisture.

continued on next page

• When I am **roasting beef, poultry and vegetables** I always decrease the temperature by 5-10 degrees Additionally, I have found that when directed to set the oven at 425-450° Fahrenheit, decreasing the heat by 25° Fahrenheit will produce better results.

• **Soups:** When I am simmering soups, I usually add a few additional cups of liquid after the first hour of simmering. Make sure to remove the scum off the top of the mixture after it comes to a boil, then add the seasonings/spices, the additional liquid and a tight-fitting lid then lower the heat to a simmer. I keep a lid on the pot to avoid too much moisture evaporation. Lift the lid occasionally to stir, taste and possibly add another pinch of this or that.

• When you **boil water** at higher elevations, it boils at a lower temperature. In areas of lower altitudes, you need to set the temperature at high, whereas in higher altitudes the water will begin to boil at medium high. This is due to the lower air pressure in higher elevations. Raising the temperature too high will only evaporate more water, so always set the temperature to boil water and/or liquids for pasta, potatoes, vegetables, soups, stews and sauces at medium to medium high. Additionally you may want to use a larger pot, adding more water to compensate for too much evaporation.

• You may have been told to decrease or increase the **baking soda** and/or **baking powder** by one fourth. I do not. What I do when measuring these two leavening agents is to make sure the amount is not measured to the top of the measuring spoon, but just a tiny speck below the top of it. To do this, indent the ingredient with your finger a tiny bit when leveling the measuring spoon. Slightly decreasing the baking powder or baking soda works best for me.

• Some recipes, when baking at high altitude, require an extra **egg** or two. I always bake with large or extra-large eggs. If using medium-size eggs, add an extra egg. This is especially true when baking cakes. Always try to use extra large eggs in cakes. The recipes found among the following pages will state at the bottom of the page whether you should add an extra egg when doubling or tripling the amounts of ingredients in that specific recipe. At high altitude an extra egg will assist the leavening agents (baking soda and baking powder) to make the dough rise.

• Beating and using **egg whites** in high altitude recipes can be a frustrating experience. I have had numerous trials and errors using egg whites throughout the years. For best results, I have found that the egg whites need to be at room temperature; also gradually increase the speed from low to medium-low while beating as they first become frothy. Continue beating at medium just until soft peaks begin to form. You do not want to beat the egg white so hard that stiff peaks (often used in sea level baking) form. The air cells will begin to fall apart, which may cause the product to collapse while baking.

• **What to do about yeast?** Although I do not bake with yeast very often, there are a few recipes in this book that call for yeast. I use dry active yeast (not rapid rising or instant), found in individual packets in the baking section of all grocery stores. Because the air is much thinner up here, yeast products (as well as many cakes) have a tendency to rise rapidly like a hot air balloon and then deflate as if the hot air was turned off, resulting in a dry, coarse and possibly deflated product. To avoid this effect, make sure that the yeast dough does not over-rise while doubling in bulk. It should take 1-1 ½ hours for yeast dough to double in bulk, not much more. I have found that yeast dough will rise better if it feels slightly warm to the touch during the early stages of doubling in bulk. Additionally, make sure to give the yeast product a tad of humidity to rise for best results. I do this by placing a steaming pot of hot water next to the bowl of dough, and refilling when the water cools.

• One of the most frustrating feats at high altitude is trying to make puddings the traditional way by using a double boiler. It simply does not work; the air is too thin and the temperature does not get hot enough to cause the starch to gel. Therefore, it is always best just to cook the pudding with the pan directly on the heat source. Remember to continuously stir the mixture until thickened to prevent burning.

• One thing I have learned when baking at high altitude is to NOT use a piece of parchment paper on a cookie sheet when baking cookies, and to avoid using paper muffin cups, as many recipes (not found in this book) may suggest. Instead, spray the pan well with pan spray, or butter the pan. The parchment paper and paper muffin cups will only absorb moisture from your product, which you do not want to happen.

Cooking and Baking Above 10,000 Feet

The best advice that I can share with those of you who reside or visit locations above 10,000 feet in altitude are to simply:

• Allow all foods to cook, simmer, roast and/or bake a few minutes longer than suggested in the following pages. I suggest not increasing the temperature, but if you feel that you must do so, allow the product a few minutes less to fully cook or bake through. When roasting foods, decrease the temperature by 15-25° F and allow to cook longer than indicated.

• The following increases or decreases are over and above the increases/decreases mentioned in the last chapter.
  • Increase flour by 2-3 tablespoons per cup.
  • Increase liquid by 2-3 tablespoons per cup.
  • Decrease sugar by 1-2 tablespoon per cup.
  • Decrease baking soda and baking powder by ¼ teaspoon per cup.
  • Decrease yeast by ¼ teaspoon per dry packet.
  • For handling the product after removing from the oven, please see the tips on pages x, xi.

Cooking and Baking Down Below
(Sea Level Tips)

Although I have neither baked nor cooked at sea level for some time, my memories and lessons were first acquired in Philadelphia, Pennsylvania. With this in consideration, it is much easier for me to share these tips than for one who has lived only at high altitude.

Adjustments for using these recipes at sea level.

COOKING at sea level:
• To prepare the following recipes in areas below 4000 feet in altitude, all you need to do is cook, simmer or roast for a shorter time period than I have indicated. For example, if you are roasting beef or simmering a soup, decrease the allotted time by one hour or so, checking the product for doneness prior to removing from the heat source. Additionally, water will boil at high altitudes at a lower temperature, so at sea level, boil water at a higher temperature setting.

BAKING AT SEA LEVEL:
• Although baking temperatures remain the same, sea level products will take less time to thoroughly bake; allow 2 minutes less time for cookies, 3-5 minutes less for muffins and about 5-7 minutes less time for brownies and cakes. Therefore, please check the product a few minutes before the allotted time for doneness by testing it with an inserted knife or toothpick. If crumbs are attached to the utensil or toothpick, the product is not through baking.

• The most important aspect that I can share with you for adjusting these recipes to be baked in areas below 4000 feet above the ocean is relative to the amount of flour and liquid used. All of these recipes will work fine as written when used in lower locations, but if you feel that you must make a pinch of an adjustment, just decrease the flour and liquid by approximately 1 tablespoon per cup required—that is all there is to it.

I know of many people who use my recipes below 4000 feet above sea level, and they make no adjustments whatsoever, none! I have made many of the following recipes at sea level and have forgotten to adjust them to "Down Below" and they turned out just fine; as delicious as when made in high altitudes. Therefore, I can conclude that there is no real difference when cooking/baking high altitude recipes at sea level, but there is indeed a significant difference in cooking/baking sea level recipes in higher elevations.

• When measuring a leavening agent such as baking soda or baking powder, make sure to level the spoon evenly with absolutely no indent in the ingredient.

• If the product appears to be too cakelike when removed from the pan, (i.e., brownies or muffins) then you may want to leave out 1 egg from the recipe the next time you bake it.

• I add a lot of fruit juice to muffins for a bit of extra moisture. At sea level, you may want to decrease the suggested amount by 2-3 tablespoons, not more, or it may affect the taste.

• For additional tips on cooking or handling baked products once removed from the oven, please see General Tips, pages vii-xi.

I Confess

Before you turn the next pages to view, read, and produce the delectable recipes found throughout the following pages, I have a few confessions to share.

First and foremost, I do not normally measure the spices and herbs that I add to recipes. Instead, I simply toss them into my food products, take a taste and usually add a smidgen more. Determining the adequate amount of spice and herbs to add was the most difficult part of writing this cookbook, for I had to actually measure these special ingredients so that you may enjoy these recipes in full flavor.

Therefore, if you find that my amount of spice is not to your liking, please adjust the amounts for your own personal preference. Additionally, I have a tendency to overuse both cinnamon and garlic by adding more than may be necessarily adequate.

Throughout the years I have learned that foods are what YOU, as the one preparing them, make them. We are all different and have our own individual tastes; some of these are based on how our mothers cooked and seasoned food, while others are based on where we reside and the fresh herbs and spices available. Therefore, again, please adjust the seasonings according to your own personal preference.

I receive much enjoyment from playing around with new and old recipes, making them as I fondly remember, or improving them and then sharing them with others. Within the following pages, there are not many fancy gourmet-type recipes, rather these are everyday recipes to be easily prepared and enjoyed at home. Sure, there are a few that are a bit extravagant that I use on special occasions, but, most are relatively simple to prepare. If you find that the following pages do not contain a recipe that you desire, please inform me, and I will try my best to develop one for you.

Last but not least: Cooking and baking should not be a stressful experience, but one filled with love, anticipation and joy! It is the little things that matter the most; the preparation of a homemade meal, a hot bowl of soup or a warm cookie that the ones you love will remember, laugh over and cherish for all time.

Sharing Mountain Recipes

The Muffin Lady's Everyday Favorites

The Whens of Food

When you first wake up in the morning, you want breakfast
When it is the middle of the day, and time for a break, you want lunch
When it gets dark at night, you want dinner
When is it freezing outside, you want a bowl of chili
When it is hot outside, you want a fresh, chilled salad
When the autumn breezes blow, you want soup
When it is spring, you want to nibble on those edible weeds
When it is Christmas, you want cookies
When it is Thanksgiving, you want turkey
When you are sick, you want a bowl of chicken soup
When your belly hurts, you want nothing to eat
When at the beach, you want seafood
When it is snowing, you want stew
When on a hike, you want trail mix
When in an orchard, you want wine or a fresh baked pie
When on a farm, you want all the fresh goodies available
When on a dairy farm, you want real ice cream
When in a wheat field, you can smell the bread
When on a diet, you want doughnuts
When on a no carb diet, you want bread
When in a foreign country or state, you want to taste their cuisine
When you are at a baseball game, you want hot dogs and beer
When you are at the movies, you want popcorn
When at a baby shower, you want quiche
When you are on a picnic, you want a basketful of sandwiches
When you want to share, you usually start with food.

Ultimate Comfort Foods

~ All of the following recipes can be doubled and tripled.
~ Make sure all butter, margarine and/or cream cheese is softened to room temperature before adding.

When I first began to think about sharing more recipes and writing another cookbook, I randomly asked people what their favorite comfort foods are. I was entirely intrigued when the majority of people stated the same three foods: Mashed Potatoes, Macaroni and Cheese, and Chocolate. So with this in mind, I decided to begin this cookbook with these culinary favorites, the Ultimate Comfort Foods.

Traditional Macaroni and Cheese, Page 12

Mom's Mashed Potatoes

While in college, after moving into a house, I made my first holiday meal for friends. Mashed potatoes were of course a desired complement to the meal and I wanted them to taste just like Mom's. When I first made them the way I thought my mother always had, they didn't taste the same. Although creamy and fluffy, I knew that something was missing. So I called Mom. That was the day that I found out that my mother's secret for her "these are the best mashed potatoes" was Muenster cheese. I continue to add it today for special occasions.

Serves 4-6

6 large potatoes or 12 small red potatoes
Enough warm water to cover the potatoes, plus a little more
½ cup milk or sweet milk (half and half) or a combo of both
⅓-½ cup (5 tablespoons to 1 stick) butter or margarine (amount depends on personal preference)
1 cup Munster cheese, shredded or thinly sliced & packed lightly (optional)
Salt and pepper to taste

1. Wash the potatoes completely under warm water. Slice potatoes into ¼-inch slices and place into a large pot. Cover with warm water and boil at medium high heat until tender and soft; about 25-35 minutes.
2. Drain and rinse the potatoes under hot water, then pour them into a large bowl.
3. Add the milk, butter/margarine and seasonings and beat with an old fashioned potato masher or an electric hand mixer until smooth and fluffy.
4. Mix the cheese into the potatoes and serve immediately.

Hint: Leaving the skin on the potatoes adds more vitamins to the product. Never use a food processor to mash the potatoes, or you will end up with too much starch and not enough fluff. Make sure that the cheese is grated or sliced into very small pieces.

Garlic Mashed Potatoes

The first time that I tasted Garlic Mashed Potatoes was at a restaurant in Denver, Colorado. I had never tasted garlic in mashed potatoes before, and my taste buds were waiting with culinary anticipation. Unfortunately, the chef in this restaurant forgot to add any garlic to the potatoes, not one clove. So what did I do? I went home still full of anticipation and I made up a batch. When I was finished with all the mashing, I immediately stuck a spoon into this recipe and my taste buds exploded with flavor. Good thing I made a small batch, as my friend and I proceeded to eat it all.

Serves 4-6

6 large potatoes or 12 small red potatoes
Enough water to cover the potatoes, plus a little more
½ cup milk
⅓-½ cup (6 tablespoons to 1 stick) butter or margarine
5 cloves garlic, peeled and crushed, or peeled and whole if cooked with potatoes
Salt and pepper to taste
¼ teaspoon of dried or a couple of sprigs of fresh parsley, for topping (optional)

1. Wash the potatoes completely under warm water. Slice potatoes into ¼-inch slices and place into a large pot with the whole garlic cloves. Cover with water and boil over medium high until tender and soft; about 25-35 minutes.
2. Drain and rinse the potatoes under hot water and then pour them into a large bowl.
3. Add the milk, butter/margarine, garlic (if you chose to use crushed) and seasonings, and beat with an old fashioned potato masher or an electric hand mixer until smooth and fluffy. Serve immediately, sprinkling a little parsley on top of each serving if you'd like.

Hint: Leaving the skin on the potatoes adds more vitamins to the product. Never use a food processor to mash the potatoes, or you will end up with too much starch and not enough fluff.

Cheese and Bacon Mashed Potatoes

For something out of the ordinary, this recipe pairs perfectly with hamburgers or chicken patties.
A little bit different than your everyday mashed potatoes and full of so much good flavor. Your children
will definitely ask for more, and your partner will lay some extra kisses on your cheek that evening.

Serves 4-6

6 large potatoes or 12 small red potatoes
Enough water to cover the potatoes, plus a little more
½ cup milk
⅓-½ cup (5 tablespoons to 1 stick) butter or margarine
1 cup grated cheddar cheese
6 slices of cooked bacon
Scant ½ cup sour cream
2 pinches cayenne pepper or a couple drops of hot sauce (optional)
Salt and pepper to taste

1. Wash the potatoes completely under warm water. (I normally leave the skin on, but peeling is a personal preference.) Slice potatoes into ¼-inch slices and place into a large pot. Cover with water and boil at medium high heat until tender and soft; about 25-35 minutes.
2. While the potatoes are cooking, fry up the bacon until crisp, but not burnt. Drain off the grease and put aside until cool. Once cool, crumble it into tiny pieces, place in a small bowl and put aside.
3. Drain and rinse the potatoes under hot water, then pour them into a large bowl.
4. Add the milk, butter/margarine and seasonings and beat with an old fashioned potato masher or an electric hand mixer until smooth and fluffy. Add the cheese and bacon to the potatoes, mix and serve with a dollop of sour cream on top.

Hint: Leaving the skin on the potatoes adds more vitamins to the product. Never use a food processor to mash the potatoes, or you will end up with too much starch and not enough fluff.

Ranch Mashed Potatoes

The flavor of ranch dressing always reminds me of the country, where fresh fruits, vegetables and herbs grow in wide open places. As one who is always experimenting with new recipes, one evening I decided to add a bit of country twang to more traditional mashed potatoes, and added some ranch dressing spices. Even cooked up in a city, this recipe served with Fried Chicken or Meatloaf can momentarily place one into the backwoods. If you shut your eyes while eating, I bet you can hear the crickets chirping and the birds singing, instead of the horns and sirens blaring from the streets down below.

Serves 4-6

6 large potatoes or 12 small red potatoes
Enough water to cover the potatoes
¼ cup milk
¼-⅓ cup of buttermilk, sour cream or yogurt
¼ cup (½ stick) butter or margarine
1 crushed garlic clove or 1 teaspoon of minced garlic
1 teaspoon each dried parsley and dill or a couple sprigs
of fresh, finely chopped
Pinch each of celery seed and dry mustard
2 pinches of dried cilantro (optional)
1 teaspoon lemon juice (optional)
Salt and pepper to taste

1. Wash the potatoes completely under warm water. (I normally leave the skin on, but peeling is a personal preference.) Slice potatoes into ¼-inch slices and place into a large pot. Cover with water and boil at medium high heat until tender and soft; about 25-35 minutes.
2. Drain and rinse the potatoes with hot water, then pour them into a large bowl.
3. Add the milk, buttermilk, butter/margarine and spices and beat with an old fashioned potato masher or an electric hand mixer until smooth and fluffy. Serve immediately.

Hints: Leaving the skin on the potatoes adds more vitamins to the product. Never use a food processor to mash the potatoes, or you will end up with too much starch and not enough fluff. You can substitute a couple of tablespoons   of ranch dressing for the buttermilk and spices.

Dreamy Cheese Mashed Potatoes

This recipe is so nice and fluffy that upon first taste you will think that you have floated up into the clouds. I first made these after taking an 8-ounce brick of cream cheese out of the refrigerator for a dessert that was never made. Instead, while preparing dinner for friends, I spotted the cream cheese and thought, "why not?" and added it to the potatoes prior to mashing for a taste of something new. Everyone thought that these were wonderful and immediately asked what I had added.

Serves 6-8

6 large potatoes or 12 small red potatoes
Enough water to cover the potatoes, plus a little more
½ cup milk
¼ cup to ½ cup (½-1 stick) butter or margarine
1 8-ounce brick cream cheese (softened to room temperature)
½ teaspoon each, onion and garlic powder
¼ teaspoon dill
Pinch of celery seed (optional)
Salt and pepper to taste
¼ teaspoon of dried or a couple sprigs of fresh parsley (optional)

1. Wash and slice potatoes into ¼-inch slices and place into a large pot. Cover with water and boil at medium high heat until tender and soft; about 25-35 minutes.
2. Drain and rinse the potatoes under hot water, then pour them into a large bowl.
3. Add the milk, butter/margarine, cream cheese and seasonings and beat with an old fashioned potato masher or an electric hand mixer until smooth and fluffy. Serve immediately, sprinkling a little parsley on top of each serving.

Hints: Leaving the skin on the potatoes adds more vitamins to the product. Never use a food processor to mash the potatoes, or you will end up with too much starch and not enough fluff.

Skinny Mashed Potatoes

There are two ways that I know of to make Skinny Mashed Potatoes.
Both can be used for those on special diets or for those who have to watch what they eat.
Additionally, these recipes are extremely easy to make and, amazingly, not too bad on the taste buds.

Serves 3-4

3 large potatoes or 6 small red potatoes
¼ cup low-sodium chicken broth (homemade if available), or ½ cup plain yogurt
A couple pinches parsley and/or chives
Pinch of garlic powder (optional)
Salt and pepper to taste

1. Wash the potatoes completely under warm water. (I normally leave the skin on, but peeling is a personal preference.) Slice potatoes into ¼-inch slices and place into a large pot. Cover with water and boil at medium high heat until tender and soft; about 25-35 minutes.
2. Drain and rinse the potatoes under hot water, then pour them into a large bowl.
3. Add the chicken soup or yogurt and spices, then mash with an old fashioned potato masher or with an electric hand beater. Serve immediately with a pinch of parsley sprinkled on top.

Hints: Leaving the skin on the potatoes adds more vitamins to the product. Never use a food processor to mash the potatoes, or you will end up with too much starch and not enough fluff.

Imitation Mashed Potatoes

Yes, these really are fake mashed potatoes, for there is not one potato fleck in this recipe.
One evening while microwaving some cauliflower, I accidentally overnuked it. The cauliflower was much too mushy,
but I was hungry so I added a bit of butter, a tad of spice and mixed it all up. Upon first bite I noticed that this bowl of
overcooked cauliflower looked and tasted similar to mashed potatoes. When watching your weight, try making
a batch of these; you may be pleasantly surprised, for this recipe is actually very good.

Serves 3-4

2½ cups cauliflower
Enough water to cover in a large microwave safe bowl
2 tablespoons butter or margarine (more if you prefer)
¼ teaspoon garlic powder
Salt and pepper to taste

1. Wash the cauliflower under warm water and cut into 1–2-inch pieces and place the pieces into a large non-metal bowl; cover with water.
2. Cook on high in the microwave for 7-10 minutes (depending the strength of your microwave) or until very tender and mushy.
3. Remove the bowl and drain off all water.
4. Add the butter/margarine and spice and mash with an old fashioned potato masher or a large fork. Serve immediately.

Traditional Macaroni and Cheese

When I first began asking friends and customers to tell me what their favorite comforts were, many immediately said, "Macaroni and Cheese, like my grandmother used to make." Having never made 'real' Macaroni and Cheese, I began asking friends for recipes, and developed this one from a combination of them.

Serves 4-6

Preheat oven to 350° F

3 cups (1 pound) macaroni or small shell noodles
1-2 tablespoons virgin olive oil
2½ cups milk
¼ cup (½ stick) butter
3 tablespoons flour
2 cups grated sharp cheddar cheese
¼ teaspoon garlic powder
¼ teaspoon Worcestershire sauce
⅛ teaspoon dry mustard (optional)
1-2 tablespoons butter or margarine
⅔ cup dried or fresh* bread crumbs or an equal amount of crushed crackers
Salt and pepper to taste

1. Grease a 9x13-inch pan or large casserole bowl.
2. Fill a large pot with water, add the oil and heat to a full boil. Add macaroni to water and boil until the noodles begin to get tender, although not completely cooked through.
3. Remove from heat, drain the water under lukewarm water and put the macaroni aside in the greased casserole bowl or pan.
4. In a small pot, heat the milk until it begins to scald or tiny bubbles appear along the sides of the pot. Put aside.
5. In another pot, melt the butter; when it begins to bubble, add the flour and spices. With a wire whisk, constantly stir this mixture until it begins to turn brown, then stir in ¼ cup milk at a time. Continue stirring until all ingredients are fully incorporated and the mixture is thick and smooth. Add the grated cheese and stir thoroughly.
6. Pour the cheese mixture over the noodles and gently stir together.
7. Melt the remaining butter and mix together with the bread crumbs. Sprinkle the bread crumbs evenly over the top of the macaroni. Bake for 15-20 minutes, or until crumbs begin to turn brown. Remove from oven and serve.

* To make fresh bread crumbs, I use hard, day-old French bread, a baguette, or crumbled darkened toast, and grate it into a bowl with a cheese grater.

Stovetop Mac and Cheese

A few years ago, while I was watching a friend's kids, it began snowing hard. The kids were outside playing, and after a couple hours I noticed that they were getting tired and would be coming in soon, cold and hungry. So I thought of making this wonderfully quick and easy recipe as I was searching for something warm to eat. It must have been good, for they hungrily finished the whole pot, and have asked for it again and again.

Serves 3-4

2 cups macaroni or similar sized pasta
¾ pound Velveeta or any soft, processed cheese, cut up into small chunks.
⅓ cup milk, a little more if you prefer this dish to be creamier
¼ teaspoon garlic
¼ teaspoon dry mustard (optional)
Dash or 2 of hot sauce
Salt and pepper to taste

1. Cook the pasta according to package directions. Drain them under hot water and leave the noodles in the pan that they were cooked in.
2. Over low heat, add the Velveeta chunks and spices to the cooked noodles. Stir until all the cheese has melted and serve immediately.

Variations:
Adding additional ingredients such as tomato sauce, chili sauce, jalapenos, chopped vegetables, or diced meats and poultry will only improve this dish and make it more flavorful and enticing.

Hint: A little bit of mild salsa and cooked ground beef truly makes this a very good dish. The kids love it.

Winnie's Mom's Mac & Cheese

While being entertained by the employees at the charming Playhouse in Jackson Hole, Wyoming I met a wonderful couple, Winnie and Dave. We immediately struck up a conversation; they told me that they worked for the school system in Florida, and I told them that I write cookbooks and am working on a second book. Needless to say, Winnie informed me that she has this terrific Mac & Cheese recipe that was her mother's and asked if I would be interested. You bet I was, so she emailed it to me. When I made up a batch, I knew instantly that I had to share this with others. This recipe is what some have since said is a "keeper."

Serves 3-4

Preheat oven to 400° F

8 ounces uncooked macaroni
2 tablespoons butter
2 tablespoons flour
1 cup milk
¼ teaspoon salt and a few grains pepper
dash of garlic powder
2 cups grated cheese, cheddar (or preferred choice)
½ cup buttered bread crumbs (½ cup bread crumbs mixed with 1 tablespoon melted butter)
2 tablespoons butter
½ teaspoon dry mustard (optional)

1. Grease an 8x8-inch pan thoroughly.
2. Fill a large pot with water, add the oil and heat to a full boil.
3. Add macaroni to water and boil until the noodles begin to become tender, but not completely cooked through.
4. Remove from heat; drain water from macaroni under lukewarm water and put aside in the prepared pan.
5. In a saucepan melt the butter at medium heat; when it begins to bubble, add the flour and spices and stir. With a wire whisk, stir this mixture constantly until no lumps are remaining. Increase the heat slightly and gradually add the milk. Continue stirring until all ingredients are fully incorporated and the mixture is thick and smooth. Put this aside.
6. Layer half of the macaroni into the prepared pan, then sprinkle with half the cheese and dot with 1 tablespoon butter and half the mustard if using. Repeat with remaining noodles, cheese and butter and mustard if using.
7. Pour all of the white sauce/milk mixture over the top layer, and then sprinkle evenly with the bread crumbs.
8. Bake for approximately 20 minutes, or until bread crumbs begin to turn golden brown, and serve.

Michelle's Mom's Macaroni and Cheese

One day while playing around with a more traditional recipe for Macaroni and Cheese, I took the results to Jane, one of my "guinea pigs," for sampling. It was so bad that she suggested not making it again. She then called Michelle, knowing that her mother's recipe is, "very, very good." Michelle shared this with me and said, "Last minute, don't know what to eat? This is quick and easy and a favorite of the kids." I came back home, tried it and it is now a favorite of mine too. For macaroni and cheese, it honestly doesn't get any easier than this.

Serves 4-6

Preheat oven to 325° F

2 cups uncooked macaroni
2¼ cups milk
1 egg
2¼ cups (10 ounces) yellow colby cheese, grated
1-2 tablespoons butter
Pinch of dry mustard (optional)
Pinch of garlic powder (optional)
Salt and pepper to taste

1. Grease an 8x8-inch pan.
2. Mix the egg thoroughly into the milk.
3. Into the prepared pan, make layers of ingredients. Evenly spread half the uncooked macaroni, half the cheese, dot the cheese with 1 tablespoon butter, then pour half of the milk mixture over this and repeat the layers with remaining ingredients, ending with the seasonings.
4. Bake for 35-40 minutes and serve immediately.

Mary's Mac and Cheese

The first time that I tasted this recipe was at Elizabeth's house. Upon my first bite, I knew that I would want the recipe and said so. Elizabeth said that it was her mother's recipe and that she has been eating it most of her life. Although, a bit different than the 'normal' macaroni and cheese, I am positive that you will be enjoying this recipe for many years to come.

Serves 4-6

Preheat oven to 400° F

1½ cups (8 ounces) uncooked macaroni or small pasta shells
1-2 tablespoons virgin olive oil
2 tablespoons butter
2 tablespoons flour
1 cup milk
¼ teaspoon salt
Pinch of pepper
½ teaspoon garlic powder or ¼ teaspoon minced garlic
2-3 tablespoons butter
½ teaspoon dry mustard (optional)
1 cup grated parmesan cheese
1 cup grated romano cheese
½-⅔ cups dry bread crumbs

1. Grease a medium-sized (2-quart) casserole dish with butter.
2. Fill a large pot with water, add the oil and heat to a full boil.
3. Add pasta to water and boil until tender (about 5-6 minutes), but still needing another 2-3 minutes to finish cooking.
4. Remove noodles from heat, drain water, and rinse noodles under hot water.
5. Mix the two cheeses together and begin to layer: Beginning with half the noodles, sprinkle half the cheese on top, dot the cheese with 1 tablespoon butter and sprinkle with ¼ teaspoon mustard. Repeat this layering with remaining ingredients, finishing with the butter and mustard.
6. Make the white sauce/roux by melting the butter in a small sauce pan. Once melted, add the flour mixed with seasonings, and stir until well blended, breaking up any lumps. Gradually add the milk to this mixture, whisk constantly until it boils, and continue whisking for another two minutes. If it is too thick, add a bit more milk, 1 tablespoon at a time.
7. Pour the sauce over the macaroni and cheese, mix the garlic into the bread crumbs and sprinkle the crumbs over the top.
8. Bake for 15- 20 minutes, or until light brown on top, remove from the oven and serve.

Whole Wheat Macaroni & Cheese

A bit of variety in your diet never hurts. Sometimes it is good to alter the way you eat, especially if you are trying to eat healthier. Substituting whole grain foods for those made with more processed flours is one way to add more nutrients to you body. The taste is just as good, if not better than what you have grown accustomed to, and ultimately you are really eating a healthier product. Many of the kids that I used to work with had special dietary needs, so I learned young how to alter favorite recipes to accommodate to their needs. This is one of the recipes that they all loved and asked for frequently.

Preheat oven to 350° F

1 pound whole wheat macaroni (about 3½ cups)
2 tablespoons virgin olive oil
2 tablespoons butter
2 tablespoons flour
½ teaspoon minced garlic
Pinch of dry mustard, (optional)
½ teaspoon dry parsley, (optional)
Salt and pepper to taste
2 cups milk
2½ cups cheddar cheese

1. Grease a 2 quart casserole dish with butter or margarine.
2. Fill a large pot with water, add the oil and heat to a full boil. Add noodles to water and boil until the noodles are tender, (about 5-6 minutes), but still needing another 2-3 minutes to finish cooking. Drain and rinse the noodles under hot water. Set aside.
3. Melt the butter in a 2-3 quart sauce pan. Add the flour and seasonings and stir constantly until smooth.
4. Gradually whisk the milk into the flour mixture until it boils again. Continue stirring with the whisk for another 2-3 minutes or until thick and smooth. If it is too thick for you, add a bit more milk, 1 tablespoon at a time, until the desired consistency.
5. Add 2 cups of the cheese to this mixture and continue stirring until melted; then thoroughly mix in the partially cooked macaroni.
6. Pour the mixture into the prepared casserole dish and bake for 25-30 minutes.
7. Partially remove the pan from the oven, sprinkle remaining cheese on top and bake for an additional 5-7 minutes or until the top is bubbly and golden. Remove from the oven and serve.

Chocolate

For centuries chocolate has been one of the most popular comfort foods, no matter where you live or how old you are. Even health professionals are agreeing that darker varieties of chocolate are better for you than once believed. (if only they had listened to us women before; we could have saved them tons of research money!) When I asked about favorite comfort foods, chocolate was the leader. When questioned about where chocolate comes from, no one knew, so the teacher in me just had to find out.

Chocolate is made from the tropical cacao tree, *Theobroma cacao*. In Greek, Theobroma cacao literally translates to mean 'foods of the Gods'. Chocolate was known as *xocoatl* by the ancient Mayan and Aztecs. They first combined the chocolate seeds with spices to make a bitter, spicy, frothy hot beverage. It was found to have stimulant and restorative properties and was used in sacred rituals as an offering to the Gods. Chocolate was even used as a form of money!

Many years later, Spanish explorers traded for the cacao seeds and began adding cinnamon and sugar. These expensive recipes were once restricted to royalty and the wealthy as a symbol of wealth and power. It took another 100 years before chocolate was again introduced to fellow Europeans by an Italian traveler, Antonio Carletti. Finally, in the mid 1700s, these expensive and treasured seeds were brought from the West Indies to the state of Massachusetts in the United States.

In the 1800s the steam engine made it possible to deliver ground cacao seeds and quickly produce cheaper versions of chocolate. It is thought that in 1847 the very first solid chocolate bar was developed and sold by Fry and Sons in England.

The cacao seed is thought to have many healthy effects, in addition to its stimulant and restorative properties. The Aztecs believed that cacao seed drinks brought wisdom. Montezuma and Giacomo Casanova believed cacao to be an aphrodisiac. Currently, dark chocolate has been found to help women during their pre-menstrual and menstrual cycles; it contains amino acids, which decrease anxiety and it releases endorphins, which reduce sensitivity to pain. Darker varieties of chocolates have been shown to improve one's mood by boosting the brain chemical serotonin, which is similar to the effects of popping Prozac. Some doctors even agree that a little bit of dark chocolate can help maintain a healthy heart and help fight cancer.

Just think, eating and enjoying an ounce or 2 of dark chocolate per day can: reduce high blood pressure; add bodily nutrients such as iron, calcium, potassium, vitamins A, B1, C, D, and E, commonly taken in supplemental vitamins; and may control pain and those mood swings, all at the same time. Personally, I prefer eating dark chocolate rather than swallowing a pill if given the choice.

Theobroma Cacao Seeds (cocao/chocolate)
Photo by Erowid, © 2002 Erowid.org

The Different Kinds of Chocolate

Unsweetened Chocolate

This kind of chocolate is often referred to as baking chocolate, bitter chocolate or plain chocolate. This is the most common type of chocolate used in baking and has been said to be the only true baking chocolate. With no added ingredients, this type of chocolate adds a strong, deep chocolate flavor to anything you add it to. Additionally, many culinary professionals use unsweetened chocolate in sauces and stews, adding more pungency to their flavor.

Bittersweet Chocolate

Bittersweet Chocolate is dark and a little sweeter than unsweetened chocolate. It is unsweetened chocolate to which sugar, more cocoa butter, lecithin, and vanilla have been added. It has less sugar than semisweet chocolate; although the two are interchangeable when baking. Bittersweet has become the preferred choice of executive chefs.

Semisweet Chocolate

Semisweet chocolate is slightly sweet, and used most often in frostings, sauces, and fillings. This chocolate is favored by everyday bakers and is commonly found in bags in grocery stores in the form of chocolate chips.

Milk Chocolate

Milk chocolate is the most popular of all chocolates. It can be found almost everywhere one goes and is most commonly used in candy bars. Whole and/or skim milk powder and more sugar are added to this form of chocolate. Although there is a burst of flavor in each bite, this is not the best kind of chocolate to use when baking: it negatively affects the texture causing the components to break down too rapidly.

German Chocolate

German chocolate is darker and sweeter than semisweet. Contrary to what you may think, German chocolate does not come from Germany; it was developed by a man named German.

White Chocolate

Many people have said that white chocolate is not really chocolate. However, since it is made from sweetened cocoa butter mixed with milk solids and vanilla, and cocoa butter is derived from the cocoa bean (cacao seed), one can only conclude that white chocolate is definitely a form of chocolate.

Cocoa

Cocoa is a powder resulting from drying and partially fermenting the fatty seeds found in the seed pods of the cacao tree; from this powder, chocolate is made. The term cocoa often refers to cocoa powder; the dry powder made by grinding cocoa seeds and removing the fat from the dark, bitter cocoa solids. It is commonly available as cocoa or Dutch processed cocoa. Dutch processed cocoa has alkali added to remove some of the acidity. While regular cocoa has a lighter color and richer flavor, I prefer using Dutch processed because I think it supplies more appeal and flavor to baked goods. The choice is one of personal taste. Another tidbit is that most people confuse hot cocoa and hot chocolate. Cocoa is made from the cocoa solids after the fat has been removed, while true hot chocolate is made from whole chocolate.

Ah, the Comforts of Hot Chocolate

Considering that the serving of hot chocolate began so very long ago, and that the savored passing of such a savvy beverage has only improved in flavor throughout the centuries, it is my feeling that a variety of recipes belong in this chapter. Hot chocolate or cocoa can be enjoyed any time of day or night, or at any time of the year. Sweet, warm and satisfying, the following hot chocolate recipes are at the top of my list of culinary comforts. Pairing deliciously with almost anything when you think about it, it can be served with breakfast, lunch, and dinner or as a snack. When you make it properly with milk or cream, you will be serving and relishing a relatively nutritional beverage. The calcium in milk, along with the vitamins and cancer-fighting antioxidant agents in dark chocolate, ultimately make this favored comfort drink much healthier than once believed.

Easy Chocolate Milk, Hot or Cold

This recipe is so very easy and a favorite beverage for all ages. You can choose to make it in a sauce pan or in the microwave, or just serve it cold; either way, the results will be delicious.

Serves 1

8-10 ounces of milk
2 tablespoons of chocolate syrup
2 large marshmallows (optional)

1. Chocolate Milk: mix the milk and syrup thoroughly together and serve.
2. For Hot Chocolate: heat the milk in a small pot until hot and steaming. (A microwave works just as well.)
3. Remove the pot from the heat, pour the milk into a large cup and pour the syrup into the milk, stirring vigorously. Serve immediately with marshmallows on top if desired.

Real Hot Chocolate

This recipe is so welcoming on cold winter nights or when coming in from the rain, that it truly is a must-have recipe in all households. For something a little special and for adults only, add a shot of Bailey's Irish Cream to each cup before serving.

Serves 2

2½ ounces of bittersweet chocolate, chopped into little pieces
1 cup boiling water
2-3 tablespoons honey or sugar (amount is of personal preference, the more the sweeter)
Dash of salt (optional)
3 cups hot milk (heated in a saucepan on the stove or in the microwave)
2 dollops of whipped cream (optional)
2 cinnamon sticks (optional)

1. Mix chocolate into the boiling water and stir until completely melted.
2. Add the honey or sugar and mix thoroughly until dissolved.
3. Add the hot milk and with a whisk and mix thoroughly.
4. Pour into serving cups, add cinnamon sticks if you like and top off with dollops of whipped cream.

Variation: (for adults only)
Add a shot of Bailey's Irish Cream, Grand Marnier or mint-flavored liqueur to the mixture for a special treat.

Mayan Hot Chocolate

This recipe is very similar to that originally developed by the Mayans and Aztecs. Much different from the more traditional hot chocolates of today, it is still very good, although quite spicy. Take a sip, close your eyes, and try to imagine what the world was like hundreds of years ago. When I first made this recipe and tasted it, for some unknown reason I felt as if the ancient ones were right there in the room, smiling down upon me.

Serves 2-4, depending on size of cup

2 cups water
1 chili pepper, cut in half, seeds removed (with gloves)
5 cups light cream (half & half) or whole milk
1 vanilla bean, split lengthwise
1 to 2 cinnamon sticks
8 ounces bittersweet chocolate, chopped finely
2 tablespoons sugar or honey, or to taste
l tablespoon almonds or hazelnuts, ground extra fine
Whipped cream

1. With gloves on, cut chili pepper in half and remove seeds.
2. In a large sauce pan, heat water to a boil and add chili pepper. Cook pepper until liquid is reduced by half, then strain and put the liquid aside.
3. In a medium saucepan over medium heat, combine cream or milk, vanilla bean and cinnamon stick until the liquid scalds or bubbles appear around the edge. Reduce the heat and add chopped chocolate and sugar or honey. Mix until sugar or honey is completely dissolved and the chocolate is melted. Remove the vanilla bean and the cinnamon sticks.
4. Adding a tablespoon at a time, mix some of the peppered water to the chocolate mixture until you reach a desired flavor. (Depending on your taste buds, you may have some extra peppered water; discard or refrigerate for another use.) Serve with a dollop of whipped cream, sprinkle the top with ground nuts.

French Hot Chocolate

I came up with this recipe, after watching the movie Chocolat, *and craving that enticingly, rich, beautifully thick liquid that was so often passed to the customers in a cup. I had been told that all it contained was solid chocolate heated with thick cream but I knew that there were more ingredients used during the preparation for such an irresistible beverage. So I played with different amounts of this and that, and finally took a sip of this amazingly luscious beverage. Ah, the glory of chocolate when warmed to perfection.*

Serves 2-3

3 tablespoons cocoa
1-1½ tablespoons sugar (amount depends on personal preference)
4½ cups milk, half and half or cream
8 ounces (1⅓ cups) dark chocolate finely chopped (⅔ cup bittersweet chocolate and ⅔ cup
  semi sweet chocolate chips or any combination)
1 teaspoon vanilla

1. In a small bowl, stir the sugar and cocoa together and put aside.
2. In a saucepan, heat the milk/cream over medium heat and bring to a slow simmer; remove from the heat, add the chocolate and stir until chocolate has thoroughly melted. Stir the vanilla into this mixture.
3. Vigorously whisk the cocoa and sugar into the hot milk until frothy and serve immediately with dollops of whipped cream, marshmallows and/or a slight sprinkle of nutmeg on top.

Miguel's Spicy Hot Chocolate

A girlfriend of mine who frequently visits a resort in Mexico brought this recipe back to me after one of her visits.
A gentleman she met named Miguel told her that the following is "mucho spicy, but, very, very good,"
and that this is an old recipe of his mother's, served often while growing up and passed down to him.
Although spicy, the flavor is one to be savored and enjoyed.

Serves 2-3

4 cups milk
½ cup cocoa
1 teaspoon flour
¼ cup brown sugar or brown sugar substitute
⅔ teaspoon crushed chili peppers
3 whole cloves, crushed or 1 teaspoon ground cloves
¼ teaspoon nutmeg
2-3 cinnamon sticks for stirring or 1 teaspoon cinnamon

1. Heat the milk to hot but not scalded.
2. Sift the cocoa and flour together into a saucepan, add a couple of tablespoons of hot milk and stir constantly until a paste forms.
3. While continuing to stir, add the sugar and spices and then pour this mixture into the heated milk. Reheat and constantly stir the milk mixture until all ingredients are thoroughly incorporated and heated; about 10-15 minutes.
4. Prior to pouring into mugs, use a slotted spoon to remove cinnamon sticks and cloves, then divide equally between 2-3 mugs. Serve with dollops of whipped cream sprinkled with chocolate sprinkles, or marshmallows.

Simplest of Hot Chocolates

Years ago I had the unusual opportunity to live in a shack with nine dogs, two cats, a horse and no water. Fortunately I kept a dozen or more jugs of water around at all times. One frigid snowy day, the power went out, leaving me with only an old Franklin woodstove to cook on. I had just run out of milk when I got an uncompromising craving for hot chocolate. So I searched the cupboards, found a bag of chocolate chips, put some in a cup, poured some water in and placed the mug on top of the stove. I stirred it every few minutes and in about 15 minutes I was drinking a mighty fine cup of hot chocolate and my craving was quenched in pure delight.

Serves 2

5 plus ounces of dark chocolate, finely chopped
   or use ⅔ cup of semi sweet chocolate chips
1⅔ cup water

1. In a sauce pan, bring the water to a light boil.
2. Add the chocolate and whisk the chocolate thoroughly into the water until completely melted.
3. Immediately pour into mugs and serve.

Mocha Hot Chocolate

The distinctive flavor of chocolate and coffee mixed together is a delight for many. So I simply felt that I had to come up with a fantastic blended drink combining these two exquisite flavors. This is a wonderful beverage to relish after a day out in the snow, and it will supply you with a burst of energy to get you through the evening ahead. Double or triple this recipe when serving company, keep the leftovers warm on the stove and when the requests for more are heard, you will be ready to oblige and refill the mugs.

Serves 2-3

2 ounces unsweetened chocolate, chopped into small chunks
1 tablespoon strong instant coffee
⅓ cup sugar
¾ teaspoon cinnamon (or ½ teaspoon cinnamon and ¼ teaspoon nutmeg)
Pinch of salt (optional)
¾ cup water
2 cups milk
2-3 cinnamon sticks
Whipped cream for topping (optional)
Sprinkle of nutmeg

1. Using a medium saucepan, mix the chocolate, coffee, cinnamon, salt and sugar thoroughly and add the water.
2. Bring this mixture to a slight simmer and stir over low medium heat until chocolate is melted and the mixture has blended.
3. Turn the heat up to a full boil, then reduce the heat back to a simmer, and continue cooking for 4 more minutes, stirring occasionally. After approximately 4 minutes, add the milk, allow to heat and pout into mugs.
4. Stir each mug with the cinnamon sticks and top with dollops of whipped cream, sprinkled with nutmeg.

Variation: (for adults only)
Add a shot of Amaretto, Kahlua, or mint-flavored liqueur for a special treat.

Hot Cocoa

Although often referred to as hot chocolate, hot cocoa is made from cocoa powder, whereas hot chocolate is made from solid chocolate. Personal preference decides which tastes better. On cold days when the rain is pouring down, I have often made this recipe and sat down by the fire to enjoy the moment. I suggest mixing the following cocoa recipes with a wire whisk, stirring vigorously, for the lumps can be cantankerous when trying to break them up in liquid.

Serves 2

¾ cup unsweetened cocoa
½ cup sugar (more or less depending on personal preference and taste)
1½ teaspoon cornstarch
¾ cup water
1½ cups milk
1 teaspoon vanilla (optional)
A dash of nutmeg or cinnamon, whipped cream or marshmallows for topping

1. In a medium sauce pan thoroughly mix the cocoa, sugar and cornstarch.
2. Set the temperature to low heat, gradually add the water and whisk vigorously. Increase the heat to medium low and add the milk. Continue stirring vigorously until the mixture begins to thicken and leaves a coat of chocolate on a spoon.
3. Stir in vanilla, if using, and serve immediately with suggested toppings.

Grandmom's Cocoa

This was my grandmother's recipe. The memories that it brings back, sitting in her kitchen, eating cookies right out of the oven and sipping this tasty drink are some that I will always cherish.

Serves 2-3

¼ cup plus unsweetened cocoa
1½ cup sugar
⅓ cup very hot water
4 cups light cream or half and half
½ teaspoon vanilla (optional)
Dash of nutmeg, cinnamon, whipped cream or marshmallows for topping (optional)

1. In a saucepan over medium heat, mix the cocoa, sugar and water together and stir vigorously with a whisk until mixture boils. Continue stirring vigorously for 1-2 minutes.
2. Stir the light cream into the cocoa mixture and make sure to stir consistently until very hot, but not boiling. Remove the saucepan from the heat and add vanilla if using and mix well. Serve immediately with topping of choice.

The sweetness of a mother's smile

A fresh baked cookie from a grandmother

A recipe from a neighbor

A laugh with a friend

A flower from a sweetheart

A day in the park with a dog

A chocolate bar broken in half

A 3-scoop cup of ice cream for 2

A piece of cake for a child

A bowl of soup for the ill

Kind looks from a stranger

The knowledge of a teacher to pass on through the years

The jokes of a comic, may bring you to tears

and

A pot of Stone Soup to add to for all times

That's a part of sharing!

Early Morning Risers

~ All of the following recipes can be doubled or tripled.
~ Use only softened butter, margarine or cream cheese, unless indicated otherwise.
~ Keep all baked goods covered in a plastic container or wrapped tightly in plastic wrap.
~ All baked goods can be frozen for up to nine days.
~ Use butter, margarine or pan spray when directed to grease the pan.
~ For a larger variety of muffins, breads, early morning fruit bars and crisps please see
Baking at High Altitude/The Muffin Lady's Old Fashioned Recipes *Cookbook*

What are early morning risers, you may ask? For me these have always been muffins, popovers, cereals, fruit bowls, toast, and if one absolutely has to, cinnamon rolls. These are the foods that many of us grab for quick breakfasts in this day of instant gratification. Rarely does a family have time to sit together at one table and eat before dashing out the door to catch the school bus or get to work on time. Have you ever noticed that on those rare occasions that this happens, if even for a minute, something inside of you smiles?

Although almost a forgotten tradition, some continue to go into their kitchens long before the light of dawn and begin to prepare breakfast. Today there are still those who rise early just to watch the sun rise, start the daily bread, get chores done early, and get some exercise in before their busy day begins. The following recipes are included for you, the early morning risers in mind. So grab a muffin as you go out the door for a run, feed the livestock, walk the dog, or get the newspaper and then come back inside and enjoy a bowl of oatmeal while reading the paper and waiting for everyone else to awaken.

Clockwise from top:
Christina's Family's Runeberg's Cakes, Page 57
Blueberry Popovers, Page 38
Pumpkin Pecan Muffins, Page 50
Pat's Oatmeal Bread, Page 59

Happiness Cake

❤ SUGAR FREE

If you begin your day with just a small slice of this cake, I can honestly guarantee that it will be a good day ahead. A recipe full of love and flavors, I have said it before, and I will again say it again, this truly is the finest cake that I make and share with others. Enjoy each and every slice and then pass this recipe on to all that you meet throughout your journeys.

Preheat oven to 98.6° F or 36 °C

Mix thoroughly:
1 cup of good thoughts
1 cup of kind deeds
1 cup well beaten faults
1 cup of consideration for others
2 cups of sacrifice
3 plus cups of forgiveness

Add:
Tears of joy, sorrow and sympathy
Flavor with love and kindly service
Fold in 4 cups of prayer and faith
Blend well
Fold into daily life
Bake well with the warmth of human kindness
And serve with a smile any time
It will satisfy the hunger of starved souls

31

Oatmeal

♥

Nothing is as simple as a bowl of hot oatmeal to begin the day and give one that burst of energy needed to get out the door. Full of goodness and healthy to boot, with the warmth of the early morning sun right in the bowl, oatmeal has been a favorite for centuries. Remember when you were young and just waking up, rubbing the sleep from your eyes, smelling the tempting fragrance of the homemade goodness waiting for you in the kitchen? This is that recipe, as it has always been; comforting, warm and full of flavor to be shared for centuries to come.

Serves 2

1⅜ milk or 1 cup milk mixed with ¾ cup water
1 cup old fashioned oats
2 tablespoons white or brown sugar, honey or sugar substitute (optional)
Pinch of sea salt
¼ cup or more additional milk, warmed in the microwave
   (amount depends on personal preference; I like mine drowned in warm milk)

1. In a 4-cup saucepan, bring the milk and/or water to a boil.
2. Add the oats and salt to the liquid, cook for about 7 minutes, stirring constantly, until most of the liquid is absorbed.
3. Spoon the cereal evenly into bowls, pour the additional milk over the oatmeal, top with sugar if you like and serve.

Variations:
• When adding the oats, also add ½ teaspoon cinnamon, nutmeg, and/or some dried fruit, such as raisins, craisins or berries for more flavor.
• While cooking, add ½ cup of chopped fresh berries, cherries or diced apple, peaches or pears, or slice a banana on top after spooning into bowls. Tastes great drizzled with maple syrup.

Great Grandmother's Baked Oatmeal

♥

My grandmother used to make this for me when I stayed overnight at her home, just as my great-grandmother had made it for my father so many years before. It always smelled so good and tasted just as good as it smelled, and I always ate a little too much; a delight I continue to do today. Quick and easy, it doesn't get any better than this. Your loved ones' bellies will leave home warm and full, while your home is filled with that country feeling of a meal well served. This is one of those special recipes that will be requested over and over again, and passed along for many years to come.

Serves 4-6

2 cups old fashioned oats
2 cups plus 2 tablespoons milk
4 eggs or liquid egg substitute
¼ cup vegetable oil
⅔ cup lightly packed brown sugar
1 teaspoon baking powder
½ teaspoon sea salt
1 teaspoon cinnamon
Sprinkle of nutmeg
½ cup plus raisins, blueberries, diced Granny Smith apples, peaches or pears

1. Grease a 1½-2 quart covered casserole dish thoroughly with margarine, pan spray or butter.
2. Mix the oats, milk, eggs, oil and brown sugar thoroughly, making sure there are no lumps of sugar.
3. Add the baking powder, salt, cinnamon and nutmeg and mix thoroughly, then add the raisins or diced fruit.
4. Cover and refrigerate overnight or for 8-10 hours.
5. Preheat oven to 350° F.
6. Remove the dish from the refrigerator; gently stir the mixture 1-2 times (not more), replace lid and bake for 55-60 minutes.
7. A creamy layer will have formed beneath the oats. Drizzle 2 tablespoons additional warmed milk on top and serve as is, or with maple syrup, butter and/or sliced bananas.
8. Store any leftovers covered in the refrigerator and reheat the next morning.

Cream of Rice

♥

Rice is right up there toward the top of the list as a food that promotes good health. I will always prefer brown rice over white, because it has much more flavor and character than white rice. Not many realize that a bowl of hot creamed rice will begin the day with a healthy supply of energy-inducing protein needed to get one through to the next meal. So for a bit of a change, try making this quick, easy, and tasty recipe and just watch the smiles appear as the bowls get rapidly emptied.

Serves 2-3

1 cup brown rice, rinsed with water and thoroughly drained
4¼ cups milk
Pinch of salt
½ teaspoon cinnamon (optional)
2 tablespoons butter
½ cup raisins or other dried fruit, blueberries, or diced apples
2 teaspoons honey, sugar or brown sugar per bowl, according to taste

1. In a medium saucepan, bring the milk and butter to a boil. Add the rice, salt, cinnamon and fruit (if using) and stir.
2. Cover the saucepan, lower the heat and simmer for approximately 10-12 minutes or until rice is chewy, not tough; remove from the heat and add the sweeteners, if using.
3. Serve immediately, with warmed milk and/or maple syrup.

Great Grandmother's Hasty Pudding

♥ SUGAR FREE

*During a visit from my parents, my father asked me if I had ever found his grandmother's recipe for
Hasty Pudding; stating that it was an old-time Colonial favorite he had enjoyed as a little boy and that he wanted
me to prepare it for him. Not knowing what Hasty Pudding was, I searched his mother's recipe box in an attempt to find it.
I found a browned card titled: Old Colonial Pudding, (Pennsylvania Dutch Hasty Pudding). I skimmed the card rapidly,
and realized that this was a simple cornmeal mush, and had been lovingly served to him decades ago, with lots of milk,
molasses or honey. I rapidly made a batch, hence the name 'Hasty' Pudding. Since my dad was diabetic, I substituted
sugar-free preserves for the molasses and honey. I must have done well, because he finished his whole bowl and
a reversal of roles occurred, for my mother then requested a recipe from me.*

Serves 4-6

2⅔ cups water
¾ teaspoons sea salt
1 cup corn meal
1 teaspoon vanilla or maple extract (optional)
Milk
1 tablespoon brown sugar or brown sugar substitute, maple syrup, molasses, honey, etc. (optional)

1. Bring the water and salt to a full boil in a medium saucepan.
2. Stirring constantly, sprinkle the cornmeal into the boiling water and reduce the heat to low. Add your extract here
   if you are using. Allow the corn mixture to simmer slowly for 35-40 minutes and then spoon it into deep bowls and
   serve with lots of milk, molasses, honey, brown sugar, maple syrup or sugar-free preserves.

Muesli

♥

Many believe that serving Muesli for breakfast began in Sweden. However, I asked a Swedish friend about this, and she sad that this nutritional breakfast cereal originated in Switzerland, created by an old doctor to assist his patients in eating healthier foods. It makes no difference where this delight originated; I am just glad that it has. Full of fruits, nuts and goodness, this cereal is a favorite way to start the day. However, do yourself a favor and make your own, beginning with one of the recipes below. Packaged versions tend to add more sugar and fat to help maintain the shelf life. When trying to eat healthier, the following recipe is just as quick and easy as opening a box, but much better for you.

Traditional Muesli

Serves 4

¾ cup old fashioned oats
½ cup barley flakes
1 cup milk
1 heaping tablespoon honey or brown sugar
1 tablespoon each chopped hazelnuts, almonds and sunflower seeds
½ cup raisins or chopped dried apricots (optional)
1 peeled, cored and grated Granny Smith apple
2 cups vanilla or plain yogurt

1. Place the oats, barley flakes and milk into a large bowl, cover and refrigerate overnight.
2. The next morning, grate the apple and add it to the oat mixture with the honey, nuts, seeds and fruits.
   Mix all together with the yogurt and serve.

Mom's Muesli

♥ SUGAR FREE

No nuts in this version. This is not just terrific tasting and very healthy for your family, it is also exceptionally easy to prepare; just never tell my father just how easy this is when you meet him in heaven, for he was old school and therefore thought all good food must take a long time to prepare.

Serves 1-2

1 cup plain yogurt
1 cup oats
½ teaspoon cinnamon
½ cup milk
1½ tablespoons sugar, honey or sugar substitute
1 peeled, cored and diced Granny Smith or pippin apple
1-2 tablespoons fresh squeezed lemon juice
1 orange or tangerine, peeled and separated into sections
and/or a handful of blueberries
1 sliced banana

1. Combine all ingredients except the banana in the order given in a large bowl. Cover and allow to sit in the refrigerator overnight.
2. Serve cool in the morning with fresh banana slices and drizzle with a small amount of milk or light cream if desired.

Popovers

♥ SUGAR FREE

The goodness in a basic recipe to which fruits, vegetables and spices are added is where most of our favorite recipes begin. Many have asked me what the difference between muffins and popovers is and the answer is rather simple. Popovers are lighter and have a fluffier texture than that of a muffin, which is a bit denser in consistency. Additionally, muffins, once removed from the oven, have a nice rounded top, whereas popovers tend to have a puffed but flat-top hat on. Looks can be deceiving though; once the suggested additions are added, I'm sure you will be pleasantly surprised with the taste, as will all that are awakened by the delicious fragrance that these bring into your home.

Makes approximately 5-6 large or 12 regular size popovers

Preheat oven to 425° F

1 cup plus 2 tablespoons flour
1 cup plus 1 tablespoon milk
¼-½ teaspoon salt
1 tablespoon butter, melted
2 eggs, or equivalent amount of egg substitute

1. Grease 5-6 large popover or 12 regular-size muffin sections.
2. Mix together the flour, salt, melted butter and milk.
3. Add the eggs, one at a time, and mix thoroughly until all ingredients are incorporated.
4. Fill each prepared section with batter until just below the top and bake at 425° F for 15 minutes, then lower the temperature to 350° F. (Do not open oven to decrease the temperature, simply decrease the temperature setting.)
5. Continue baking for approximately 23-25 minutes or until an inserted knife or toothpick comes out clean. Remove from the pan within 1-2 minutes and serve.

Variations:
Add ½ cup or more chopped fruits, nuts or finely chopped vegetables of choice; ¼-½ teaspoon of spice: vanilla, maple extract, almond or lemon extracts, cinnamon, nutmeg, ginger or cloves with the fruit or nuts; garlic, chili pepper, basil or dill weed with the vegetables. If adding chocolate chips, use only mini chips, as the larger ones will sink to the bottom of the popover.

Cheddar Apple Popovers

♥ SUGAR

Apples and cheddar cheese make a perfect combination of flavors to begin a new day. So very easy to make, this brings the taste of autumn into a house even on the warmest of summer days. Although rare anymore, there are days when I get up before dawn, make this recipe while the sun rises, and you can bet I grab one right out of the pan as I am heading outside to mix the horse's morning mash. You see, I think that these are best eaten hot, when the blend of flavor is at its peak.

Makes approximately 6-8 large popovers

Preheat oven to 425° F

2 extra large eggs, or equivalent amount of egg substitute
1 cup plus 2 tablespoons flour
Pinch of salt (optional)
1 cup milk
½ teaspoon vanilla
1 tablespoon butter, melted
1 Granny Smith or pippin apple, peeled, cored and diced
⅓ cup sharp cheddar cheese, grated

1. Thoroughly grease 6-8 large muffin or popover sections.
2. Thoroughly mix together the eggs, flour, salt (if used) and milk. Add the melted butter and vanilla and gently stir in the grated cheese and diced apples.
3. Divide the batter evenly between the prepared sections and bake for 15-17 minutes at 425° F and then lower the oven heat to 350° F (Do not open the oven to decrease the temperature, simply decrease the temperature setting.)
4. Continue baking for 23-25 minutes or until golden and an inserted knife or toothpick comes out clean. Cool for a couple of minutes, remove from the pan and serve.

Variation:
Omit the apples, and add ¼ cup fresh chopped basil leaves and simply mix it all together when adding the melted butter. These are a super complement to soups.

Maple Cinnamon Popovers

♥

The taste of maple, a pinch of cinnamon and raisins makes this recipe one of my very favorites to start the day with.
Years ago when I would arise at 2 a.m. to begin preparing the treats that had to be delivered later that morning,
I would often make this recipe up just for myself, to help me get through the morning grind.
These are much too good not to share, so please pass them around!

Makes approximately 5-6 large or 10 regular size popovers

Preheat oven to 425° F

1 cup plus 2 tablespoons flour
1 cup plus 1 tablespoon milk
¼-½ teaspoon salt
1 tablespoon butter, melted
2 eggs, or equivalent amount of egg substitute
1 teaspoon maple extract
1 teaspoon cinnamon
½ cup raisins (optional)
1-2 tablespoons maple syrup for topping

1. Grease 5-6 large muffin/popover or 10 regular size muffin sections.
2. Mix together the flour, milk, melted butter, cinnamon, salt and maple extract.
3. Add the eggs one at a time, and mix thoroughly until all ingredients are incorporated; gently mix in the raisins.
4. Fill the prepared sections with batter to just below the top and bake at 425° F for 15 minutes, then lower the temperature to 350° F. (Do not open the oven to decrease the temperature, simply decrease the temperature setting.)
5. Continue baking for 23-25 minutes or until an inserted knife or toothpick comes out clean. Remove from pan within the first minute, place on a piece of waxed paper, drizzle a little maple syrup over the top of each popover and serve.

Ann's Blueberry Breakfast Popover

SUGAR

Ann is a wonderful woman whom I met during a journey to the southwestern portion of Colorado. She also has been baking and cooking for years, and has shared many of her recipes with those who live on the southwestern slope and beyond. We both have a fondness for the glorious scents that good foods bring into a home, as well as all the smiles that such endeavors bring. When I asked if she would share some of her recipes for publication in this book, she enthusiastically complied. The following is one of her favored, delicious recipes. Easy, and full of flavor, this recipe is sure to become an early morning favorite for many years to come.

Serves 4-6

Preheat oven to 450° F

1 cup flour
3 eggs
1¼ cups milk
1 tablespoon butter, melted
Pinch of salt
1 cup frozen blueberries
2 tablespoons additional butter

1. Melt 2 tablespoons butter in a 9-inch cast iron skillet.
2. Place flour and next four ingredients into a blender and blend on high for two minutes.
3. Pour the batter into the prepared skillet and sprinkle the top with blueberries.
4. Resisting the urge to open the oven too early, bake for 35-40 minutes. If the oven is opened too soon, you take the risk of having a collapsed popover, so wait until 35 minutes have passed before checking the product. You will know they have finished baking when the top is lightly browned and crisp or when an inserted toothpick or knife comes out clean.
5. Serve immediately with warm maple syrup.

Simple Bowl of Fruit and Yogurt

♥ **SUGAR** FREE

This may be one of the easiest recipes there is on earth. It can be used anywhere, no matter what country or altitude one lives in. No cooking or heating is required. All you need do is pick out your favorite fruits, chop the larger fruits into pieces and mix with the brief list of ingredients. Quick, simple and full of nutrition, even younger children can prepare and enjoy this dish while watching early morning cartoons, waiting for you to begin the day ahead.

Serves 1

½-¾ cup chopped fruit (if using berries do not chop them)
½ cup plain low-fat yogurt
1 teaspoon honey or 1 scant teaspoon sugar substitute (optional)

1. Place fruit into a single serving bow, top with yogurt and honey.
2. Mix it all up and serve.

Variation:
Sprinkle with granola for a bit of crunch and an extra dose of nutrition.

Early Morning Fruit Bars

♥ SUGAR FREE

This is one of those recipes that can honestly be enjoyed any time of day. However when I first began making these, many said that they were like a breakfast cereal bar, only better. So for all of you out there who begin the day with prepackaged breakfast items, why not start early with a bit more nutrition supplied from these easily assembled, scrumptious, fruity treats?

Makes 9-12 bars

Preheat oven to 350° F

1½ cups (3 sticks) canola oil or melted margarine
3 cups plus 2 tablespoons oats
2⅔ cups flour
¾ cup brown sugar or brown sugar substitute
1½ teaspoons cinnamon
4 cups blueberries, fresh or frozen, thawed and drained of juice
2 cups raspberries, fresh or frozen, thawed and drained of juice
1½ tablespoons flour
1 cup raspberry jam (sugar-free jam works fine)
1½ tablespoons flour

1. Mix together the oil/margarine, oats, flour, sugar and cinnamon until ingredients hold together and crumbs begin to form. The dough will be somewhat moist.
2. Remove 1¼ cups of this mixture and place in a small bowl to use for the topping
3. Grease a 9x13-inch pan with butter, margarine or pan spray.
4. Evenly press the remaining crumbs onto the bottom of the prepared pan and bake crust for 20 minutes while preparing the filling.
5. For the filling, place the blueberries, raspberries, jam and 1½ tablespoons of flour into a medium bowl and gently mix until the jam is thoroughly incorporated.
6. Remove the bottom crust from the oven after 20 minutes and immediately spread filling evenly and completely over crust.
7. Remix the reserved crumbs to further break them up, sprinkle them over the filling and bake another 20 minutes or until the topping is golden. Allow to cool prior to cutting into 9 or 12 pieces. Cover the leftovers in the pan with plastic wrap.

Variations:
Raspberry jam with blackberries; apricot jam with peaches; blueberry jam with blackberries; or any combination of the fruits given. (Strawberries get too mushy in this recipe.)

Bob's Favorite Blueberry Muffins

♥ SUGAR ~~FREE~~

Of all the blueberry muffins that I have made throughout the years this specific recipe remains the favorite, especially for Bob, one of my original test tasters. Originating from my Great-Grandmother's Blueberry Coffeecake, this recipe has been enjoyed in a variety of shapes and sizes for more than a century. Nice, light and good for you too, what better treat could you ask for early in the morning or anytime throughout the day?

Makes 8 large or 12 regular size muffins

Preheat oven to 375° F

TOPPING:
2 tablespoons sugar or sugar substitute
2 tablespoons flour
1 teaspoon cinnamon
2 teaspoons butter or margarine (optional)

1. Thoroughly combine and set aside.

MUFFIN BATTER:
½ cup (1 stick) butter or margarine
1½ cups sugar or 1⅓ cup sugar substitute
1 tablespoon vanilla
4¼ cups flour
5 teaspoons baking powder
2 cups plus 2 tablespoons milk
1½ cups fresh or frozen blueberries

1. Thoroughly mix together the butter, sugar, vanilla, milk, flour and baking powder.
2. Add the blueberries gently, and at slow speed, mix berries thoroughly into the batter.
3. Grease 8 large or 12 regular-size muffin sections.
4. Fill each muffin section with batter and sprinkle topping on top of each muffin.
6. Bake 20-35 minutes (depending on muffin section size) or until they are golden and feel firm on top or until inserted knife or toothpick comes out clean.

Variations:
RASPBERRY MUFFINS
Substitute raspberries for the blueberries.

PEACH MUFFINS
Substitute chopped peaches (peeled fresh or canned) for the blueberries, and add ¼ teaspoon nutmeg to the batter and a pinch of nutmeg to the crumb topping.

Lemon Poppy Muffins

When I first began to bake and distribute my treats around town, a customer asked if I could bake her some Lemon Poppy Muffins. Not knowing what I was getting myself into, I responded with, "Sure I can." So I went home, experimented with ingredients and came up with a poppy seed muffin. Then I added some lemon juice, peel and extract to the recipe. The look was there, but the flavor wasn't quite lemony enough for me. That is when I thought to add a bit of lemon curd to the batter. The next day, I took this customer a Lemon Poppy Muffin and she was delighted, as many others have been since this recipe was developed.

Makes 5-6 large or 10-12 regular size muffins

Preheat oven to 375° F

¼ cup (½ stick) melted butter, margarine or canola oil
¾ cups sugar or sugar substitute
2½ tablespoons lemon juice
2 teaspoons lemon extract
1 heaping tablespoon lemon curd
2 eggs
1 cup milk
2¼ cups flour
1 tablespoon baking powder
½ teaspoon soda
¼ cup poppy seeds

1. Thoroughly mix the butter, sugar, eggs, milk, lemon juice, lemon extract and lemon curd in a large bowl.
2. Add the dry ingredients and poppy seeds to the egg mixture. Thoroughly mix batter until all ingredients are fully incorporated.
3. Grease 5-6 large 10-12 regular-size muffin or 2 dozen mini muffin sections.
4. Fill each muffin section ⅞ full with the batter.
5. Bake 15-35 minutes (depending on size of muffin sections) until firm to the touch or until inserted knife or toothpick comes out clean.

Variation:
LEMON FRUIT MUFFINS
Omit the poppy seeds and add 1 cup fresh raspberries or blueberries sprinkled with a pinch of flour prior to adding to the batter.

High altitude only: If doubling this recipe, add an extra egg, bringing the total to 5 eggs. If tripling, add two extra eggs, bringing your total to 8 eggs.

Orange Muffins for Valerie

Last year while attending an International Association of Culinary Professionals (IACP) conference I met a new friend, Valerie. Valerie was at the conference representing Chef's Choice, a company dedicated to supplying some of the finest home and commercial kitchen appliances available. After we were introduced we immediately began talking, and soon learned that we had much in common. She asked if I had a recipe for orange muffins, to which I replied not yet but I would come up with one for her. Upon returning home, I began to play around with ingredients, and eventually developed this recipe. When I took samples to my tasters, all responded brightly and many asked what had taken me so long.

Makes 6 large or 12 regular size muffins

Preheat oven to 375 ° F

6 tangelos or 5 oranges
¾ cup sugar
2 tablespoons Grand Marnier (optional)
1 tablespoon orange extract
2 eggs
½ cup canola oil
2 cups plus 2 tablespoons flour
1 teaspoon baking powder
½ teaspoon baking soda
1 inch-long twig of orange balsam, finely minced (if available)
Possible additions: ½ cup raisins, craisins, chopped pecans, mini chocolate chips, blueberries or cranberries

1. Leaving the rind on each orange, cut the top and bottom from each orange. Cut each orange into sections and using a food processor fitted with a grating wheel, process all but 2 oranges. You should have 1 cup of pulp. Squeeze the juice from remaining 2 oranges into the pulp to a make 1½ cups total. You may need to squeeze another half of an orange into the measuring cup to get this much.
2. Grease 6 large or 12 regular-size muffin sections..
3. Thoroughly mix together the eggs, sugar, oranges, oil, Grand Marnier and orange extract. Add flour, baking powder, baking soda and orange balsam. Mix together until thoroughly incorporated.
4. Using a rubber/plastic spatula, scoop the batter and fill each prepared muffin section ¾ full and drizzle the top of each muffins with a small amount of additional juice.
5. Bake for 25-30 minutes or until an inserted knife or toothpick comes out clean.

Variation:
ORANGE CRANBERRY MUFFINS
Add ¾ cup fresh cranberries and ½ cup chopped walnuts (optional) to the batter for a different flavor.

Apple Crumb Muffins

SUGAR FREE

I am perplexed as to why I even came up with this recipe; but I am glad that I did. It was on a cold, snowy autumn day and I had turned the oven on for some extra heat when I spotted a couple of apples that I had intended to use for baked apples. I stared at the apples for the next few seconds, and then decided to play. So I added a bit of this and a tad of that. I thought that the top looked boring, so I added a quick crumb topping and put them into the oven to bake. They came out looking as gorgeous as they do when I bake them today; and they taste just as great as they look!

Makes 6 large muffins

Preheat oven to 375° F

MUFFINS:
2 cups diced apples
¾ cups sugar or sugar substitute
¼ cup (½ stick) melted butter, margarine or canola oil
2 eggs
1 cup plus 1 tablespoon milk
2 teaspoons vanilla
2½ cups flour
1 tablespoon baking powder
½ teaspoon baking soda
¾ teaspoon cinnamon
¼ teaspoon nutmeg
¾ cup raisins or chopped walnuts (optional)

CRUMB TOPPING:
2 tablespoons sugar or sugar substitute
1 plus tablespoon butter or margarine
¼ cup flour
¼ teaspoon cinnamon

1. Grease 6 large muffin sections.
2. In a small bowl, using 2 knives or forks, mix all topping ingredients together until crumbly and put aside.
3. Thoroughly mix together the eggs, butter, sugar, milk and vanilla.
4. Add the chopped apples to the egg mixture and mix gently.
5. Gradually add the flour, baking powder, baking soda and spices and mix thoroughly. Add the raisins or nuts.
6. Fill each muffin section almost to the top with the apple batter.
7. Top each with a sprinkle of Crumb Topping.
8. Bake for 30-35 minutes or until inserted knife or toothpick comes out clean.

Hint: If using raisins, soak them in very hot water for a minimum of 10 minutes prior to adding to a batter or dough.

High altitude only: If doubling this recipe, add an extra egg, bringing the total to 5 eggs. If tripling, add two extra eggs, bringing your total to 8 eggs.

Cheddar Muffins

♥ SUGAR FREE

*Personally, I think that these muffins are a perfect accompaniment to a bowl of soup or chili.
However, many customers would grab these out of my delivery basket early in the morning. They used to tell me
that the cheesy taste and moist texture, in addition to a few vegetables, made these a great food to start the day with.
A versatile recipe, whereby one can add different vegetables, meats or fruits and a variety of seasonings according
to what the muffins are accompanying, making this an exceptional addition to all recipe collections.*

Makes 4-5 large muffins

Preheat oven to 375 ° F

½ cup (1 stick) melted butter, margarine or canola oil
  (I use margarine)
2 tablespoons sugar or sugar substitute
2 cups plus 2 tablespoons flour
3 diced scallions
2 eggs or equivalent liquid egg substitute

2 teaspoons baking powder
¾ cup plus 1 tablespoon milk
¾ cup shredded Cheddar or Swiss cheese
2 ounces cream cheese, cut into pieces
½ teaspoon garlic powder (optional)
¾ teaspoon dill (optional)
Salt and pepper optional

1. At slow speed, mix all of the ingredients until thoroughly combined.
2. Grease 4-5 large muffin sections.
3. Fill each muffin section ⅞ full with the batter.
4. Bake 25-35 minutes or until toothpick comes out clean but moist. Serve warm for best flavor.

Variations:
CHEDDAR APPLE MUFFINS
Leave out scallions, dill, and garlic powder, and add ¾ cup chopped apples, 1 teaspoon cinnamon and ¼ teaspoon nutmeg to the batter. One half cup of raisins or chopped nuts can also be added.

SPINACH CHEESE MUFFINS
Add ¾ cup cooked and chopped spinach.

BACON CHEESE MUFFINS
Add 3 large slices of crumbled bacon or ⅔ cup of diced ham.
Jalapeno Cheddar Muffins: Add 2 drops of hot sauce, 2 teaspoon chopped, diced jalapenos and ¼ cup diced green pepper. With this combination, use cheddar or pepper jack cheese.

CHEDDAR BROCCOLI MUFFINS
Add ¾ cup chopped broccoli, cooked and drained to the batter.

High Altitude Only: If doubling this recipe, add an extra egg, bringing the total to 5 eggs. If tripling, add two extra eggs, bringing your total to 8 eggs.

Buttermilk Corn Muffins

Way up on the mountain, there are many days when I often wish that I was down in Mexico, sitting by the sea. One morning long ago, I decided to make a recipe that could momentarily fulfill my wish. I came up with this recipe to go with a batch of Huevos Rancheros. Later that morning, when I began to eat, I shut my eyes, and instantly I could hear reggae music, waves crashing against the shore and the sweet accent of the natives in a Mexican resort. Never doubt the power of one's imagination, for when paired with different cuisines, it can take you anywhere, without even leaving your home.

Makes 8 large or 12 regular size muffins

Preheat oven to 375° F

3 cups corn meal
3 cups flour
⅓ cup sugar
1 tablespoon baking powder
1½ teaspoons baking soda
1½ teaspoons cayenne pepper
5 eggs
3⅓ cups buttermilk
¾ cup (1½ sticks) melted butter
3 teaspoons diced jalapenos (optional)

1. Mix the dry ingredients together in a large mixing bowl.
2. Add the eggs, butter and jalapenos to the dry ingredients and then gradually add the buttermilk and mix the batter thoroughly.
3. Grease 8 large or 12 regular size muffin sections.
4. Fill each muffin section to the top with the batter.
5. Bake 25-35 minutes or until inserted toothpick comes out clean.

Variation:
CHEESE CORN MUFFINS
Using the recipe above, add 1 cup shredded cheddar and ½ cup corn kernels with the eggs and buttermilk.
Jalapenos optional.

Pumpkin Pecan Muffins

This grand recipe is so spicy, moist and bursting with flavor, one might think that these muffins were pulled right off the vine in a pumpkin patch. This recipe will provide a beautiful path to an early morning walk, even on the dreariest of days. Your senses will be filled with the fragrance of earthy spice while your palate is enveloped in the nutty essence mingled with the pumpkin.

Makes 8-10 large or 24 regular size muffins

Preheat oven to 350° F

2 eggs
1 cup (2 sticks) butter (do not substitute)
1½ cups sugar
1¾ cups flour
1 teaspoon baking soda
1 tablespoon cinnamon
2 teaspoons ginger
½ teaspoon nutmeg
½ teaspoon cloves
⅓ cup ice cold water
2 cups plus 2 tablespoons canned pumpkin
⅔ cup chopped pecans (reserve 2 tablespoons)

1. Cream together the butter, sugar and eggs.
2. Add the dry ingredients, spices and chopped nuts to the egg mixture in two parts, alternating with the water. Mix between each addition until just blended.
3. Lightly mix the ingredients while slowly adding the pumpkin. Thoroughly mix all the ingredients for 3 minutes on medium speed in the electric mixer.
4. Grease 8-10 large muffin pan sections and fill with batter. Sprinkle each top with the reserved nuts.
5. Bake 40-45 minutes or until an inserted knife or toothpick comes out clean.

Variation:
PUMPKIN BREAD
This recipe can also be made into a loaf of bread, simply by substituting a 9x5-inch bread pan and one 4-inch bread pan for the muffin pans and baking for 60-75 minutes or until an inserted knife or toothpick comes out clean. This recipe also works wonderfully as mini bread loaves.

Cinnamon Sugar Muffins

SUGAR

Almost every Sunday my grandparents would come over to our house. More often than not, Grandfather would come by early and bring us a box of fresh doughnuts, eat a few, then return home to gather both grandmothers and bring them back over. I usually went for the cinnamon sugar doughnuts, for those were my favorite. So a few years back, with a craving for those special doughnuts, I came up with this recipe. Although not in the shape of a doughnut, the taste came so very close—warm, soft and sweet—that for a split second I thought I saw my grandfather.

Makes 8-9 large or 18 regular size muffins

Preheat oven to 350° F

½ cup (1 stick) butter or margarine
⅔ cup of sugar or equivalent amount of sugar substitute
2 eggs
2¼ cups flour
2 teaspoons baking powder
⅔ cup milk
¾ teaspoon cinnamon
¼ teaspoon nutmeg
3-4 tablespoons melted butter (do not substitute oil)
½ plus cup of sugar, or equivalent amount of sugar substitute
1½-2 teaspoons cinnamon

1. Grease 8-9 large or 16-18 regular-size muffin sections.
2. Cream together the butter and sugar, and then add the egg and mix thoroughly. Add the flour, spices and baking powder to the egg mixture, alternating with the milk. Continue mixing until these ingredients are incorporated.
3. Fill each muffin section almost to the top of each muffin section and bake for 25-30 minutes or until inserted knife or toothpick comes out clean.
4. While the muffins are baking, melt the 3-4 tablespoons butter. In a small bowl, mix together the sugar and cinnamon.
5. When muffins are done, allow them to cool for a minute, then remove one by one, dip all sides of each into the melted butter, and roll in the cinnamon sugar. Serve immediately for best flavor.

High altitude only: If doubling this recipe, add an extra egg, bringing the total to 5 eggs. If tripling, add two extra eggs, bringing your total to 8 eggs.

Ann's Seeded Carrot Muffins

This is a fabulous recipe to start your day with. It is so good and healthy that as you head out for your early morning walk or run, the scents of vegetables, fruits and spice coming from this delicious treat may temporarily place you into a vegetable garden, rather than the sidewalk of a busy street. Enjoy the moment!

Makes 12 regular size muffins

Preheat oven to 375° F

10 ounces (2-3 medium carrots), unpeeled, cut into chunks
6 tablespoons pumpkin seeds
6 tablespoons raw sunflower seeds
3 large eggs
1 cup plus 2 tablespoons canola oil
¾ cup drained, canned, crushed pineapple
2 tablespoons vanilla extract
2¼ cups flour
1 to 1½ cups granulated sugar
1 tablespoon ground cinnamon
2½ teaspoons baking soda
⅔ cup raisins (optional)

1. Using a steamer or a double boiler, steam the carrots until tender, about 25 minutes. Remove and cool for a few minutes before mashing. A few remaining lumps are okay. Allow mashed carrots to drain in a strainer for 15 minutes or so to remove all excess water. If you need to, use the back of a large spoon to push the excess water through the mesh.
2. Toast the seeds in a small cake tin in a toaster oven or oven at 325° F until lightly browned, about 8-10 minutes. Allow seeds to cool.
3. In a medium bowl, beat the eggs. Add oil, carrot puree, pineapple, seeds and vanilla, mixing thoroughly. In a separate bowl, stir together dry ingredients. Make a well in the dry ingredients and pour in egg mixture. Stir just until all ingredients are fully incorporated.
4. In a regular size muffin pan, grease 12 muffin sections well with butter, margarine or pan spray.
5. Divide the batter evenly among the prepared muffin sections and bake about 22 minutes or until tops spring back when lightly pressed with your finger. Cool in pan 10 minutes before serving with lots of butter.

Cherry Almond Muffins

I think cherries and almonds go together like a hand and glove, which makes this recipe my all time favorite muffin. When I had my delivery route, these muffins were one of the first recipes that went into the oven. The almond fragrance would take over the kitchen, and the first bite would explode with the juice of sweet, dark cherries and the crunch of nutritious almonds. After one of these muffins, I knew I'd get everything done and make it through the day just fine. For those who wake early and who love cherries, then this recipe is a must-have in your collection.

Makes 4-5 large or 12 regular size muffins

Preheat oven to 375° F

¼ cup (½ stick) melted butter, margarine or canola oil
¾ cups sugar
2 teaspoons vanilla
1 teaspoon almond extract
2 eggs
1 cup milk

2¼ cups flour
1 tablespoon baking powder
½ teaspoon baking soda
2 cups fresh and pitted or frozen and partially thawed dark, red cherries (do not drain)
⅓ cup sliced almonds

1. Grease 4-5 large or 12 regular-size muffin sections.
2. Thoroughly mix the melted butter, sugar, eggs, milk, vanilla and almond extract. Add the dry ingredients to the egg mixture alternating with the cherries.
3. Fill muffins sections ⅞ full with the batter. Sprinkle almond slices on top of each muffin and bake 20-35 minutes (depending on muffin size) or until inserted knife or toothpick comes out clean.

Hint: If you do not like almonds or have an allergy to nuts, delete the almond extract and nuts, and bake as directed.

Variations:
ALMOND POPPY SEED MUFFINS
Omit the cherries, add 1 additional tablespoon of milk and 3-4 tablespoons of poppy seeds to the batter and bake as directed.

ALMOND CHOCOLATE CHIP MUFFINS
Omit the cherries and add ⅓ cup mini chocolate chips to the batter and bake as directed.

PEACH MUFFINS
Substitute chopped peaches for the cherries, omit the almond extract and add ¼ teaspoon nutmeg to the batter.

High altitude only: If doubling this recipe, add an extra egg, bringing the total to 5 eggs. If tripling, add two extra eggs, bringing your total to 8 eggs.

Buttermilk Rhubarb Muffins

There is a beautiful area in Colorado where wild rhubarb grows right next to a creek. One day while visiting this location, I decided to pick some of the rhubarb to bake a pie that evening. Evidently I picked too much and had lots of leftovers to play around with. I remember thinking to myself that if rhubarb tastes so good in pies, maybe it would taste just as good in muffins. After several trials this recipe came out of the oven and to my delight tasted pretty darn good. This recipe does not work well with frozen rhubarb, because it gets too stringy and mushy, so use only fresh rhubarb.

Makes 6 large or 12 regular size muffins

Preheat oven to 375° F

2¼ cups flour
1 cup sugar
¼ cup canola oil
2 teaspoon baking powder
½ teaspoon baking soda
2 eggs
½ cup plus 1 tablespoon buttermilk
1 teaspoon vanilla
½ teaspoon cinnamon or ½ teaspoon freshly grated lemon rind
Sprinkle of nutmeg (optional)
Scant 2 cups fresh rhubarb, chopped

1. Grease 6 large or 12 regular-size muffin sections.
2. Mix together the eggs, oil, sugar, buttermilk, vanilla in a mixing bowl until thoroughly incorporated.
3. Gradually add the flour, baking powder, baking soda and spices, then add the chopped rhubarb. Mix all ingredients together until incorporated.
4. Fill the prepared muffin sections evenly with the batter and bake for approximately 25-40 minutes (depending on chosen pan size) or until firm to touch and an inserted knife or toothpick comes out clean.

High altitude only: If doubling this recipe, add an extra egg, bringing the total to 5 eggs. If tripling, add two extra eggs, bringing your total to 8 eggs.

Mom's Banana Chocolate Chip Muffins

These vanishing muffins are standard staples for early morning risers. Quick, easy and good, the scents escaping from these muffins fill your home, and may make it easier to arouse all out of bed. It always worked for me while growing up. I hated to get out of my warm bed in the morning. Occasionally my mother would awaken early and make up a batch of these. The aroma always came through my closed door and was so enticing that I had to sneak down to the kitchen, grab one and then sneak back up to my room to enjoy this treat before anyone else. I didn't know for many years that I was not alone in this venture, for my father would also sneak down to the kitchen, grab one right out of the pan and then go back upstairs.

Makes 8-9 large, 14 regular size or 2 dozen mini muffins

Preheat oven to 375° F

6 large, ripe bananas
3 eggs
¾ cups (1½ sticks) butter or margarine
½ cup milk less 1 tablespoon
1 tablespoon vanilla
¾ cup sugar
3 cups plus 2 tablespoons flour
1½ teaspoons baking powder
1½ teaspoons baking soda
2 teaspoons cinnamon
¾ cup chocolate chips
Additions: blueberries or raspberries

1. Mash the bananas in a mixing bowl.
2. Add the butter, eggs, sugar, vanilla and milk to the mashed bananas and mix thoroughly.
3. Add the dry ingredients and choice of an addition and mix batter thoroughly.
4. Grease 8-9 large, 14-15 regular-size or 26-30 dozen mini muffin sections.
5. Fill each muffin section to the top and bake 20-35 minutes (depends on size of muffin pan section) or until muffins feel firm to touch and an inserted knife or toothpick comes out clean.

Oatmeal Muffins

♥ SUGAR

Healthy and moist with lots of flavor, what more could one ask for to begin a busy day ahead?

Makes 6 large or 12 regular size muffins

Preheat oven to 350° F

TOPPING:
½ cup oats
⅓ cup flour
⅓ cup brown sugar or brown sugar substitute
¼ cup (½ stick) butter or margarine
½ teaspoon cinnamon

1. Mix all topping ingredients together until crumbly and then set aside.

MUFFIN BATTER:
⅓ cup canola oil
½ cup sugar or sugar substitute
2 eggs or equivalent liquid substitute
1 cup plus 2 tablespoons oats
1½ cups whole wheat flour
1 tablespoon baking powder
1½ teaspoons cinnamon
½ teaspoon nutmeg
1 cup plus 2 tablespoons milk
½ cup raisins and/or chopped walnuts, blueberries or diced peeled apples

1. Thoroughly mix the oil, eggs, and sugar. Add the remaining ingredients alternately with the milk. Gently but thoroughly mix the batter together.
2. Grease 6 large or 12 regular-size muffin sections..
3. Fill the muffin sections almost to the top with the batter and then sprinkle the top of each muffin with crumb topping and bake 20-30 minutes (depending on size of muffin section) or until an inserted toothpick comes out moist but clean.

High altitude only: If doubling this recipe, add an extra egg, bringing the total to 5 eggs. If tripling, add two extra eggs, bringing your total to 8 eggs.

Christina's Family's Runeberg's Cakes

Christina, my lovely friend from Stockholm, Sweden, shared this recipe with me after finding it on the internet during a search for family information. She calls them "Little Finnish Cakes" and sent me a short tidbit relative to how these delicious little cakes became a traditional treat in Finland in celebration of the birthday of Johan Ludvig Runeberg, a famous 19th century Finnish poet. Evidently, Johan enjoyed beginning his day with these little sweet cakes. So delicious they were, (and still are) that their reputation grew wide and today you can buy these wonderful little cakes everywhere in Finland; that is if you get to the bakeries early enough, as they have a tendency to sell out quickly.

Makes 12 individual cakes

Preheat oven to 350° F

¾ cup (1½ sticks) butter or shortening
¾ cup sugar
2 eggs
½ teaspoon almond extract
¾ cup plus 1 tablespoon flour
¾ cup toasted bread crumbs
1 teaspoon cinnamon (optional)
½ teaspoon cloves (optional)
1 teaspoon baking powder
¼ cup cream or half and half
A variety of fruit preserves
¼ cup water
¼ cup sugar
¼ teaspoon almond or rum extract
½ cup powdered sugar
1½ teaspoons water or milk

1. Cream together the butter and sugar. Add the eggs one at a time, then the almond extract. Add the flour, bread crumbs, baking powder and spices alternately with the cream and mix thoroughly, making sure all ingredients are fully incorporated and smooth.
2. Grease 12 regular size muffin sections or fill each section with a paper muffin cup.
3. Divide the batter evenly between the muffin sections and with a floured thumb make an indentation into each cake and fill each with the preserves and bake for 15-20 minutes or until an inserted knife or toothpick comes out clean.
4. While the cakes are baking, mix together the water, sugar and remaining almond extract to make a syrup. After removing each cake from the pan, brush each generously with this sugar mixture.
5. Mix together the powdered sugar and water and either pipe a ring around the jam or dollop a small amount on top of each cake and serve warm.

Pat's Whole Wheat Bread

Pat Congden is a fine, elderly woman whom I have had the pleasure to meet, share times with, and devour her treats. Years ago she would make the bread for me during the brief period of time that I had a bakery/deli affectionately called The Shop. I had never tasted homemade bread like hers before, nor had my customers. Her loaves sold out daily; they made the best bread for sandwiches that I have tasted since moving to Colorado so long ago. When started first thing in the morning, the heavenly scent of the following homemade breads will linger in your home throughout the day, enticing all who enter to request a slice or three.

Makes 2 loaves

2 packages of dry active yeast
2 cups warm water
½ cup honey
½ cup brown sugar
¼ cup (½ stick) butter
2½ teaspoons salt (must use, do not delete)
3½ cups whole wheat flour
3½-¾ cups all purpose flour
½ cup raisins, previously soaked in hot water, drained and patted dry (optional)
Egg wash (1 egg white to 2 tablespoons water, mixed well)
1-2 tablespoons melted butter

1. Sprinkle the yeast into ½ cup of warm water, cover, and allow to sit for 10 minutes or until it bubbles. Add the remaining water, the honey and brown sugar; cover and allow to rest for about 15 minutes.
2. In a large mixing bowl, add the butter to the yeast mixture, then gradually add the flours, salt and raisins (if using). Mix thoroughly until all ingredients are incorporated. Remove the dough from the bowl and knead it on a floured surface 8-10 times.
3. Gather the dough and place it in another large greased bowl. Cover this bowl with a warm damp cloth,   and place in a warm spot to rise to double in bulk, about 1½ hours.*
4. Thoroughly grease two 9x5-inch bread pans with pan spray or butter.
5. Once the dough has doubled, remove it from the bowl, shape it into 2 loaves and place the loaves into the prepared pans. Cover with a warm, damp cloth and allow the loaves to rise to double again in a warm area, about 1 hour.
6. Preheat oven to 350° F.
7. With a pastry brush, brush the egg wash all over the top of loaves and bake at 350° F for approximately 1 hour or until golden on top and when tapped with your hand it sounds hollow inside. You may check for doneness by inserting a knife into the center of a loaf. If it comes out clean, your bread is done.
8. Remove the pan from the oven and spread a small amount of melted butter all over the top. Cool the bread in the pan for approximately 10-15 minutes, remove and serve or allow cooling for a longer period and place into a large plastic bag.

*****Hint:** The dough should feel slightly warm during first rising.

Pat's Oat Bread

*Ah, the glory of the mingled taste and scent of homemade bread! This recipe is much too good not to share with others;
I feel very fortunate that Pat has shared this with me to pass along to you! For many of you who watch what you eat,
this is a recipe full of whole grain goodness and a taste that will have those you serve coming back for more. In addition to
the authentic, wholesome flavor, this recipe is full of healthy oats that help to reduce cholesterol, hypertension, and high
blood pressure, increase fiber, and overall, maintain a healthy heart. All this goodness wrapped up in a moist, rich,
satisfying loaf of everyday bread will make this recipe a favorite in your household for generations to come.*

Makes 2 loaves

2 cups warm water
2 packages dry active yeast
¼ cup sugar
½ cup oats, quick or old fashioned
1 cup milk
1 tablespoon butter, melted
¼ cup (½ stick) butter
4¾-5 cups flour, plus an additional 4-5 tablespoons
  used when kneading dough

½ cup raisins, previously soaked in hot water,
  drained and patted dry (optional)
1 teaspoon cinnamon (optional)
2 teaspoons salt
Egg wash, made of 1 egg white and 2 tablespoons water,
  mixed together

1. Sprinkle the yeast into ½ cup of the warm water, cover and allow to sit for 10 minutes or until it bubbles. Add the sugar and remaining water and allow to rest for a few more minutes.
2. While the yeast is dissolving in the warm water, heat the milk to a boil, stir in the oats and melted butter, stirring over medium heat for a little more than 1 minute, or until the oats have absorbed most of the milk. Allow the oats to cool until just warm.
3. In a large mixing bowl, add the butter to the yeast mixture, then gradually adding the flours, oats, salt cinnamon and raisins (if using). Mix thoroughly until all ingredients are incorporated.
4. Gather the dough, and knead it 6-8 times on a floured board while adding the additional tablespoons of flour.
5. Place the dough into another large greased bowl. Cover this bowl with a warm damp cloth, and place in a warm spot until the dough doubles in bulk, about 1½ hours.*
6. Thoroughly grease two 9x5-inch bread pans with pan spray or butter.
7. Once the dough has doubled, remove it from the bowl, shape it into 2 loaves and place the loaves into the prepared pans. Cover with a warm, damp cloth and allow the loaves to rise to double again in a warm area, about 1 hour.
8. Preheat oven to 350° F.
9. With a pastry brush, brush the egg wash over the top of the loaves and bake for approximately 1 hour, or until golden on top and when tapped with your hand it sounds hollow inside. You may check for doneness by inserting a knife into the center of a loaf: If it comes out clean, your bread is done.
10. Remove the pan from the oven, spread a small amount of melted butter all over the top, allow the bread to cool in the pan for approximately 10-15 minutes, remove from the pan and serve or allow to cool longer for sandwich slicing.

***Hint:** The dough should feel slightly warm during first rising.

Aunt Gert's Cinnamon Rolls

My Aunt Gert was my grandmother's dearest friend. Born before 1900, both of these women shared a life-long friendship in addition to a common joy for baking. I continue to be thankful to these wonderful women, for they shared their gift of enjoyment, incredible skill and treasured recipes with family members throughout the years. I feel blessed that I am one of those to receive such delicacies, especially this recipe, for these are the finest cinnamon rolls that I have ever tasted. Splendidly moist and undeniably characteristic of the best of the best in the cinnamon roll department, I guarantee that these will disappear quickly and requests for more will be frequent.

Makes 18 cinnamon rolls

2 dry active packages yeast or 2 yeast cakes
1½ cups scalded milk, cooled to warm
3 tablespoons sour cream (must be at room temperature for adequate results)
¼ cup sugar
6⅓ cups flour
½ cup (1 stick) butter
1 heaping tablespoon vegetable shortening or lard
¾ cup sugar
4 eggs

FILLING:
½ plus cup (1 stick, plus more) butter
1-1⅓ cup sugar (amount depends on how sweet you want your filling)
3-4 tablespoons cinnamon
1 cup raisins and/or chopped walnuts or pecans
4 tablespoons brown sugar
4 extra tablespoons brown sugar (optional)
Egg wash, made of 1 egg white and 2 tablespoons water, mixed together

ICING:
1½ cups powdered sugar
2-3 tablespoons milk
½ tablespoon vanilla

1. In a small bowl, sprinkle the yeast into the sour cream mixed with *half* the milk; cover and allow to rest for 10 minutes. Add the rest of the milk to the yeast.
2. While the yeast is resting, sift 2 cups of flour and ¼ cup of sugar into a mixing bowl. Add the yeast mixture, stir thoroughly, cover and let rest for an hour. Dough should appear a little bubbly after the hour.
3. Cream the butter and vegetable shortening, beat in ¾ cup sugar and then the eggs, then gradually add the yeast mixture, stirring in   large spoonfuls alternately with the remaining flour. The dough should be slightly sticky. Cover this bowl with a warm damp cloth and set in a warm place to rise to double in bulk, approximately 1-1½ hours.*

4. Once the dough has doubled, divide it in half and roll each half out on a floured board until rectangular and ¼-inch thick. Dot ¼ cup of butter all over the surface of the first half of dough (I usually put a dot every half inch all over the dough), then sprinkle on ½-⅔ cup of sugar, 2 tablespoons cinnamon, the raisins and/or nuts and top this by sprinkling 2 tablespoons brown sugar over all.

5. Beginning at the longest side, roll the dough up tightly; seal by pinching the edge against the mass. Pinch the   side edges to seal.

6. Repeat this procedure with the remaining dough.

7. Butter two 10x2-inch round cake pans thoroughly. Sprinkle 1 tablespoon extra brown sugar all over the bottom of each buttered pan.

8. With a serrated knife, cut the dough into 1½-inch sections, and place cut side down into the prepared pans, making sure that the rolls do not touch one another.

9. Cover each pan with a warm damp cloth, place in a warm spot and allow the dough to rise another hour to almost double in bulk.

10. Preheat the oven to 350° F.

11. Using a pastry brush, brush the egg wash all over the top of the rolls, sprinkle 1 tablespoon extra brown sugar over the top of them and bake for approximately 25 minutes or until an inserted knife or toothpick comes out clean.

12. Allow to cool in the pan for about 15 minutes and then invert onto a plate and re-invert to turn right side up. *Handle gently. OR* simply remove individually from the pan.

13. Make up the icing by mixing the powdered sugar with the milk and vanilla and spread or drizzle over the tops of the rolls.

*Hint: The dough should feel slightly warm during first rising.

This recipe freezes well. I have often frozen several rolls at a time by wrapping them together tightly in plastic wrap, then placing them into a large freezer bag.

Oatmeal Cinnamon Rolls

Considering that cinnamon rolls are my all-time favorite baked product, and that I have a tendency to eat too many of them, which results in excess poundage around the waist, I knew that I must go on a mission to decrease the fat in these incredible tasting treats. I played and played and threw out lots of disasters until one day a thought came to me. If one can use oats to make bread, why not try it in cinnamon rolls; and instead of using butter, what if I used a high-quality margarine spread? The day this mission came to an end and these fabulous scented treats came out of the oven, did I let them cool? Nope! I dug in immediately and then invited a friend over and told her that maybe I should go into baking for a living, for I am pretty darn good at it. She enthusiastically bobbed her head as she gobbled down her second roll.

Makes 12 cinnamon rolls

DOUGH:
2 packages of dry active yeast or 2 yeast cakes
½ cup warm water
1 teaspoon sugar
1 cup oats
3 tablespoons butter, margarine or canola spread
2 cups plus 2 tablespoons water, boiled
⅔ cup brown sugar
1½ teaspoons salt (do not omit)
1 egg or equivalent amount of liquid egg substitute
5 cups plus 2 tablespoons flour
Egg wash, made from 1 egg white and 2 tablespoons water, mixed together
2 tablespoons extra brown sugar (optional)

FILLING:
⅔-¾ cup cinnamon sugar (approximately ⅔ cup sugar mixed with 2 tablespoons cinnamon)
½ cup (1 stick) butter, margarine or canola spread
⅔ cup raisins or chopped nuts
2 tablespoons brown sugar

1. Dissolve yeast and 1 teaspoon sugar into ½ cup warm water, cover and let rest for 7-10 minutes or until bubbly.
2. In a mixing bowl pour the boiling water over the oats and 3 tablespoons of butter/margarine. Stir until butter/margarine is melted. Set aside for a few minutes.
3. Add the yeast mixture, brown sugar and salt to the oats, stir and gradually add the egg and remaining flour, ½ cup at a time. Knead the dough on a floured surface 8-10 times. Place in a greased bowl, cover with a warm damp cloth and allow to double in bulk, about an hour.*
4. Once the dough has doubled, roll each half into a rectangular shape on a floured surface until ¼-inch thick. Dot ½ cup butter/margarine over the surface of the dough, (I usually put a dot every half inch all over the dough), sprinkle the cinnamon-sugar mixture to cover all the dough, then sprinkle the raisins and/or nuts over the cinnamon sugar. Top this by sprinkling 2 additional tablespoons brown sugar over the top of the dough.

5. Starting from the long side, roll the dough up tightly and seal by pinching the edge against the mass. Pinch the side edges to seal.

6. Grease one 10x2-inch round cake pan and one 9x5-inch bread pan thoroughly with butter or margarine.

7. With a serrated knife, cut the dough into 1½ inch sections; place 9 rolls cut side down into the large prepared pan, and 3 into the prepared bread pan. Make sure that the rolls do not touch one another.

8. Cover each pan with a warm damp cloth, place in a warm spot and allow the dough to rise another hour to almost double in bulk.

9. Preheat the oven to 350° F.

10. Using a pastry brush, brush the egg wash all over the top of the rolls; sprinkle 2 tablespoons extra brown sugar over the top of rolls and bake for approximately 25 minutes, or until an inserted knife or toothpick comes out clean.

***Hint:** The dough should feel slightly warm during first rising..

Aunt Sylvia's Babka

Which would you prefer with a fresh cup of milk, hot coffee or tea early in the morning; an old fashioned Polish sweet bread, full of warm, fruity, sugary, nutty flavor, or a prepackaged sweet? I would always choose homemade, and this is a recipe I longed to have in my morning routine. Something told me that there just had to be a family recipe, but I was unable to find one in my grandmother's treasured recipe box. So I called my aunt too many times; she always said that she didn't have a recipe, until one day when I caught her in her kitchen and she patiently recited me this recipe which was developed by her aunt a long time ago. I immediately made the high altitude adjustments, made a batch, and upon the second try my longing was pleasantly fulfilled.

Makes 2 loaves

DOUGH:
1 package dry active yeast or 1 yeast cake
¾ cup plus 2 tablespoons scalded milk
¾ cup plus 1 tablespoons warm water
½ cup sour cream (must be at room temperature)
¼ cup sugar
½ teaspoon salt
½ cup (1 stick) butter
2 heaping tablespoons vegetable shortening
¾ cup sugar
4 eggs
5¾-6 cups flour

FILLING:
¾ cup (1½ sticks) butter, more if needed
1 cup sugar, more if needed
3-4 tablespoons cinnamon
¾ cup raisins
6 tablespoons brown sugar
½ cup sliced almonds

ICING:
1½ cups powdered sugar
½ teaspoon vanilla
2-3 tablespoons milk

1. Mix together the scalded milk and warm water. Measure out ½ cup into a separate bowl, allow it to cool, and then mix in the yeast. Cover this and let it rest for 10 minutes, then add the remaining milk mixture and the sour cream.
2. In a different bowl, mix together 2 cups of the flour, the salt and ¼ cup of the sugar. Gently stir this into the yeast mixture, cover and set aside until bubbles begin to form.

The Egg

There are many varieties of edible eggs available throughout the world today, including those from quail, ducks and geese, found delicately served in many fine restaurants. However, the most frequently used variety of eggs are those laid by the chicken. These are the eggs that are normally served for breakfast, in sandwiches; salads when used discreetly, they can magically turn a plain simple dish into one of sublime magnificence. Eggs can be prepared in many ways; fried, poached, steamed, baked or scrambled are universally the most common means for preparing an everyday egg. But how to prepare an everyday egg is a question that needs to be addressed, so here we go.

The Fried Egg

This is the easiest of all eggs to prepare. I'm sure that many have heard the expression, "It is so hot outside that you could fry an egg on the sidewalk." There is some truth to that statement, for all one needs to fry an egg is a hot surface, such as a frying pan or a clean flat pavement, previously washed with rain, and an egg. Many have asked how to prevent the yolk from breaking: My response is to break the egg into the frying pan carefully, or one could poke a small hole into the egg shell, using a small pin, prior to cracking the shell. The means for cooking a fried egg is as follows:

1. Over medium heat, melt a tablespoon of butter or margarine into a frying pan and swirl it around to coat the bottom of the pan.
2. Poke a small hole into the egg shell with a pin, crack the egg against the side of the pan and gently pour the insides into the pan. Allow to cook for 2-3 minutes or until the white has solidified and the yolk is still soft. Run a spatula around the edges of the whites, to make sure that the egg is not sticking to the pan, and gently lift the egg out of the pan, or slide it out of the pan onto a plate and serve.

Courtney's Bird's Nest Eggs

This is a delightfully easy, attractive recipe that I first saw prepared by a young teenager. I was down in the city one morning, around 11:00 when I stopped by friends to say hello. Their beautiful 13-year old daughter was slowly crawling her way out of bed and into the kitchen to make herself some breakfast. Within minutes she was sliding this pretty toast and egg concoction onto a plate. When I asked her what it was she said Bird's Nest Eggs and offered to make me one, which I gladly accepted.

Serves 1

1 slice of bread
1 tablespoon butter, melted
1 tablespoon butter
1 egg
Salt and pepper to taste

1. With your fingers or using a 2-inch cookie cutter , make a 2-2½ inch hole out of the center of the bread. Spread the slice on each side with melted butter.
2. Over medium heat in a frying pan, melt the remaining tablespoon butter and toast the bread slice on one side, flip over, crack the egg into the center hole, and cover and cook until egg whites are set, about 2-4 minutes.
3. Remove from the heat, and very gently so as not to break the egg yolk, slide onto a serving plate.

The Steamed Egg

The steamed egg is often confused with its close cousin, the poached egg. *"What are you talking about?"* Many have asked when I point out that they are actually steaming the eggs when using the little sectional pan often sold as an egg poacher. The following descriptions should clear up the mystery:

Poached eggs are cooked in a small amount of lightly simmering water until the whites solidify. Steamed eggs are made by cracking the raw eggs into sectioned pans and either microwaving as is, or cooking in the sectional pan above simmering water.

Both varieties taste very much the same. The only true differences between them are the cooking procedures and the appearance. In each of the following recipes that call for poached eggs, one can substitute steamed eggs. Many feel that the steamed egg is easier to prepare, and visually more attractive, for they pop out of the pan sections in a pretty round shape, rather than the lumpy mass of a poached egg.

The Poaching of the Egg

How to describe the poached egg? This is a question my ears have heard many times and I often ponder how to answer it adequately. Do I answer that poached eggs are easy to prepare; that they are colorful; sensational when made properly; that some consider them to be elegant; and absolutely delicious? Or do I tell them that these eggs are considered festive by many, to be served during Sunday brunch and holidays with a variety of meats, vegetables, seafood and a sauce or just as is? I guess the answer lies in the palate of the one who fulfills the temptation derived from its presentation.

2 eggs
Water
1 tablespoon vinegar

1. Fill a medium sized skillet with 3 inches of water. (Make sure the skillet has a lid, or you could use a plate as the lid.) Cover and cook over medium high heat until the water boils. When the water boils, remove the lid and add 1 tablespoon of vinegar (this helps the eggs maintains their shape), lower the heat to medium low and allow water to cool to a simmer.
2. In the meantime, gently crack each egg into a custard cup, a tea cup or a cup of similar size and place close to the skillet.
3. Very carefully (being cautious not to burn your fingertips) slightly dip a tilted edge of the cup into the boiling water and allow the egg to slide out into the water, repeat with other egg and immediately cover the skillet. Allow to cook for 3-4 minutes, and then using a slotted spoon remove the eggs from the pan, one at a time. Make sure to allow any excess water to drain from the egg/spoon before placing on a plate or piece of toast, meat or vegetable. Season with salt and pepper if you like, or drizzle with a sauce such as hollandaise.

Hints: For runnier yolks, cook a few seconds less, for harder yolks cook a bit longer. If you do not like taste of vinegar, while the egg is still in the slotted spoon, dip the spoon and egg into a bowl of lukewarm water, drain and then place upon the plate.

Eggs Florentine

This creamy, lush phenomenal tasting treat looks splendid on all Brunch and Holiday tables. But why would you want to wait until Sunday or a Holiday to enjoy its superb flavor, when you can enjoy it anytime a craving arises?

Serves 4

CREAMED SPINACH:
1½ fresh bunches or 9-10 ounces of washed and chopped spinach.
½ teaspoon powdered garlic, (optional)
2 ounces (½ stick) butter, divided in half
2 tablespoons flour
¼ teaspoon each salt and white pepper (black pepper works fine)
1 cup milk
¼ teaspoon nutmeg

8 eggs
4 English muffins or croissants
2 cups creamed spinach
3 tablespoons butter, melted (to spread on breads)
Hollandaise Sauce (p. 74)*

*Make the hollandaise sauce before the eggs and keep warm by covering with a lid.

1. Steam or cook the spinach with the garlic and 2 tablespoons butter in water until dark green and tender, put aside. (I usually fill a large bowl with chopped spinach and 2 tablespoons butter, fill the bowl with water and microwave the spinach for 9-10 minutes) Drain the water from the spinach, reserving a couple tablespoons in a small bowl — you may or may not need this excess water.
2. Make a white sauce by melting 2 tablespoons butter over medium heat, adding the flour, salt and pepper, whisking these into a paste and continue to whisk while adding the milk. Cover and stir until thick, add the drained cooked spinach and nutmeg, mix thoroughly, cover and keep on top of very low heat, stirring occasionally. (If this becomes too thick, add a couple of teaspoons of excess water left over from cooking the spinach.)
3. While lightly toasting each half of the muffins or croissants under the broiler, or in a toaster oven using the "top brown" setting, fill a medium-sized skillet with 3 inches of water. (Make sure the skillet has a lid, or use a large plate as the lid.) As you are waiting for the water to boil, using a pastry brush, lightly brush each half of toast with melted butter and put aside.
4. You can poach 3-4 eggs at a time or simply use a poaching pan. To poach fill a medium-sized skillet with 3 inches of water. (Make sure the skillet has a lid, or use a large plate as the lid.) Cover and cook over medium high heat until the water boils. When the water boils, remove the lid, add 1 tablespoon of vinegar, (this helps the eggs maintains their shape), lower heat to medium low and allow the water to cool to a simmer. In the meantime, gently crack each egg into a custard cup or tea cup and place these close to the skillet. Very carefully slightly dip the cup into the simmering water and allow the egg to slide out into the water, repeat with other egg and immediately cover the skillet. Allow this to cook for 3-4 minutes, and then using a slotted spoon remove the eggs from the water. Drain any excess water to from the egg/spoon.
5. During the time that it takes to poach the eggs, working rapidly, evenly spread each slice of toast with the spinach, then top each with a poached egg and drizzle with hollandaise.

Variation:
Add a slice of Swiss, Emmenthaler or Gruyere cheese on top of the spinach prior to adding the egg.

Eggs Benedict

My friend Elizabeth says that this divine brunch favorite should be restricted to Sunday mornings and holidays, but I feel that it can be made any day or any time of day whenever a craving for its warm, rich, satisfying splendor arises. Years ago I was told that the original recipe was developed in the early 1890s at either the Waldorf-Astoria or at Delmonico's Steak House, both located in New York City. One story says that a Mrs. Benedict requested something different on the menu, while another version says that a Mr. Benedict requested bacon and poached eggs served with small pitcher of hollandaise sauce, to help cure his hangover. Although this debate continues a century later among culinary historians, I am just glad that someone by the name of Benedict initiated the development of this mouthwatering dish.

Serves 4

Warm water
1 tablespoon vinegar
8 eggs
8 slices of Canadian bacon
4 English muffins
3-4 tablespoons butter, melted

HOLLANDAISE SAUCE:*
3 large egg yolks
2 tablespoons fresh squeezed lemon juice
A pinch each salt and white pepper
A couple drops of hot sauce or Worcestershire sauce (personal preference)
1 tablespoon water
1 cup (2 sticks) clarified butter, melted, no substitutes
  (To clarify butter, melt and strain in a measuring cup through a cheese cloth or very fine sieve.)
Add ¼ teaspoon paprika to hollandaise sauce for a pinker color.

*Make the hollandaise sauce before the eggs and keep warm by covering with a lid.

1. Using a double boiler, fill the bottom section with 2 inches of warm water. Heat the water to a gentle simmer, not a full boil, put the top section on, and let it warm for a few seconds. Whisk in the eggs yolks, juice, hot sauce or Worcestershire sauce, spices and water and continue to whisk until all ingredients are incorporated. It is very important to keep whisking, making sure that the eggs do not begin to cook and solidify.
2. Gradually add the melted butter 1 tablespoon at a time and continue whisking until all butter is used. If very thick, whisk in an additional tablespoon of water or cream. Once thickened, remove from the heat and cover to keep warm until the eggs are prepared and ready to be served. (If the sauce cools too much, reheat this top pan over very low heat, stirring constantly until warmed. If it begins to separate, whisk an egg yolk in a separate bowl or cup and then whisk into the sauce.)
3. Toast the English muffins lightly under the broiler, or in a toaster oven, "top brown" setting.

4. While the muffins are toasting, in a large frying pan brown the Canadian bacon on each side over medium heat. Divide the toasted muffins evenly between four plates, brush each half with the melted butter and top each with a slice of the browned bacon. Put aside and poach the eggs.
5. Follow the directions given previously to poach the eggs. Make sure to allow any excess water to drain from the egg/spoon and then slide each egg directly onto the bacon already placed on one half of each English muffin.
6. Drizzle or smother each with hollandaise sauce and serve immediately.

Variations:

Eggs à l'Oscar

Follow the recipe for Eggs Benedict, making the following changes:
• Substitute croissants for English muffins if desired;
• Omit the Canadian bacon and replace with 8 stalks of asparagus, cut in half, and 4 large crab legs, meat removed, or ½ pound of crab meat (Check crab meat for any lingering shells and remove them.)
1. While the croissants are toasting, steam the asparagus until just tender and put aside.
2. Divide the toasted croissants evenly between four plates, top each slice with asparagus stalks and put aside while poaching the eggs. Place the egg on the asparagus, and top the eggs with the crabmeat and hollandaise sauce.

The Basics of Scrambled Eggs

Throughout the years as a baker, I have been asked how I get my scrambled eggs to taste so good.
Only taking a few minutes to mix and add ingredients, scrambled eggs are one of the most common and versatile,
nourishing and comforting of all breakfast foods. You can add anything from vegetables, fruits and herbs, to meat
and/or cheese to them, only making them taste better. Simple, quick and easy, this is my basic recipe for scrambled eggs.

Serves 2-3

6 large eggs
¼ cup milk
Salt and pepper to taste

1. Grease a medium-sized frying pan by adding a small amount (less than 1 tablespoon) of butter, margarine or pan spray; heat over medium heat.
2. Crack the hard shell of the eggs and pour into a bowl. (Remove any egg shells that may have fallen into the bowl.)
3. Begin to break down the eggs by mixing vigorously with a fork or whisk while adding the milk and spices.
4. Continue mixing until all of the eggs and milk are a uniform color.
5. Pour the egg mixture into the preheated frying pan and, with a heat resistant spatula, continue mixing until all the egg mixture is cooked and solidified.
6. Immediately remove from the pan and serve while hot.

Variations:
Add any of the following: sausage, bacon, ham, Canadian bacon, chorizo, shrimp, crab, lobster, smoked salmon, haddock, or most any flaky fish, broccoli, peppers, mushrooms, tomatoes, onions, scallions, potatoes, grated carrots, spinach, artichokes, jalapeños, chili peppers, olives, hot sauce, chili sauce, salsa, country gravy, hollandaise sauce and/or a variety of cheeses and/or tofu and variety of herbs & spices.

Grandmom's Custard Eggs

Grandmothers can be really sneaky when they have to, and one of mine was more often than not. When I was a little girl, I was a very fussy eater, usually preferring sweets above all else. I later discovered that she often disguised certain foods so that I would eat them. One of these foods was scrambled or fried eggs, for I thought that the yolk of the egg tasted nasty. Being the grandmother that she was, and knowing that eggs are full of protein and good for you, she often made this recipe when I stayed over at her home, hiding honey and cinnamon in the eggs; knowing instinctively that I would gobble it all down without a second thought. I was completely shocked when, as an adult, I found a small index card in her recipe box entitled Custard Eggs for Randi. I thought back to those times, and laughed out loud at how deceitful she had been. God Bless grandmothers and their instinctive adaptations to everyday life!!!!!!!

Serves 2-3

5-6 eggs
½ cup milk
1 tablespoon butter
2-3 teaspoons honey
Salt and pepper to taste
¼ teaspoon cinnamon
Pinch of nutmeg

1. Melt the butter in a frying pan over medium heat, add the honey and melt it into the butter.
2. Beat the eggs thoroughly with the milk and spices, lower the heat in the pan to low, pour the egg mixture in and cook as for scrambled eggs or until set and moist.
3. Serve immediately with toast, preferably cinnamon raisin toast.

My Route's Favorite Egg Sandwiches

My route was where my culinary career began; these were the people and businesses that I would deliver to each and every morning, these were my guinea pigs, my taste testers; and I filled their bellies every morning with a variety of magnificently prepared treats. Because my deliveries were early in the morning, several of these wonderful folks began to request breakfast-type sandwiches in addition to the sweets and breads I usually filled my basket with. So I assembled these two wonderfully easy sandwiches in response to their demands. Although nothing truly special, these are as easy as it gets, and can be eaten at the table or taken on the go.

Bacon, Egg and Cheese on an English Muffins

Serves 4

4 English muffins (toasted or not, a personal preference)
8 eggs
1-2 tablespoons butter or margarine
¼ cup milk
Salt and pepper
8 slices bacon
1 cup grated cheddar cheese

1. In a frying pan, brown the bacon until crisp and place onto 4 sides of the English muffins.
2. Melt the butter in a frying pan over medium heat, mix the eggs, spice and milk thoroughly, and the eggs until moist and just beginning to set. Sprinkle the cheese over the eggs, cover the pan, allow the cheese to melt, and then evenly divide the cheesy eggs between the 4 bacon lined muffins.
3. Put the other half of the muffin on top of the cheesy egg and serve.

Kielbasa and Egg Wrap

Serves 6

Preheat oven to 400° F

½ package of puff pastry sheets, partially thawed and cut into 6 squares
18-20 ounces of kielbasa sausage, cut into 6 sections
12 eggs
1-2 tablespoons butter or margarine
½ cup milk
Salt and pepper
Sprinkle of garlic powder
A couple drops hot sauce (optional)
1½ cup grated cheddar cheese
Egg yolk wash; mix 1 egg yolk with 2 tablespoons water, put aside

1. Grease a cookie sheet or large baking dish with pan spray or butter.
2. In a skillet over medium to high heat, brown the kielbasa on all sides and remove from the pan.
3. Beat the eggs, milk and spices thoroughly, while melting the butter in a separate frying pan. Cook the eggs over medium until very moist and just beginning to set, remove from heat.
4. Layer each puff pastry square with one section of kielbasa, then some egg and then a sprinkle of cheese. Roll the puff pastry tightly around the kielbasa, and pinch edges to seal. (Some of the kielbasa should be protruding from both ends of the roll.)
5. Using a pastry brush, brush each roll with the egg wash and bake on a greased cookie sheet or pan for 12-15 minutes or until pastry is golden.

The Omelet

According to the Oxford Dictionary, omelet *is defined as "beaten eggs cooked in a frying pan and served plain or with a savory or sweet filling." That sounds like plain ol' scrambled eggs with added ingredients to me. I consider an omelet to be eggs cooked in the round, filled with a scrumptious variety of fresh ingredients and then folded over and served hot. Although there are a massive variety of different ingredients that can be used to fill an omelet, I have listed only the most commonly used.*

Utensils:
6-8 inch non-stick frying pan, (oven-proof, if you want to melt extra cheese on top)
Wire whisk
Rubber spatula
Paper towels (to wipe off the pan after making each omelet)

Makes one omelet

3 eggs per omelet or an equivalent amount of liquid egg substitute
  (Works best if eggs have been removed from refrigerator 30 minutes before using.)
2 tablespoons milk or half and half (use cream for richer flavor)
1 tablespoon butter or oil per omelet
Salt and pepper to taste
½ cup of diced or chopped meats; bacon, ham, sausage, chorizo, etc.
¼ cup or more of grated cheese; American, cheddar, Colby, Monterey Jack, cream cheese (cubed), Swiss, provolone, etc.
⅓ cup of diced or julienned vegetables, fresh or sautéed in butter until tender
¼ teaspoon garlic powder or minced, basil, dill weed, parsley, rosemary, thyme, paprika, Tabasco, etc. (optional)

1. Have all fresh ingredients diced and prepared before cooking the eggs. If sautéing, lightly oil a frying pan, place vegetables into pan, and cooked at medium heat until tender. Put aside.
2. Melt butter or oil over medium heat in the frying pan.
3. As the butter begins to melt, beat the eggs with a wire whisk while gradually adding the milk and spices.
4. Pour the egg mixture into the heated pan, let cook for a few minutes prior to adding the fillings. The bottom of the egg mixture will begin to cook quickly; use a plastic/rubber spatula to gently lift the outer edges of the eggs while slightly tilting the pan, allowing the center liquid to flow out towards the sides and drizzle over the edge of the cooked egg.
5. When the eggs are partially set, begin with the cheese and evenly sprinkle the fillings onto one half of the eggs, leaving the other half empty. (The cheese can be divided by adding half onto the eggs, and the remaining half on top of the vegetables and/or added meats.)
6. Once the eggs appear evenly cooked through, gently fold the empty half of eggs over the fillings on the other half. There may be a tiny bit of liquid that flows out, not to worry it will finish cooking from the heat of the eggs.
7. Immediately serve on a warm plate.
8. If desired, immediately cover the omelet on the plate with any type of a heated sauce, such as hollandaise, mornay, country gravy, cheese, green chili, maple syrup, etc. and serve. See Accessories chapter for these recipes.
9. Wipe pan down with a paper towel prior to preparing another omelet.

Popular Omelet Fillings

SPICES	FRUITS & VEGETABLES	MEATS	CHEESES
Minced garlic	Onions	Bacon	American
Basil	Scallions	Ham	Cheddar
Rosemary	Tomatoes	Canadian bacon	Colby
Thyme	Potatoes	Mexican chorizo	Monterey Jack
Salt	Broccoli	Spanish chorizo	Muenster
Pepper	Spinach	Chicken	Swiss
Paprika	Peppers	Turkey	Jarlsburg
Chives	Asparagus	Shrimp	Gruyere
Celery salt	Mushrooms	Lobster	Marbled
Tabasco	Celery	Crab meat	Cream cheese
Hot sauce	Carrots	Salmon	Brie
Salsa	Artichokes	Haddock	Camembert
Lemon juice	Refried beans	Pork sausage	Feta
Parsley	Chilies	Italian sausage	Tofu
Worcestershire sauce	Pimento		Blue cheese
Mustard	Olives		
Nutmeg	Apples		
Cinnamon	Pears		
Dill	Peaches		
Powdered garlic	Cherries		
Chervil	Berries		
	Bean sprouts		
	Alfalfa sprouts		

Popular Omelets

All of the following omelets are to be prepared as on page 80. This is simply the list of ingredients to fill the most popular omelets, found in many restaurants today. The quantities listed are per three-egg omelet. The following fillings can be altered to meet personal tastes, but whichever you choose, remember to place your fillings on only half of the omelet, so the empty side will fold over easily. For best flavor, serve the omelet immediately or keep on a warm plate in an oven on very low heat until ready to be served.

Although fresh fillings are preferred, I usually sauté raw vegetables in a tablespoon of butter or oil prior to using in an omelet.

Bacon and Egg Omelet

2-3 pieces of cooked bacon
½ cup cheddar or American cheese
1 teaspoon of minced onion or 1 tablespoon diced onions (optional)

Hint: This recipe goes perfectly with Country Gravy (p. 340).

Ham and Cheese Omelet

½ cup diced or 2 pieces of sliced ham or Canadian bacon
½ cup cheddar, American, or Swiss cheese
1 teaspoon of minced onion or 1 tablespoon diced onion (optional)
Pinch of garlic (optional)
Salt and pepper to taste
3-4 fresh sliced mushrooms (optional)

Hint: This recipe goes perfectly with Country Gravy (p. 340) or Cheese Sauce (p. 339).

Three Cheese Omelet

⅔ cup assorted cheeses, grated
¼ teaspoon basil (optional)
Salt and pepper to taste
I like to use cheddar, Monterey Jack and Swiss, but you can use what suits your fancy.

Variation:
Add 1 tablespoon diced scallions and a ¼ teaspoon dill or hot sauce.

Hint: Fabulous served with Green Chili Sauce (p. 342), or Hollandaise Sauce (p. 74)

Western Omelet

½ cup diced ham
2 teaspoons diced onions, preferably sautéed
2 teaspoons finely diced green peppers
¼ teaspoon diced jalapeños (more if you prefer)
¼ cup grated hash browned potatoes (already cooked)
2 tablespoons diced tomato
¼-½ cup of cheddar or pepper jack Cheese
Salt and pepper to taste
A couple drops of hot sauce
Pinch of garlic
Pinch of cayenne pepper
Layer the potatoes first, then the ham, then the vegetables, ending with the cheese.

Hint: This recipe goes great served with Green Chili Sauce (p. 342), a dollop of sour cream and a slice or two of avocado on top

Denver Omelet

½ cup diced ham
1 teaspoon diced onion or scallion
1 tablespoon diced green peppers
⅓-½ cup grated American or Cheddar cheese
2 slices of tomato for the top (optional)
Salt and pepper to taste
¼ teaspoon garlic powder or minced garlic
Couple drops of hot sauce

Spinach and Cream Cheese Omelet

2-3 ounces cut up cream cheese, add this directly to the egg mixture
¾ cup of fresh chopped spinach, packed firmly
3-4 sliced mushrooms (optional)
½ teaspoon minced garlic
1 teaspoon finely diced scallion
Pinch or 2 each dried dill, basil and/or parsley
Couple drops of hot sauce
½ cup cheddar or Monterey Jack cheese (optional)
Salt and pepper to taste

Hint: This recipe goes beautifully with Cheese Sauce (p. 339), or Hollandaise Sauce (p. 74)

continued on next page

Garden Omelet

Sauté the first 5 ingredients in 2 tablespoons butter or oil.
½ cup chopped broccoli
2 teaspoon diced onion
3-4 sliced mushrooms
1-2 asparagus spears, cut into ¼-inch slices
1 tablespoon diced green pepper
4-5 large fresh leaves spinach, cleaned
Your choice of herbs. Basil, thyme, cilantro, dill and garlic work great in this.
2 slices fresh tomato
¼-½ cup cheddar or pepper jack cheese
Salt and pepper to taste
Pinch each garlic, celery salt, basil, dill and parsley

Remove vegetables from heat and drain the oil or excess butter from vegetable; add the spinach to the pan. Mix together until spinach just begins to wilt, place on the omelet, ending with the cheese. Top omelet with 2 fresh slices of tomatoes.

Hint: This recipe goes beautifully with Cheese Sauce (p. 339), or Hollandaise Sauce (p. 74)

Spicy Cajun Omelet

⅓-½ cup of hot, spicy bulk sausage, sautéed until brown with the next four ingredients.
1 tablespoon diced onions
1 tablespoons each diced green peppers and diced red peppers
A drop or 2 Tabasco or hot sauce
Pinch each of cayenne pepper and dried cilantro
Salt and pepper to taste
½-¾ cup cheddar, Pepper Jack, Asiago cheese or combination of each

Italian Omelet

½ cup mild or hot Italian sausage, previously cooked and drained of grease
2 teaspoons sautéed onions
Dash each of minced garlic, basil, marjoram and parsley
2 tablespoons each grated provolone, mozzarella and Asiago cheese
2 teaspoon parmesan cheese to sprinkle on top
Salt and pepper to taste
Add a ¼-⅓ cup of Marinara Sauce (p. 198) on top (optional)

Seafood Omelet

¾ cup fresh or frozen, thawed and drained seafood (fresh fish, crab, lobster, shrimp, single or any combination is fine)
1 teaspoon of diced scallions
1 teaspoon fresh-squeezed lemon juice
¼ teaspoon garlic, minced or powder (optional)
¼ teaspoon of Old Bay seasoning
2 tablespoons cubed cream cheese
¼-½ cup of grated cheese, I prefer swiss or Gruyere
Salt and pepper to taste

Variation:
For a richer flavor add 3-4 ounces sliced Brie or Camembert cheese, (rind gently removed) to the eggs during the last minute of cooking. Serve with Hollandaise (p. 74), Newburg (p. 338) or Mornay Sauce (p. 339).

Salmon and Cream Cheese Omelet

Although you may be up in the mountains or on the high plains, this will taste as if you are in a Jewish deli right by the sea.

4 ounces of smoked salmon (Lox)
2-3 tablespoons cut up cream cheese
1-2 tablespoons diced scallions
¼ teaspoon dill
A pinch of garlic minced or powdered
A drop or 2 Tabasco (optional)
Salt and pepper to taste
This recipe goes wonderfully with Hollandaise Sauce (p. 74)

Variation:
Add a couple chopped leaves of fresh spinach to the egg mixture before cooking.

The Sweet Omelet 1 (a personal favorite)

Add 2 teaspoons sugar or sugar substitute and 1 tablespoon brandy, Grand Marnier or 1 teaspoon lemon juice
    to the egg mixture before cooking.
⅔ cup of fresh berries, cherries, diced peaches, apricots or a combination of for the filling.
¾-1 cup of grated Swiss, Monterey Jack or cheddar cheese
Salt and pepper to taste
Serve immediately with powdered sugar or Hollandaise Sauce (p. 74)

Variation:
For a richer flavor add 4 ounces sliced Brie or Camembert cheese to the eggs, (rind gently removed), during the last minute of cooking.

continued on next page

The Sweet Omelet 2

Life can be OOH so good sometimes. This recipe is perfect to serve to your mother or father or a special someone for their birthday breakfast.

Add 1 tablespoon brown sugar or sugar substitute and 1 tablespoon brandy (optional) to the egg mixture.
Sauté in 2 tablespoons of butter or oil:
1 tablespoon diced onion
1 peeled and diced apple
1 teaspoon lemon juice
¼ teaspoon cinnamon
A pinch of nutmeg
Salt and pepper to taste
Continue sautéing until apples become tender, place on half of omelet
½-⅔ cup grated cheddar cheese
Serve immediately with powdered sugar or cinnamon sugar.

Variations:
For a richer flavor add 3-4 ounces sliced Brie or Camembert cheese to the eggs, (rind gently removed), during the last minute of cooking. Or, add ⅓ cup cooked breakfast sausage with the apples.

The Other Tortilla

The tortilla is popularly known as an unleavened, round, flat Mexican bread, commonly used as the base for burritos, tacos, enchiladas, quesadillas and various other Mexican culinary delights. However, while dining in a Mediterranean restaurant, I learned that far across the ocean from Mexico, in Spain, the tortilla is defined as an omelet that looks like a cake. Out of curiosity I ordered this special omelet and found it so pleasing that I asked to speak with the chef to learn how to prepare it. Fortunately for me, he honored my request and quickly scribbled down the instructions, while stating that any ingredient added to a traditional omelet can also be added to the Spanish Tortilla. This recipe is made with the same ingredients as the one that I first tasted, savored and requested.

Serves 2

¼ cup extra-virgin olive oil
3 cups diced new or red potatoes
½ cup finely diced onions
5 eggs
Salt and pepper to taste

1. Set the temperature to medium low and heat the oil in a skillet. Once the oil is hot, add the potatoes and cook them about 10-15 minutes. Add the onions, reduce the heat to low and continue cooking for 30 minutes or until the potatoes are crisp but tender. Drain the oil from the pan into a small bowl. Set aside the potatoes and onions to cool.
2. Beat the eggs with salt and pepper, and then gently add the potato/onion mixture.
3. Using a paper towel, wipe the crumbs and oil from the skillet, pour the previously used oil back into the pan, heat over medium low until hot, then add the egg mixture.
4. Swirl the pan around to evenly disperse the eggs and cook for 6-9 minutes.
5. With a plastic/rubber spatula, gently lift the edges of the egg mixture to make sure that it is not sticking, and then place a large plate over the pan, and turn the eggs over onto the plate, then gently slide it back into the skillet. Cook the eggs for 4-6 more minutes or until set but still moist. (Make sure that you do not overcook them.) Serve hot or warm.

Fancy Breakfast Cups

A different way to serve scrambled eggs, this is one of those fancy recipes that your loved ones will think you spent hours at, instead of just a few minutes. So very lovely, for you can add the same variety of ingredients as with scrambled eggs, but when served with a side of fresh fruit and fresh-cut flowers on the table, your loved ones will feel the essence of sitting in an elegant 5-star restaurant. For an added sparkle, serve juice in wine glasses alongside the plates, with a slice of orange or lemon slipped onto the rim of each glass.

Serves 4-6

Preheat oven to 400° F

½ package of frozen puff pastry sheets
2 tablespoons butter or margarine, melted
12 eggs
½ cup milk
1 cup grated cheese, cheddar or Swiss
  (or personal choice)

6 previously cooked sausage patties, slices of bacon,
  Canadian bacon or ¾ cup diced ham
2 tablespoons diced scallions or onions
¼ teaspoon each dill and garlic
Salt and pepper to taste
A couple drops or more hot sauce (optional)

1. In a large frying pan, fry the bacon, sausage or Canadian bacon thoroughly, and place on a plate. Do not drain the pan, just put it aside for now. (If using diced ham, just put it aside for now as well.)
2. Thoroughly grease 6 large muffin sections in a pan and then fit each square gently into each prepared muffin section. Partially thaw the puff pastry sheet, roll it out a little and then cut into 6 squares. Place one square in each muffin section.
3. Using a pastry brush, brush each square thoroughly with the melted butter and bake until golden, about 13-18 minutes. Remove the pan from the oven and lower the temperature to 350° F.
4. Allow the puff pastry to cool for a few minutes, remove from the pan and set aside.
5. Mix the eggs, milk, ⅔ cup grated cheese, diced onion and spices until all ingredients are incorporated. (If using ham put it into the egg mixture.)
6. In a large frying pan, cook the egg mixture over medium heat, stir until just gelled together; continue stirring and remove from the heat.
7. Place the puff pastry cups onto an oven-safe plate, and then place a sausage patty, bacon slice or Canadian bacon slice onto the bottom of each cup. Fill each cup with the egg mixture, sprinkle remaining cheese on top and bake for just a couple minutes to heat and melt cheese. Serve immediately.

Suggestion: serve with Country Gravy (p. 340), or Hollandaise Sauce (p. 74).

Variations:
• Substitute the meat with broccoli, diced peppers, diced tomatoes or chopped cooked spinach and just mix in with the eggs.
• Substitute 6 slices of sliced bread for the puff pastry, and cook for 8-10 minutes or until golden.

Bacon and Egg Casserole

The glory of a casserole is that no matter if you make it early in the morning or after work late in the day, it takes almost no effort to toss a few fresh ingredients together, stir in a few spices, pour them into a pan and bake. This is one of those casseroles, offering a variation of the traditional bacon and egg filled breakfast plate, and just as easy to make. I often make this recipe, put it into the oven, grab a cup of coffee and then go back to bed to watch the morning news.

Serves 6-8

Preheat oven to 325° F

6-8 slices bacon, crisply cooked and crumbled
3 cups small croutons, preferably unseasoned
2 cups grated cheddar, marbled Monterey Jack, Swiss or Colby cheese
7 eggs or equivalent amount liquid egg substitute
3 cups milk
Salt and pepper to taste
½ teaspoon dry mustard
1 teaspoon diced scallions or ½ teaspoon onion powder
A couple drops hot sauce

1. Thoroughly grease a 2-quart casserole dish with pan spray, butter or margarine.
2. Place the croutons into the bottom of the casserole dish, sprinkle the grated cheese on top of the croutons.
3. In a bowl, thoroughly mix the eggs, milk, scallions, mustard, salt and pepper and pour over the cheese and croutons. Sprinkle the crumbled bacon on top.
4. Bake uncovered for 45-55 minutes or until eggs are set. Serve immediately.

Variations:
• Substitute the bacon with ¾ cup diced ham or 1 cup fresh broccoli, chopped asparagus and/or spinach.
If using ham, use Swiss cheese for best flavor.

Hint: Leftovers can be stored in the refrigerator and reheated up to 36 hours later.

Mushroom and Sausage Breakfast Bake

I found this recipe in my grandmother's treasured box full of recipes, many of which date back to long before I was born. One Saturday morning, while searching for something different to make, I saw this recipe on a folded piece of paper, opened it, saw the date 1948, and the words Woman's World *at the bottom of the page. It sounded good, so that night I made a batch as instructed and placed it in the refrigerator to be baked the next morning. It smelled so good while baking, filling the house with a wholesome country scent, that my ex and I were salivating in anticipation, while our hunger grew with each passing minute. The wait was definitely worth the time, for we determined that this dish was full of country flair and goodness, and one that he requested many more times.*

Serves 6

8 slices of French or Italian bread, cubed
1 pound ground sausage
8 ounces mushrooms, sliced
1-2 tablespoons butter, margarine or oil
2 cups grated cheddar or Colby cheese
6 eggs
2½ cups milk
Salt and pepper to taste
1, 10–12-ounce can condensed cream of mushroom soup
½ can milk

1. In a frying pan or skillet cook the sausage until brown and crumbly.
2. Sauté the mushrooms in the butter until they just begin to get tender, and remove from the pan.
3. Grease a 2-3 quart casserole dish with butter, margarine or pan spray.
4. Combine the bread cubes, cheese, sausage and mushrooms in the casserole dish. Beat the eggs and spices into the milk, stir well and then pour this over the bread mixture. Cover and refrigerate overnight.
5. The next morning preheat the oven to 325° F.
6. Mix the soup with ½ can of milk and pour all over the bread/egg mixture, and bake for 65-75 minutes or until an inserted knife come out clean.

Egg and Potato Breakfast Casserole

On one hand, this is a recipe for the purest of meat and potatoes eater. No matter what time of day or what meal may be served at the time, this recipe is for you. On the other hand, if made without the bacon, most people still rave about the flavor and cannot understand how a dish as easy as this one can taste so incredibly good. So if you enjoy meat and potato dishes, this one is for you and for all those who have chosen not to eat meat, then this recipe can also be made for you. ENJOY!

Serves 6-8

Preheat oven to 325° F

5 medium potatoes, thinly sliced
8 ounces bacon
¼ cup diced green peppers
¼ cup diced red peppers
¼ cup diced yellow peppers or ½ cup chopped broccoli
¼ cup diced onion
7 eggs
¼ cup milk
Salt and pepper to taste
⅓ cup canola or vegetable oil
3 tablespoons flour
3 cups milk
4 ounces grated cheddar or Colby cheese,
   or American cheese slices
Salt and pepper to taste

1. Fry the bacon in a frying pan or skillet until brown and crisp.
2. Thoroughly grease a 2-quart casserole dish with butter, margarine or pan spray.
3. Begin to layer the ingredients into the prepared dish; first the potatoes, then the peppers and onion and then the bacon, if using.
4. Beat the eggs with the milk and spices. Pour this over the potatoes, meat and vegetables, making sure that the egg mixture is evenly dispersed throughout the pan, if not, shake the pan a little to assist.
5. Bake for approximately 35-40 minutes or until eggs have set. In the meantime, make the sauce.
6. In a medium saucepan, mix the oil and flour together until thick and no lumps remain. Over medium heat, heat this mixture while adding the cheese and milk. Stir constantly until the sauce begins to thicken, allow sauce to simmer for 1-2 more minutes, stir in the spices and pour over individual servings of the egg dish.

The Overnight Cheesy, Veggie Egg Casserole

The delight of simplicity defines this pretty dish. It is fabulous to bring to the office for an early morning meeting or just for a morning get together with friends. Although nothing extraordinary, what makes this recipe unique is that one can use almost any combination of vegetables and/or fruits and the outcome only gets better and better.

Serves 6-8

Preheat oven to 350° F

10-12 slices whole wheat bread, crust removed and cut into little cubes
2 tablespoons butter, margarine or oil.
1½ cup chopped broccoli
½ cup grated carrots (optional, I add them for color)
½ cup diced onion
1½ cup chopped fresh spinach
14 eggs or equivalent amount of liquid egg substitute
½ cup milk
1 teaspoon mustard (optional)
½ teaspoon basil
¼ teaspoon each parsley and dill
Salt and pepper to taste
1 pound of Cheddar, Swiss or Monterey Jack cheese, cubed
1 tomato sliced thinly.

1. Sauté the vegetables in butter, margarine or oil until still crisp but tender, drain of fat and put into a large bowl.
2. Add the bread cubes, eggs, milk, seasonings and cheese to the vegetables and mix thoroughly.
3. Grease a 9x13-inch pan and pour the egg mixture into the pan. Cover with plastic wrap or foil and refrigerate 7-9 hours.
4. First thing in the morning, preheat the oven to 350° F. Remove the pan from the refrigerator, allow to sit for about 30 minutes while slicing the tomato. Place tomato slices on top of eggs and bake for 45-55 minutes or until eggs barely jiggle.
5. Cool for 5-10 minutes; allowing the eggs to completely set and serve.

For something extra special, this recipe pairs splendidly with Hollandaise Sauce (p. 74).

Variations:
• Substitute diced apples and/or blueberries for the broccoli and carrots, and add a ½ teaspoon nutmeg in place of the spices.
• Substitute 3 tablespoons finely diced jalapenos or green chilies, for the broccoli, spinach and carrots, ¾ teaspoon cayenne pepper, 1 teaspoon cilantro, ½ teaspoon parsley, a pinch or 2 of cumin and few drops of hot sauce in place of the herbs, and if you like, add ½-¾ pound cooked and crumbled chorizo.

Crust for Quiche

I developed this flaky, delicate crust especially for the Quiche Lorraine, Spinach Mushroom and Seafood Quiches recipes on the following pages.

Makes one unbaked deep dish pie crust (approximately 9-10 inches round)

1½ cups flour
½ teaspoon salt
2-3 tablespoons cold water
½ cup plus 1 tablespoon cold shortening

1. Sift together the flour and salt in a medium bowl.
2. With a pastry blender or two forks, cut the shortening into the flour/salt combination until little beads begin to form. Using a fork, work the water into the flour and shortening mixture until the dough begins to form into a ball. *Do not overwork the dough.*
3. Press the dough into a flat ball and roll out onto a floured surface. Turn the dough carefully over two or three times during the rolling process.
4. Once the dough is rolled out, gently lift and fit the dough into a 9 or 10-inch deep dish pie pan.
5. Trim off any excess dough and either flute the edge or press the edge with the tines of a fork to the side of the pan.

Spinach Mushroom Quiche

---

*I believe that a quiche, often described as a custardy, cheesy, egg pie, should be smooth, silky and satisfying,
as well as being full of fresh ingredients that can sustain one until the next meal. My first experience tasting its elegance
was an unfulfilling event, for I was served this skinny, triangular piece of baked egg mixed with vegetables, which tasted
as bland as could be. Upon leaving the restaurant, still hungry, I knew that I could come up with a terrific recipe.
Since that day, over 30 years ago, I have used this recipe often, adding a special ingredient to enhance the flavor,
that until now, I have kept an uncompromised secret, sharing it with no one, not even my closest friends.*

Preheat oven to 350° F

One pie crust recipe (p. 93).

THE FILLING:

12-14 eggs or equivalent amount of liquid egg substitute

⅔-¾ cup milk, half and half or cream
  (the thicker the cream, the richer the pie)

1½ chopped bunches of fresh spinach or 10 ounces of
  bagged spinach, washed thoroughly

8 ounces of sliced mushrooms, washed and rinsed

2 tablespoons butter

Sprinkle of garlic powder

1 bunch of scallions sliced, include some of the green part

1 teaspoon minced garlic

1 teaspoon dill

1½ cups grated Swiss or Emmentaler cheese

1½ cups grated Gruyere cheese

2½ tablespoon Blue Cheese Salad Dressing
  (p. 334 , my secret ingredient)

2 teaspoons blue cheese crumbles (optional)

Salt and pepper to taste

1. Steam or cook the spinach and mushrooms with the butter and a sprinkling of garlic until dark green and tender.
   (I usually do this by placing all into a microwave-safe bowl, filling it with water and microwaving for 9-10 minutes.)
   Drain all water from the cooked spinach and mushrooms.
2. Mix all the filling ingredients thoroughly together, pour into the prepared pie crust/shell and bake for 55-65 minutes
   or until the center just barely jiggles.
3. Allow to cool for a few minutes and serve.

Variation:
Substitute 1½ cups chopped broccoli for the spinach or 1½ cups of mixed chopped broccoli, julienned zucchini and
diced yellow peppers and thinly shredded radicchio leaves.

Hint: Any leftovers can be stored in the refrigerator for a couple of days or frozen for up to 1 month. To freeze, remove
from the pan, wrap in plastic wrap, then foil; or place wrapped in plastic wrap into a freezer-safe baggie.

Quiche Lorraine

The delectable quiche, often referred to as an open-faced French Tart, actually began long ago in Germany, in the Duchy of Lothringen, and was later renamed Lorraine in France. Although where it originated is only a concern to the culinary historians, many are simply happy to just delve into its luscious offering. Today one can find this enticing dish on menus throughout the world, for it is the type of majestic dish that can truly be served anytime, day or night.

Preheat oven to 350° F

One pie crust recipe (p. 93).

THE FILLING:
12-14 eggs or equivalent amount of liquid egg substitute
⅔ cup milk, half and half or cream (the thicker the cream, the richer the pie)
10 pieces of bacon, fried and crumbled or 1¼ cup diced ham
¾ cup thinly sliced or diced onions
1 teaspoon minced garlic
½ teaspoon dill
½ teaspoon parsley
¼ teaspoon nutmeg
1½ cups grated Swiss or Emmenthaler
1½ cups grated Gruyere cheese
2½ tablespoon Blue Cheese Salad Dressing
    (p. 334 , my secret ingredient)
2 teaspoons blue cheese crumbles (optional)
Salt and pepper to taste

1. Mix all the filling ingredients thoroughly together, pour into the prepared pie crust/shell and bake for 55-65 minutes or until the center just barely jiggles.
2. Allow to cool for a few minutes and serve.

Variation:
Substitute 3 cups grated cheddar, Colby or marbled for the Swiss and Gruyere.

Seafood Quiche

*Whenever I make this, I shut my eyes and take just a second to allow the enticing aroma to fill my senses.
My imagination takes me to a beach and I can even hear the waves breaking as I anxiously await this sensational dish to
come out of the oven. This specific recipe pairs perfectly with a side of Country Potatoes (p. 114) or a simple salad of mixed
greens and cherry tomatoes. For an aura of pure decadence, serve next to a pretty basket of fresh croissants.*

Preheat oven to 350° F

One pie crust recipe (p. 93).

THE FILLING:
12-14 eggs or equivalent amount of liquid egg substitute
⅔ cup milk, half and half or cream (the thicker the cream, the richer the pie)
5-6 ounces of cleaned shrimp, steamed or boiled, cut into pieces or 4 ounces salad shrimp uncut
4-5 ounces bay scallops, steamed or boiled
5-6 ounces of crabmeat (leg or lump, either works fine)
½ cup diced red onions
½ cup finely diced green or red pepper, broccoli or julienned zucchini (optional)
1-2 teaspoons minced garlic
2 teaspoons fresh squeezed lemon juice
1 teaspoon dill
½ teaspoon parsley
½ teaspoon basil
½ teaspoon Old Bay seafood seasoning
1½ cups grated Swiss or Emmenthaler
1½ cups grated Gruyere cheese
2½ tablespoon chunky Blue Cheese Salad Dressing (p. 334, my secret ingredient)
2 teaspoons blue cheese crumbles (optional)
Salt and pepper to taste

1. In a saucepan, steam or boil the shrimp and scallops until opaque or done.
2. Mix the filling ingredients thoroughly together, pour into the prepared pie crust/shell and bake for 55-65 minutes or
   until the center just barely jiggles.

Suggestion: Drizzling Mornay Sauce (p. 339) over each slice only enhances the appeal of this dish.

Huevos Rancheros

This is a hearty, spicy, favored Mexican breakfast dish, often devoured with intent to sustain one throughout the day or to cure the results from overindulging the night before. Considered to be large in portion and intended for the hungry, this dish is not for those who choose to eat very small portions. But, then again, one plateful can ideally be shared between two if you enjoy eating lightly or to leave some room in the belly for other morning flavors. Personally, I enjoy this dish for its blending of spices, variety of ingredients and for the pure enjoyment of being contentedly full after indulging in its grace.

Serves 4

Preheat oven to 325° F

8 eggs, fried or scrambled with a few drops of hot sauce
2-3 tablespoons butter or margarine
½ pound chorizo or 8 slices of crispy bacon, crumbled
½ pound grated cheddar, Monterey Jack, Colby or
    marbled cheese
2 cups canned refried beans

4 large flour, corn or whole wheat tortillas
2-3 cups of canned or homemade Green Chili (p. 342)
    OR 1 small jar of salsa or make your own salsa
    (see recipe below)
1 avocado, sliced into 8 sections
⅓-½ cup of sour cream

1. Wrap the tortillas in foil and warm at 300° F until ready to use in the preheated oven; or, you could fry the tortillas for about 30 seconds per side, over medium to high heat in ½ cup vegetable oil. Remove from the pan, and drain on a set of paper towels.
2. Microwave in a bowl or heat the refried beans in a frying pan over medium heat, stir occasionally to distribute the heat. Place the chorizo or bacon crumbles on top of the beans, reduce the heat setting to low and cover to keep hot. In a separate pan, heat the green chili or warm the salsa.
3. While the tortilla, beans and chili are heating, fry, poach or scramble the eggs in a tablespoon of butter until cooked to your liking.
4. Remove the tortillas from the oven and wrapping and place each on a plate. Spread the heated beans and meat evenly on top of each tortilla, place the eggs on top of the beans and meat, sprinkle the grated cheese all over the eggs, top with hot green chili or warmed salsa, a couple slices of avocado and a couple dollops of sour cream.

QUICK HOMEMADE SALSA
1 large tomato, diced
6-7 leaves of fresh cilantro, finely chopped
1 jalapeno, diced or one 4-ounce can diced jalapenos
2-3 tablespoons diced onion
½ teaspoon minced garlic (more or less depending on personal taste)
½ teaspoon oregano
1 teaspoon hot sauce
Pinch of cumin

1. Mix all together, put aside for immediate use or refrigerate for later use.

Mesa Verde Eggs

In the southwestern corner of Colorado there is a beautiful, natural, monumental National Park called Mesa Verde. When you follow the road or trails around this amazing park, you get the opportunity to view the old dwellings where the ancient ones lived hundreds of years ago. If you are one who believes that spirits surround us, you can actually see and hear the ancient ones around such dwellings. As I was leaving there one warm, sunny afternoon, I heard them, the ancient ones, whispering the following recipe. Please do not ask how or why, it just was, and I immediately pulled over, wrote down the instructions and once I got back home made the dish. Since that time, many moons ago, I have prepared this exceptional olden dish time and again, and have actually had the audacity to change it just a little, for the sack of simplicity.

Serves 4-6

THE SAUCE:

1 pound of pork (roast, butt or shoulder),
  cut into ½–1-inch size chunks, fat removed
½ pound chorizo or ground sausage
3-4 large tomatoes, diced
1-2 garlic cloves or 1 heaping teaspoon, finely diced

½ teaspoon cumin
1 teaspoon dried cilantro
8 ounces of fresh chilies, finely diced, or one 8-ounce can
  of diced chilies
¼-½ teaspoon oregano
Couple drops of hot sauce (optional)

1. In a large skillet, brown the meats, and then add the remaining ingredients, cover the pan, simmer at medium low about 40-50 minutes or until the tomatoes are tender.
2. Prepare the eggs 5-8 minutes before sauce has finished cooking.

THE EGGS:

12 eggs
½ cup milk
1 teaspoon Tabasco or any chosen hot sauce
1 tablespoon butter or margarine
6-8 ounces grated cheddar or Monterey Jack cheese

1 bunch fresh cilantro, chopped
Salt and pepper to taste
1 thinly sliced avocado
⅓-½ cup sour cream
6 flour, whole wheat or corn tortillas

1. Beat the eggs, milk and spices thoroughly together. Melt the butter in a frying pan over medium heat and pour in the egg mixture. Scramble the eggs until moist but set. (Be careful not to overcook the eggs, making them too dry.)
2. Remove the eggs from the heat, divide evenly between the serving plates, and sprinkle with a few pinches of chopped cilantro, then the cheese, and the warm sauce. Top each with a dollop of sour cream and a couple slices of avocado and serve with warmed buttered tortillas.

Hints: To warm the tortilla, wrap in foil and heat in the oven, or heat them at a very low setting directly in a pan on the stove, or wrap them in a paper towel and microwave for just a few seconds. This sauce tastes great over a simple bowl of noodles, too!

Juanita's Breakfast Burrito

I have noticed that this fabulous simple treat has grown in popularity over time. Years ago when I first moved to Colorado, you could only find a true breakfast burrito in a Mexican restaurant or on the Sunday brunch menus in a variety of restaurants. Today one can find and purchase them anywhere: in restaurants, from street vendors, at convenience stores, and in the subway, airports and train stations. I do not think that they have placed them into vending machines to date, but if it is possible, they will, sooner or later. There are so many varieties of breakfast burritos, but when I chose to make my own, I first consulted with a Mexican grandmother. She told me that this recipe can be prepared in its full glory by smothering it in green chili, or it can be prepared as is, making it much easier to, "fill, roll and walk."

Serves 2

Preheat oven to 350° F

2 large flour or whole wheat tortillas
4 eggs
¼ cup milk
1 teaspoon diced jalapenos, fresh or canned
¼ teaspoon cumin
½ teaspoon cilantro
½ teaspoon garlic
¼ teaspoon oregano

Salt and pepper to taste
1-2 tablespoons butter or margarine
1 large russet potato, cut into small chunks
2 tablespoons (or more) green pepper, diced (optional)
6 ounces ground sausage or chorizo
⅓-½ cup grated cheddar, Monterey Jack, or marbled cheese (optional)
½ plus cup refried pinto beans (optional)

1. Wrap the tortillas in foil and warm for 15 minutes in the oven. If using the refried beans, heat them in a saucepan or in the microwave until hot.
2. While the tortillas are warming, brown the sausage/chorizo until crumbly and remove the meat from the pan; add the onions, potatoes and peppers and cook over medium heat until tender. Meanwhile, beat the eggs thoroughly with the milk and spices, melt the butter in the pan with the vegetables and add the eggs; scramble and cook until set but moist.
3. Remove from heat and stir in the meat.
4. Remove the tortillas from the oven; working with one tortilla at a time (the other should be kept wrapped to keep warm), spread half the beans onto the tortilla, half of the cooked meat onto the beans, and then half of the egg mixture onto the center of the tortilla, sprinkle with cheese and roll up tightly, tucking the edges toward the center as you roll.
5. Place each burrito on a plate, cover with cheese and smother with warm Green Chili (p. 342)

Hint: If choosing to serve with green chili sauce (p. 342), Juanita says, *"You may also want to add a couple tablespoons of fresh diced tomatoes and/or avocado to the top of the sauce, with a couple dollops of sour cream."*

Pop Pop's Fried Matzo

*Growing up we always called my mother's father, Pop Pop, a common term used for one's grandfather.
I remember the first time he made this dish for me, thinking that it would be "yucky" as I watched him make
enough for himself, for my grandmother Doe and me. Boy, was I ever surprised when I took the first bite, —this dish
tasted so good, that I actually ate the whole plateful (a rarity back then). Years later, I prepared this recipe for a friend,
who responded very much like I had when she first heard what I was making. As she took her first tiny bite,
I knew from her look that she liked it and immediately she looked up smiled and sang,
"This is yummy!" while drizzling more maple syrup onto her plate.*

Serves 2-3

3 full pieces matzo (whole wheat is fine)
6 eggs
¼ cup milk
½ teaspoon cinnamon
Salt and pepper
2 tablespoons butter or margarine

1. Melt the butter in a frying pan or skillet over medium heat.
2. Beat the eggs, milk and spices together. Break the matzo into 1–2-inch pieces and stir these into the egg mixture. Allow the mixture to sit for a minute or two.
3. Pour into the heated pan and fry up as you would scramble eggs. Do not over cook the eggs; they should be moist but solidified.
4. Serve steaming hot, with choice of maple syrup, fruit flavored syrup, powdered sugar, sour cream and/or fresh fruits.

French Toast

Considered to have been developed in New York by a gentleman named Joseph French a few hundred years ago,
French Toast is popularly served daily all over the world today. Although varying in name according to which country
you may be dining in, the taste gets more gratifying from the addition of various ingredients added to this basic recipe using
slices of day old bread, dipped into an egg mixture and fried in a pan until golden. So very simple to prepare,
even the little ones can help assemble this golden dish. For total fulfillment, serve with fruits, bacon or sausage
and smothered in syrup, for then it will be guaranteed to sustain one until the next meal.

Serves 2

4 slices of bread, preferably day old (wheat, white, oat, cinnamon raisin or French)
2 eggs
2 tablespoon milk
2 tablespoons butter or margarine
¼ teaspoon cinnamon (optional)
Sprinkle of nutmeg (optional)
½ teaspoon vanilla (optional)

1. In a large shallow bowl, beat the eggs, milk and spices, dip the bread into the egg mixture, turn over and allow to briefly soak while melting the butter in a frying pan over medium to high heat.
2. Gently lift the soaked bread slices and place into frying pan, allow the bottom to cook until golden about a minute or two, turn over and cook the other side until golden.
3. Immediately remove from the pan, divide between plates and serve with choice of topping.
4. Serve warm with fresh fruits, flavored syrups, honey or preserves.

Hint: If you have leftover egg, add a small amount of butter to the same pan after removing the bread and scramble until moist and set.

Grandmom's Challah French Toast

I always felt as if I was eating something special whenever a plateful of these appeared on my grandmother's table. I often wondered what different kinds of ingredients she used to make them crisper, yet still soft and chewy, than more traditional everyday varieties of French toast. Years after growing up and moving away, I found this recipe in that overstuffed, tin recipe box of hers. While reading the tinted index card, I saw that she used fresh challah bread and cornflakes to get that lip-smacking crispy outer coating that I so fondly remembered. While serving this to family and friends, I quickly learned to make a few extra slices, for extras were always requested.

Serves 4-6

6 thick slices of fresh challah (about 1-inch thick each)
1 cup cornflake crumbs
   (put 2 cups corn flakes into a baggie, and roll or pound with a rolling pin until crumbly, continue until you can measure out 1 cup, or purchase the crumbs at the grocery)
6 eggs
¼ cup milk or water
1 tablespoon sugar
1 tablespoon plus 1 teaspoon vanilla or 1 tablespoon vanilla and 2 teaspoon maple extract
Pinch sea salt
2 tablespoons butter or margarine

1. Beat together the eggs, milk, sugar and vanilla until frothy.
2. Place the bread slices into a large shallow pan, pour the egg mixture all over the bread, and then turn each bread slice over and allow the bread to soak for 10-15 minutes or until all the egg mixture has soaked into the bread. You will want to flip the bread over once again while soaking.
3. In a small, shallow pan, spread the corn flake crumbs, then working rapidly with one slice at a time, coat both sides and the edges of each slice. With the palm of your hand gently press the crumbs into the bread.
4. Over medium high heat, melt 2 tablespoons butter into a frying pan, place a few slices of the coated bread into the pan, and fry until golden on both sides, about 3-4 minutes per side. Serve warm with fresh fruits, flavored syrups, honey or preserves.

Celestial French Toast

A divine special occasion dish that I came up with years ago after returning from my route with a couple of croissants left over. What to do with leftover croissants—which in my opinion only stay fresh for about 18 hours—perplexed me, for I did not want to throw these buttery, finely-shaped treats out. The next morning, a Saturday, they were still sitting on my counter and between the growls in my belly and the continuous opening and shutting of the refrigerator in search of something substantial to eat, the following recipe began to develop in my brain. So I played around with this and that, cooked up my concoction, and not just impressed myself, but also my friend, who requests this on special occasions and who continues to say that this is one of the finest breakfasts he has ever had.

Serves 2

2 large croissants
2 eggs
2 tablespoon milk
2 tablespoons butter or margarine
¼ teaspoon cinnamon (optional)
Sprinkle of nutmeg (optional)
½ teaspoon vanilla (optional)
2 tablespoons butter or margarine
4 ounces of cream cheese, whipped
6-8 strawberries, washed and thinly sliced
¼ cup fresh blueberries (optional)

1. Slice each croissant almost in half, so that when opened it resembles a butterfly shape.
2. Beat the eggs, milk and spices together; in a separate bowl whip the cream cheese until smooth, or use pre-whipped cream cheese.
3. Spread the cream cheese on both sides of each croissant, and top with strawberry slices and blueberries, pushing the fruit slightly into the cream cheese. Fold the croissant back into full shape.
4. Melt the butter into a large frying pan over medium to high heat; dip the filled croissants into the egg mixture, allow them to soak in the egg mixture for a couple of seconds; turn the croissants over and allow the egg mixture to soak into the other side.
5. Gently lift the filled croissants out of the egg mixture and place into frying pan. Fry one side until golden, turn over and fry the second side until golden, about two minutes for each side.
6. Serve warm with fresh fruits, flavored syrups, honey or preserves.

Variation:
Use thinly sliced fresh peeled peaches, raspberries, blackberries, lingonberries or blueberries in place of strawberries.

Berry Baked French Toast

In addition to tasting absolutely fabulous, this recipe is delightfully easy to make for it is actually prepared the night before, making life so much easier come morning. Personally, I think that one should hold out on preparing this dish for special occasions, such as birthdays, Christmas, Easter, Father's Day, Mother's Day, etc.; then the ones you cook for will really appreciate it as an exceptional dish only to be served on special days to special people.

Serves 4-6

1 large loaf French bread, sliced into 12 sections (any sandwich type bread will also work)
10 ounces cream cheese
12-14 eggs
2 cups milk (for richer flavor use half and half)
⅓ cup maple syrup or dark corn syrup
1 teaspoon vanilla or maple extract
1 scant teaspoon cinnamon
1¼ cup fresh berries (do not use strawberries, they get too mushy)

SYRUP:
1 cup sugar
2 tablespoons plus ¼ teaspoon corn starch
1 cup plus 1 tablespoon water
1¼ cup fresh berries
1-2 tablespoons butter or margarine

1. Thoroughly grease a 9x13-inch pan.
2. Break up six of the bread slices into smaller pieces and spread all over the bottom of the prepared pan.
3. Cut the cream cheese into little bits and spread over the bread pieces, then spread the berries all over the cream cheese, then repeat breaking up the remaining bread slices into smaller pieces and sprinkling them over the berries.
4. Beat the eggs, milk, vanilla, syrup and cinnamon thoroughly and pour over the bread ingredients, cover the pan and refrigerate overnight.
5. The next morning, preheat the oven to 350° F and bake this dish for 35 minutes, remove the cover and bake another 15-20 minutes.
6. While it is baking, prepare the syrup by mixing the sugar, corn starch and water in a medium-sized sauce pan. Heat this over medium, stirring vigorously with a whisk to break up any lumps. Once the lumps are gone, add the berries and butter. Continue stirring until hot and serve drizzled over the bread and egg mixture.

Hints: You can substitute 1-2 apples for the berries, just peel, core and dice them to about the same size as that of a blueberry or raspberry. You can use any flavored syrup in place of the berry syrup, or this dish is lovely served with Pecan syrup (p. 331)

The Pancake

The fragrance of a fresh stack of pancakes right off the griddle can tempt even the strongest of dieters;
the rationalization being that it is only a few pancakes, she can start again later. As the dieter gets ahold of herself
and begins to walk away, she turns and once again glances, and then stares at the stack of temptation: spread with fresh
whipped butter (or margarine), oozing with berries and drizzled with the finest of pure syrups. Then the moment comes
when she begins to salivate and she is torn between being good and eating good. What should she do?
"Oh forget the diet," *she says,* "Hand me a fork!"

Serves 4

1⅔ cups flour
1 tablespoon baking powder
2 tablespoons sugar
1½ cups plus 1 tablespoon milk
3 eggs
1 tablespoon canola oil
3 tablespoons butter, melted
½ teaspoon salt
1-2 teaspoons vanilla
½ cup or more fresh diced fruits or berries, raisins, chopped nuts, chocolate chips, etc. (optional)

1. Preheat griddle to medium high, or heat a skillet over medium high heat. Spread the pan or griddle with oil or melt the butter into it. You will know when it is hot enough by sprinkling a couple drops of water onto it; if the drops sizzle, the pan is hot enough.
2. In a bowl, thoroughly mix the flour, sugar, baking powder and salt.
3. In a large mixing bowl, beat the eggs and milk until light yellow, then mix in the melted butter, oil and vanilla.
4. Add the flour mixture to the eggs and mix by hand with a fork or large spoon until all ingredients are incorporated and the batter is smooth. Do not overmix the batter. It should only take about a minute or so.
5. Using ¼ cup at a time, pour individual cakes onto the prepared pan, cook for 2 or 3 minutes or until the batter begins to bubble; flip over and cook opposite side for another 2 minutes.
6. Keep the cakes warm by storing them in a 250-300º F oven, until all batter is gone.
7. Serve warm with, butter, fresh fruits, flavored syrups, honey or preserves.

Hint: Add more butter, margarine or oil to the pan as needed until all batter is gone.

Buttermilk Fruit Pancakes

Personally, I think that this recipe made with or without the fruit makes some of the best homemade pancakes I have ever tasted. I found it amazing how just the addition of a few choice ingredients can change the taste of this favored, hearty breakfast dish into one of incredible satisfaction. Years ago, on a warm summer morning, I was much too hungry from skipping dinner the night before. My belly was growling for something substantial, so I stared into my kitchen cabinet, into the fridge, and onto the shelves. I saw some fruit, and my mind began to churn the following ingredients into this recipe. Since that day the following has been requested and prepared many more times than I can begin to count.

Serves 4

¾ cup buttermilk
2 eggs
2 tablespoons butter, melted
1 cup plus 1 tablespoon flour
1 tablespoon sugar or 1½ teaspoons sugar substitute
1½ teaspoons baking soda
1 teaspoon cinnamon
2 bananas, sliced
2 fresh peaches, peeled and diced or 1 can light peaches, drained of all liquid and diced
¼ teaspoon nutmeg
Extra butter, margarine or vegetable oil for cooking

1. Thoroughly mix the eggs, buttermilk and melted butter together. Add the remaining dry ingredients and stir well, then gently fold in the fruit.
2. Heat approximately 1 tablespoon, butter, margarine or oil into a large frying pan or a griddle over medium to high heat until hot. Test the heat by sprinkling a drop or 2 of water onto the pan; if it sizzles, the pan is hot enough.
3. Using ¼ cup of batter at a time, pour the batter into rounded circles onto the pan; when the tops begin to bubble, flip the individual cakes over and continuing cooking for about 1 minute, or until the bottom is golden.
   Serve immediately with butter, flavored syrups or with a sprinkling of powdered sugar.
4. Keep cakes warm by storing them in a 250-300º F oven, until all batter is gone.
5. Serve warm with fresh fruits, flavored syrups, honey or preserves.

Hint: Add more butter, margarine or oil to the pan as needed until all batter is cooked.

Variation:
Add ¾ cup fresh berries, raisins, cranberries, or 1 large peeled, cored and diced apple, chopped nuts and/or chocolate chips.

Corey's Buckwheat Pancakes

We should all feel very blessed for the friends that we have. Corey is a friend whom I met during my adventures as an author. She has been a tremendous support and has blessed me by sharing some of her recipes, so that I may share with you. This is one of her recipes, welcomed with open arms and heart. For all of you out there whose bodies cannot process many wheat products, then this tempting recipe is for you. I am sure that all will be pleasantly surprised at how something so hearty and relatively healthy can also be as light, fluffy and pleasing as these sensational cakes. Corey adds, "Berries or sliced bananas or peaches may be added to the batter or on top for an even yummier breakfast. Go for it!"

Makes eight 5-inch pancakes

⅓ cup buckwheat flour
1⅔ cup spelt flour or combination of spelt & whole wheat flour
1 teaspoon baking powder
1 teaspoon baking soda
1 teaspoon salt
3 tablespoons canola oil
2 eggs or equivalent amount liquid egg substitute
¾ cup plain non fat, plain yogurt
1¼ cup rice or soy milk (whole or skim milk works fine too)
Canola oil for the griddle
Sliced fruits and/or berries for topping or batter (optional)

1. Mix all dry ingredients in a medium-sized bowl, make a well in the center and add the wet ingredients.
2. Whisk all ingredients together, until just mixed. There may be some lumps. The batter should be fluid and may thicken slightly to a pudding consistency. If this happens add a tiny bit more liquid, 1 tablespoon at a time.
3. Over medium to high heat, heat approximately 1 tablespoon canola oil in a large frying pan, cast iron skillet, or on a griddle. You can test the heat by sprinkling a drop or two of water onto the pan; if it sizzles, the pan is hot enough.
4. Using ¼ cup of batter at a time, or a ladle, pour the batter into rounded circles into the pan. When the top begins to bubble, flip the individual cakes over and continuing cooking for about 1 minute, or until the bottom is golden. Serve immediately with butter, flavored syrups or with a sprinkling of powdered sugar.
5. Keep cakes warm by storing them in a 250-300° F oven, until all batter is gone.
6. Serve warm with fresh fruits, flavored syrups, honey or preserves.

Hint: Add more butter or oil to the pan as needed until all batter is gone.

Carolyn's Multi-Grain Pancake Mix

The magnificent ease in mixing a bunch of grains and storing them in a jar, to be used with additional ingredients at a later date, is what makes our busy days go so smoothly at times. Much better for you than prepackaged foods to which preservatives have been added, this homemade recipe stores easily for a couple of months, and is just as easy to prepare when ready. Carolyn thinks the final product is best served with fresh pineapple or mango slices; I think that adding any fruit on top of these scrumptious, wholesome, breakfast cakes will only enhance the nutritional benefits and add diversity to the flavor.

Makes approximately 24 prepared pancakes

1 large tightly sealed jar (glass or plastic)
1 cup all-purpose flout
1 cup whole wheat flour
1 cup oat flour
1 cup rice flour
1 cup rye flour
½ cup quick oats flour
½ cup bran
½ cup sugar (brown sugar will work too) or sugar substitute
1 tablespoon sea salt
Scant ½ cup baking powder
1 tablespoon cinnamon (optional)

1. Mix above ingredients together thoroughly and store in the jar.
2. When ready to use, measure out 1 cup and add:
    1 extra large egg
    ¾ cup milk (soy or almond milk work well, too, rice milk I do not think works well in high altitudes)
    2 tablespoons melted butter, margarine, vegetable or canola oil
3. Whisk all ingredients together, making sure to remove any lumps.
4. Heat approximately 2 tablespoons butter, margarine or oil into a large frying pan or a griddle over medium to high heat. (You can test the heat by sprinkling a drop or 2 of water onto the pan; if it sizzles, the pan is hot enough.)
5. Using ¼ cup of batter at a time, pour the batter into rounded circles into the pan, when the top begins to bubble, flip the individual cakes over and continuing cooking for about 1 minute, or until the bottom is golden.
6. Keep cakes warm by storing them in a 250-300º F oven, until all batter is gone.
7. Serve warm with butter, fresh fruits, flavored syrups, honey or preserves.

Mom's Oatmeal Pancakes

After my father had his first heart attack, my mother had to relearn how to cook for him, using healthier ingredients than the ones he had grown fond of and accustomed to. One of the doctors suggested using more whole grains, such as oats, in many of her recipes as they can assist in lowering one's cholesterol levels. Dad always loved to have a full breakfast on Sundays, before he became engrossed with the bouncing ball of the televised basketball games, often forgetting to eat lunch. So my mother came up with this recipe. While visiting, I tasted these and immediately asked for the recipe and told her these were better than the ones she used to make when I was little. Although I have not had a heart attack, I continue to enjoy these on Sunday mornings, with memories and giggles of my parents, may they rest in peace!

Serves 3-4

2 cups old fashioned oats
2½ buttermilk cups or plain yogurt
½ cup plus 1 tablespoon flour
¾ cup whole wheat flour or all purpose flour
2 teaspoons sugar or 1 teaspoon sugar substitute
1 teaspoons baking powder
1 teaspoons baking soda
Pinch of sea salt
2 eggs or equivalent amount of liquid egg substitute
¼ cup canola oil, melted butter or margarine
Sprinkle of cinnamon (optional)
2 tablespoons butter or oil (more may be needed for cooking)

1. Mix the oats, yogurt or buttermilk together, cover and refrigerate overnight.
2. In the morning, mix together the flours, baking soda and baking powder and salt into a medium-sized bowl.
3. In a small bowl, whip the eggs until frothy, then add the oil, mix thoroughly and pour into the oatmeal mixture, mix and then add the dry ingredients, working rapidly. The batter will be very thick, you may want to add another tablespoon of yogurt or buttermilk.
4. Heat approximately 2 tablespoons butter, margarine or oil, in a large frying pan or griddle over medium to high heat. You can test the heat by sprinkling a drop or 2 of water onto the pan; if it sizzles the pan is hot enough.
5. Using ¼ cup of batter at a time, pour the batter into rounded circles into the pan, when the top begins to bubble, flip the individual cakes over and continuing cooking for about 30-60 seconds or until the bottom is golden. Serve immediately with butter/margarine, flavored syrups, or choice of fruits.

Hint: Add more butter or oil to pan as needed until all batter is gone.

Larry's Oat Cakes

I first tasted these hearty treats decades ago while camping with friends. Larry, a fine camping cook and dear friend, made a huge batch for breakfast. We ate them with butter and syrup, just like a pancake, I noticed that these were a bit dense, yet tasty. I ate and went about my business, as did the rest of us, while he continued to fry up these little cakes, wrap them and tuck them away. Later that day, while hiking, we stopped for a rest, and Larry pulled from his knapsack the stashed little breakfast cakes, some peanut butter, jam and a couple of bananas. He surprised us all, for these small cakes made quite a tasty little snack, much better than the bags of chips and candy bars the rest of us had stashed. While preparing a batch, make a few extras so later in the day the children can make their own snack while you take a break. Wow, what a concept!

Serves 4-6

1½ cups quick oats
1½ cups plus 1 tablespoon flour
½ teaspoon cinnamon (optional)
¾ teaspoon baking soda
¼ teaspoon salt
3 tablespoons dark brown sugar
2¼ cups milk
¼ cup (½ stick) melted butter margarine, or canola oil
¾ cup or more raisins or chopped nuts
Extra butter, margarine or oil for cooking the cakes

1. In a small bowl, mix the sugar, milk and butter, in a separate larger bowl, mix the oats, flour, baking soda, salt and cinnamon, if using.
2. Add the milk mixture to the dry ingredients and stir until combined. There may be a couple of small lumps.
3. Heat approximately 2 tablespoons butter, margarine or oil into a large frying pan on a griddle over medium to high heat. You can test the heat by sprinkling a drop or 2 of water onto the pan; if it sizzles, the pan is hot enough.
4. Using ¼ cup of batter at a time, pour the batter into rounded circles into the pan, when the top begins to bubble, flip the individual cakes over and continuing cooking for about 30-60 seconds or until the bottom is golden.
5. Add more butter or margarine to the pan as needed until all batter is gone.
6. Serve immediately with butter, flavored syrups and/or fresh fruits.

Suggestions for snacks:
Spread with peanut butter, honey, dried fruits or fresh berries, sliced bananas, chopped nuts and seeds, chocolate chips, or just plain with some butter or flavored butter.

Hint: These store well for up to 24 hours if wrapped tightly in plastic wrap or placed in an airtight container.

Chef's Choice Authentic Belgian Waffles

I tasted this terrific recipe at a friend's home one day. We had been reminiscing about the fun times we each had at the beach back east, and she decided to make the memories better by making up a batch of waffles and ice cream, a favored beach dessert. When she pulled out her waffle iron, I noticed that it was Chef's Choice, a company I knew and had met employees of in the past. I asked my friend what recipe she used and she stated the one that came with the waffle iron for they were the best she had ever tasted. So I contacted Chef's Choice and asked permission to reprint their recipe in this cookbook. Without hesitation they generously granted me permission and forwarded their recipe. In my opinion, these are the best of the best in the department of waffles, whether made for breakfast or any time of the day.

Serves 6

1 cup granulated sugar
1 cup butter (2 sticks), melted
4 eggs, separated
1⅔ cups flour (1½ cups at sea level, use self-rising flour)

1. Preheat the waffle iron to appropriate setting.
2. Place the granulated sugar in a medium-sized bowl. Mix in the melted butter. Mix in the 4 egg yolks. Add and thoroughly mix in the flour.
3. In a medium-sized bowl, beat the egg whites until stiff. Fold the whites into the flour mixture until all is well blended. If necessary, add a little more flour to stiffen the batter. The batter should flow off a spoon, but only slowly.
4. Pour one full measured cup of batter onto the preheated waffle grid. Close and latch the lid. Bake until the signal indicates the waffle is done.
5. Remove waffle and place on wire rack for 30 seconds or so and then serve immediately. Because this batter has so much butter, some batter could seep out of the sides and front of the waffle maker during the baking process. This is normal. The waffle will be soft and fragile when "ready", but it will stiffen quickly when removed from the griddle. Because it is very sweet and filling (like a butter cookie), you will find that three waffles will satisfy a group of 6 to 8 people.

Ann's Cheesy Cornmeal Waffles

God Bless Girlfriends! I will be honest, I know how to prepare many different foods, but waffles are not one of them. I don't even own a waffle iron. Please forgive me, for if I want waffles, I go for the quick fix; I pull them out of a box in the freezer. Fortunately, I have a friend who also lives at high altitude and is a food professional; she very generously shared this recipe with me, stating that she only gets requests for more, and never a complaint. I asked a mutual friend of ours how they taste, and as her smile grew wide, she responded, "SENSATIONAL."

Serves 4-6

3 large eggs
1¾ cups buttermilk (soy or rice milk work fine)
2 tablespoons canola oil
1 cup flour
2½ teaspoons baking powder
½ teaspoon baking soda
½ teaspoon salt
1 tablespoon sugar
1 cup cornmeal
½ cup shredded/grated cheddar or Monterey Jack cheese
½ cup canned or frozen corn kernels
Tabasco Sauce to taste
2-3 tablespoons fresh chopped cilantro
Toppings: Salsa, grated cheese, sour cream, avocado chopped or sliced

1. Spray the waffle iron with pan spray and heat.
2. Beat the eggs until lemony in color, stir in the buttermilk and oil. In a separate bowl, mix together the flour, baking powder and baking soda, salt and sugar, and then mix this into the eggs.
3. Gradually stir in the cornmeal, cheese, corn and Tabasco until all ingredients are incorporated.
4. Spoon batter onto the waffle iron, spreading it to the edges if necessary and bake as usual.
5. Top each with chopped cilantro, salsa, some more grated cheese, a couple dollops of sour cream and some chopped or sliced avocado.

Great Grandmother's Buttermilk Biscuits

This recipe was most likely developed in the late 1800s, and passed down through the generations for everyone's enjoyment. Heavenly is the only world I can think of to describe these mouthwatering, puffy, little breads. Double the batch, for these have a tendency to vanish right before your very eyes.

Makes 9-12 biscuits

Preheat oven to 400° F

2 cups plus 2 tablespoons flour
¼ cup sugar
1 teaspoon baking powder
¼ teaspoon baking soda
½ teaspoon sea salt
⅓ cup shortening
¾ cup buttermilk

1. Grease a 10x2-inch round pan with butter or margarine.
2. Mix the dry ingredients until combined and then using two knives, forks or the whip in an electric mixer, cut the shortening into the dry ingredients until coarse and crumbly. Gradually add the buttermilk and mix until all ingredients are incorporated.
3. Knead the dough a few times on a lightly floured surface and pat the dough out to about 1-inch thick.
4. Use a variety of 2–3-inch serrated-sided cookie cutters to cut out various shapes.
5. Place each biscuit onto the prepared cookie sheet and bake for 15-18 minutes or until golden on top.

Biscuits and Country Gravy

Considered to be thick and hearty, this wholesome dish is guaranteed to please and leave one with at least one notch loosened on their belt. When I first made the gravy, a friend stopped by to say hello, saw what I was making, and claimed that she did not eat meat anymore. As I asked her to take just a small taste of the gravy around the meat, she reluctantly dipped a sliver of bread into the sauce, then another, then another and another. As she was insisting that she could not eat meat because it upset her stomach, she continued dipping slivers of bread into the saucepan. Later that day she asked me to write down the recipe, stating that her kids would just love it as she did.

Make a batch of Great Grandmother's Buttermilk Biscuits on the previous page. Wrap in foil to keep warm while preparing the gravy.

COUNTRY GRAVY:
Pure old fashioned country sustenance, not intended for those who prefer to eat lightly.

Makes approximately 2½ cups

½ pound of pork sausage
¼ cup sausage drippings (mixed with melted butter if necessary to measure ¼ cup)
4 tablespoons flour
2 cups milk
Salt and pepper to taste
Couple drops hot sauce (optional)

1. Brown the sausage in a frying pan until a few small chunks remain and the rest is crumbly. Drain ¼ cup of the excess fat/grease into a heat-proof cup. If there is not enough grease, add enough melted butter to make ¼ cup. Pour the grease into a small/medium saucepan while leaving the cooked sausage in the frying pan for now.
2. Add the flour to the saucepan, heat the pan over medium heat and stir the flour into the grease, making a paste. Remove the pan from the heat and stir in the milk, return the pan to the heat and continuing stirring until it begins to thicken. Add the sausage and spices, and then stir until hot and thick.
3. Serve immediately by pouring the gravy over the biscuits.

Hint: Pre-butter the biscuits for best flavor.

For a full meal, serve with choice of eggs, sausage links, patties or slices of crisp bacon. *Or,* serve over a plate of freshly made Hash Brown Potatoes (p. 116), with a side of eggs.

Steve's Corned Beef Hash and Eggs

*About 20 years ago I dated a neighbor who lived just down the road, and one morning we both awoke hungry
and in need of food. He was the financial manager at a local restaurant, and his benefits were plenty. He pulled a chunk of
corned beef out of the refrigerator that he had brought home the night before, and for the next half hour or so, I watched, listened
and learned while he made this terrific dish. When he turned to get the eggs, my fork chose to dive into his concoction, and then
by instinct this same fork lifted itself into my mouth. Oh so good it was, that my fork again chose to continue its tasting
venture, until it was suddenly taken from my fingers and I was abruptly instructed to wait until the eggs were cooked.
Some may call this a 'Heavenly Hash', while I just call it 'Good Stuff', no pun intended.*

Serves 2-3

2-3 Russet potatoes, cleaned, peeled and into ½-inch chunks
¼ cup (½ stick) butter or margarine
1 onion diced
8 ounces corned beef, finely chopped and/or pulled
1 teaspoon horseradish (more if you prefer)
½ teaspoon minced garlic
Salt and pepper to taste
Couple drops of hot sauce (optional)
¼ cup cream
4 steamed or poached eggs
2-4 pieces of toast or fresh biscuits (optional)

1. In a large skillet, cover the potatoes with warm water, heat on medium high and bring the water to full boil.
   Decrease the heat to low and simmer the potatoes for 7-8 minutes. Drain all water from the pan, and sprinkle the
   potatoes with salt and pepper. Remove the potatoes to a bowl and put aside.
2. Wipe the residue out of the pan with a paper towel, and fill with butter and onions. Over medium heat, cook the
   onions in the butter for about 6-7 minutes, and then stir the corned beef, horseradish, garlic and potatoes into the
   pan. Press down until flat and compacted together.
3. Reduce the heat to low/medium and drizzle in the cream. Cook for another 12-15 minutes, then flip the mass, pat it
   down flat and cook for an additional 15-20 minutes or until bottom has browned.
4. Serve immediately topped with a steamed or poached egg or two.

Hash Brown Potatoes

Quick and easy to prepare, needing only a skillet or frying pan, a little butter or bacon fat and fresh shredded potatoes, this basic recipe has become a favorite side to serve with breakfast any time of day, evening or night. The old way was to fry the shredded potatoes in reserved bacon fat. Though this is still the favored means of preparation, supplying one with the full flavor intended, in today's modern world, where many are concerned with the amount of fat intake, this crispy side dish can be made with margarine, canola, safflower, sunflower, corn or vegetable oil to lower the cholesterol.

Serves 4-6

3-4 large baking potatoes
¼ cup bacon fat, butter, margarine or oil
Salt and pepper to taste
Sprinkle of garlic powder or garlic salt (optional)

1. Scrub the potatoes clean under warm water, leaving the skins on.
2. Shred the potatoes in a food processor using a large-holed grated.
3. Heat the butter, fat or oil in a large skillet or frying pan, over medium high heat. Once hot, add the shredded potatoes to the pan and spread them out evenly. Sprinkle with seasonings, and fry until the bottom is crisp and brown about 6-7 minutes.
4. Flip the potatoes over, (in sections if easier for you), add a tiny bit more fat or oil if necessary and fry this side until browned and crisp.
5. Serve immediately, or place on an oven-proof plate and keep warm in a preheated oven.

Variation:
Add ⅓ cup diced onion, 1 teaspoon minced garlic, and/or a couple drops of hot sauce.

Kathleen's Mother's Hash-Brown Pie

While visiting a friend in Ohio, he insisted that his mother make this old-fashioned dish for me. At the same time, knowing me too well, he whispered to me to at least give it a try, and not crinkle my nose at the prospect of tasting something unfamiliar. Kathleen began to prepare this while sharing that her mother would make this for a few neighboring men folk when they took their breaks from the local factories, often eating meals at each other's homes. She said that the men always welcomed the sight of this pie, and would eagerly gobble it all and then would go back to work nourished, full and happy. I, being the fussy eater that I am, was pleasantly surprised that it tasted as terrific as I had been advised.

Serves 4-6

Preheat oven to 350° F

4-5 large baking potatoes
1 medium onion, diced
2 large eggs
½ cup sour cream
Salt and pepper to taste
¾ teaspoon garlic powder
Couple pinches nutmeg
Heaping ½ cup grated Monterey Jack or marbled cheese

1. Lightly grease a 2–3-quart casserole dish.
2. Shred the potatoes in a food processor with a large-holed grater.
3. Add the remaining ingredients and mix thoroughly. Pour all into the prepared dish.
4. Bake for 60-70 minutes, or until the top is crisp and crunchy.

Suggestion: Serve hot as is or with a side of Country Gravy (p. 114), or Green Chili (p. 342) to add a bit more spice to the day.
Accent with a side of crisp bacon, sausage patties or links.

BJ's Breakfast Taters

BJ was very special to me, and is one person whom I regret losing touch with too many years ago. He was the finest hunter I have ever met and an even better cook. He would usually make a large breakfast, whether on a hunting and camping adventure or just for the sake of eating large and well. I fondly remember watching him whip up these savory potatoes, making sure to add extra spice, and even going as far as pushing a few taters to the side of the pan for me, prior to adding the green peppers to the pan, knowing that I refused to eat them. Today these continue to be my favorite, not just because they are the best breakfast potatoes I've ever had, but because each time I make a batch, my mind smiles back to cherished memories from long ago.

Serves 4-6

4-5 large baking potatoes
½ cup (1 stick) butter
1 onion sliced thinly or diced
1 medium green pepper diced (optional)
Salt and pepper to taste
1 teaspoon minced garlic
Paprika (optional)

1. Wash the potatoes until clean, leave the skins on and cut into 1 inch chunks
2. Melt the butter over medium high in a large skillet or frying pan, and add all ingredients.
3. Fry all the ingredients together until crisp on the outside, but tender in the center and serve hot with choice of breakfast meats and/or eggs.

Suggestion: Serve smothered in Green Chili (p. 342), a couple sprinkles of grated cheese with a few dollops of sour cream for a different full meal any time of the day.

Corey's Breakfast Skillet Potatoes

A vegetable lover's delight! Corey says, "This recipe was developed in my early years in Telluride, prior to a big day of skiing. The cheese and salsa warmed me and stuck with me so I didn't have to stop for lunch. If you have leftover ham, it works really well in this too." *I have made these many times since Corey first shared it with me, a fabulous blend of ingredients, truly leaving one satisfied and full.*

Serves 2-3

3 medium-large potatoes, red ones work great, but any variety will do, chopped into 1-inch chunks
1 small-medium onion, diced
½ green pepper, diced
1 small zucchini, diced
1 large clove garlic, minced
1 tablespoon canola oil
½ teaspoon Spike seasoning (found on grocery shelves in the seasonings section)
½ cup grated cheddar or Monterey Jack cheese
Salsa (optional)
Sour cream (optional)

1. Heat the oil in a skillet (cast iron works best) on medium heat.
2. Add chopped potatoes to the skillet and cover. Chop the onions, and add to the potatoes, then the peppers, and then the zucchini; stirring each time you add another ingredient and covering. While adding the last of the zucchini, sprinkle the spice all over the top; chop and the garlic.
3. Continue coking until all of the vegetables and potatoes are tender and browned, then top with grated cheese and cover until melted.
4. Serve with salsa and sour cream if desired.

Variation:
For an even heartier breakfast, enjoy with an egg or two, cooked the way you like them.

The cake with morning coffee, commonly called the Coffeecake

Being raised in Philadelphia, I learned at a young age to appreciate a long-held tradition of serving sweet, rich breads, commonly prepared with a crumb or streusel topping. At some point in history, these rich, cake-like breads were affectionately termed Coffeecakes for they were often served accompanied by a hot cup of coffee or tea. Usually served at the end of breakfast or as an afternoon snack, these lovely, sweet cakes can be found everywhere; in the bakery, at an aunt's house, even prepackaged in the convenience stores. Many will rave about the breakfast you serve, some may even request a recipe or two, but a well-made coffeecake may be talked about for decades to come.

The Crumb Cake

This is it, a true crumb cake whereby the crumbs are what make the cake so lusciously desirable. The topping of the cake, the crumbs, should be pea size, crumbly but thick, and sweet enough to entice one to scoop up any crumbs that drop off with their fingertips or fork. The crumbs should not be hard, but rather dense and soft. In the opinions of my taste testers, this cake generously meets all necessary requirements and should be shared for the benefit of all.

Serves 4

Preheat oven to 325° F

CAKE:
3¼ cups flour
1 cup sugar
1 tablespoon plus 2¾ teaspoons baking powder
3 eggs
1 cup plus 2 tablespoons milk
1 tablespoon vanilla
¼ cup (½ stick) melted butter, margarine or canola oil

CRUMB TOPPING:
2½ cups flour
1 cup lightly packed dark brown sugar
1 scant tablespoon cinnamon
¼ teaspoon nutmeg (optional)
1 cups (2 sticks) melted butter, slightly cooled
  (no substitutes)
3-4 tablespoons powdered sugar
½ cup chopped nuts, raisins or mini chocolate chips
  (optional)

1. Thoroughly grease a 9x13-inch pan with butter, margarine or pan spray.
2. In a large measuring cup or bowl, mix together the flour, sugar and baking powder.
3. In a mixing bowl, beat the eggs, milk, melted butter or oil and vanilla until all ingredients are incorporated, then gradually add the dry ingredients mixing on a low speed until all ingredients become incorporated.
4. Spread the batter evenly into the prepared pan and make the Crumb Topping.
5. For the topping, place the flour, brown sugar, and spices into a bowl and mix with your fingers or a strong fork, breaking up any and all brown sugar lumps. Pour the melted butter on top and stir until crumbly. The crumbs should be larger than a pea, but not as large as a coin.
6. Sprinkle the crumbs over the cake batter and bake for 30-40 minutes or until an inserted knife or toothpick comes out with maybe 1-2 crumbs attached. Sprinkle the powdered sugar all over the crumbs and cool for 15-20 minutes prior to covering with plastic wrap; then cool a bit longer prior to serving for best flavor.

Great Grandmother's Cinnamon Streusel Cake

You know, many will rave about the breakfast you serve, some will even request a recipe or two, but a well made coffeecake, as previously said, may be talked about for decades to come. This is one of those coffeecakes; for it has been enjoyed, talked about and requested for over 100 years! It has been said to be outstanding, fabulously perfect with a cup of coffee or tea and is as impressive as can be. I can only hope that you relish its distinctive flavor as many have before you and that it is baked, savored and shared among your family and friends for at least another century.

Preheat oven to 350° F

TOPPING AND FILLING:
2½ cups packed brown sugar
½ rounded cup flour
½ cup (1 stick) butter
3 tablespoons cinnamon
Mix these three ingredients together to make the streusel, and put aside in a separate bowl.

CAKE:
1 cup (2 sticks) butter
1⅓ cups sugar
6 eggs
3 cups plus 2 tablespoons flour
2 teaspoons baking powder
2 teaspoon baking soda
2 cups sour cream, or plain yogurt if you don't like sour cream

1. Cream together the butter, sugar and eggs. Add the flour, baking powder and baking soda to the butter mixture. Mix the batter thoroughly.
2. Grease a 9x13-inch pan or 10x2-inch round pan with butter, margarine or pan spray.
3. Spread half of the batter into the pan. Sprinkle half of the streusel all over the bottom layer of batter.
4. Repeat with remaining ingredients, batter and then streusel on top.
5. Bake approximately 45-55 minutes or until an inserted knife or toothpick comes out clean. Let cool in the pan an hour for best flavor.

Peach Cobbler Cake

This is my favorite to delve into right out of the oven. Rarely is there ever a time when I bake a cake that I do not allow it to cool before tasting. But when I make this luscious cake, I cannot resist. These uncontrollable moments when my taste buds have much less patience than my attitude and the fork develops a mind of its own are what I call the Force of Enticement. This Force takes over and I lose all control; it just appears as if a driving force, unknown to me, just pushes that fork right into this cake, takes out a small amount and delivers it into my mouth. So if you ever feel this powerful Force take over, do not hesitate, but first blow on the food on the fork, cooling it slightly avoiding any tongue burning prior to delivering this small amount of pleasure to your awaiting senses.

Preheat oven to 350° F

STREUSEL:
1 cup brown sugar
¼ cup flour
¼ (½ stick) cup butter
2 tablespoons cinnamon
¼ teaspoon nutmeg

1. Mix and set aside in a separate bowl.

CAKE:
8 cups (8-10 peaches) sliced and skinned fresh peaches
   or use four 15-16 ounce cans light peaches, drained
   (to skin fresh peaches, soak them in hot water for
   10-15 minutes and immediately peel the skin off)
1 cup sugar
½ cup (1 stick) butter
2 eggs
1 tablespoon vanilla
3 cups plus 2 tablespoons flour
4 teaspoons baking powder
1 cup plus 2 tablespoons milk

1. Cream together the butter, sugar, eggs and vanilla.
2. Add flour and baking powder to the butter mixture, alternating with the milk. Mix the batter thoroughly.
3. Grease a 9x13-inch pan with butter, margarine or pan spray.
4. Spread a little less than half of the batter onto bottom of the prepared pan. You will use every bit of the batter, so when spreading batter into the pan and again on top of peaches, have a bowl of about 1 cup of flour available and a rubber spatula. Constantly repeat dipping the back of the spatula into flour to help to spread the batter. (It will seem like there is not enough batter, but there really is enough.)
5. Sprinkle half of the streusel over the batter, and then cover the streusel with half the peaches, completely covering the bottom half of batter.
6. Gently spread the second half of the batter over the peaches.
7. Place the remaining peaches on top of the batter, and sprinkle the remaining streusel over the peaches.
8. Bake 40-50 minutes or until inserted knife comes out clean.

Variation:
Plums, fresh or canned can be substituted for the peaches.

The Philly Streusel Cake

*Throughout Pennsylvania, one can find prepackaged cakes and treats, manufactured by a company titled Tasty Kakes.
I grew up on Tasty Kakes; they were available wherever one went and we always had a few packages around the house to
nosh on. After receiving our driver's licenses my oldest girlfriend and I would normally stop at a convenience store on the
way to school, grab some coffee and a package of Tasty Kake Coffeecake, a plain, light cake with crumbly cinnamon topping.
After moving to Colorado where Tasty Kakes were not freshly available, I went on a mission to duplicate the taste.
It took years, but one day the following came out of the oven and is as close I have come to reproducing
those little treats that my taste buds so fondly remember and crave.*

Preheat oven to 350° F

STREUSEL TOPPING:
⅔ cup brown sugar
½ cup flour
1½ tablespoons cinnamon (use a little less if you prefer)
½ cup (1 stick) cold butter
1 cup chopped nuts and/or raisins, optional

Mix until crumbs become coarse or smaller than large peas and set aside.

CAKE:
½ cup (1 stick) butter or margarine
8 ounces cream cheese
1 cup sugar
2 eggs
1 tablespoon vanilla
⅓ cup milk
1½ cups plus 3 tablespoons of flour
1 teaspoon baking powder
½ teaspoon baking soda

1. Cream together the butter, cream cheese and sugar.
2. Add the eggs and vanilla to the butter mixture and continue mixing. Add the remaining ingredients
   and mix thoroughly.
3. Grease a 9x13-inch pan with butter, margarine or pan spray.
4. Spread batter evenly into pan. Sprinkle the streusel topping all over the batter.
5. Bake 30-40 minutes or until inserted knife comes out clean. Allow to cool 30 minutes prior to serving.

An old Irish prayer, shared with me to share with you!

May the road rise up to meet you.

May the wind always be at your back.

May the sun shine upon your face,

And the rains fall soft upon your fields.

And until we meet again,

May God hold you in the palm of His hand.

Afternoon Delights

~ All recipes can be doubled or tripled.
~ Make sure to thoroughly clean all vegetables and fruits before adding to any of the following recipes.
~ Use butter, margarine or pan spray when directed to grease the pan.
~ Leftovers can be covered in plastic wrap or placed in plastic containers and stored in the refrigerator for a day or two.

Many are familiar with the growl of the belly when the noon sun shines and the time comes for a break in the daily routine. But what one should eat has long been a question of design. These foods commonly served in the middle of the day are what I refer to as The Afternoon Delights. Easily served or packed in a container or bag and taken to work or school, many of these midday delights can also be served at a table setting or taken to a friend's home to share with others.

Shrimp Salad, Page 152

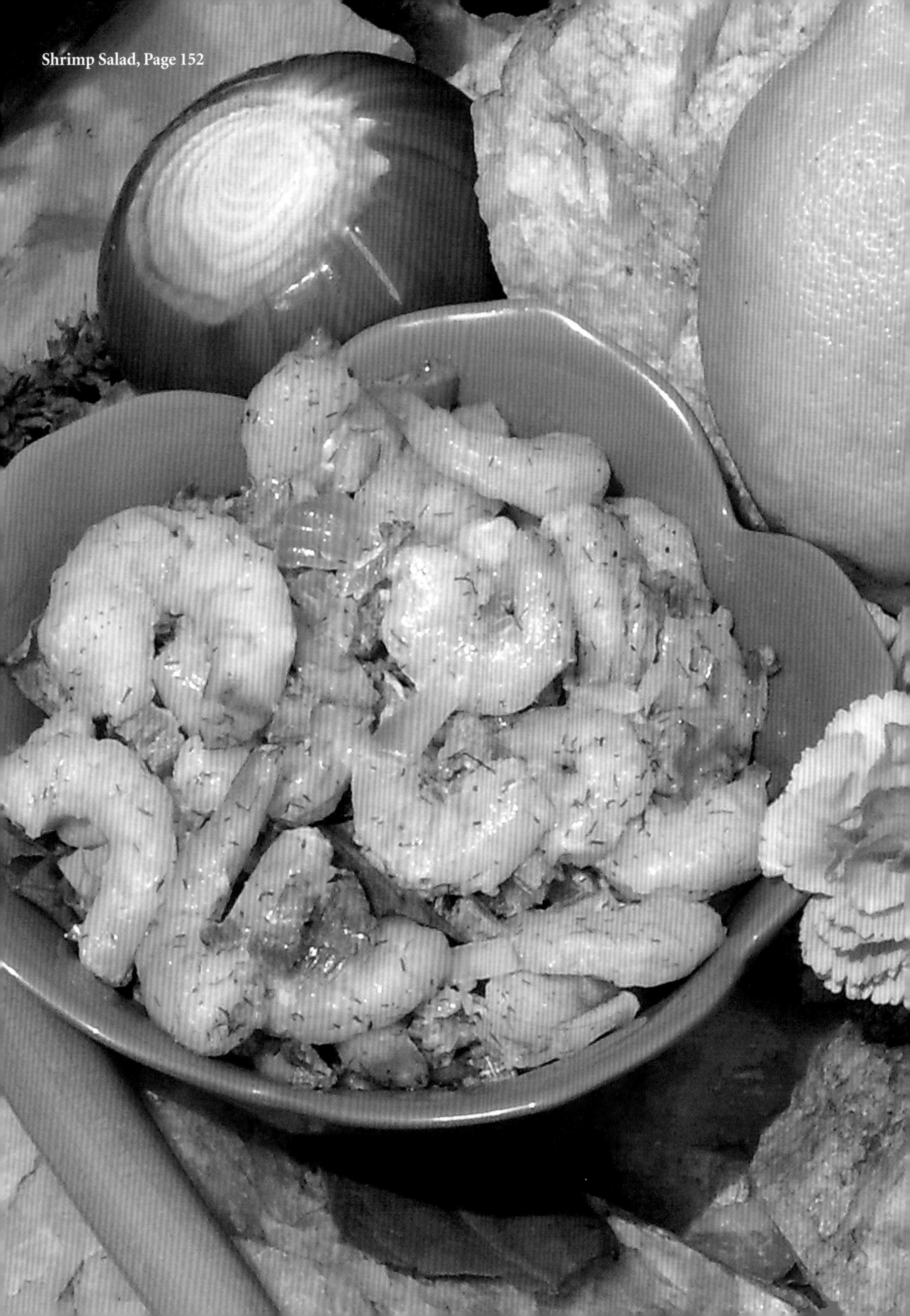

My Favorite Leafy Salad Combination

*Preparing a leafy salad has never been easier than in today's modern world where one can purchase
a bag full of prewashed greens, pour the leaves into a bowl or onto a platter and add whatever their palate desires.
I like my salads with a variety of ingredients, offering a diversity of fresh flavors while enhancing the visual appeal.
We all have our personal favorite salad additions; the following are some of mine, usually prepared
and eaten as a whole meal with a side roll or slice of bread. For Salad Dressing Recipes, see pp. 334-337.*

Serves 1-2

3 cups of leafy salad greens, chopped (any combination is fine)
1 hard boiled egg, chopped
1 small stalk of celery diced
1 tablespoon chopped cooked/canned beets
2 tablespoons grated cheese, preferably Muenster, Gruyere, Monterey Jack or provolone
1-2 tablespoon peas
1-2 tablespoons diced red onion
1-2 thinly sliced radishes
1-2 tablespoons garbanzo beans (chick peas)
Handful alfalfa sprouts
1 tablespoon sunflower seeds
1-2 tablespoons raisins
2 tablespoons chopped pecans

1. Gently toss all ingredients together and drizzle with your favorite dressing.

Mom's Cobb Salad

*Whenever I would see my mother preparing this pretty salad, I knew that the Lovely Ladies
(my aunts and neighbors), would be coming over for their weekly mah-jongg or canasta game and I was
required to disappear rapidly. I always obliged, (well almost) and either went out or up to my room, but not before
picking a few personal delights out of the salad and complimenting her for making the best salad ever. A Cobb Salad is one
of the most popular salads; there are likely hundreds of recipes written, shared and made easily available, but this specific
one has been requested, so once again, years later I must oblige. Even my aunt has asked what my mother had listed
in the ingredients of her Cobb Salad with the hope of finding the coveted ingredient, a tiny bit of lemon juice.*

Serves 4-6

7-8 cups of finely chopped lettuce greens (a mixture of iceberg, romaine, watercress or curly endive leaves work well) or one 16-ounce bag of mixed lettuce leaves
½ lemon
6 slices of bacon (optional)
4 hard boiled eggs
2 tablespoons fresh minced chives
1 clove garlic, finely diced

12 ounces sliced cooked turkey, or 6 ounces sliced turkey and 6 ounces of sliced ham
2 diced tomatoes or 1 small basket of cherry tomatoes
4-6 ounces of sliced sharp cheddar cheese or Monterey Jack cheese
4 ounces of Roquefort or blue cheese crumbled
½ cup chopped pecans or walnuts (optional)

1. Hard boil the eggs by placing them into a saucepan, cover with cool water and heat at medium high until the water reaches a full rolling boil. Lower the heat slightly and allow the eggs to boil for 20 minutes, drain and rinse the eggs several times with very cold water. Allow the eggs to sit in the saucepan full of cold water for at least 20 more minutes, before cracking and peeling off the shell.*
2. Fry the bacon in a frying pan or skillet until brown and crisp, remove from the pan, and pat dry with a paper towel. Once cool enough to handle, crumble into a small dish and put aside.
3. While the eggs and bacon are cooling, thoroughly wash and dry the lettuce with paper towels, then finely chop the leaves into bite-size pieces. Sprinkle the leaves with the juice of half a lemon and toss. Cover with a paper towel and put aside in a large bowl or platter.
4. In the meantime, chop the chives and large tomatoes; slice the turkey, ham, and cheese into strips, making sure all ingredients are prepared to be placed into the salad.
5. Remove the paper towel from the leaves, and place all ingredients on top of the lettuce in a pleasing pattern such as in stripes or in the pattern of a wheel, ending by sprinkling the bacon crumbs, nuts and crumbled cheese over the top. Serve with a variety of dressings.

*Hint: My grandmother always said that it is best to roll the eggs between the palms of your hands several times before cracking and peeling the shell. She told me that this helps loosen the shell from the skin of the egg, making the tedious job of peeling the shell easier.

Caesar Salad

The first time I tasted this splendid salad was at a restaurant called Fagan's. Not only did the employees and customers grow to be dear friends and teach me how to drink whiskey in a coffee cup (I was only 17), they introduced me to a glorious variety of foods, including Caesar Salad. The waitress would actually come to your table with a large wooden bowl and proceed to use the back of a wooden spoon to rub the bowl with anchovies and spices before tossing in the remaining ingredients, also brought to the table. The experience was a pure culinary delight and one that will always be treasured. I developed this recipe from memory and whenever I prepare it, I fondly remember those days long gone and am thankful that the memories and friendships remain strong today.

Serves 4

Preheat oven to 350° F

2 cups day-old French or Italian bread, broken or cut into ½ inch cubes
1 tablespoon plus 1 teaspoon butter
Scant ½ cup extra virgin olive oil
4-5 cloves of garlic, more if you like, peeled, crushed or minced
1 teaspoon sea salt
1 tablespoon lemon juice
½ teaspoon Worcestershire sauce
1 tablespoon red wine vinegar
3 anchovy fillets (optional, but does enhance the flavor in a true Caesar Salad)
Fresh cracked pepper to taste
1-2 eggs boiled for 4-5 minutes only, *no longer!*
1 large head of romaine lettuce, finely chopped
½ cup grated Parmesan cheese

1. Make croutons by heating the butter, oil and 2 cloves of garlic in a skillet over medium heat until the butter melts. Remove the pan from the heat; remove the garlic cloves and place them into a large bowl, preferably a wooden bowl. Toss the bread cubes into the butter mixture, spread onto a baking sheet and bake for 14-16 minutes or until golden brown. Remove from the oven and set to cool.
2. Make a paste by mashing the salt, anchovies and all of the garlic cloves into a large bowl with the back of a large wooden spoon. (A wooden bowl is best, but any bowl will work fine.) Add the juice, Worcestershire sauce, vinegar and cracked pepper and blend all together thoroughly. Separate the eggs and add only the egg yolks into the bowl; mix until all ingredients are thoroughly incorporated.
3. Gently toss the chopped lettuce with this dressing, making sure all leaves are covered, toss in the cooled croutons and top with grated cheese.

Fruity Spinach Salad

This beautiful cornucopia of goodness is an offering of Mother Nature's nutritional benefits at their peak of freshness. You will be pampering yourself in the benefits of anti-oxidants from the berries, iron and vitamins from the lovely, dark, greens leaves of freshly picked spinach, the magnificence of natural protein from the meat and eggs, much needed calcium supplied from the cheese and of course, and the crunch of fiber from the walnuts; which have been found to lower blood level cholesterol concentrations when eaten in small amounts. Astonishing isn't it, that while supplying your body and mind with the nutrients of Mother Nature's intentions, you are also indulging in the mingle of the phenomenal flavors provided from such design.

Serves 2

4 cups of spinach leaves, washed and rinsed thoroughly and stems removed
3 hard boiled eggs
3-4 slices of bacon, browned crisp and crumbled
⅓ cup blue cheese or feta cheese, crumbled
¼ cucumber, diced
¼-⅓ cup sliced mushrooms, previously washed
¼ cup chopped walnuts
⅓ cup fresh blueberries

1. Wash and drain the spinach leaves thoroughly, then pat dry with a paper towel and chop into bite-sized pieces. Fry the bacon over medium heat until crispy brown. Allow bacon to drain and cool on top of paper towels.
2. Peel the hard boiled eggs and chop into ½ inch pieces.
3. Place the chopped spinach into a bowl or platter, top with the eggs, crumble the bacon and cheese over the top, and then sprinkle with walnuts and blueberries.
4. Serve tossed with your favorite dressing.

Variation:
This is a great salad without the fruit and/or nuts too.

Crunchy Chunky Spinach Salad

This personal favorite of mine is full of all kinds of goodies. Satisfying crunch in combination with small bites of poultry elicits a scrumptious variety of tastes with each bite, making this an exceptionally fine and nutritious salad to serve for years to come.

Serves 2

½ small bag of baby spinach leaves, washed, drained, patted dry, stems removed and chopped
1-1½ cups diced cooked chicken or turkey
One 15-ounce can mandarin oranges, thoroughly drained
3-4 slices bacon, browned and crisp, crumbled (optional)
2 hard boiled eggs, shelled and chopped
¼ cup cashews, chopped
⅓ cup crispy Chinese noodles
2 tablespoons diced scallions or finely diced red onions
Small can water chestnuts, drained

1. Toss all ingredients together and serve with favorite dressing.

Suggestion: This salad pairs exquisitely with Hot Bacon Dressing (p. 336), or Raspberry Vinaigrette Dressing (p. 337).

Wheatless Burrito Salad

The fabulous ease of opening up a couple cans and cooking some ground beef, chicken or shrimp manifests itself in this appetizing salad. I have often had an urge to grab a huge burrito in the middle of the day, but then my conscience takes over and I begin to think that I may not want to be too full for the remaining afternoon. We all are familiar with the bulge in our bellies from eating too much of a good thing and the resulting desire to simply lie around afterward. Unfortunately, many of my afternoons are fully scheduled, and the act of relaxation is just not possible. So, one cool day, when a craving for a large burrito began to grow stronger, I decided to fulfill my urge with a simple salad; made from the same ingredients, minus the carbs from the tortilla.

Serves 2

1 cup, cooked and crumbled ground beef, chopped chicken or medium-sized shrimp
2-3 drops hot sauce
4-5 cups shredded lettuce
1 can refried beans, black or pinto
½ cup (more if you prefer) canned or homemade Green Chili Sauce (p. 342)
½ cup grated cheddar, marbled, Colby, Monterey Jack, Pepper Jack or grated Mexican cheese combination, more if desired
3 teaspoons diced green chilies or jalapenos (optional)
2-3 dollops sour cream
6-8 black olives, thinly sliced
½ tomato, seeded and diced
1 avocado, peeled, pitted and sliced

1. Divide the lettuce evenly between plates or bowls. Heat the refried beans until hot, either in a microwave-safe bowl or in a sauce pan. Spread or dollop the refried beans onto the lettuce.
2. Heat the meat, chicken or shrimp until warm/hot. Mix with a couple drops of hot sauce and place evenly on top of the refried beans.
3. Smother each plate with warmed green chili sauce, sprinkle with cheese, and garnish with jalapeños (if using) a couple dollops of sour cream, black olives, tomatoes and avocado.

Dad's Favorite Oriental Salad

Although Dad and I enjoyed each other's company, whenever we got into a car without other riders, our standard arguments would naturally erupt. One day, he appeared pretty stressed when he started in on me, but fortunately we were in the old neighborhood when I remembered his favorite Chinese restaurant, only a few blocks away. I suggested we go get his favorite salad and the tension in the car miraculously flew out the window. While eating, I excused myself and somehow convinced the young cook to share the recipe, as it had saved me from the wrath of my father. The cooked laughed out loud as he scribbled down the recipe, telling me that my father was a good guy and frequent customer. Months later, while visiting Colorado, our arguments began again while in the car; as we passed a grocery I asked him to stop to purchase our lunch ingredients. Just as before, this salad saved me from his wrath, for his anger again flew out the car's window as he laughed at my conniving nature when I told him how I obtained this recipe to prepare his lunch.

Serves 3-4

1 pound chicken breast or tenders, previously cooked with 1 teaspoon lemon pepper, cooled and chopped
6 cups Napa cabbage, chopped into bite-sized pieces or shredded
1 small red pepper, julienned (cut into small strips)
1 small yellow pepper, julienned (cut into small strips)
1 cup pea pods
½ cup scallions, diagonally sliced
¼ cup toasted sesame seeds*
⅓ cup dried apricots, diced
1 tablespoon fresh grated ginger, or 1 teaspoon ground ginger
¼ cup chicken broth (preferably homemade)
¼ cup rice vinegar
¼ cup soy sauce (preferably low sodium)
1½ tablespoons sugar or sugar substitute
1½ tablespoons sesame oil
1 cup crispy chow mein noodles

1. In a large bowl, mix all ingredients but noodles together thoroughly.
2. Divide the salad evenly between plates or bowls and top each with a sprinkling of the chow mein noodles and serve.

Variation:
⅔ cup chopped broccoli can be added, as can ⅔ cup toasted sliced almonds*.

***Hint:** To toast sesame seeds or almonds, preheat oven to 400° F, butter a cookie sheet well, spread the almonds or seeds flat on the sheet and bake for 1-2 minutes or just until the seeds, or nuts begin to brown. Allow to cool prior to adding to the salad.

Kathleen's Layered Salad

The beautiful colors viewed in the layers of this delightful salad can light up an entire room.
The flavors are as fresh as can be and the taste is even more pleasing than its appearance.
Absolutely perfect when serving a group of people or as a take along to a get-together.

Serves 6

SALAD:
7-8 cups leafy greens, chopped into bite-size pieces, divided in two
5 hard boiled eggs, shelled and chopped
⅔ cup diced red onions
1 large thinly sliced cucumber
⅔ sliced radishes
1½ cup frozen peas, thawed and drained
1½ cup diced cooked ham, bacon (crumbled), chicken or turkey
1 cup shredded Colby or Swiss cheese
1 large sliced tomato (optional)

DRESSING:
1 cup mayonnaise
1 cup sour cream or yogurt
Juice from 1 lemon
1½ teaspoons Worcestershire Sauce
½ teaspoon dry mustard
2 teaspoons fresh finely chopped dill

1. In the order listed, layer all salad ingredients into a clear bowl, ending with half the lettuce.
2. Whisk the mayonnaise, sour cream, lemon juice, Worcestershire sauce, mustard and dill in a bowl until thoroughly blended.
3. Spread the dressing over the layers and then sprinkle with cheese. Cover with plastic wrap and refrigerate for 24 hours. Just before serving, top with a tomato slice if you like.

The Shower and Potluck Salad

My apologies to all men reading this, for this attractively tasty salad is not one that you may eat often, so believe me when I say, you are missing out on some of the good stuff. Now this statement does not just imply that you are missing out on the wonderful flavors that the mingled ingredients elicit, but also on the gossip, jokes, tears and fashion statements that commonly surround the serving of this salad at Baby and Bridal Showers, Sweet 16 parties and the occasional Pot Lucks; which are frequented more by women then by yourselves. So, next time you guys get together for a card game or to watch a sporting event, toss the beer and pizza aside, grab a glass of wine, layer the following ingredients into a bowl, check out each others shoes and clothing, talk about each other and the kids, and have a good cry on your buddy's shoulder.

Serves 4-6

1 large head romaine or iceberg lettuce, chopped well or shredded
½ cup diced celery
½ cup diced yellow, red or green peppers, veins and seeds removed
1 medium red onion, thinly sliced
1 bag frozen peas, thawed and drained
1 pound cooked ham, turkey or chicken diced (2-3 cups)
1¼ cups grated Cheddar, Swiss, Gruyere or yellow Colby cheese
¼-⅓ cup mayonnaise
1 tablespoon sugar
1-2 teaspoon lemon juice
½ teaspoon minced garlic and/or dill
Small basket of cherry tomatoes

1. Layer all the ingredients, except the mayonnaise, sugar, lemon juice, spices and tomatoes, into a bowl in the order given.
2. Mix the mayonnaise, sugar, lemon juice and garlic/dill thoroughly together and pour over the layers.
3. Cover and refrigerate until serving. Once ready to serve, place a few cherry tomatoes on top.

Variation:
Add ½ cup raisins and ½ cup pecans as another layer.

Someone's Seafood Louie Salad

There are not enough words throughout the varied languages around the world to express the gratitude and love felt each time I find new treasures in my grandmother's recipe box. This tin box, filled with an admiration for good, well-prepared foods; a love toward all she served; and a love for sharing, offers an unconditional offering of my grandmother's affection. The following recipe came out of her box, written on an index card dated 1947, with the handwritten words, For Lenny, (my father), above the date. I have no idea whose recipe this was, but once I saw the list of ingredients, you can bet I went to the grocery, bought supplies, came back home and made it. Upon lifting the fork to sample the magnificent flavor of this special salad, I looked up towards the grace above and said, "Hello," to both my father and grandmother, knowing that they were smiling down at me.

Serves 3-4

SALAD:
1 head iceberg or romaine lettuce, chopped or shredded (prepackaged greens can also be used)
16 ounces lump crabmeat and/or medium shrimp
1 avocado, peeled, pitted and chopped into chunks
1 medium tomato, cut into wedges or a few cherry tomatoes
2-3 hard boiled eggs

1 lemon, cut into wedges

THE LOUIE DRESSING:
1½ cups mayonnaise
¼ cup chili sauce
3 tablespoons finely minced green onions (include some green tops)
2 tablespoons finely minced green pepper
1 tablespoon fresh lemon juice
1½ teaspoons Worcestershire sauce
¼ teaspoon hot sauce

1. Put the chopped lettuce greens in a large bowl.
2. Make sure to search the crabmeat for any loose shells and remove them. Mix the crab with the next three ingredients, and place on top of the lettuce in the bowl.
3. To make the dressing, whisk together all ingredients in a bowl. Gently toss with the salad or use dressing of choice and gently toss into the salad, serve garnished with lemon wedges.

Grandmom's Cucumber Salad

Whenever I prepare this salad I am reminded of the lunches spent with my grandmother at the little coffee shop in her apartment building. I specifically remember one rainy day when she ordered this salad. Knowing that I did not eat many vegetables, I was required to take a little taste. Both of us were shocked when I stated that I liked it and proceeded to take a couple forkfuls from her plate. Years later, while searching for something in her recipe box, I came across a card entitled Pres. Cuc. Salad, *and thought, "Why not?" for it seemed so easy to prepare. Upon first bite my memory went back in time to the day that I first tasted this. How she got a hold of this recipe I will never know, but many taste buds are awfully glad that she did!*

Serve 3-4

2 cucumbers
½ large red onion
1½ cups water
½ cup white or rice wine vinegar
1½ teaspoons sugar or 1 teaspoon sugar substitute
½ teaspoon sea salt or seasoned salt (see below for recipe)

1. Peel and slice cucumbers into ⅛-inch thick rounds.
2. Peel and slice the onion, into ⅛-inch thick slices. Toss cucumbers and onions together in a bowl.
3. In a small bowl or jar with a tight fitting lid, stir or shake the water, vinegar, sugar and seasoned salt.
   Once thoroughly mixed, pour mixture over the vegetables and chill for 1 hour.

SEASONED SALT:
¾ cup salt
¼ teaspoon white pepper
1 teaspoon pepper
¼ cup garlic powder
½ teaspoon oregano
1 teaspoon paprika
⅛ teaspoon celery seed

1. Mix ingredients together and store in a tightly sealed jar or plastic container.

Hint: This salad may be served cool or at room temperature, but it only remains fresh for 1 day.

Mom's Mozzarella Tomato Salad

My mother would occasionally prepare and serve this to the Lovely Ladies during their card games and I would often see a bowlful on the table during various parties at the house. There was never a tomato left in the bowl, and each bite consumed was accompanied by many oohs and aahs, so I can only surmise that this salad was savored by all that indulged in its delicacy. Honestly, I never tasted her salad, thus I cannot share a description of its flavor. But I will say that the scent that filled the air around the bowl was so terrific that I would often dip a piece of bread into the bottom of the bowl for a taste of the essence left behind.

Serves 4-8

1½ pounds tomatoes, thinly sliced
1 small seedless/English cucumber, peeled and thinly sliced
1 bunch green onions, thinly sliced including the stems
2 tablespoons fresh basil or 1 tablespoon fresh basil and 1 tablespoon fresh lemon basil, finely chopped
1 tablespoon fresh parsley, finely chopped
3 tablespoons olive oil, preferably extra-virgin
3 tablespoons red wine vinegar
½ pound Mozzarella cheese, cut into small cubes
Salt and pepper to taste

1. Place all prepared ingredients into a bowl and mix together thoroughly.
2. Cover and refrigerate overnight and/or for up to 2 days prior to serving. Remove from refrigerator at least 1 hour before serving for best flavor.

Tabbouleh

This old Middle Eastern favorite has become popular worldwide and can now commonly be found in many grocery stores throughout the west. A marvelous choice of ingredients, marinated with a blend of lemony oil, makes this a delightful mid-day meal.

Serves 4-6

4¼ cups boiling water
1¼ cups bulgur wheat
3 tomatoes, diced
½ cup canned garbanzo beans
¾ cup diced red onion or scallions
1 cucumber sliced and diced
1½ cups fresh parsley, chopped
2-4 tablespoons fresh chopped mint (amount depends on personal preference)
½ cup fresh squeezed lemon juice (or more if you like)
¼ cup olive oil
1 teaspoon sea salt
¼ teaspoon pepper

1. Place the bulgur into a large bowl and cover with boiling water. Let this stand for an hour or more until the bulgur is light and fluffy, then drain well by pressing all excess liquid through cheesecloth or a fine mesh sieve. Put softened grain back into the bowl and add the remaining ingredients, stir well and refrigerate for at least 1 hour so that the flavors have time to marinate.

Waldorf Salad

To add the nuts or not to this old fashioned favorite is a matter of personal preference. I first tasted this at a friend's home during a holiday meal, immediately asked for the recipe and was astonished that she didn't have one written down. I reproduced my interpretation, took her some and was blatantly informed that she rarely adds the celery, never the nuts, and only adds mayonnaise to hold the apples and raisins together. She took the container and immediately noticed some nuts had been added, and got quite persnickety until I pointed out that there were only nuts in half of the container; one side didn't have any. Later, we chatted and giggled as girlfriends do, while we ate the whole container, nuts and all.

Serves 4

½ head lettuce, shredded
2 cups apples, peeled, cored thinly sliced or diced
2 cups celery diced
1 cup dark or golden raisins or dark dried cherries
1 cup chopped pecans or walnuts
3-4 tablespoons mayonnaise (more if you like)

1. Place the lettuce into the bottom of a bowl. Mix the remaining ingredients together in a separate bowl and spoon onto the lettuce.
2. Serve immediately or refrigerate for a couple of hours until serving.

Variation:
Add 1 plus cup chopped cooked chicken or turkey breast.

Cherry Salad

The luscious beauty of blending the red of cherries, the slight tan of an almond and the pale green, curly, red-tipped lettuce is what makes the following a welcome addition to all recipe collections. This salad is not just divine in flavor, but will add a touch of elegance to all tables onto which it is placed.

Serves 4-5

1 head of red leaf lettuce, thoroughly washed and patted dry with papers towels
3 cups pitted sweet dark or Rainier cherries
1 cup chopped or slivered almonds
1 cup diced celery
¾ cup mayonnaise
3 tablespoons powdered sugar
1 teaspoon vanilla

1. In one bowl toss together the cherries, almonds and celery; in a separate bowl, mix the mayonnaise, sugar and vanilla thoroughly. Pour the mayonnaise mixture over the cherries, and gently stir until combined. Refrigerate for 45-60 minutes.
2. Divide the lettuce evenly between plates or bowls and spoon cherry mixture onto the leaves and serve immediately. This can also be served in a large bowl rather than on individual plates.

Variation:
• Honey yogurt can be used instead of the mayonnaise and sugar.
• Peaches and pecans or walnuts can be used in place of the cherries and almonds.
• Spinach can be substituted for the red leaf lettuce.

Hint: If you cannot find honey yogurt, simply add 2-3 teaspoons of honey to plain yogurt and mix.

Sunshine Salad

*Many of us get that familiar craving for fresh summer fruits in the depth of the frozen winter months.
Long ago, I came up with the following to soothe this craving, for each time I toss these ingredients together during
the frost of winter, I look out at the snow falling, shut my eyes and I can truly feel the warmth of the sun shining on
my face as my imagination travels to the fragrant orchards and gardens where these fruits are grown.*

Serves 2-4

2 pink grapefruits, peeled and sectioned
2 tangelo oranges, peeled and sectioned
1 cup red or green seedless grapes
1 cup blueberries
½ fresh pineapple, peeled and chopped
¾ head romaine lettuce, washed and patted dry with paper towels and chopped into bite size pieces
1 small lemon
½ cup mayonnaise
¼ cup light corn syrup
1 tablespoon fresh grated orange peel
½ teaspoon fresh finely chopped orange balsam (optional)
2 teaspoons finely chopped lemon basil (optional)
½ cup chopped walnuts, golden raisins and/or chopped dates (optional)

1. In a bowl, place the lettuce leaves onto the bottom, mix the four fruits together and place on top of the lettuce.
2. Grate the peel of the lemon into a separate bowl, then squeeze all the juice from the lemon into the bowl. Add the mayonnaise, corn syrup, orange peel, orange balsam and lemon basil and thoroughly mix together.
3. Pour the lemon mixture over the fruits and lettuce, and gently toss to coat. Sprinkle with walnuts, raisins and/or dates. Serve immediately.

Pasta Salads

I am trying to imagine the descriptive words commonly associated with hundreds of recipes developed from mixing fresh vegetables, meats, poultry, fish, fruits and various shaped pastas. Fresh, flavorful and versatile first come to mind; quickly followed by creamy yet chunky; smooth and rich; spiced and herbed; absolutely delicious; and satisfying enough to sustain one through the afternoon. Commonly created as a side dish or served on a bed of lettuce as a meal, pasta salads are a favorite to bring to picnics and summer barbecues when the harvest of vegetables is at its peak.

To begin, you must choose a pasta; elbow macaroni, ziti, rigatoni, small colored flavored wheels or small shells are the preferred shapes. Then use your imagination and choose some colorful vegetables, meats and cheeses. It is this use of your imagination that will begin to form a worthy salad. Additionally, keep in mind that the dressings used to mix, spice and hold the chosen ingredients together are partially what makes these creamy salads so delectable.

Mom's Deli Pasta Salad with Meat

Serves 2-4

SALAD:
One 8-ounce package small pasta such as elbow macaroni, shells, cheese tortellini or tri-colored shapes
8 ounces thinly sliced cooked ham, hard salami, turkey,
   chicken, or various seafoods
8 ounces provolone cheese, cubed
1 small can sliced black olives, drained
1 small red onion, diced
1 medium zucchini, julienned (cut into small thin strips)
1 thin carrot, julienned (cut into small thin strips)
½ cup chopped green pepper or peas
½ cup chopped sweet red pepper
2 medium tomatoes, diced

DRESSING:
¼ cup fresh parsley, finely chopped
⅓ cup grated Parmesan cheese
½ cup olive or vegetable oil
¼ cup cider or red wine vinegar
1-2 teaspoons minced garlic
1 teaspoon dry mustard
1 teaspoon each dried basil and oregano (preferably
   lemon basil for it truly complements this recipe)
Salt and pepper to taste

1. Cook pasta according to package directions, drain thoroughly under cool water; and place into a large bowl.
   Add all vegetables, meats and cheeses to the cooked pasta and stir together.
2. Combine the oil, vinegar, garlic, mustard, and seasonings in a container with tight-fitting lid, and shake well.
   Pour all dressing over the salad and gently toss to coat.
3. Cover the bowl with plastic wrap or a lid and refrigerate for 8 hours or overnight. Toss once again before serving,
   making sure all ingredients are coated with dressing.

Variation:
½ cup of peas, frozen and thawed can be added, as can ½ cup corn kernels

Deli Pasta Salad

Serves 2-3

2 cups elbow macaroni, cooked, drained, and chilled
⅓ cup red onion chopped
⅓ cup celery chopped
½ cup frozen peas, thawed and drained (or if available, use freshly shelled peas)
⅔ cup chopped broccoil
½ cup diced red pepper (optional)
½ cup diced tomato
½ cup mayonnaise
½ teaspoon each dry mustard, dill, powdered garlic and parsley
2 tablespoons cider vinegar
Salt and pepper to taste

1. Cook pasta according to directions on the package, drain under cool water and place into a large bowl. Add vegetables to the pasta and stir together.
2. In a small bowl, whisk together the mayonnaise, mustard, spices and vinegar until thoroughly incorporated.
3. Using a rubber spatula, pour mayonnaise dressing over the pasta and vegetables, and gently stir together, making sure that all ingredients are covered.
4. Refrigerate at least 2 hours to give the flavors time to mingle; serve as is, or on a bed of mixed lettuce leaves.

Variations:
• Add 1 cup chopped cooked turkey, chicken, shrimp, crab meat or lobster.
• Add ½ cup sliced black olives, or 4 ounces fresh sliced mushrooms, or 1 cup fresh blueberries or red seedless grapes

ALTERNATE DRESSING FOR DELI PASTA SALAD:
½ cup red wine vinegar
1 teaspoon pepper
¾ cup olive oil
2-3 teaspoons oregano
½ teaspoon basil

1. Thoroughly mix and stir into the cooked pasta before adding meats and vegetables.

Stir-fried Linguini Pasta Salad

In the words of Rhonda, one of my incredible editors, "Much too good, do not pull this one out of the book!"

Serves 2-3

8 ounces linguini noodles
1½ tablespoons butter
1½ tablespoons olive or vegetable oil
Juice from 1 lemon
Grated peel from 1 lemon
1½ cups chopped broccoli (or ¾ cup each chopped cauliflower and broccoli)
1 zucchini, julienne (cut into thin strips)
1 small carrot, julienne (cut into thin strips)
½ small red onion, diced or ½ bunch scallions diced
¼ cup honey
1 teaspoon dried basil (preferably lemon basil)
1 teaspoon oregano
1-2 teaspoons minced garlic or 2 garlic cloves, finely chopped
¼ cup each grated Parmesan and Romano cheese
Salt and pepper to taste

1. Cook linguini according to package directions, drain under cool water and place in a large bowl.
2. In a large skillet, heat the oil and butter over medium, add the broccoli and garlic and stir-fry for 3-4 minutes, stirring occasionally.
3. Lower the heat to low and add remaining vegetables and spices; do not add the cheese. Allow mixture to simmer for 5-7 minutes or until tender. Stir gently once each minute.
4. Once the vegetables are tender, pour over the pasta and gently stir to incorporate.
5. Refrigerate for at least 2 hours to allow flavors to blend. Sprinkle with Parmesan and Romano cheese before serving.

Variation:
Asparagus can be used in place of broccoli.

Mom's Potato Salad

Growing up as a fussy eater, I refused to taste this salad until I was a teenager; and then I couldn't get enough. I never liked salads made with pickle juice, so naturally I thought that one potato salad tasted like all the others. Foolish me, for Mom's was different and the best I had ventured to taste; though I didn't taste many, only the obligatory one or two teeny bites at a friend's house. Although nothing individually extraordinary, this is just a fine, simple blend of everyday ingredients that when mixed together produce an amazingly palatable experience. Truth be told, this is one of the recipes which sold-out daily during the brief period that I had a shop. The recipe requests have been persistent if not demanding; and one of the motivating factors towards writing this cookbook.

Serves 4-6

5 large russet potatoes, washed, peeled (if desired) and cut into 1–2-inch chunks
5 hard boiled eggs, peeled
¾ cup celery, diced
¾ cup red onion, diced
1-2 teaspoons minced garlic
2 teaspoons dill
½ teaspoon celery salt
Salt and pepper to taste
⅔ cup plus mayonnaise (you do not need an excessive amount, just enough to hold everything together,
    plus a bit more for creaminess)
Sprinkling of paprika for the top (optional)

1. Fill a large pot with warm water and heat to a full boil over medium heat.
2. Place the potatoes into the boiling water and cook until tender, but not as soft as for mashed potatoes,
    about 15-20 minutes. Rinse and drain thoroughly under cold water and pour into a large bowl.
3. Cut the eggs into small chunks and add to the potatoes, along with all other ingredients except the paprika.
    Stir gently, breaking up some of the potatoes, while leaving most in chunks.
4. Sprinkle the top with a bit of paprika, cover with plastic wrap and refrigerate at least 2 hours before serving.

Stephen's Grandmother's Hot German Potato Salad

Stephen is a professional chef, a webmaster and a friend. We met by chance through the internet and immediately shared our passion for good foods and swapped cookbooks with one another. This recipe comes with his blessing and permission, just as he has it listed in his cookbook, Recipes from a German Grandma, *published by The Kitchen Project in 2001. This book is full of delicious, admired and treasured recipes, originating from German decent and written for all to enjoy. With this recipe you will not have to go out to eat to feel the essence of being in a foreign country, all you need to do is prepare this enticing salad for a taste of German cuisine.*

Serves 4

4 large potatoes
5 thick slices bacon, diced
1 cup diced onion
¼ cup vinegar
¼ cup water
¼ cup sugar
Salt and pepper to taste

1. Thoroughly wash the potatoes, slice and then boil them in their jackets in a large pot of water until tender.
2. Fry the diced bacon in a large skillet over medium heat until almost crisp; add and stir the chopped onions to the skillet and cook until slightly golden brown.
3. Add the oil, water and sugar to the hot skillet, continuing to heat and stir the mixture until the sugar dissolves.
4. Add the sliced potatoes and mix together thoroughly. Season with salt and pepper, continue cooking for 10-15 minutes or until the potatoes have absorbed all the liquid and are heated through. Continue stirring and flipping the potatoes over for another 5-10 minutes, remove from the heat and allow the flavors to stand for a few more minutes to blend completely before serving.

Egg Salad

I am astonished at how such a simple mix of vegetables and eggs can always make me feel better. When I was a little girl and ill, my mother would make a batch of this cool, refreshing egg concoction, which always felt so nice and smooth while flowing down my sore throat. Years later, after a surgery, I specifically asked her to make me a bowlful of this amazing salad, just as she did when I was little and ill. Today, my mother may be gone, but this still has the same effect; whenever I am down or under the weather, this salad endlessly continues to brighten up the day, cool a sore throat and ultimately make me feel better. I believe that the magic of a mother's love blended into this recipe is what may induce the healing power. Who knows? I'm just glad that it is as good today as when she made it long ago!

Serves 3-5

10-12 hard boiled eggs
1 cup celery, diced
1 cup red onions diced
½-⅔ cup mayonnaise
1-1½ teaspoons dill (amount is of personal preference)
Salt and pepper to taste
Sprinkle of paprika (optional)

1. Peel the eggs, and chop into chunks.
2. Add remaining ingredients and mix gently but well.
3. Cover and refrigerate until serving. Serve on a plate of lettuce or between slices of bread with lettuce and tomato slices. Store leftovers covered in the refrigerator.

Variation:
Add ½ cup grated carrots and/or ½ cup raisins or dried cherries.

Tuna Fish Salad

A beautiful, light, healthy salad commonly served on a bed of lettuce with some fresh vegetables and/or between or on top of slices of bread. Considered a favorite salad among those watching their caloric intake, yet still popular among those who enjoy full-flavored foods.

Serves 4-6

24 ounces canned albacore tuna, packed in water, drained
1 cup celery, diced
1 cup red onion, diced
1 teaspoon dill
1 teaspoon minced garlic
¼ teaspoon celery seed or salt
¼ teaspoon pepper, more or less to taste
A couple drops of fresh squeezed lemon juice

1. Mix all ingredients together in a bowl and refrigerate for at least 1 hour, allowing all ingredients to mingle and blend for full flavor.

Chicken or Turkey Salad

*Okay, I confess, this is my favorite of all the chunky salads available throughout the world.
I make this recipe all the time, for I never seem to get enough. Many have their own favorites in the department
of Chicken Salad, for the variations are plentiful, but this recipe makes my mouth begin to water just at the thought of it.
Excuse me, for now I must go get a plateful. Be right back!*

*Ah, the enjoyment of satisfaction from this heavenly blend of flavors has once again quenched the desires of my palate!
Bon Appetite!*

Serves 4-6

4 cups cooked chicken or turkey
1 cup celery, diced
1 cup red onions, diced
1 cup red grapes, sliced in half
½ cup plus mayonnaise
1 healthy teaspoon minced garlic
¼ teaspoon celery seed or salt
1½ teaspoons dill
Salt and pepper to taste
½ cup chopped pecans, walnuts or almonds (optional)

1. Chop the chicken into 1-inch chunks, shredding the largest of these by simply rubbing them apart between your fingers. (This shredding procedure is important, for it assists in making this salad creamier, while still keeping some chunks in the final product.)
2. Add and mix together all remaining ingredients but the nuts.
3. Refrigerate the salad for at least 2 hours allowing the flavors to blend. Sprinkle the nuts on top prior to serving.

Kathleen's Curried Chicken Salad

If you ever need to make a good impression on a new friend or family member, this is a perfect salad to serve. Kathleen told me that when she first got married, her mother-in-law was rather cantankerous and never thought any woman was good enough for her son. This was very frustrating to Kathleen, because she longed to improve this horrid relationship with her husband's mother. One day Kathleen invited her to lunch and spent the morning preparing a few of her mother-in-law's favorites, including this spicy, fruit-filled chicken salad. It worked! As soon as his mother took a bite of this recipe, she instantly raved about how good it tasted, and eagerly ate to her heart's content. When she got up to leave, it gave great pleasure and relief to Kathleen when this woman kissed her on the cheek while saying, "Welcome to the family!"

Serves 4-5

4 pounds chicken, previously cooked, boned and skinned
1 Granny Smith apple, peeled, cored and diced
½ cup plus celery, diced
3 scallions diced or 1 tablespoon finely diced red onion
1 cup seedless red grapes, sliced in half
½ cup toasted sliced almonds*
1 tablespoon curry powder
1⅓ cups mayonnaise
Salt and pepper to taste

1. Chop the chicken into 1-inch cubes and place into a large bowl.
2. Add all remaining ingredients to the chicken and stir well. Cover and refrigerate until serving.

*To toast almonds, preheat oven to 400° F, butter a cookie sheet well, spread almonds to lay flat on the sheet and bake for 1-2 minutes or just until the nuts begin to brown. Allow to cool prior to adding to the salad.

Shrimp Salad

I will never forget the first time I tasted this scrumptious salad. I was visiting my parents at the beach and my mother handed me twenty dollars to go buy sliced meats at the local grocery store. As I approached the deli counter, a divine salad displayed in a shell-shaped platter grabbed my attention. Just arriving from the Rocky Mountains the night before, I craved fresh seafood and this beautiful shrimp salad was calling out to me. So what's a girl to do, obey her mother or feed her appetite? I chose both, for I purchased 1/4 pound each of sliced turkey and corned beef and a full pound of the salad. When I returned to the house and pulled the packages out of the bag, I noticed the familiar look of annoyance on Mom's face while she shook her head. She didn't say much, just handed me another twenty with a command to go back to the store and get what she had requested, as company was coming over shortly. When I again returned to the house, meats in hand, the container of 'my' shrimp salad was in a neighbor's hand and almost gone. Everyone shared in the laughter, for once again I had to walk back to the store, this time at my expense, of course. I'll tell you though, the following recipe was worth every step I took that day; and I'd do it again in a New York minute.

Serves 3-4

16-20 ounces medium shrimp, cooked, peeled and deveined
¾ cup diced celery
¾ cup diced red onion
1 teaspoon dill
1 teaspoon minced garlic
1-2 pinches Old Bay Seafood Seasoning
1 tablespoon fresh squeezed lemon juice
¼ cup mayonnaise (only enough to moisten the salad)

1. Place all ingredients into a bowl and gently mix together.
2. Serve as is, on a bed of lettuce with tomato wedges, lemon wedges and/or with bread slices.

Variation:
This can also be prepared with a combination of fresh cooked lobster and/or crabmeat.

Bob's Ham Salad

Bob says that this easy salad is splendid for an everyday get together with friends, family and colleagues. He once told me that years ago when he still worked at a lumber yard, he would frequently bring a large bowl of this salad to work with him, knowing that his boss enjoyed anything made with ham. The boss loved this recipe and actually informed Bob that if he would write it down for his wife, Bob could have the weekend off. Evidently his wife was not a very good cook, and he stated so to Bob. Isn't it wonderful how the sharing of food can bring out the good in people!

Serves 2-4

2-2½ cups diced ham
1 cup grated Cheddar cheese (Swiss works well too)
2 medium stalks celery, diced
½ red onion, diced
½ cup peas
2 tablespoons sweet relish or finely diced kosher pickles
½ cup mayonnaise
1 scant tablespoon spicy mustard (optional)
½ teaspoon pepper

1. Mix all ingredients in a large bowl.
2. Refrigerate for at least 2 hours, allowing the flavors to blend and serve with lettuce and tomato wedges or on slices of bread.

Variation:
Add 1 cup cooked macaroni or small shell noodles and 1-2 more tablespoons mayonnaise.

The Sandwich

With each sandwich I indulge in, I continue to be thankful that someone long ago, whether a rabbi or the 4th Earl of Sandwich, decided that placing meats and cheese between slices of bread was an incredibly delicious creation. For hundreds of years a 'Sandwich' has often been considered an Afternoon Delight of irreplaceable esteem. Sure, you can assemble a sandwich for breakfast as well as for dinner, but one usually indulges in the magnificence of a well-prepared sandwich during the midday hours.

Most sandwiches are served with lettuce, tomato, onion, mayonnaise, mustard, potato chips, French fries or cottage cheese, and a pickle on the side. Any of the following recipes can be served wrapped in a tortilla, or pushed into a pocket of pita bread instead of being placed between slices of bread. The variety of meats, cheeses and vegetables used to assemble sandwiches is vast; use your imagination and taste buds to create is the best advice I can give. For convenience I have supplied a list of favorites.

Each recipe makes 1 sandwich

The Reuben

4-6 ounces sliced corned beef
2-3 tablespoons Thousand Island dressing
¼ cup sauerkraut
2 slices rye bread

1. Grill the sandwich before serving.

The Special

4-6 ounces sliced pastrami
2-3 tablespoons Russian dressing
¼ cup coleslaw
2 slices rye bread

Poultry Special

4-6 ounces sliced chicken or turkey
2-3 tablespoons Caesar salad dressing
2 slices of bread

The Club

2-3 slices cooked bacon
4 slices turkey
2 slices cheese
3 slices bread

1. Place turkey and cheese on bottom slice of bread, top with second slice of bread; place bacon on top of second slice of bread and top with the third slice.

The Combo

6 ounce combination of chosen meats, such as sliced turkey, ham, roast beef, pastrami, or other meat
2-3 slices Swiss cheese
2 slices bread

The Salami Special

3 ounces each hard and Genoa salami
2-3 slices provolone cheese
1 round roll

Tuna Salad Special

⅓-½ cup Tuna Salad (p. 149)
⅓ cup potato chips
2 slices bread or 1 round roll

Special Egg Salad

⅓-½ cup Egg Salad (p. 148)
¼ cup sprouts
2 tablespoons sunflower seeds
2 slices marble rye bread

Open-Faced

4-6 ounces sliced meats, poultry, fish or vegetables
2-3 slices of cheese
1 slice of bread

1. Melt the cheese on top of the other ingredients
   and serve warm.

Grilled Cheese

4-6 ounces cheese
2 slices of breads

1. Place the cheese and choice of vegetables between 2
   slices of bread and grill until the cheese has melted
   and bread is golden.

BLT

4-5 slices of cooked bacon
Lettuce and tomato
2 slices of bread

Avocado and Cheese

4-6 ounces Brie cheese
4 slices avocado
2 slices pumpernickel bread
(Sliced turkey can be added if you like.)

Bagel, Lox and Cream Cheese

4 ounces sliced Nova Lox salmon
2 ounces cream cheese
1 bagel

Top the cream cheese and lox with sliced onions,
tomatoes and thinly sliced cucumbers.

BBQ

4-6 ounces warm pulled beef, pork or poultry to which
   a BBQ Sauce has been added.
1 round roll

Vegetable

4-6 ounces thinly sliced vegetables
2-3 tablespoons salad dressing
2 slices bread

A Few Favorite Submarine Sandwiches

(Also commonly referred to as Hoagies, Heroes, Po'Boys or Grinders)

Before I supply a short list of favorites, I must inform you that what separates a very good sub sandwich from all the others is the oil drizzled on just before folding the long roll over the scrumptious ingredients inside. The oil used on the sandwich adds a bit of tang, enhancing the flavor of combined ingredients in each and every bite. The oil is primarily used on cold subs, while hot subs are often made with warm BBQ or tomato sauce. Most subs are prepared with lettuce, tomato, onion, sweet peppers, mayonnaise, mustard and/or oil.

Sub Sandwich Oil

Per 1-2 sandwiches

3 tablespoons olive oil
1 tablespoon red-wine vinegar
½ teaspoon dried oregano, crumbled
Sprinkle of garlic powder
Salt and fresh ground pepper to taste

1. Mix all thoroughly together and put aside in a small bowl or container. Store leftovers in a jar or plastic container with a tight fitting lid.

The Italian

2 ounces each Cappicola ham, Genoa salami, hard salami, Proscuitto and/or peppered ham, provolone cheese

Chicken

1 grilled chicken breast
2-3 tablespoons blue cheese crumbles
Caesar dressing

Turkey

4 ounces sliced turkey
2-3 slices cooked bacon
2 ounces sliced cheddar, Brie or provolone cheese

The Deli

2 ounces each roast beef, corned beef, hard salami
2 ounces Provolone cheese

The Veggie

6 ounces thinly sliced zucchini, carrots, peppers, tomatoes, onions, mushrooms, and/or sprouts
3-4 slices avocado or ⅓ cup guacamole or Marinara Sauce
2 ounces feta, cheddar or provolone cheese, or tofu
   (Heated and melted for best taste)

Hint: The vegetables can also be grilled in Sub Oil, before placing onto the bread.

The Tuna

½ cup or more Tuna Salad (p. 149)
2-3 ounces provolone cheese
1. Melt cheese over the tuna

Meatball

Meatballs, smothered in Marinara Sauce (p. 198)
2-3 ounces sliced provolone and/or Mozzarella cheese.

Sausage

1 Italian or Polish Sausage, smothered in Marinara
   Sauce (p. 198)
2-3 ounces sliced provolone and/or mozzarella cheese.

BBQ

Hot pulled beef or poultry smothered in BBQ Sauce,
with a side of coleslaw.

The Cheesesteak

6 ounces thinly sliced round steak or roast, grilled with just
   a smidgen of vegetable oil and onions added to the pan
2-3 ounces provolone cheese

Peppers, mushrooms and tomato sauce are sometimes
added upon request.

The Burger

Being that the burger, like a sub, is available almost everywhere one goes these days, I believe that it may be the most popular type of sandwich around the globe. With the growing surge in the restaurant industry, some fast food, some slow and elegantly designed, the prices, shapes and varieties of the burger are endless. Many are served thin, flat and tasteless; and sell for as little as one dollar. Others are huge and piled high with exotic flavors and sell for over $50. Cooking or grilling a thick, juicy, succulent burger at home prepared exactly to your liking is a sublime delight if ever there was one. I am sure that many have experienced the satisfaction of removing a hot burger from the grill, piling a few choice ingredients on top and taking that first savory bite while the juice flows down your chin. A well-prepared burger is an eating experience like no other.

The creation of the hamburger dates back almost 1800 years to a time when the Mongols, known as Taters in Russia, carried flat patties of raw lamb and mutton under their saddles for food. When they invaded Moscow they brought these meats them, which were soon adopted as a fine cuisine and referred to as "Steak tartare". Years later these meats were shared with Germans when the Russian Ships would dock at the ports in Hamburg Germany. Germans were infamous for naming foods after their towns and cities, hence the origin for the term Hamburger. These fine tasty meats fondly referred to as Hamburg Steaks were shared among many. At times these fine meats were served on a Brotchen', a round bun-shaped bread. The Germans also shipped goods to ports in New York and fortunately while immigrating to the United States, many brought their fondness for the Hamburg Steak with them which soon developed into the wonderful delights of today, The Burger.

In today's health-oriented world, with the variety of diets and availability of diverse ingredients, it is now an accepted practice for a burger to be made from an assortment of ingredients, such as ground meats, turkey/chicken, salmon, and/or vegetables. When preparing any burger, plan on using one pound of meat per 3-4 burgers. Common toppings include: lettuce, tomato, onion, pickles, various cheeses, mushrooms, peppers, sprouts, cucumbers, avocado, salsas, chilies, guacamole, salad dressings, pineapples, mayonnaise, mustards, pesto, tomato based sauces, and on and on. A burger is often served with a side of potato chips, French fries, a salad or cottage cheese. Just use your imagination and your palate to create The Incredible Burger.

My Cheeseburger in Paradise

No Heinz 57 here, but just as fabulous, and pairs perfectly with a beer, margarita, wine spritzer, a bottle of soda pop or iced tea.

Makes 3-4 burgers

1 pound lean ground beef
2 teaspoons minced garlic
1-2 tablespoons Worcestershire sauce
Kosher salt and pepper to taste
2 tablespoons of olive oil
½ of a small red onion, thinly sliced
½ pound of mushrooms, thinly sliced
12 ounces of Camembert cheese, rind carefully removed
½ cup or more alfalfa sprouts
1 sliced avocado (8 slices)
3-4 kaiser rolls
mayonnaise

1. Heat oil over medium heat, add the mushrooms and onions and cook until tender, about 7-10 minutes. Put aside in small bowl or plate.
2. Mix the ground beef with the garlic, Worcestershire sauce, salt and pepper. Make 3-4 round patties out of the meat and grill or fry the patties until cooked to your liking.
3. While cooking the burgers, slice the rolls in half, and spread the cheese evenly on both sides of each roll. Heat the rolls in the oven or on the outer rim of the grill, if desired.
4. When the burgers have cooked to your liking, place each onto the bottom of a roll, slather it with mushrooms and onions, then place the sprouts on top. Spread the avocado slices right onto the cheese, then spread some mayonnaise if you like and place the roll on top of the other ingredients. With the palm of your hand, lightly squish it all down and serve.

Teriyaki Burger

An astonishing combination of flavors, eliciting pure tropical bliss with each and every bite.

Makes 3-4 burgers

1 pound ground meat, ground turkey works exceptionally well in this recipe.
¼ cup finely diced red onion
¼ cup teriyaki sauce
1-2 teaspoons minced garlic
6-8 slices cheese of choice
3-4 sliced pineapple rings
3-4 rolls, English muffins or croissants

1. Mix all ingredients but the cheese, pineapples and rolls thoroughly together and shape into 3-4 patties.
2. Grill, cook or fry the patties until cooked to your liking. Place each patty onto the bread, top it with cheese, then a pineapple slice, and finish with condiments to your liking.

Dad's BBQ Burgers

My father took great pride in this sauce and in his techniques at the grill. Throughout the years, many requested this recipe and were told there was none. Fortunately, years later, with a tendency towards being sneaky but resourceful when necessary, I hid behind the slightly ajar kitchen door, watching with notepad in hand while he made a batch. A few months later, while he was visiting Colorado, several friends came over for a BBQ and I was laughing when I brought this sauce to the grill saying it was my Dad's Recipe. Dad gave me an engaging look, but his grin grew wide as I reminded him that his mother taught me that recipes are for sharing not hoarding and that he always told me to use my resources and imagination to get along well in life.

Makes 3-4 burgers

DAD'S BBQ SAUCE:
One 28-ounce can tomato paste or 1 bottle ketchup
¼ cup hot or chili sauce
½ teaspoon minced garlic
2 teaspoons Worcestershire sauce
1 tablespoon light or dark corn syrup
⅓-½ cup cool water
2 tablespoons cornstarch
Pepper to taste

THE BURGER:
1 pound of ground beef, turkey or chicken
¼ onion, finely diced
1 teaspoon minced garlic
Salt and pepper to taste
3-4 rolls

1. Prepare the sauce in a medium saucepan by combining the tomato paste or ketchup, hot sauce, garlic, Worcestershire sauce, and corn syrup. Heat this mixture over medium, stirring constantly until it reaches a full boil, then lower the heat and simmer for 10-15 minutes, stirring occasionally.
2. In the meantime, mix the water into the cornstarch until the starch dissolves. Stir just a little bit of the hot sauce into the cornstarch, and then add all to the saucepan with the remaining sauce.
3. Reheat mixture to a full boil, continue to stir until it begins to thicken, and remove from the heat. Season with salt and pepper.
4. Prepare the burgers by mixing all the fixings for the burger and dividing the meat in 3-4 patties. Place onto a grill or fry the burgers in a frying pan. A few minutes before the meat has finished cooking, spread the BBQ sauce on top of each burger. If using cheese, place the cheese under the sauce, directly on top of the burger. Continue cooking until the meat is cooked to your liking and assemble your burgers.

Variations:
Dad's BBQ sauce also tastes fabulous on BBQ ribs, chicken, turkey and beef steaks. Pulled/shredded chicken or beef mixed with this sauce will produce terrific BBQ sandwiches too. Just make sure you have plenty of napkins on hand.

Hidden Surprise Burgers

Absolutely delicious to eat, rave about and share with all friends, family and customers.

Makes 3-4 burgers

1 pound ground beef, turkey or chicken
¼ cup finely diced onions
2 scant teaspoons minced garlic
1 tablespoon Worcestershire sauce
Dash of lemon pepper
6 ounces blue cheese crumbles, cheddar or provolone cheese (if using chunk cheese, cut into very small cubes)

1. Thoroughly combine all ingredients but the cheese. Shape the meat into 3-4 patties and with your thumb, insert a hole in the center of each patty. Make sure that you do not insert your thumb all the way to the bottom of the patty, rather about ⅔ of the way through.
2. Divide the cheese crumbles or cubes evenly into 3-4 piles and gently press the cheese into the indentation. Using surrounding meat to fully cover the cheese completely, making sure that there is at least ⅓-inch of meat over the cheese.
3. Grill, fry or cook the burgers until done to your liking and serve on a kaiser roll or croissant with condiments of choice.

Variations:
A combination of grilled peppers, onions and mushrooms pair splendidly with this recipe, as does a spreading of avocado slices on the roll prior to adding the cooked burger.

Hint: Tiny cubes of cheese can also be mixed into the meat, before shaping into patties. Just make sure that the meat covers the entire outside of the burger and that no cheese is visible for it could affect the final result. If you notice a bit of cheese on the outside of the patty, simply push it towards the center and cover with meat.

Mom's Heart-Wise Turkey Burger

After my father's first heart attack, my mother had to alter many of her recipes, accommodating his diagnosed condition and dietary needs. My father had several favorite foods that he wasn't very happy about giving up (Oreo Cookies and ice cream after devouring a large beef burger, to name a few), but Mom was a great cook and found many ways to appease his appetite. She came up with this recipe after lunching with the Lovely Ladies at a restaurant, and until the day he passed, this was always a personal favorite of his.

Makes 3-4 burgers

1 cup green cabbage, shredded
2 tablespoons julienned carrots (cut into small strips)
2 tablespoons julienned zucchini (cut into small strips)
1 tablespoon fresh minced parsley
1 teaspoon fresh sweet or lemon basil, finely minced
1 cup plain fat-free yogurt
1 pound ground turkey or chicken
¼-⅓ cup finely diced red onion
2 teaspoons minced garlic, or 2 cloves crushed
Sea salt and pepper to taste
1 cup fresh spinach
3-4 tomato slices, more if preferred
4 whole wheat, multi-grain or oat rolls

1. In a medium bowl, mix together the cabbage, carrots, zucchini, parsley, basil and ½ cup of the yogurt. Cover the bowl with plastic wrap and refrigerate until serving.
2. Thoroughly mix the turkey, remaining yogurt, onion, garlic, salt and pepper. Shape the mixed meat into thick patties and grill or fry until done to your liking.
3. Place each burger on bottom side of each roll, top the burger with the vegetable mixture, then the tomato slices, spinach and remaining half of the roll.

Mom's Easy Salmon Burgers

I always had a difficult time calling this recipe a burger, but the shape is there, the cooking method is the same, the condiments used are the same, and the taste, though significantly different, is still one to be savored. The health professionals suggest adding more fish to one's diet for the nutritional benefits, so why not start with this delicious recipe, full of flavor and tasty enough to satisfy even the pickiest of eaters?

Makes 3-4 burgers

1 pound salmon filet, poached or cooked in microwave
4-6 ounces sliced cheese of choice (optional)
2 teaspoons fresh squeezed lemon juice
½ cup finely diced red onion, scallions or shallots
1 tablespoon fresh minced parsley
½ teaspoon dried dill
1 teaspoon minced garlic or a garlic clove crushed
2 eggs or equivalent amount of liquid egg substitute
¼ cup mayonnaise or yogurt
½ cup plain bread crumbs
3-4 large lettuce leaves
6-8 thin slices of tomato
6-8 thin slices of cucumber
3-4 whole wheat, multi-grain or oat rolls

1. In a medium bowl, breakup the salmon and remove any lingering bones. Sprinkle the salmon with lemon juice, add the diced onions, parsley, dill and garlic and mix thoroughly.
2. In a small bowl. beat eggs into the mayonnaise or yogurt and blend into the salmon mixture.
3. Gradually add the bread crumbs to the salmon mixture, just a little at a time until the mixture is thick enough to shape into patties.
4. Shape the mixture into 3-4 patties and either fry them in a pan prepared with just a smidgen of oil or grill them for 3-4 minutes on each side.
5. Place each patty on bottom side of roll, top with cheese, tomato, cucumber, lettuce and the top half of roll.

Elizabeth's Portabella Veggie Burger

A fabulous, full flavored alternative for anyone who wishes to cut fatty meats and/or all animal products from their diets. I first tasted this recipe during a BBQ at Elizabeth's. I arrived late and the kids had already eaten all of the meat burgers, leaving only these huge mushroom caps to be grilled. Elizabeth knows me too well. She immediately advised me to, "Stop being so picky and try something new, you may like it," and grilled up one of the best sandwiches I have ever tasted.

Makes 4 burgers

4 large portabella mushroom caps
⅓ cup olive oil
3 tablespoons balsamic vinegar
1-2 garlic clove, minced
1 teaspoon minced fresh thyme leaves or ½ teaspoon dried thyme or lemon thyme
Salt and freshly ground black pepper
1 medium-sized red onion, halved lengthwise and thinly sliced
3-4 tablespoons grated provolone or a mixture of grated Romano and Parmesan cheeses
4 rolls or buns

1. In small bowl, combine the oil, vinegar, garlic, thyme, and salt and pepper to taste. Place the mushrooms and onions in a shallow bowl and pour the marinade over them. Marinate for 1 hour at room temp, turning once.
2. Preheat the grill or broiler. Place the mushrooms and onions on the grill, or put them on a baking sheet and place under the broiler; reserve the marinade. Turn them over once while cooking and baste them with the remaining marinade.
3. Grill or broil the mushrooms about 10 minutes or until tender and browned.
4. Meanwhile, split the rolls open and toast them on the grill or under the broiler until golden brown.
5. Place one mushroom cap on each bun, top with the onions and cheese and serve.

Snacks

Whether serving afternoon tea, having a chat in the break room or waiting for the kids to return from school, afternoon snacks are welcome and the varieties are plenty. Sure, many have heard not to snack between meals, but every now and then a little snack may supply you with an extra burst of energy to easily finish off the afternoon work, chores, reports and homework assignments. So grab a glass of milk, make a cup of tea or brew a fresh pot of coffee and pamper yourself with a few late day Afternoon Delights.

Cheesy Lemon Bars

Lemon bars were always a favorite among my customers and I often made up several batches a day to appease their appetites. However, a couple years ago I wanted a change, and came up with an alternative filling. I had no idea what the response would be, but I thought a change might be good. Evidently it was, for these creamy lemon bars were welcomed and relished and have now become a standard treat whenever the opportunity arrives for something a bit more extraordinary than the norm.

Preheat oven to 350° F

1 package of super moist lemon cake mix
⅓ cup canola oil, melted butter or margarine
1 egg or equivalent amount of liquid egg substitute
2 teaspoons fresh squeezed lemon juice
8 ounces cream cheese (Neufchatel can also be used)
⅓ cup sugar
1 tablespoon fresh squeezed lemon juice
1 egg or equivalent amount of liquid egg substitute

1. Blend the cake mix, oil, egg and 2 teaspoons lemon juice until crumbly, although the dough will begin to gather slightly. Remove 1 cup of crumbs from the bottom of the bowl.
2. Grease a 9x13-inch pan. Press the remaining cake mixture into a the pan and bake for 15-20 minutes or until the top just begins to brown.
3. While the batter bakes, beat together the cream cheese, sugar, juice and egg until smooth and creamy.
4. Immediately upon removing the cake from the oven, spread the cream cheese filling on the top, then sprinkle the reserved crumbs on to the filling and return to the oven to bake for an additional 15-20 minutes or until the crumbs just begin to brown. Allow to cool completely before slicing into 9-12 bars.

Variation:
Gently fold ⅔ cup fresh blueberries or raspberries into the cream cheese filling prior to spreading it on the crust.

Honey Nuts and Fruit Bars

When I used to work with kids, I would often see them munching on candy bars, soda pops and various other sugar-saturated treats, only leading to an extensive amount of energy and an over-sugared brain, which ultimately disturbed their thought processes and learning. Granted, I worked with a unique group of kids, who already portrayed an abundance of learning disabilities, often associated with attention deficits on top of a dash of hyperactivity. So to make my job easier and their learning experience more productive, I felt that I had to come up with an alternative sweet but healthier snack; this was one of the recipes I would often bring to them.

Preheat oven to 350° F

4 eggs
½ cup canola oil
1 cup honey
1 cup plus 1 tablespoon flour, sifted once and remeasured
½ cup oats
¼ teaspoon baking soda
1 teaspoon cinnamon
1 teaspoon vanilla or maple extract
1 pound assorted fruits, such as dried apricots, dark and golden raisins, dried cherries, fresh dates or figs,
   ground together in a food processor
1 cup chopped almonds or walnuts

1. Beat the eggs until frothy, add the oil and honey and stir. Add the flour, oats, baking soda and spices and mix well,
   then gradually add the fruits and nuts to the mixture.
2. Grease a 9x13-inch pan. Spread the batter evenly into the pan and bake for 25-30 minutes.
3. Cool the bars for a couple minutes and then tightly cover with plastic wrap. Makes 9-12 fruit-studded bars.

Cinnamon Roll Cake

*While meandering my way through the various folded pages, book parts and index cards in that treasured
tin recipe box of my grandmother's, a page from a magazine dated 1938 caught my attention. The print was extremely
small, and Grandmom's chicken scratch was just as difficult to read, but the faded photo resembled some sort of swirled
cinnamon cake. Fortunately, I have an ancient magnifying glass that was also hers, so I put the recipe up to the glass and
wrote it down. I was delighted when I realized that the recipe was for some sort of Cinnamon Roll Cake and eagerly
waited for it to finish baking. A girlfriend stopped by and asked what I had in the oven for she could smell something
baking from outside the door. A short while later, as we sat enjoying the warmth of flavors almost gone, she perfectly
described this lovely cake, "Not too big, not too sweet, but just right; may I take some home to the kids?"*

CAKE:
1 yeast cake or 1 small package of dry yeast
¼ cup lukewarm water
3 tablespoons melted shortening or butter
½ cup plus 1 tablespoon warm buttermilk
⅓ cup sugar
2 eggs, slightly beaten
1½ teaspoon salt
3¼ cups flour sifted
½ cup (1 stick) butter
½-⅔ cup dark brown sugar
1-2 teaspoons cinnamon
1 cup raisins and/or chopped walnuts

ICING:
1 cup powdered sugar
2-3 tablespoons milk
¼ teaspoon cinnamon

1. Crumble the yeast into the water, cover and allow to sit for 10 minutes.
2. Thoroughly mix together the buttermilk, shortening, sugar and salt. Add the eggs and yeast and mix thoroughly.
3. Sift the flour into the buttermilk mixture, mix thoroughly, remove from the mixing bowl and place into a greased bowl, cover and allow to double in bulk in a warm place (1½-2 hours).
4. Once the dough has doubled, roll it out on a floured surface to a 12x20-inch rectangle and spread the butter over it. Sprinkle the brown sugar all over the butter and then sprinkle the cinnamon on top of the brown sugar. Top this with raisins and/or chopped walnuts, and beginning at the longest edge, roll it all up tightly like a jelly roll. Pinch the edges and ends to seal.
5. Grease a 9-inch bundt pan well.
6. Cut the roll into 2-inch sections and place each, cut sides up, right next to each other in the prepared pan. Cover and allow the dough to rise to double again. (1-1½ hours)
7. Preheat oven to 350° F and bake for 30-40 minutes or until inserted knife comes out clean, and top is firm.
8. Mix together the icing ingredients and drizzle all over the top

Cream Cheese Filled Coffeecake? Almost!

---

*It was early spring when the temperature dropped significantly and the rain turned to snow.
The weather supplied an opportune moment to create and test new treats on friends who were coming by later
in the day. I had wanted to develop a recipe for a cream cheese filled coffeecake similar to those prepackaged at the grocery,
so I went on a mission. The first batch doesn't need to be discussed, but the second was quite a tasty surprise. When I removed
it from the oven, once again that "Force of Enticement" took over my senses. I lost all control and suddenly found a fork
within my fingers, diving into the cake. As I noticed the creamy cheese layer was nowhere in sight, that fork was delivering
a luscious sensation to my palate. Later that day, as the last crumbs were being fought over, my friends and
I concluded the mission was a success, for although we couldn't see the filling, we sure could taste it.*

Preheat oven to 350° F

CAKE:
1 cup (2 sticks) butter
2¼ cups flour
2 cups sugar
1 tablespoon plus 1 teaspoon baking powder
¾ teaspoon cinnamon
1 tablespoon vanilla
2 large eggs
1 cup plus 1 tablespoon milk

FILLING:
12 ounces cream cheese
¾ cup sugar
2 medium eggs (do not use large)
2 teaspoons vanilla

1. Grease a 9x13-inch pan well.
2. Beat the butter, flour, sugar and baking powder until small crumbs form. Remove ¾ cup of crumbs from the bowl
   and mix the eggs and milk thoroughly into the remaining crumbs in the bowl.
3. In another bowl, beat the filling ingredients until smooth.
4. Spread half the batter into the prepared pan. You may want to continuously dip the back of a rubber spatula into
   flour to help spread the batter.
5. Spread the filling over the bottom layer, top with remaining batter and then sprinkle the remaining crumbs all
   over the top.
6. Bake 40-50 minutes, or until an inserted knife or toothpick comes out clean.

Orange/Blueberry Bread

♥ SUGAR

I am often astounded at the amazing collection of recipes that I continue to find in my grandmother's tin box. She must have had great fun, searching and cutting various recipes out of newspapers and magazines and then preparing them for my father. The day I found this recipe, it was neatly cut and folded, but appeared to be old for I could view the fashion of the day along the creases. This was enough to intrigue me to open the folds (gosh, the fashions were lovely back then), and as I turned the page over, I saw this recipe. I called my dad and asked him if it was any good and he happily stated, "Absolutely, it was a favorite of mine and I haven't had any in years. Make me a loaf, ship it FedEx and charge it to my account." So I did. His employees actually called to tell me how good it was, and to request a copy of the recipe, which I kindly recited to them.

Makes 1 loaf

Preheat oven to 350° F
2⅔-¾ cups flour
2 eggs or equivalent amount of liquid egg substitute
1 cup milk
½ cup sugar or sugar substitute
⅓ cup orange juice
1 tablespoon grated orange peel or fresh orange zest
½ cup canola oil
4½ teaspoons baking powder
¼ teaspoon baking soda
1¼ cups blueberries

1. Cream together the eggs, milk, sugar, orange juice, orange peel, and oil.
2. Sift the flour together with the baking powder and baking soda and then add to the egg mixture and mix together thoroughly.
3. Mix 1 tablespoon of extra flour with the blueberries to coat and gently stir them into the batter.
4. Grease a 9-inch loaf pan, pour in the batter and bake 55-60 minutes or until inserted knife comes out clean. Allow to cool 15 minutes prior to serving.

Blair's Zucchini Bread from Cheryl

I received this message while checking my e-mails one day:
"Returned from vacation and finally got a chance to respond to my emails.
While on our trip, came across this wonderful zucchini recipe and wish to share it with all."
Later that day, I picked up a few ingredients on my way home and baked this recipe. Those that have enjoyed
this spicy and flavorful treat agree that this recipe is DE-LICIOUS and really should be shared.

Makes 1 loaf

BREAD:

3 large eggs, lightly beaten
1½ cups granulated sugar
3 cups shredded zucchini (1½ pounds)
¾ cup canola oil
2 teaspoons vanilla extract
2 cups plus 2 tablespoons all-purpose flour
1 cup whole wheat flour
½ cup wheat germ

¼ cup nonfat dry milk powder
1 teaspoon salt
1 teaspoon baking soda
1 teaspoon baking powder
2 teaspoons ground cinnamon
½ teaspoon ground nutmeg
¼ teaspoon ground cloves

1. Grease two 8x4-inch loaf pans.
2. Combine the first five ingredients in a large mixing bowl and stir together.
3. In another bowl, mix the flour and the next nine ingredients together thoroughly.
4. Add the zucchini mixture to the flour and mix until all is well blended.
5. Pour batter evenly into the prepared pans.
6. Bake for 45-50 minutes or until a knife or toothpick inserted in center comes out clean. Allow to cool for a few minutes before drizzling on the icing.

ICING:

1 cup sifted powdered sugar
½ teaspoon vanilla extract
2 tablespoons milk
¼ cup chopped pecans, toasted

1. Combine powdered sugar, vanilla, and milk, stirring until smooth. Drizzle evenly over loaves; sprinkle with toasted pecans.

Molasses Bread

This bread, full of molasses, has just enough spice to fill your home with the feel of old country goodness. The flavor always makes me think of how simple but delicious life must have been like over a century ago, before modern technology, prepackaged and/or fast foods became the norm. I often envy those harder times, for in many ways they seem so much simpler. Whenever I need to get away from the daily hustle and bustle of modern life, I'll make a loaf of this recipe, dream of what life must have been like long ago and then walk to a neighbor's to say hello and share a few slices; just like they did before cars, fast foods and cell phones.

Makes 1 loaf

Preheat oven to 325° F

¾ cup brown sugar
⅔ cup dark molasses
1 egg
3 cups plus 2-3 tablespoons flour
1 teaspoon baking powder
½ teaspoon baking soda
1½ cups buttermilk
1 tablespoon cinnamon
½ teaspoon nutmeg
½ teaspoon cloves
¾ cup dark and golden raisins and/or chopped walnuts

1. Grease a 9x5-inch loaf pan well with pan spray, butter or margarine.
2. In a mixing bowl, cream together the sugar, molasses and egg.
3. Add the dry ingredients to the molasses mixture alternating with the buttermilk, and mix well between each addition.
4. Pour all of the batter into the prepared pan and bake for 55-65 minutes or until an inserted knife or toothpick comes out clean.

Mom's Favorite Strawberry Yogurt Bread

♥

Once my mother realized that I was in this profession for the long haul, she frequently put in requests for this and that. It didn't matter that she was 2000 miles away and a tad overweight; she wanted treats, and in her mind, I was her personal baker and must oblige her demands. One day she called with a craving for berries, but didn't want any more fruit bars, and the fruit muffins did not ship well. I had just picked some strawberries (before the deer gobbled them all), so I came inside and created this lovely, lowfat recipe. I shipped it later that day on Dad's FedEx account and the next day Mom called to inform me that the Lovely Ladies just loved it and to send more next week.

Makes 1 loaf

Preheat oven to 350° F

½ cup (1 stick) butter, margarine or canola spread
¾ cup sugar
2 eggs or equivalent amount of liquid egg substitute
1 tablespoon vanilla
Scant ⅔ cup plain yogurt
1¾ cups plus 2 tablespoons flour
½ teaspoon baking soda
½ teaspoon baking powder
¾-1 teaspoon cinnamon
1 plus cup fresh chopped strawberries
⅔ cup chopped walnuts

1. Grease a 9x5-inch loaf pan well with pan spray, butter or margarine.
2. In a mixing bowl, cream the butter and sugar, then add the eggs, yogurt and vanilla and mix thoroughly.
3. Add the remaining ingredients and mix thoroughly together.
4. Pour the batter into the prepared pan and bake for 55-65 minutes.

Scones

♥ **SUGAR**

*My first experience in commercial baking was at a natural food market's commissary; I was given
the 2 a.m. chore of mixing a huge container of ingredients, and making it into little round mounds called scones.
I found them too dry and boring and swore that if I ever baked scones, they would not be dull, rather full of flavor.
When customers began requesting scones, I thought of those early mornings, years back, and was determined to develop
a very good recipe, to be enjoyed, remembered and requested. So I played and played, tossed out a lot of disasters,
until one day when I saw a package of cream cheese softening on my counter. I added just a smidgen, then a little
more and the final result continues to be described as awesome by many; including that natural grocery market.*

Makes 8 scones

Preheat oven to 375° F

⅓ cup (6 tablespoons) of butter or margarine
3 ounces cream cheese
¼ cup sugar or equivalent amount of sugar substitute
1 teaspoon vanilla (almond, maple, lemon or orange extracts can be substituted)
2¼ cups flour
1 egg or liquid egg substitute
2 teaspoons baking powder
½ cup of milk, minus 1 tablespoon
1 cup berries, cherries, dried or fresh fruits, chopped nuts, and/or mini
Chocolate chips

1. Grease a cookie sheet well with pan spray, butter or margarine.
2. Cream together the butter, cream cheese, sugar and vanilla until smooth and fluffy.
3. Add the flour, baking powder, egg and milk to the butter mixture and mix. Add your choice of fruits and/or nuts
   and flavors. Mix all thoroughly together until the dough begins to pull away from the sides of the bowl.
4. Remove the dough from the mixing bowl and knead it on a floured surface about 10-12 times. Once the dough has
   been kneaded, gently pat it into an 8-10-inch circle and place the circle onto the prepared cookie sheet.
5. With a serrated knife, slice dough into 8 triangular slices. (*Do not separate the slices.*) Using a pastry brush or a fork,
   brush the dough with a tablespoon of extra milk or water.
6. Bake the scones for 16-18 minutes or until they begin to turn golden.
7. Remove cookie sheet from the oven and let the scones cool for 4-5 minutes, then gently pull apart the slices.
   Allow to cool for at least 5 minutes prior to serving after the pieces have been separated.

Hint: When using a nutty flavored extract, add some of the same nuts to the batter. If using a fruit flavored extract,
add about 1 large tablespoon of lemon curd or preserves to the batter for flavor enhancement.

Fruit Burritos

♥ SUGAR FREE

When I began to think about what recipes I have that can be prepared as an afternoon snack and that are also kid-friendly, there was no question about including this recipe at the end of this chapter. The kids, those lovely little people that we love with all our hearts, who seem to have endless energy, massive needs and bottomless bellies, usually want a snack after returning from school. But taking the easy way and allowing them to grab prepackaged snacks is not quite the ideal answer in my mind. This snack, on the other hand, is perfect to suit their needs.

Serves 4-6

4-6 large whole wheat tortillas
½ cantaloupe, seeded and chopped into bite-size pieces
1-2 bananas
¾ cup sliced strawberries
¾ cup blueberries
¾ cup raspberries or blackberries
2 kiwi fruits, peeled and sliced
1 apple, peeled cored and diced
A couple drops of fresh lemon juice
½ cup chopped pecans or walnuts (optional)
8 ounces Neufchatel (low-fat) cream cheese
¼ cup or less honey

1. Mix all the fruit together with the lemon juice in a large bowl.
2. Whip the cream cheese until smooth, and then spread a few tablespoons on each tortilla.
3. Sprinkle ⅔-¾ cup fruit onto each tortilla and drizzle the fruit with approximately 1-2 teaspoons of honey per tortilla.
4. Roll up as you would a burrito and ENJOY!
Store leftovers covered in the refrigerator.

Hint: Fruits can be adjusted according to individual likes and dislikes. For the sake of ease, the honey can be whipped into the cream cheese, ultimately creating less mess.

The Glory of Food

You've got to shop a little,
Pick a little
And even smell the fruits, a little

And then you've got to

Clean a little
Dice a little,
And even stir the sauce, a little

You've got to

Fry a little
Bake a little
Take a taste, well just a little

And then you've got to

Laugh a little
Cry a little
And even burn the roast, a little

As long as there's a mouth to feed
You've got their palate in your hand
So don't forget to spice the dish
For you won't serve your efforts bland

So you've got to

Eat a little,
Drink a little
And even share your bread, a little
That's the glory of Food

Don't forget the extra spoonfuls of love!

The Simmers of Love

~ All recipes can be doubled or tripled.
~ Store all leftovers in the refrigerator or freezer.
~ At high altitude, the pots should be covered, at sea level you have the option to cover a pot of soup or not.
~ Most of the following can be prepared in a stock pot, crock pot, pressure cooker and/or Dutch oven.

I have often heard, *"My mom's chicken soup is the best,"* or, *"My dad's stew is to die for,"* and these words are absolutely correct to each of us. Often these praises surround the complex flavors delivered from the exceptional, savory dishes that must be simmered or cooked at a slow boil for an extended period of time. These slow simmered foods, prepared with an appreciation for eating well and heartily, are what I have affectionately titled, *The Simmers of Love.* The following recipes have been found to be irresistible and unforgettable, and are shared to fill your home with the magnificent flavors and scents of homemade love.

Carl's Favorite Chunky Italian Sauce, Page 199
French Onion Soup, Page 189

Susan's Garlic Chicken Soup

One snowy day, when the roads were much too icy to venture far from home, I decided to simmer a batch of this soup. Oh my, I found it so tasty that I called a neighbor to see if she wanted any. She had earlier gotten stuck in her driveway during an attempt to venture out for groceries; and I had so much soup, that I suggested that we meet halfway up the road, because this soup was much too good not to share. We met, shared, and quickly departed, for the weather was getting worse. About 30 minutes later she called, informed me how much she enjoyed the soup and asked if there was any more. Evidently she enjoyed the flavor so much, that she was willing to go back out into the snow and cold for more.

3 to 4 servings

1 bay leaf
3-4 large cloves garlic
1 medium onion
1 cup milk
2 cups chicken broth
2 tablespoons balsamic vinegar
2 tablespoons butter
1 teaspoon salt
½ teaspoon pepper
4 slices white sourdough bread
One 16-ounce package spinach, cleaned and stems removed
2 to 3 pounds boneless, skinless chicken breasts, washed, patted dry and cut into bite-size pieces.

1. Peel and finely chop the garlic and dice the onion.
2. Put the garlic, onion, milk, broth, vinegar, butter, bay leaf, salt and pepper in a large saucepan. Place pan over medium low heat and slowly bring to a slight simmer (about 25-35 minutes); reduce heat to low.
3. While the soup is heating, tear the bread into small pieces and set aside. Clean and pat dry the spinach leaves and chop into bite-sized pieces.
4. Stir the bread pieces, spinach and chicken into the soup pot, then cover and simmer 20-30 minutes on low heat, making sure that it never boils. Remove lid and turn chicken pieces over. Cover and simmer 20 more minutes or until chicken has cooked through, and serve.

Doe's Chicken Soup

I still remember the thrill I felt the first time I spelled my name in the alphabet noodles resting on the bottom of my bowl of this excellent soup. Doe, one of my grandmothers, was a sweet, tiny woman who could cook up a storm if asked to. She believed in the old way of cooking, you start in the morning and you don't stop till it's all done. Many of my holiday memories surround a huge steaming white pot, filled to the brim with this recipe. She always came to the house early in the morning and began cleaning and dicing the ingredients, putting them all into that pot. Within hours, the house smelled absolutely delicious, but we knew it would take many more hours until it was ready to be served. Once the chicken tenderly pulled away from the bones, most of the ingredients were strained from the pot, and then separated onto a large, oval plate. She knew us well and while saying that, "There is plenty more where this came from," each individual bowl was filled with soup, love and a smile.

Serves 10-12

One 18–20-quart pot, with a lid
1 large chicken (preferably bought from the butcher), whole or cut into pieces. Leave the skin on.
1-1½ pound chunk of stew meat (thick short ribs were often used)
1 large onion, peeled, with first layer removed
1 bunch fresh parsley (2-3 ounces)
1 bunch fresh dill (2-3 ounces)
1 bunch celery, washed
1 pound carrots, washed and chopped into 3–4-inch lengths
1⅓ cup lima beans
1 whole sweet potato, washed and peeled
1 plus tablespoon kosher salt, more may be added later if needed
Pepper to taste

1. Thoroughly wash the chicken, place it into the pot and cover with water. Bring the water to a boil and skim the foam from the top.
2. Tie the parsley, dill and celery bunch with a small string and place into the pot of boiling water, along with all remaining ingredients. Bring the water back to a boil, skim the scum from the top again, add 2-3 more cups of warm water, and lower the heat to a very slow simmer, covering with a lid. Allow this to simmer for 6-8 hours, tasting after about 3-4 hours and adding more seasonings if you like. This soup is finished cooking when the chicken is tender and begins to pull away from the bones. Before removing anything from the pot, remove any excess fat from the top of the soup by placing two paper towels on top of the broth, let it sit for a few seconds and discard. Then remove the bunch of herbs and celery.
3. Using a colander or large sieve and slotted spoon, remove all ingredients from the broth, allowing them to drain over the pot; place on a large plate. You may want to separate the vegetables, the beef and the chicken into three separate piles or plates, tossing out any visible bones.
4. Serve in individual bowls with previously prepared thin egg noodles, alphabet noodles or rice, with the chicken and vegetables placed in the bowls or served on a separate plate as the main course.

Hints: If freezing the broth, I suggest freezing half of it in a large container and then dividing the remaining broth between separate containers to be used in various recipes and culinary creations. You can also remove the fat from the top of the soup, by placing two paper towels onto the top of the soup and dragging them across the liquid, hence, absorbing up the excess fat. It is sometimes easier to allow the soup to cool, and then remove the fat after it solidifies. The cooked chicken, beef and veggies freeze well; but my aunt will tell you to remove the carrots before freezing for they get too mushy.

Variation:
I often make this soup almost the same way, but omitting the beef, lima beans and the sweet potato, and it tastes just as exquisite as when Doe used to make it.

Aunt Lil's Matzo Ball Soup

I truly wish I had a dime for each time I heard, "Your Aunt Lil makes the best matzo balls on earth;
no others can compare," from one of the Lovely Ladies and/or anyone else who has had the luxury of tasting these fabulous
little matzo meal balls. Unfortunately I never received a cent for these statements, although once I finally found out her
secret I knew that it must be shared. Ready? Here it is; she freezes them after boiling, then a short while before serving
her soup she takes the balls out of the freezer, allows them to thaw for just a bit, and then tosses them into the pot
of soup to finish them. That is all there is too it, a simple technique that offers much flavor and praise.

Serves 10-12

MATZO BALLS:
4 eggs, separated (place whites into a mixing bowl, yolks into a small bowl)
1 cup matzo meal

1. Beat the whites until peaks form (high altitude you will get soft peaks, sea level you will get stiffer peaks).
2. Salt and break the yolks with a fork, pour them into the mixing bowl and carefully fold them into the whites.
   Add the matzo meal and gently fold in until all is thoroughly combined.
3. Refrigerate this mixture for 5-10 minutes, while bringing a large pot of salted water to full boil.
4. Remove the batter from the fridge, wet your hands with cold water and using about 3-4 tablespoons at a time, roll
   dough between the palms of your hands into firmly packed balls, a little larger than an average golf ball. You should
   get about 10-12 balls from the batter.
5. Put the balls into the boiling water, bring the water back to a boil, cover the pot and allow the balls to cook for
   45-55 minutes.
6. Using a slotted spoon, remove the balls from the water, allow them to cool and then place them onto cookie sheet
   and freeze. Once frozen, place them into a freezer-safe baggie and put them back into the freezer. When ready to use,
   take out the desired amount, partially defrost and toss into the hot soup (below) 30-45 minutes before serving.

Aunt Lil's Matzo Ball/Chicken Soup

One 16–18-quart pot
1 large, whole chicken, plus 2 large chicken breasts
1 large, peeled onion
¾-1 pound carrots, cut into 2-inch chunks
1 small bunch celery, bottom removed and left as is, or cut into 3-inch chunks
2 bunches fresh dill, folded in half and wrapped in a clean rubber band
1½ tablespoons kosher salt
Pepper to taste

1. Rinse and pat dry the chicken. Put it in the large pot and cover with enough water so that the pot is about ¾ full. Bring the water to a boil and skim the foam from the top.
2. Add salt and pepper, chunks carrots, celery, the whole peeled onion and the bunch of dill.
3. Cover the pot, set the temperature on low and simmer for 2½-3 hours, add the matzo balls and continue simmering until the carrots are fairly soft but not mushy, and the chicken is tender but still attached to the bone.
4. Turn heat off, take out the dill, and press all its juices back into the pot, using the pot's lid and a fork. Carefully remove chicken, place into a colander or sieve over the pot, drain any juice and place separately on a plate. Next, remove the carrots, onion and celery, draining each over the pot just as you did the chicken and place on a plate separate from the chicken.
5. Bring it all hot to the table, fill each soup bowl with the broth and matzo balls and serve.

Variations:
• You could remove the chicken and vegetables before adding add the matzo balls to the broth and allow them to slow simmer for 45-55 minutes.
• If removing broth from the freezer and in the mood for some matzo balls for additional goodness and grace, thaw both, and as the broth comes to a slow boil, add the matzo balls and allow to simmer until soft and hot.

Hints: If freezing, take out carrots for they do not freeze well in chicken soup. You will want to separate the ingredients after the soup has finished cooking for in Aunt Lil's words: *"Now some like the soup with celery, but if you and yours do not like it, then take the celery out after simmering and throw it out."*

Beef Broth

When simmering a good beef broth, choose the ingredients based on your culture, personal likes and dislikes; then allow to simmer in a stock pot for hours on end. A good beef broth, just like that of a well made chicken broth, is eaten as a soup, but the leftovers (if any), can be used to enhance the flavor in an enormous number of recipes.

Makes approximately 8-10 cups

2-3 pounds of beef (brisket, chuck, sirloin or round roast), trimmed of fat
2-3 tablespoons flour
¾ cup plus reserved beef roast juice or 3-4 beef bouillon cubes
3 quarts of water (plus 2-3 cups more added after skimming the foam)
2-3 celery stalks, chopped into 2-inch sections
2-3 carrots, chopped into 2-inch sections
1 medium-large whole onion, first layer peeled away

½ tomato, seeded and diced
1 tablespoon finely diced green pepper
1-2 ounce bunch fresh parsley
1-2 ounce bunch fresh dill
2-3 teaspoon minced garlic
1 tablespoon Worcestershire sauce
2 teaspoons teriyaki sauce (optional)
1 bay leaf
1 tablespoon kosher salt, more can be added for taste
Pepper to taste

1. To prepare the beef, braise it by dredging it in the flour and then heating in a large pan until brown on all sides, or cover the beef in cool water and allowing it to sit for 30-45 minutes before heating.
2. Tightly tie the parsley, dill and bay leaf with a string.
3. After the beef is braised, cover it with water, and heat over medium high until the water boils. Skim the foam from the top of the water and add remaining ingredients, plus 2 cups extra water and bring it back to a boil.
4. Decrease the heat to low and simmer until beef is tender and can be easily pierced with a fork, 5-7 hours, or longer if necessary.
5. Using a colander or large sieve and slotted spoon, remove and drain the ingredients over the pot and place them onto a large plate. You may want to separate the vegetables from the beef and place into separate piles or plates. Discard the bunch of herbs.
6. Serve the broth in individual bowls, with previously prepared thin egg noodles, alphabet noodles or rice; or cut the beef into small bite size pieces, add the pieces and the vegetables to individual serving bowls and serve.

Hints: If freezing the broth, I suggest freezing half of it in a large container and then dividing the remaining broth between separate containers to be used in various recipes and culinary creations. You can also remove the fat from the top of the soup, by placing 2 paper towels onto the top of the soup and dragging them across the liquid, hence absorbing the excess fat. It is sometimes easier to allow the soup to cool; then remove the fat after it solidifies.

Bob's Favorite Minestrone Soup

I didn't know what I was preparing when I began, but I remember a day at the shop when I had a few vegetables that needed to be used immediately. I placed most into a stock pot to simmer in some reserved beef broth, took a taste and looked around for something to add substance. I spotted a couple cans of different beans, added them for diversity, and some pasta for a heartier appearance. Bob as usual, showed up at the back door to sneak in and take a taste of the aroma he sniffed outside the door. As I turned and saw him standing over the pot, equipped with chef cap and large spoon, he informed me that I was making one of the best minestrone soups he had ever tasted, but it needed more pasta for authenticity and so he put some in. Delighted by his enthusiasm, I brought him a bowl to fill and as he went to the sitting area he told folks all about the amazing soup in the back. A few minutes later there was no soup left!

Serves 8-10

¼ cup butter
⅓ cup olive oil
3 carrots, diced
3 celery stalks, diced
1 onion, peeled and diced
1 large or 2 medium zucchini, diced
2 medium potatoes, peeled and diced
1 tomato diced
½ head green cabbage, shredded
6 cups beef broth or 6 beef bouillon cubes soaked in 6 cups water
One 16-ounce can kidney beans, drained
One 16-ounce can cannelloni beans, drained
One 16-ounce can chick peas, drained
1 teaspoon minced garlic
Salt and pepper to taste
1½ cup small tubular shaped pasta (tubetti or ditilini), or small shell pasta
Grated Parmesan cheese for topping

1. In a large 2-3 gallon pot, heat the butter and oil over medium heat. Add the carrots, celery, potatoes, onion. Cook and stir these until lightly browned, then add the broth, the remaining vegetables and spices and heat until boiling.
2. Reduce the heat to low, cover the pot, stir occasionally and simmer for 50-60 minutes or until vegetables are tender, but not mushy. Add the drained beans to the broth.
3. Simmer for an additional 10-15 minutes and add the pasta. Continue simmering at low heat until the noodles are tender. Serve each bowlful with a sprinkle of Parmesan on top.

Marley's Meema's Best Veggie/Beef Soup

I have heard Marley state too many times that her Meema (grandmother) made the best soup on earth.
So I asked her if she would share the recipe and she kindly obliged. I have made and tasted this delicious soup many times,
but I feel that Marley's description explains it best: "I remember this seeming to cook FOREVER (all day was more like it!),
because it smelled so wonderful and patience was hard to find. If it doesn't all vanish right away, it gets better each day.
Perfect with a slice or two of warm fresh-baked bread and butter!"

Serves 10-12

2 pounds beef chuck (or ribs from rib roast) previously cooked, left whole or chopped into 1–2-inch pieces
5 quarts water
Salt and pepper to taste
1 teaspoon parsley
1 teaspoon thyme
1 cut up onion, any color
1 can chopped tomatoes
1 (or more) cup cabbage, shredded
⅓ cup celery, cut up
1 package of mixed vegetables (frozen) or use your choice of favorites such as: 1 small can whole corn, or fresh corn,
   cooked and removed from cob; 1 small can or 1 cup frozen peas; 1 cup carrots

1. Cook all ingredients on medium high until the water boils.
2. Reduce the heat to low and allow to simmer for 1-2 hours or until the flavor reaches its peak and soup is ready to serve.

Bean Soup

There are many varieties of beans available on the grocer's shelves these days. You can find dried beans, canned beans and fresh beans in the produce section; and many varieties of bean soups, stews and mixes all perfectly lined up on the shelves. But a homemade bean soup is a rarity indeed in today's fast-paced, quick-fix society. Sure, lots of folks know how to make bean soup, but they do not take the time, for it is much easier to pick up a can at the store, heat the contents in the microwave, add the spoon and eat it. Personally, I prefer homemade over the canned varieties, so I came up with my own luscious recipe with a little help from my friends. Some suggested soaking the beans overnight, while more advised to allow all flavors to incorporate slowly at a low temperature. I must have done something right, for many have enjoyed a bowl or two at one sitting, many more have asked for the recipe and I know a few who will no longer open a can of bean soup; they call me instead.

Serves 10-12

One 2-3-gallon pot
2 large meaty ham shanks
1½ cups pinto beans
1½ cups small red kidney/red beans
1½ cups navy beans
1½ cups black eyed beans
1 drained can garbanzo beans (optional)
1 large onion, peeled and left whole or thinly sliced
3 cloves garlic finely diced or 1 tablespoon minced garlic
1 small bunch celery, chopped or left whole, bottoms trimmed off
¼ cup parsley, chopped

1. Drain the liquid from all beans and place into the pot. Tightly tie the parsley and celery together with a string, or tie just the parsley if using chopped celery. Add all ingredients except the garlic to the pot, and fill the pot with warm water to just below the rim.
2. Bring to a boil over medium heat, skim the scum from the top of the water, then add the garlic. Cover the pot and decrease the heat to low. Allow to simmer for 5-7 hours or until the meat pulls away from the bones and the beans are tender. Serve hot and store leftovers in the refrigerator.

Victor's Favorite Tomato Soup

I admit, normally when I make soup I make the kind that simmers for a period of time, at least longer than 30 minutes. However, there was a night long ago when Victor had a craving for tomato soup and asked me to make him some. When he went to gather more firewood, I quickly fulfilled his request by opening a can and adding a pinch or two of spice. A while later, as he was soaking up the last drops of this recipe, he enthusiastically claimed that this was the greatest bowl of tomato soup he had ever eaten, and I should to make it more often.

Serves 1-2

One 10-12-ounce can condensed tomato soup
1 full can of milk
¼ teaspoon minced garlic
¼ plus teaspoon Italian seasoning
1 plus teaspoon grated Parmesan cheese

1. Pour the soup contents into a saucepan, fill the can with milk and pour into the soup.
2. Heat the soup and milk over medium, stirring occasionally. Add the garlic and seasoning, and stir until steaming hot. Lower the heat and allow to simmer for 7-10 minutes, stirring occasionally to avoid burning.
3. Pour all into a large bowl, sprinkle the top with Parmesan cheese and serve immediately.

French Onion Soup

French Onion Soup is one of the reasons that I love to go out to eat. But finding a well-prepared one can be a challenge, unless you know where to go. When I was living back east, acquiring my first graduate degree, I found a restaurant that made the finest I have yet to taste. I went there often, just to revel in a bowlful between classes. A couple years later, back in Colorado, I had not forgotten that taste and I craved to reproduce it. One early autumn day it began snowing hard and the temperature was dropping rapidly. I spotted a bagful of onions and knew the time was ripe to play with a new recipe and so I did. Ah, this tasted heavenly! A word of advice; don't skimp on the cheese.

Serves 4-6

½ cup (1 stick) butter
7-8 cups thinly sliced sweet yellow onions
¾ teaspoon sugar
3-4 tablespoons flour
2½ quarts beef broth
1 teaspoon Worcestershire sauce
1 cup white wine
¼ cup brandy or cognac (optional)
½ teaspoon sage
1 bay leaf
Salt and pepper to taste
1 loaf French bread
1½-2 cups shredded Swiss or Gruyere cheese for topping
⅓ cup grated Parmesan for topping

1. Melt the butter in a large pot at a medium low temperature, then stir in the onions, coating them with melted butter. Cover the pot and allow the onions to simmer for about 20 minutes, until they are translucent and tender. Stir the sugar into the onions, raise the heat to medium high, and continue simmering, stirring frequently until the onions have caramelized or turned a golden brownish color.
2. Lower the heat back to medium low, stir in the flour and 2 cups of beef broth and stir or whisk consistently until the mixture has thickened. Add the remaining broth, Worcestershire sauce, wine, sage and bay leaf; cover the pot and allow all to simmer for 40-50 minutes or until all flavors have mingled to your liking.
3. Just before the soup has finished simmering, prepare the topping. Slice the French bread into ½-¾ inch slices, butter both sides of each slice and brown both sides under a broiler or in a toaster oven.
4. If using cognac or brandy, stir it into the soup just before serving. Place individual bowls onto a cookie sheet, fill each bowl with soup, place a slice of the toasted bread onto the top of the soup and top the bread with a healthy sprinkling of the cheese. Place the bowls under the broiler until the cheese has melted and is golden brown; about 5 minutes, possibly longer. Carefully remove the cookie sheet and bowls from the heat and serve immediately.

Potato Soup

A wholesome, hearty bowl of this favorite soup takes only a little longer than one hour to thoroughly cook, and is superb to serve at the beginning of a meal or alongside a sandwich. Not quite as thick as a chowder or as thin as a broth, but just right. Pleasantly gratifying when served on a cold, wintry day or at a rainy, summer get-together.

Serves 6-8

4 pounds peeled potatoes (about 7-8 potatoes)
¾ cup (1½ sticks) butter
2 cups chopped celery
½ cup diced parsnips
2 cups thinly sliced onions
1½ cups diced carrots
¼ cup flour
2 quarts chicken broth
½ teaspoon marjoram
1 tablespoon minced garlic
Salt and pepper to taste

1. Place the potatoes in a large pot, cover with water and a lid, bring to a boil and cook for 10 minutes. Drain out the water and chop the potatoes into 1-inch chunks.
2. Over medium high heat, melt the butter in the pot. Add the potatoes, celery, onions, carrots and parsnips and cook, stirring occasionally, for about 10-15 minutes or until lightly browned.
3. Sprinkle the flour over the vegetables and stir in to coat all. Add the broth and seasonings and heat uncovered until the liquid boils, stirring frequently.
4. Reduce the heat to low, partially cover the pot and allow the soup to simmer for 30-40 minutes or until vegetables and potatoes are tender and easily pierced with a fork. Serve hot.

Variation:
Add a few shreds of cheddar or Colby cheese, with a sprinkle of paprika to the top of each bowl before serving.

Bob's Favorite Cheddar Broccoli Soup

I admit that I am a fussy eater and not much into canned, condensed soups that have been stuck in a metal container for an unknown amount of time. I will try to make most things from scratch before subjecting myself to a bowl of prepackaged condensed soup. One day, Bob asked if I could make Cheddar Broccoli Soup; my response was sure, give me a couple of days and I will figure it out. Once again, I began to play around with the necessary ingredients and to my astonishment and his delight I came up with the following flavorful recipe.

Serves 2-4

½ cup (1 stick) butter
2 cups broccoli, chopped into chunks
½ onion, diced
½ cup plus 2 teaspoons flour
¾ teaspoon paprika
½ teaspoon celery seed
1 teaspoon minced garlic
8 cups chicken broth (homemade works best)
8-9 ounces grated cheddar cheese
1 quart half and half
1½ teaspoons Worcestershire sauce
Salt and pepper to taste

1. Melt the butter in a large pot. Add the broccoli, stir and sauté until the broccoli is coated with the butter. Add the flour and spices and cook over medium heat until this mixture is bubbly.
2. Add the chicken broth and stir until the mixture is smooth. Cover the pot and simmer this mix at medium low heat for 60-75 minutes, allowing the flavors to blend.
3. Heat the half and half to warm in the microwave or in a saucepan. Add the cheese, warmed half and half and Worcestershire sauce to the simmering broth. Stir constantly until all of the cheese has melted and the soup is heated through. Serve hot.

Hint: To reheat, heat the pot at a low temperature, stirring constantly until heated through, but do not allow it to boil. You may want to increase the temperature slightly, but not a lot or you will risk burning at the bottom of the pan.

Clam Chowder

This is the white kind of clam chowder. Rich, thick and creamy, a hot bowl of this soup is often considered the comfort food of the fisherman's soul. However, one does not need to be a fisherman to wrap your hands around a hot bowlful and take in the fragrance of the sea while devouring a taste of heaven. In my opinion, the secret for preparing a batch of clam chowder is to use only heavy cream and make sure that the soup does not boil, but rather allow it to simmer slowly at a low temperature.

Serves 4

½ cup (1 stick) butter
2 cups celery, diced
2 cups sweet onions, finely diced
2 tablespoons minced garlic
⅓ cup flour
2 cups plus 2-3 tablespoons clam juice
3-4 large potatoes, peeled and cut into 1-inch chunks
2 teaspoons thyme
2 bay leaves
1 tablespoon or less Tabasco or a favorite hot sauce
Salt and white pepper to taste
1 quart heavy cream
4 cups minced clams and juice (If you cannot get fresh clams, you can use the canned variety.)

1. Melt the butter in a large pot at medium high heat. Add the celery, onions and garlic and sauté until the vegetables are tender and slightly golden.
2. Stir the flour into the pot, making sure it coats all the vegetables. Add the clam juice, potatoes and spices, but not the hot sauce, to the pot and heat until this mixture begins to boil.
3. Reduce the heat to medium low, allowing the boil to reduce to a simmer and add the cream. Simmer the mixture about 25-30 minutes or until the potatoes are tender, but not mushy. Make sure to stir the mixture occasionally to prevent sticking and burning at the bottom of the pan.
4. Stir in the clams and hot sauce, increase the heat slightly and simmer until the clams are fully cooked and turn opaque, about 10-15 minutes. (Do not overheat at this stage or your soup may curdle.)
5. Remove the pot from the heat, take out the bay leaves, ladle into bowls and serve piping hot.

Ann's Cheesy Corn Chowder

When Ann first shared this recipe with me, I knew it must taste marvelous, because she is such a fine cook.
While this soup was simmering one day, a friend stopped by to say hello, but said that she couldn't stay for very long.
Then she started sniffing the air and unconsciously followed her nose into the kitchen. I was one step behind her when her
nose took a dive toward the top of my soup pot and then, between grovels and moans, she turned and asked, "Ok, where's
your phone? This smells too good to pass up." She canceled whatever it was she had scheduled, took off her coat and we
waited anxiously until the soup was ready to serve. A short time later, the two of us smiled bright and wide, for we had
finished most of the soup, leaving our bellies pleasantly full and taste buds completely satisfied. Good Stuff!

4 bacon slices, cut into ¾-inch pieces
1 cup finely chopped onion
1 tablespoon unsalted butter
2 teaspoon ground cumin
3 tablespoons flour
4 cups broth (chicken or vegetable, or French Onion Soup)
2-3 cloves garlic, chopped
½ red bell pepper, chopped
1 large boiling potato, diced
½ cup evaporated milk
One 10-ounce package frozen corn kernels
8 ounces grated Pepper Jack cheese

1. Cook the bacon pieces over moderate heat in a 3-quart pan, stirring until crisp. Transfer with a slotted spoon
   to paper towels to drain excess grease.
2. Add the onion and butter to grease in pan and cook until onion is softened. Add cumin and flour and cook over
   medium heat, stirring constantly for 1-2 minutes. Whisk in the broth and bring this mixture to a boil.
3. Stir in garlic, pepper and potato, cover and simmer for 10 minutes or until potato is cooked through, stirring occasionally. Stir in evaporated milk and corn and return to a gentle simmer. Add cheese and stir until just melted. *Do not boil!*
4. Ladle into individual bowls and serve topped with bacon crumbles.

Crab Bisque

I came up with this recipe around 13 years ago after FedEx delivered a few pounds of crab claws to my house. At first I had no idea what was in the box I signed for, and then I noticed that it came from Florida, where my parents were vacationing at the time. Patience was nowhere in sight and I tore the package open and immediately called a friend over to join me in this fresh, luxurious taste of the sea. Oh my, we ate as much as we could, but there was truly no room left in our bellies and still about a pound left of this delectable treat. Not wanting to freeze or dispose of the remains, I put the leftovers into the refrigerator for the time being. The next day, snow pounded the streets and pastures and hunger began to grow. Soup sounded good and with a little advice from my friend, the following phenomenal soup was created.

Serves 4

¼ cup (½ stick) butter
6-7 scallions, finely diced
¼ cup flour
3 cups milk
1½ cup heavy cream
½ teaspoon nutmeg
¼ teaspoon paprika (optional)
¼ teaspoon minced garlic
1 teaspoon Old Bay Seasoning
Salt and white pepper to taste
1 plus pound crab meat, preferably fresh, but canned works too

1. Melt the butter in a large saucepan over low heat; add the scallions and sauté for 4-5 minutes. Whisk the flour into the scallions and continue cooking for another 5-6 minutes.
2. Pour the milk and cream into the flour mixture, whisk vigorously until the liquid begins to warm. Stir in the spices and turn up the heat slightly. (You do not want this mixture to boil, or even slightly simmer; you just want it to heat evenly or it could curdle.)
3. Over a plate or bowl, pick through the crab meat with your fingers, removing any remaining pieces of shell; gently place the crab into the liquid. (Do not stir the crab meat into the soup for it will break up too much.)
4. Heat the soup until hot and serve with warm homemade bread.

Nana Mildred's Oyster Soup

Elizabeth and I are as close as sisters, and although quite opposite from each other, we share a desperate longing for the same beach. She once fed me a bowl of this soup, knowing that I greatly missed that beach and needed a taste of its cuisine. This soup was delightfully yummy and we said so as we were placing whelk shells from that beach up to our ears to listen to the sounds of the sea. This recipe was her grandmother's and best described in the words of a granddaughter: "My grandmother, Nan to me, Mildred to others, made this often for us in the fall and winter months, when we weren't at the beach, to remind us of the seashore, our fun and adventures from the summers past and those to come! It was a BIG favorite and she always made A LOT more than two servings. Guaranteed to warm you up in cold weather!"

Makes 2 Servings

2 cups freshly shucked oysters
2 tablespoons butter
1 tablespoon Worcestershire sauce
3 cups scalded milk
¼ teaspoon celery salt
¼ teaspoon salt
¼ -½ teaspoon pepper
¼ teaspoon cayenne pepper
Oyster crackers, for the top

1. Drain all liquid from the oysters into a small bowl.
2. Place the butter, oysters and Worcestershire sauce into a heavy saucepan and cook at medium high heat. Continue cooking until the oysters' edges just begin to curl. Make sure to stir or shake the pan a little while cooking to prevent any burning.
3. Add the oyster juice and scalded milk to the saucepan, stir and add the seasonings. Turn the heat down and simmer for 5-10 minutes to blend, ladle the soup into bowls, top each bowl with a few oyster crackers and serve steaming hot.

Doe's Beef Stew

*A slow-simmered favorite that offers a taste of wholesome, hearty, homemade love with each and every bite.
I think that this was originally my mother's grandmother's recipe, but I am unsure and all are now up above. So please,
when you get to heaven, seek out my Doe and ask her to send me a message, informing me if this luscious stew, is hers or my
great-grandmother's recipe. Also, please don't forget to tell her that I send many hugs of thanks for sharing this with me.*

Serves 4-6

1 garlic clove
2-3 tablespoons oil
1-2 tablespoons flour
2 cups homemade beef broth
1½ pounds beef stew meat or chuck roast cut, trimmed of fat and cut into 1-inch pieces
2-3 large carrots, chopped into 2-inch chunks
1 medium onion, chopped
2-3 large celery stalks, chopped into 2-inch chunks
3-4 garlic cloves, diced or 1 plus tablespoon minced garlic
1½ tablespoons Worcestershire sauce
2 bay leaves
Dash of celery seed
1 cup red wine
¼-⅓ cup molasses
1 cup fresh string beans
1 cup fresh, canned or frozen corn kernels, drained
1 plus cup fresh or frozen peas

1. Cut the garlic clove in half and rub the sides and bottom of a large pot with the garlic. Discard the used garlic clove.
2. Heat the oil in the bottom of the pot over medium heat. Add the meat, sprinkle it with the flour and slightly brown the meat on all sides. Add the broth and enough warm water to bring the level to two inches above the beef.
3. Bring this mixture to a boil, skim the scum from the top, add an additional cup of water or broth and decrease the heat to low.
4. Add all remaining ingredients and allow the stew to simmer until the meat is tender, soft and easily pulls apart with a fork.

Variation:
Chopped venison, elk or moose meat can be substituted for the beef.

Hint: If this stew is not thick enough to your personal liking, add an additional tablespoon of flour to the finished product, stir it in and allowing it to simmer without a lid until the juice has thickened. You can also thicken the stew with ½ cup of mashed potato flakes.

The Brothers' Provence-Style Beef Stew in Red Wine

*While attending a culinary conference, I met a new friend and colleague, Brendan O'Farrell.
As we spent time chatting about our upcoming cookbooks and passion of sharing recipes, I inquired if he had
a recipe for a good, old fashioned stew that I may use. His smile was bright as he showed me a recipe in his cookbook,
saying that this classic French stew is sometimes called "The Mother of all Stews" and one that he was positive my readers
will approve of. With Brendan's permission, I have included it in these pages for your enjoyment, just as he sent it to me.
This recipe is outstanding and each bite will be immensely appreciated, raved over, prepared and talked about for years to come.*

Serves 8-10

4-5 pounds lean stewing beef, cut into 1-inch cubes

2 onions

4 carrots cut into ½-inch pieces

1 tablespoon Herbes de Provence (*see below for recipe)

Salt and pepper to taste

1½ cups full bodied red wine

2 tablespoons cognac or brandy

1 cup thick diced bacon

1 tablespoon olive oil

3 garlic cloves

Zest of half orange, sliced

2 bay leaves

2½ cup beef broth

½ cup pitted black olives

1 cup fresh parsley, chopped

1. Season the beef cubes with the Herbes de Provence, salt and pepper. In a bowl, combine the beef, half the onions, half the carrots, red wine and brandy. Be sure the wine and cognac cover most of the meat and vegetables, as a marinade. Cover and refrigerate for at least 6 hours.

2. Separate the beef from the marinated vegetables and wine with a slotted spoon. Set the vegetables and wine aside for later use. Pat the beef dry with paper towels. Sauté the bacon in a large Dutch oven or pot over medium high heat until golden. Remove bacon and set aside, leaving the bacon fat in the pot. Add the oil, and brown the beef on all sides in batches (do not crowd the pan), about 10 minutes. Remove the last batch of beef. Sauté the unmarinated onions and carrots in the same pan, stirring frequently until golden, about 10 minutes. Remove from heat.

3. Preheat the oven to 275 ° F. Return the bacon and all the beef to the Dutch oven or pot. Add the reserved wine marinade and vegetables, garlic, orange zest, bay leaves and beef stock. Cover with a tightly fitting lid and braise in the oven for 3 to 4 hours, until beef is fork tender. Remove from oven and skim off excess surface fat. Adjust seasoning with salt and pepper to taste. Add the olives. If making a day ahead, cool to room temperature and refrigerate overnight. Remove from the refrigerator and let stand until returned to room temperature before reheating over low heat. Serve in shallow bowls with a sprinkling of parsley over each serving.

*Herbes de Provence is a blend of Mediterranean herbs made up of a scant ½ teaspoon each of: basil, thyme, marjoram, rosemary, savory and crushed bay leaves with an optional pinch of lavender, fennel seeds and sage. This will yield 1 tablespoon.

This recipe is from the wonderful cookbook *Brothers in the Kitchen - A Celebration of Friendship, Fine Food and Entertaining*, by Michel Deville and Brendan O'Farrell, published July 2006.

Marinara Sauce

The Italian Market in South Philadelphia is a seductively fragrant area, offering the finest in Italian cuisine and culture. One day a friend and I strolled through the Market, munching contentedly on pastries, when he suddenly pulled me over to a stand owned by his cousin. As these two caught up on family matters, I noticed a humble elderly woman across the way, squishing tomatoes between her fingers into a large simmering pot. Curiosity got the best of me, so I excused myself and walked over to watch. She looked up and offered a wide, toothless smile and urged me to come closer. She spoke kindly to me in broken English while demonstrating the technique for producing true Marinara Sauce; squish the tomatoes through the fingers. When my friend came to gather me, the old woman and I hugged, then she handed me a jar of sauce, smiled that brilliant smile of hers, and pointed to her heart, saying, "Mangia! Mangia!"

Serves 4

2-3 tablespoons olive oil
1 large onion, chopped
2-3 garlic cloves, minced
4-5 stewed tomatoes, peeled and cooled or one 28-ounce can Italian tomatoes
1 teaspoon sweet basil
1 teaspoon oregano
2-3 tablespoons tomato paste
½ cup red wine
½ cup water
1-2 teaspoons sugar or honey, or 1 teaspoon baking soda

1. Slice an extra garlic clove in half and rub it all over the inside of a 1-2 gallon pot. Dispose of the clove after using.
2. Heat the oil in the pot over medium heat, add the garlic and onion and sauté until slightly browned.
3. Squish and crush the tomatoes between your fingers directly into the pot. Stirring constantly, add all remaining ingredients and allow the sauce to simmer for 3-5 hours, stirring often to prevent burning and sticking to the bottom of the pot.
4. Serve this sauce over pasta or in various casseroles and dishes made with pasta.

Hint: I usually taste this sauce after the first hour or so of simmering, and then add a pinch more spice and wine for my personal taste.

Carl's Favorite Chunky Italian Sauce

This is one of those recipes best described in the words of my adopted big brother: "Where'd you learn how to make sauce this good?" Carl and I adopted each other more than 25 years ago; I needed a big brother and he needed a little sister always looking over his shoulder. Today, I feel quite lucky that such a unique friendship has survived the passage of time. A fine cook he is and believe me, he does not hand out compliments on others' cooking generously, so when he said that, I knew I had done well.

Serves 6

2-3 tablespoons virgin olive oil
1 plus pound Italian sausage, cut into 1–2-inch chunks (mild or hot)
1 plus pound ground beef
1 medium onion, diced
5-7 garlic cloves, diced
Two 28-ounce cans tomato sauce
18 ounces tomato paste
⅓-½ cup red wine
½ green pepper, seeded and finely diced
1 teaspoon oregano
1 teaspoon sweet basil
Scant ½ teaspoon marjoram
Scant ½ teaspoon thyme
Scant ½ teaspoon sage
2 tablespoons grated Parmesan cheese
1 tablespoon honey, 2 teaspoons sugar OR 1 teaspoon baking soda
2 medium zucchinis, sliced into ¼-inch slices

1. Cut an extra garlic clove in half and rub the sides and bottoms of a 2-gallon stock pot with it, then discard the garlic.
2. Heat the oil in the pot over medium heat, add the garlic and onion and sauté until slightly browned.
3. Add the meats to the pot and stir the ingredients until they begin to brown. Add all remaining ingredients but the zucchini. Cover the pot, decrease the heat to low and allow to simmer for 4-5 hours. Unless using a crock pot or pressure cooker, make sure to stir the sauce occasionally while simmering, to prevent any sticking or burning on the bottom of the pan.
4. Approximately 30 minutes before removing the sauce from the heat add the sliced zucchini.
5. Serve this sauce over pasta, potatoes and/or rice or use it in a variety of dishes such as Lasagna, Chicken Parmesan, Zucchini Pasta, etc.

Hint: Taste the sauce after the first 2-3 hours or so of simmering and then add more seasoning if desired. I will usually stir an additional ⅓ cup wine into the sauce at this time.

Red Chili

Thick, hot and spicy, with a touch of Southwestern flair, this recipe has been said to cure all that may ail you, even if you are as healthy as an ox. I have made this recipe more times than I can count, to the pleasure of many. I must share the secret; make a potful and store it in the refrigerator over night, giving the ingredients an opportunity to continue blending, resulting in an even more pungent and appetizing flavor. But, if you are impatient, and must immediately gratify your hunger with a bowlful, go for it.

Serves 6-8

2-3 tablespoons oil
1 medium onion, diced
1 teaspoon minced garlic
1 plus pound ground beef
½ pound ground chorizo
Two 28-ounce cans tomato sauce
One 12-ounce can tomato paste
One 16-ounce can pinto beans, drained
One 16-ounce can kidney beans, drained
One 16-ounce can garbanzo beans, drained
1 teaspoon cilantro
1 teaspoon chili powder
¼ teaspoon cayenne pepper
Few drops hot sauce
¼ teaspoon parsley
2-3 teaspoons finely diced canned jalapenos

1. Heat the oil in a large pot over medium heat, add the garlic and onion and sauté until slightly browned.
2. Add the meats to the pot and stir until they begin to brown. Add all remaining ingredients, decrease the heat to low, cover the pot and allow all to slow simmer for 1½-2½ hours. Make sure to stir occasionally to prevent sticking and burning on the bottom of the pan unless using a crock pot of pressure cooker.
3. Serve hot with shredded cheddar cheese, a couple dollops of sour cream and a Cheddar Muffin (p. 48).

Neighbor John's Green Chili

One bitter cold evening, while visiting with John, he heated a container of his fabulous spicy Green Chili to warm the chill away. Warmed by the pungent jolt of spice, I asked him to write down the recipe, so that I may share it with my readers. Impressed with himself and the compliment, he obliged my request and graciously wrote the following down on the back of an envelope, right then and there. Be prepared, for this chili is a tad spicy, but guaranteed to warm even the coolest of souls. Best served with lots of cheese, sour cream and a few slices of avocado; these additions help to temper the heat of this piquant delight.

Serves 6-8

1 pound ground buffalo or ½ pound each ground beef and ground pork
5 garlic cloves, diced
2 tablespoons olive oil
½ large onion, thinly sliced or diced
1-1½ teaspoons chili powder
1 tablespoon fresh diced cilantro
Salt and pepper to taste
2 pounds fresh green chilies, roasted, peeled, deveined and seeded
One 32-ounce can tomatillos (Mexican green tomatoes) in juice
12 ounces (1½ cups) chicken broth, canned or homemade
5 ancho jalapenos (dried)
One 16-ounce can black beans, undrained
One 12-ounce beer (optional)

1. Over medium heat, heat the olive oil and sauté the garlic and onions in a large pot until slightly brown. Add the ground meats and dry spices. Decrease the temperature and allow this mixture to simmer for a few minutes, stirring occasionally.
2. Cover the ancho jalapenos with warm water and allow them to soak for 10-15 minutes. In the meantime, place the seeded fresh chilies into a blender or food processor, add the tomatillos and chicken broth and blend until smooth. Add the pre-soaked jalapenos to the blender mixture and blend them in.
3. Add the mixture from the blender and the black beans to the pot of meat mixture and simmer at a low temperature for 60-90 minutes. For more liquid and flavor, add the beer during the last 45 minutes of simmering. Serve hot with cheese and sour cream.

Carl's Cowboy Chili

Hold onto the bull, grab a bowl and have a seat, for this special recipe is soft enough for a toothless cow, scented enough to lead a horse and strong enough to beat that bull. The taste will leave you yeehawin' in between the yippy-yaw-ki-yeas and yawhoos soon to follow.

Severs 5-6

1½ pounds sirloin pork, trimmed of fat and cut into 1-inch cubes
1 medium onion, chopped
2 garlic cloves
Two 15-ounce cans tomatoes or tomatillos, including liquid
1 teaspoon plus chili powder
¼ teaspoon cayenne powder
½ teaspoon cilantro
2 tablespoons diced green chilies, canned or freshly roasted and diced
1½ cups beef broth (homemade tastes better)
1 or 2 dashes Worcestershire sauce
1 tablespoon masa corn flour
3 tablespoons water

1. Over medium heat, cook the onions and meat in the bottom of a stock pot, once the meat begins to brown, drain out all the fat. Add all remaining ingredients but the masa corn flour and water to the meat, cover and simmer for 2½-3 hours, stirring occasionally.
2. If you prefer a thinner chili, then skip the next step and just allow the chili to simmer until meat is tender and easily pierced with a fork. However if you prefer your chili a tad thicker, whisk the corn flour and water together in a small bowl, add a cup of broth from the stock pot, whisk it into the flour mixture and then add to the pot of chili. Continue stirring for 2-3 minutes and cook all for an additional 15 minutes or until the chili has slightly thickened.

Stone Soup

This soup is the tastiest soup that has ever been made. Although, it has been treasured and passed on by many, there is no true documentation or copyright associated with its recipe and associated folk tale. Some will say that this soup originated in France, while others say it originated in Russia. However it really doesn't matter where or who developed the following, what matters is that it be passed on and savored for a lifetime.

It has been said that many years ago a great famine occurred in Eastern Europe. Cold and hungry villagers hoarded whatever foods they could for survival. Although friends and neighbors remained, the foods were not shared as they once were; rather they were stashed in secret hiding places, only to be shared among immediate family members.

One chilly day, tired and hungry from days on the road, a young man wondered into a village looking for a place to rest and some food as he hadn't eaten in a couple of days. As he went from door to door asking for a crust of bread and a place to rest his weary head, he was sent away with the words: *"We have no food for ourselves, thus nothing to share, and all beds are full from wanderers before thee"*. Desperate, hungry and cold, he went and sat on a rock by the creek, built a small fire and pulled a large kettle out of his sack. He filled the kettle with water from the creek, placed it over the fire and then began searching the ground until he found just the right sized stones. The villagers watched in awe as he added the stones to the heated water. As the water began to boil, he smelled that soup as if it was the best thing in the world. Of course this got their curiosity, so very slowly the town's folk approached the young man and inquired as to what he was doing. *"Making Stone Soup of course"* he said! *"Since you do not have any food, I shall make a pot of Stone Soup for all! Ah, a fine soup it is, but would taste much better if I had a little cabbage to add to it."* Fortunately, one of the villagers, a generous soul she was, did not think twice, went to her supply of stashed food and brought this stranger a head of cabbage.

As time went by, more and more villagers came to see what this young man was doing. As he stirred his soup, he commented that a good soup needs a bit of salt to enhance its flavor, and once again a villager volunteered some salt. Soon the villagers were bringing carrots, onions, potatoes, turnips and parsley to add to his pot of simmering stones.

As the villagers began to smell the delicious aroma rising over the brim of the kettle, they were full of wonderment that a few stones could produce such a good soup. As they voiced this to the young man, he mentions that if he only had a bit of salt beef, then this soup, made from stones, would be fit for a *"rich man's table"*. The villagers all looked to the butcher who miraculously managed to find some spare beef, which he generously added to the pot of stones.

A short while later, the young man tasted his soup and declared to all what a fine soup he had brewed. He requested that the villagers join him in such a fine meal and shared his soup with all. Amazingly some went to into their homes and brought him some bread, others offered wine, cider and cheese. Soon everyone was sitting at the tables enjoying a wonderful meal indeed! There was much good will passed that eve; with full bellies, all sang and danced into the night. The young man was offered a warm bed and invited to stay the night. In the morning he was given breakfast and some food to carry him on his journey. The villagers gather to see him off and to thank him for his generosity. One villager offered a hand and a hug as he said *"We will never go hungry again, now that we know how to make soup from stones."*

Recipe for Happiness

1 heart full of love

A set of open eyes

2 heaping cups of patience

3 overflowing cups of forgiveness

2 handfuls of generosity

Lots of warm smiles

A cup of humor

A tablespoon of tears

2 arms that bear hugs

1. Mix all ingredients evenly with kindness.

2. Add an abundance of faith and mix well.

3. Spread this mixture each and every day;
no matter where you go or who you
may meet along your journeys,
for this is one recipe to be shared with all.

What's for Dinner?

~ Store all leftovers covered in the refrigerator or freezer.
~ Make sure all butter, margarine and/or cream cheese is softened to room temperature before adding.
~ Foods will take longer to cook, roast or bake at high altitudes. For use at sea level please adjust cooking times accordingly and always test the product for doneness before removing from the heat source.

Many think that preparing dinner is a long and ingratiating process. I have heard dozens of women talk about how they had made their husband's or kids' favorite foods, and then afterwards felt as if their efforts were expected or taken for granted. They would spend hours dicing, basting and stirring until their arms felt like they would fall off; setting the table; tossing the salad; and bringing the hot foods to the table; only to have it consumed in a matter of minutes without a second thought. Well folks, I hate to inform you, but you are wrong! Although, an appreciation for your efforts may not be noticed at the time the meal is served, a well-prepared dinner is one that is cherished, remembered and passed on to be reproduced with memories for generations to come.

Bon Appetit!

Mom's Brisket, Page 207

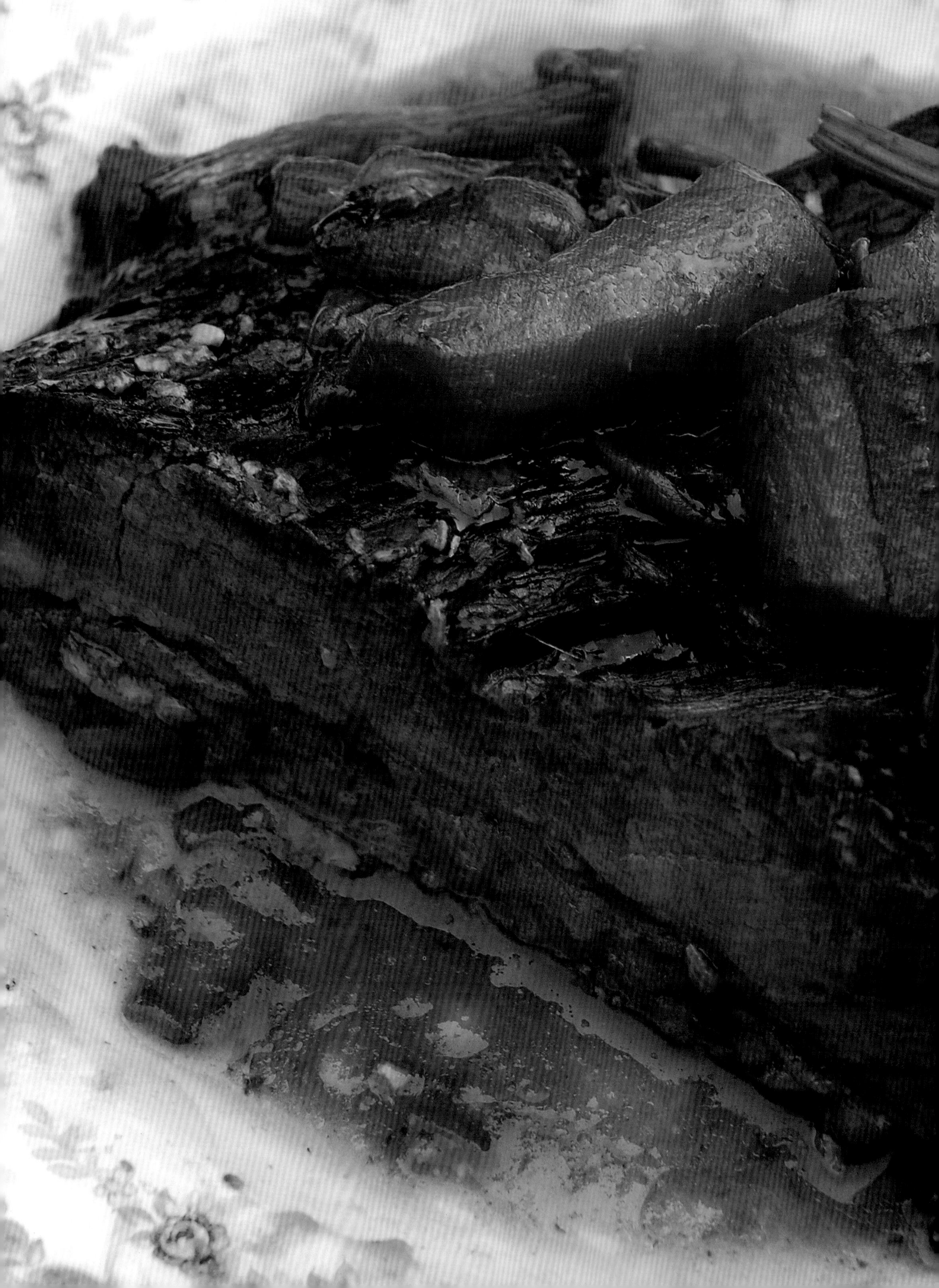

Mom's Brisket

This notable recipe produces that lovely impression as if you have died and gone to heaven with each bite; but it took me years to perfect high up in the mountain. Whenever I made a brisket, it always came out of the oven tough and without that melt-in-your-mouth tenderness that I longed for. Then the proverbial light bulb came on in my head and I thought, if I lower the temperature just a smidgen and allow the beef to roast a little longer, maybe it would turn out correctly. It took an extra hour or two and a lot of patience, but the aroma was mouth-watering, as was each and every bite. Lesson learned from this experience: roasting a magnificent piece of beef at high altitude takes a bit longer and a slightly lower temperature than it does to roast at sea level, but it is well worth the time, effort and patience, for the results are outstanding.

Serves 6-8

Preheat the oven to 325° F

One 4–5-pound fresh brisket of beef
3-4 large carrots cut into 3-inch pieces
1 medium to large onion, thinly sliced
3-4 garlic cloves, diced or 2 tablespoons minced garlic

1 scant tablespoon Worcestershire sauce
2 pinches of paprika, more if you like
Warm water
Salt, pepper and a dash of celery seed to taste

1. Butter or use pan spray and coat a large roasting pan.
2. Place beef into pan with the fat side up. Smear with the spices and Worcestershire sauce.
3. Pour enough warm water over the beef so that it comes about ¾ up the sides of the beef; add the carrots and onion slices.
4. Cover the pan with foil, baste the beef at least every half hour or so for approximately 5-6½ hours, until tender and easily pierced with a fork. If necessary, add a little bit more water during the cooking process, so that there is always a bit of excess liquid in the pan. You may need to add 1 or more cups of extra liquid twice, once after the first 2 hours and again after 3½ hours.
5. Slice the beef diagonally against the grain and serve with the vegetables and the excess juice or thickened gravy.

BEEF GRAVY
Skim the fat from the juice/drippings (about 3 tablespoons) and place them into a skillet. Then add:
3 tablespoons butter or margarine
3-4 tablespoons flour
1 teaspoon minced garlic
5-6 cups of juice or beef broth
1. Heat ingredients over medium low heat.
2. Consistently whisk mixture until all ingredients are incorporated and the gravy reaches the desired consistency. Serve hot over the sliced beef.

Hints: Reserve excess juice in the freezer for use in beef broth or gravies at a later date. A ¼ cup of ketchup can be rubbed on top of the brisket before roasting.

Sea Level: Set the temperature at 325° F and shorten cooking time for 60-90 minutes.

Cherry Burgundy Brisket

*This positively awesome recipe was developed one day as I cleaned out the refrigerator.
I found a recently opened bottle of wine and because I don't drink wine, I wasn't sure what to do with
the rest of the bottle until I remembered the piece of brisket thawing on the kitchen counter. I enjoy experimenting with
food, so I poured the wine over the beef and left it in the fridge to marinate overnight. The next morning, I spotted a bag
of thawed cherries I was going to use for something that had been forgotten about the night before, so tossed them into the
pan with the wine and beef. Hours later, the house smelled great and with the first bite I knew that my creation was
a success and impressive enough to serve royalty, while easy enough to serve to family and friends.*

Serves 6-8

Preheat oven to 325° F

One 4-5-pound brisket
¾ bottle of Burgundy
1 tablespoon minced garlic
1 medium onion, thinly sliced
1-2 teaspoon Worcestershire sauce
One 16-ounce bag frozen cherries, thawed
Salt and pepper to taste

1. Place the brisket, wine and garlic into a large roasting pan, cover the pan tightly with foil and let marinate in the refrigerator overnight or for at least 8 hours.
2. When ready to cook, preheat oven, add the Worcestershire sauce, cherries and onions to the pan, cover tightly with foil and allow to roast for 5-7 hours or until tender and easily pierced with a fork.
3. Slice the beef diagonally across the grain, pour a little juice over the slices and serve with choice of vegetables and potatoes, pasta or rice.

Hint: Reserve leftover juice in the freezer for later use.

Sea Level: Set the temperature at 325° F and shorten cooking time for 60-90 minutes.

Pot Roast

This is what I consider pure comfort food for the soul. Use a crock pot, pressure cooker, Dutch oven or roasting pan; all one needs to do is add the ingredients and simmer at a slow temperature all day long. The wait for a taste to thy palate may be an impatient one, but well worth it, for this slow cooking method is what produces the superior essence that will be requested and savored often in the years to come.

Serves 6-8

Preheat oven to 325° F

4-5 pounds beef chuck, bottom or top round, pork, venison or elk roast (the thicker the cut, the better)
1 garlic clove
1-2 tablespoons flour
2 tablespoons oil or 3 tablespoons butter
2 garlic cloves, finely minced (a pinch more if using wild game)
1-2 carrots, chopped
1-2 celery stalk, chopped (optional)
½ teaspoon cloves and or nutmeg
1 medium onion
2 cups beef broth
½ cup red wine (optional)
1 large bay leaf
2 teaspoons Worcestershire sauce (a pinch more if using wild game)
2-3 tablespoons butter
Salt and pepper to taste

1. Cut any excess fat away from the meat and rub the meat all over with the garlic clove. Discard the clove.
2. Heat the oil or butter in a 9 or 10-inch skillet over medium, dredge the meat in the flour and slightly brown it on all sides. Remove from the pan, and place it into the pan that it will be simmered in; add a cup of warm water.
3. Add all remaining ingredients, cover tightly with foil or the pot's lid, and simmer until tender and easily pierced with a fork, about 5-7 hours.
4. If using a roasting pan or Dutch oven, remove the lid 30-40 minutes before removing from the oven, turning the roast once in the pan.

Hints: If using wild game, pound it a few times with the back of a large spoon or mallet to tenderize the meat before cooking. You can also poke a few holes all over the top with the prongs of a fork. Additionally, spread 2 tablespoons butter or top of the meat if using wild game. Reserve the leftover juice in a tightly fitted container and freeze it to use later as it makes a wonderful addition to or base for beef broth.

Sea Level: Set the temperature at 325° F and shorten roasting time by 60-90 minutes.

Grandmom's Fruity Pork Roast

*I first tasted this at my grandmother's apartment after I had unexpectedly stopped in to say hello.
There were a few neighbors enjoying each other's company and my grandmother was serving this wonderful dish.
She asked me to stay while placing a platter full in front of me, leaving me no choice but to sit and eat. As these women cackled
and laughed about and to each other, I sat quietly, ate and relished their tales. A few decades later, I found this recipe in that
magical tin box of hers, and knew that I would be making it during the rainy downpours predicted for the next day.
I served this to friends on the same dishes that Grandmom had used years ago and as we shared old tales
with each other, we consumed the glorious culmination of this terrific recipe.*

Serves 6-8

One 4–5-pound pork roast, trimmed of fat
¼ cup oil
½ cup white wine
1 cup apple cider or apple juice
2 tablespoons fresh squeezed lemon juice
1 teaspoon minced garlic
Scant ¼ teaspoon rosemary
Scant teaspoon thyme
A few drops soy sauce
2 tablespoons finely diced onion or scallion
3 tablespoons brown sugar
¾-1 cup dark and golden raisins (dry cherries can also be used)
½-⅔ cup diced dried apricots
2 Granny Smith apples, peeled, cored and sliced

1. Combine all ingredients except apple slices into a roasting pan, cover with plastic wrap and marinate overnight.
2. The next day, preheat oven to 325° F, exchange the plastic wrap for foil and cook the roast until tender and easily
   pierced with a fork, (2½-4 hours). About 30-45 minutes before serving, remove the foil, add the apples to the pan,
   and continue roasting until done.
3. To serve, place the roast on a large platter, pour the juice and fruits into a bowl and serve alongside.

Hint: This can also be prepared in a crock pot or pressure cooker set a slow temperature.

Corned Beef and Cabbage

It was years ago and just a few days before St. Patrick's Day that I first read this recipe in my grandmother's magical tin box. I wasn't searching for anything specific, just meandering through the folded papers and cards, when this little, amber newspaper page caught my attention. I gently picked it up and it magically unfolded right before my eyes. I swear my grandmother somehow led me to this recipe; she must have sensed that I had no idea how to prepare corned beef and cabbage to celebrate the holiday. Although, the recipe was difficult to read, for the letters and words were faded with age, I deciphered what I could, compensated for what I couldn't and ended up preparing a marvelous dinner. As company was leaving with containers full of leftovers, among the hugs, kisses and thank yours, I overheard one say, "Great food, we'll be back next year, same time, same place, same meal," and they were!

Serves 8-10

1 roasting pan with lid and steaming rack
One 4–5-pound corned beef brisket, trimmed of fat
    (remove the packet of spices and refrigerate for another use or discard)
2 bottles Guinness Draught Beer
1½-2 teaspoons coriander seeds
1-2 teaspoons mustard seeds or 1 teaspoon ground mustard
1-2 bay leaves
½-1 teaspoon minced garlic
Dash cinnamon
Dash nutmeg
Dash ground cloves
Dash cardamom
Salt and pepper to taste
4 large potatoes, washed and chopped into quarters
5-6 carrots, chopped into ½-inch slices
3-4 turnips, washed and sliced
1 large cabbage, cut into wedges

1. Pour one of the beers into the bottom of a roasting pot, add the spices and all the juice from the corned beef package. Place the steaming rack in the pan, then sit the beef on the rack and fill the pot with warm water, just to the top of the rack.
2. Set the temperature to medium high and bring the liquid to a boil. Decrease the heat to low and simmer on top of the stove for 4-6 hours or until tender and easily pierced with a fork. After the 2-3 hours of simmering, add the second beer to the broth and enough water so that the liquid level remains even with the steaming rack.
3. Remove the beef onto a plate, add the potatoes and vegetables to the broth under the steaming rack, and place the cabbage wedges on top of the steaming rack, replace the lid and simmer for 15-25 minutes or until vegetables are tender but not mushy.
4. Remove all remaining ingredients from the broth and place into a bowl. Ladle a little juice over the beef and the vegetables, and pour the rest into a gravy bowl. Slice the beef against the grain and serve.

Roast Beef

This recipe can be summed up rapidly; if you are one who enjoys a good chunk of beef and savors the leftovers for sandwiches or another meal, then it just doesn't get any better than this. To top it off, this is so wonderfully easy that even those of you who claim you can't cook can make this irresistibly succulent beef with no trouble.

Serves 8-10

Preheat oven to 325° F

One 5-pound sirloin roast (the kind that is wrapped in a net)
1-2 tablespoons butter
1-2 teaspoons minced garlic
Salt and pepper to taste

1. Leaving the netting on the beef, place it into a large roasting pan and using a fork, poke holes all over the top of the beef.
2. Spread the butter over the top of the beef and then spread the garlic all over the butter and season with salt and pepper.
3. Place the pan into the preheated oven and allow the beef to roast for approximately 2 hours or until cooked to your liking.
4. Slice to desired thickness. Pour excess juice into a gravy bowl and reserve leftovers for gravy or beef broth.

Hint: When sliced very thin, almost paper thin, this beef makes exceptional roast beef sandwiches.

Carl's Swiss Steaks

Remember those old-fashioned diners that used to dot the highways and byways long ago?
There may still be a few of these Mom-and-Pop style restaurants around, but they come few and far between.
However, when you walk into one, see the tables full of food and the happy faces, you know that you are in a fine food
establishment indeed. The jukebox may be on; the red and white plastic tablecloths may have an occasional tear; but the
food is some of the best you could ever indulge in. Carl used to cook at one such place and this dish was a frequent request.
Though a bit time-consuming, the basics are easy and the taste produces that lip-smacking goodness that you can't get
enough of until the buckle of the belt needs to be nudged just a hole or three, offering more room for the belly to expand.

Serves 4-6

2 pounds beef round steak, trimmed of fat
¼ cup flour
½ cup (1 stick) butter
2 medium onions, sliced
8-10 large mushroom caps, washed thoroughly
1 plus cup warm water
Salt and pepper to taste
1-2 teaspoons Worcestershire sauce
¼ cup red wine

1. Using a meat tenderizer or mallet, pound the flour into both sides of the meat and then cut the meat into 3x1-inch strips.
2. Over medium heat, melt the butter in a large skillet, a Dutch oven or a 1-gallon stock pot. Add the onions and sauté until tender but not brown. Add the mushrooms and continue sautéing another 7-8 minutes or until the mushrooms are tender. Remove the vegetables from the skillet, add the floured meat and brown each slice on both sides.
3. Add the onions and mushrooms back to the skillet, pour in the warm water, cover and cook for 25-30 minutes.
4. Add all remaining ingredients, cover, lower the heat to low and allow to simmer for 60-80 minutes or until the meat is tender. You will need to stir the mix occasionally to prevent sticking and burning.
5. Serve over pasta, mashed potatoes, rice, or alongside a baked potato or salad.

Hint: I often make a double or triple batch and freeze what is leftover for an easy meal at a later date.

Mom's Shepherd's Pie

Truth be told, this is one of my very favorite comfort foods and I am positive that it will become one of yours and your family's as well. Honestly, this is one of the easiest and most satisfying recipes I have ever made. Although not quite the traditional Shepherd's Pie that you may relish at a restaurant, as there is no true comparison; this meal will warm your bones, pleasantly fill your belly, and the recipe will be requested many times over, as it often was in the house I grew up in.

Serves 4-5

Preheat oven to 350° F

1 plus pound ground beef
½ cup diced onions (optional)
2 cups canned or frozen peas, drained or thawed and drained
1½ cups corn kernels (optional)
1 batch Mom's Mashed Potatoes (p. 5)
2 cups canned, jarred or Homemade (Beef) Gravy (p. 340)

1. Brown the beef and onions in a skillet or frying pan, until the beef is cooked through. Drain the fat from the pan.
2. Have all ingredients ready to be layered. In a deep bowl or pie plate layer the mashed potatoes, then the peas, the browned beef and onions, then the corn kernels, if adding, and smother the top with heated gravy.
3. Place the bowl in the oven to heat for about 10 minutes and serve hot.

Mom's Pepper Steak

My honest nature says that I must tell you that I have never tasted this recipe; I do not like peppers. However, I specifically remember my mother making this often because my father just loved it; as did other family members and friends. Additionally, when I have made this for a few friends, they also find it wonderful. When I thought about adding it to these pages, one of these friends, who sometimes knows me too well, responded with these exact words, "Absolutely, just because you won't eat it, doesn't mean that its goodness shouldn't be shared!"

Serves 4-5

1¼-pound beef round steak or flank steak, sliced into thin pieces
2 tablespoons oil
2 garlic cloves, crushed
1 cup beef broth
2 tablespoons cornstarch
2 tablespoon water
1 tablespoons soy sauce
1¼ cup green peppers, seeds and veins removed and thinly sliced
½ teaspoon ginger
Sea salt and pepper to taste

1. Heat a skillet over medium and add the oil and garlic. When the garlic begins to brown, add the beef slices. Allow the beef to cook for 3-4 minutes and add the broth, then season with salt and pepper. Turn the temperature down to low and stir occasionally.
2. Mix together the cornstarch, water and soy sauce in a saucepan; heat over medium and stir constantly until this thickens, then add the peppers and ginger to the sauce. Once this mixture gets hot, and the peppers are crisp but tender, add all of the sauce into the skillet with the beef, and heat at a low temperature until the heat is evenly distributed among the ingredients.
3. Serve the beef and pepper mix over white or brown cooked rice.

Cream of Mushroom Dinner

This recipe is so very easy. If you do not eat meat, chicken or seafood, you can prepare this with a variety of sautéed vegetables. The flavor is very good and fulfilling, and the process is much too simple to be true. What more can you ask for during the busy days of meeting deadlines, getting the kids to this or that after-school activity, finishing chores and trying to take some 'me' time, to recharge your energy for the evening ahead?

Serves 4

1 plus pound ground beef/turkey, London broil sliced into thin strips, chicken tenders or 2-3 cups vegetables chopped
1 10–12-ounce can condensed Cream of Mushroom soup
8 ounces mushrooms, washed and sliced
½ soup can milk
½ onion diced
2 cups chopped broccoli or cauliflower (optional)
½ teaspoon or more minced garlic
1 teaspoon Worcestershire sauce
Salt and pepper to taste
One 16-ounce package pasta (any kind)

1. Brown the beef or chicken in a large skillet over medium heat.
2. Add the soup and milk and stir it into the meat.
3. Decrease the heat to low, add all remaining ingredients, cover the skillet and allow mixture to simmer for 35-45 minutes.
4. While the mixture is simmering, prepare the pasta according to package directions. When it is finished cooking, drain and place into a large shallow bowl. Top the pasta with cooked meat or chicken mixture and serve.

Doe's Stroganoff

Almost a lifetime ago, I stepped out of the elevator in an apartment building to a mélange of individual scents streaming out from under each door. Each scent let me know who was roasting chicken, who was making soup, and who was baking to their heart's delight. As I approached my grandparents' door, I was hit with an aroma that made my mouth begin to water. When I walked in, Doe was just finishing loading a plateful of this creamy beef dish for my grandfather. I took a taste right out of the pan, then another and knew that I would be staying longer than anticipated—to my grandparents delight. As we were finishing up, a neighbor (who evidently had been the one baking when I arrived earlier), stopped by with a plate of warm cookies. Finished with dessert, I hugged each one of them, thanked them for sharing some of the goodness that life offers, said my farewells, and then raved about this meal at my next stop.

Serves 6-8

2 pounds sirloin beef, trimmed of fat and cut into bite-size cubes
2 tablespoons flour
1 teaspoon sea salt
½ cup (1 stick) of butter or margarine, divided in half
1 cup chopped onion
1 teaspoon minced garlic
⅓ cup flour
2 tablespoons tomato paste
2-3 cups beef broth
2 cups sour cream
¼ cup white wine or sherry
8 ounces wide egg noodles, cooked according to the package directions, thoroughly drained and placed into
    a large shallow bowl

1. Combine the flour and salt and then coat the meat entirely in this mixture.
2. Melt 4 tablespoons butter in a skillet over medium heat, add the meat and brown.
3. Add the onions to the skillet and cook until the meat is done and the onions are soft and tender. Remove the meat and onions from the pan. Add remaining butter, flour and the tomato paste, mix slightly, then blend in the beef broth. Cook and stir constantly over medium high heat until the mixture thickens and becomes bubbly. Return the meat and onions to the pan, stir to evenly coat with the broth mixture and then decrease the temperature to low.
4. Stir the sour cream and wine into the meat mixture and stir occasionally until heated through, about 6-10 minutes. (Do not allow Stroganoff to boil!)
5. Pour the meat mixture over the cooked noodles or stir the noodles into the skillet and serve.

Mom's Spaghetti and Meatballs

This recipe is highly recommended after a hard day of work, play or just for the sake of a good, hearty meal. Splendidly delicious and being relatively easy to prepare makes this a favorite in many households. All you really need is a good sauce, a few of these meatballs, a large plate of spaghetti to serve it over, a bit of cheese to sprinkle on top, and you've got an excellent meal, certain to please all. By the way, this recipe gets better if the sauce and meatballs are made a day in advance, allowing the flavors to mingle together overnight.

Serves 4

3-4 cups of Marinara Sauce (p. 198) or your favorite jar of tomato sauce
10-12 ounces spaghetti, cooked according to package directions, drained and covered to keep warm

1 tablespoons butter or margarine
2 tablespoons oil
½ cup diced sweet yellow onion (Vidalia preferred)
¼ cup diced green pepper (optional)
1½ teaspoons minced garlic
1½-2 pounds ground beef
¼ cup dry bread crumbs
¼ cup minced fresh parsley
2 tablespoons minced fresh basil
3 tablespoons grated Parmesan cheese
2 tablespoons A-1 Steak Sauce
3 eggs
Sea salt and pepper to taste
2 tablespoons oil
¼ cup combined shredded Parmesan and Romano cheese

1. Over medium high heat, melt the butter and oil in a large skillet. Add the onions and pepper, sauté until tender but crisp, about 5-7 minutes, and then transfer the vegetables to a large bowl.
2. In a different bowl, beat the eggs until frothy and mix all of the ingredients (except the pasta, sauce, oil and cheese) thoroughly into the eggs with your hands. Season with salt and pepper and then roll into tightly packed meatballs, about 2 inches in diameter. You should get about 8-10 meatballs.
3. Begin to heat your sauce over medium low heat, stirring occasionally.
4. Heat 2 tablespoons oil in a large skillet over medium high heat. Brown the meatballs in the skillet, turning them often so that they cook evenly for about 5-7 minutes and then place each ball into the warmed sauce.
5. Allow the meatballs to heat in the sauce for 15-30 minutes and then ladle the sauce and meatballs over a plate of spaghetti. Sprinkle the cheese over the top and serve.

Hint: The meatballs can simmer in the sauce for a longer period if you like.

Meatloaf

I never like my mom's meatloaf, so I had no choice but to come up with a recipe of my own when customers began requesting it at my shop. Not having a clue as to what I was doing, I came up with this recipe. The greatest feedback came from a customer who frequented my shop often to purchase dinners to go. One day after purchasing a whole meatloaf and a few desserts to go, she proudly informed me that her husband of 43 years always thought that she made the best meatloaf in the world, until he tasted mine. Now that is what I call a compliment!

Serves 4-6

1½ pounds ground beef
¾ cup plus 2 tablespoons milk
¼ cup ketchup
2 eggs, beaten
⅔ cup unseasoned bread crumbs
⅓ cup finely diced onion
½ teaspoon garlic powder
Salt and pepper to taste
½ cup ketchup
3 tablespoons brown sugar
¼ cup water
Salt

350

1. Mix together the milk and ¼ cup ketchup and pour this over the bread crumbs. Allow the crumbs to soak up the milk, then add the ground beef, eggs, onions, garlic, salt and pepper and mix it all up with your hands or with an electric mixer.
2. Grease a 9x5-inch loaf pan well with pan spray, butter or margarine, shape the beef mixture into a loaf and place into the prepared pan.
3. Thoroughly mix together the remaining ketchup, brown sugar, water and salt and pour all over the top of the beef loaf.
4. Bake for approximately 1 hour and 10 minutes, remove from the oven, gently remove the loaf from the pan, pour any remaining juice on top and serve.

Yams and Ham

This is another recipe from that magical tin box of my grandmother's. The magazine page was torn, but it intrigued me when I saw the faded date 1939 and the words country flavor; I had to give it a try. Oh my, a few hours later the fragrance in my house was phenomenal. Tasting this luscious combination, with an added touch of sweetness, made me think of what life must have been like back then, and how the goodness of simplicity remains priceless today.

Serves 4-5

Preheat oven to 325° F

1-2 tablespoons butter or margarine
1 large uncooked slice of ham, 1 plus inch thick
¼ cup dark brown sugar
5 medium yams
¼ teaspoon nutmeg
Pinch of cinnamon
1-2 tablespoons pure maple syrup or 2 teaspoons maple extract

1. Melt the butter in the bottom of a large skillet or pan and then drizzle with the maple syrup or extract. Add the ham slice and brown on both sides, about 2-3 minutes per side.
2. Remove the ham from the pan and place it into a large covered casserole dish or deep pan and cover with foil. Bake for a little less than 2 hours or about 110 minutes. Do not discard ham drippings; just put the skillet aside for now.
3. While the ham is baking, wash and peel the yams thoroughly, and then boil them in a large pot filled with warm water until they just begin to tender.
4. Approximately 30 minutes before the ham has finished baking, heat the drippings over medium heat, then lower the heat, quarter the yams and add them to the heated drippings. Sprinkle with brown sugar and spices and cook the yams slowly, turning them over often until good and browned.
5. Remove the ham from the oven and serve it on a large platter surrounded by the yams.

Joanne's Wiener Schnitzel (Breaded Veal)

*I met Joanne's son while participating in a book signing, and he mentioned what a fabulous cook his mother was.
I told him that I was writing another cookbook and was always looking for new recipes shared by others to add to the pages.
A couple of days later this young man's mother, Joanne, contacted me. We had a lovely conversation and she kindly said that
she was pleased to share her family's favorite, a recipe for Wiener schnitzel. A few days went by and I received this fabulous
recipe in the mail and I made it up the next day. Although I had never tasted Wiener schnitzel before, this recipe
is remarkable and I send hugs of thanks to her for sharing it.*

Serves 4

4 veal or pork cutlets
Worcestershire sauce
1 teaspoon Coleman's English dry mustard
Grated parmesan cheese
2 cups white cracker crumbs (any kind of white cracker, i.e., Saltines)
2 beaten eggs
2 tablespoons oil

1. Pound only one side of the meat with a meat tenderizer or mallet until it is ¼-inch thick.
2. Sprinkle drops of Worcestershire sauce all over the meat, then an even sprinkling of mustard, followed by a sprinkling of parmesan cheese.
3. Dip each cutlet into the beaten eggs and then press each side of the cutlets in the cracker crumbs.
4. Heat the oil over medium high heat (350° F if using an electric skillet), add the cutlets and fry about 3 minutes per side or until brown. Serve immediately with coleslaw, creamed potatoes, baked squash, carrot raisin salad or steamed carrots.

Franks and Beans

A long time ago, I introduced scratch cooking to a group of teens at a residential facility with this recipe.
One day their activities had been canceled due to weather, so I asked the cook if we could use the kitchen.
When I showed her this recipe, she hesitantly began to pull out the ingredients. I showed the kids how to measure,
stir and cook, as the cook quietly watched from the background. The kids were so impressed that their endeavor produced
such an awesome flavor, that they personally brought the cook a bowlful and joyfully gave her hugs of thanks
for the opportunity. After we had finished cleaning up, the kids went back to their quarters and the cook
smiled as she turned to me and said, "In 66 years I have never tasted better."

Serves 8-10

½ cup (1 stick) butter or margarine
1 large onion, thinly sliced
¼ cup plus 1 teaspoon flour
2 cups homemade tomato sauce
2 cups beef broth
2-3 tablespoons molasses
¼ cup vinegar
1 plus tablespoon Worcestershire sauce
1½ teaspoons brown sugar, or substitute with baking soda
2 teaspoons chili powder
2 pounds of frankfurters, cut into diagonal pieces
4 cups drained kidney beans (or a combination of pinto and kidney beans)
Salt and pepper to taste

1. Melt the butter in a large pot over medium heat; add the onions and sauté until tender.
2. Blend the flour into the tomato sauce, broth, molasses, vinegar, Worcestershire sauce, sugar and chili powder with a whisk. Stir this blend into the onions.
3. Decrease the heat to medium low, add the frankfurters and beans, cover the pot and simmer for 20-25 minutes or until all ingredients are thoroughly heated. Serve in bowls with a side salad.

Hint: Whisk in a little more flour if this is not thick enough to your liking.

Lemon Roasted Country Chicken

This pleasant recipe is full of wholesome, country goodness, while the flavor is certain to please any king or queen, even the little ones around your table.

Serves 4-6

Preheat oven 350° F

1 large chicken
2 lemons, cut into wedges
3-4 carrots, sliced in 3-4 sections
3-4 celery stalks, sliced into 3-4 sections
1 small onion, cut into wedges
6 new potatoes
2-3 tablespoons butter, margarine or olive oil
1 teaspoon rosemary, or 4 rosemary stems
½ teaspoon thyme
2-3 garlic cloves, sliced
Salt and lemon pepper to taste

1. Grease a large roasting pan with butter, margarine or pan spray.
2. Clean the chicken well under warm water; remove the skin if you prefer. Place the chicken into the prepared pan.
3. Rub the entire chicken with 1-2 of the lemon wedges. Stuff the open cavity with the remaining lemon wedges. Mix the rosemary and thyme into the butter/oil and rub this mixture all over the chicken. If there is excess, just add it to the open cavity with the lemon wedges.
4. Place the chicken into the prepared pan, cover with a lid or with foil and roast for 20-30 minutes and then add   all vegetables to the pan.
5. Allow all to roast for another 45-60 minutes. Pierce the chicken in a thick leg area, if the juices run clear and the vegetables are tender, the chicken is ready to be removed from the oven, carved and served. Place the vegetables into a serving bowl, carve the chicken on a large plate, and pour the reserved juice into a gravy bowl and serve.

Variation:
Rub the chicken with preferred choice of herbs; stuff it with chopped onions, carrots and celery, mixed with one generous cup dry bread cubes and roast for time allocated.

Mom's Creamy Chicken Bake

Growing up, I was often underfoot in my mother's kitchen, watching and learning as she prepared dinner every night. I was aware that this drove her nuts and such was stated often, but I was learning more than she ever knew. Much of what I saw and learned is now stored and cherished in my memory. As the years have passed, I often access these memories; I can picture in my mind just how and what she would use when making the terrific dinners prepared from scratch when I was growing up.

Serves 4-6

Preheat oven to 350° F

6 boneless chicken breasts, skins removed if desired
1 10–12-ounce can condensed Cream of Chicken soup
1 10–12-ounce can condensed Cream of Celery soup
1 cup chopped broccoli or sliced asparagus
¾ cup mushroom caps (optional)
1 teaspoon garlic powder
½ teaspoon dill (optional)
1 teaspoon poultry seasoning
2 tablespoons fresh diced parsley
¾ cup plus 2 tablespoons white wine or chicken broth

1. Grease a 9x13-inch pan well with butter, margarine or pan spray.
2. Place all ingredients except the chicken into the prepared pan and stir vigorously until thoroughly blended.
Place the chicken breasts on top of the sauce and bake for 60-75 minutes or until chicken is tender.
3. Best served over small shaped pasta or wide noodles.

Variation:
About 10 minutes prior to removing from oven, add 1-1½ cups shredded cheese to the top of the chicken and sauce.

Hasty Chicken Stew

*Have you ever had one of those days when you truly do not feel like cooking, fast food delivery is not available in your area, the kids are hungry and antsy, and your husband is coming home soon? The important statement here is that **you** do not feel like cooking, so what are you supposed to do? Why not toss together this fast and tasty recipe and smile between clenched teeth? Then sit back pleased with yourself and enjoy the moment as your tension miraculously flows away. Your family will share giggles and their daily tales between bites.*

Serves 4-6

2-3 tablespoons butter, margarine or oil
1-1 ½ pounds skinless, boneless chicken or turkey breasts, washed and fat removed
1-2 pounds potatoes, cut into ½–1-inch chunks
¼ teaspoon dill
½ teaspoon garlic powder
¼ teaspoon celery seed
Pinch of paprika
2-3 tablespoons cooking sherry, wine or unsweetened apple juice
Two 12-ounces jars, cans or 3-4 cups homemade chicken gravy
One 16-ounce package of frozen mixed vegetables, any variety
⅔ cup water
Sea salt and pepper to taste

1. Melt the butter or oil in a large skillet over medium high heat. Lower the temperature slightly, add the chicken, potatoes and spices and continue cooking while frequently stirring until the chicken is golden brown and the potatoes are tender, about 10-15 minutes. Add the sherry, wine or apple juice and continue stirring until most of the liquid evaporates.
2. Stir the gravy, frozen vegetables and water into the chicken and bring the mixture to a boil, then decrease the heat to medium low, cover and allow to cook for another 7-10 minutes. Serve hot with a side rolls or biscuits.

Rhonda's Raspberry Balsamic Chicken

Amazingly fabulous to taste and one of the fastest homemade dinners one could ever wish to prepare. I thank Rhonda dearly for this recipe; it is so very good that when served to friends or family all will think that they are eating the daily special from an eloquent restaurant. Why not turn off the TV, light the candles, put on soft background music, dim the lights, and revel in the excellence of this dish, which you once thought was time-consuming and could only be found in the eloquence of an expensive restaurant?

Serves 4

1 teaspoon vegetable oil
½ cup red onion, chopped
1½ teaspoons fresh thyme, minced or ½ teaspoon dry thyme
½ teaspoon sea salt, divided
4 skinned, boneless chicken breasts
⅓ cup seedless raspberry preserves
2 tablespoons balsamic vinegar
¼ teaspoon black pepper

1. Heat the oil in a large skillet over medium high heat. Add the onion and sauté for about 5 minutes. Sprinkle thyme and ¼ teaspoon salt over chicken. Add chicken to onions and sauté for 6 minutes on each side or until done. Remove chicken from pan; keep warm by wrapping or covering in foil.
2. Reduce the heat to medium, add the remaining salt, preserves, vinegar, and pepper to pan, stir constantly until preserves melt. Spoon the sauce over chicken and serve immediately with potatoes, pasta or rice.

Hint: Other fruit preserves, such as apricot, blackberry, peach, or cherry will also work in this recipe.

Easy Chicken

This recipe is much too easy to taste this good, but it really is. I often served this as a 'Dinner to Go' at the shop. It always sold out with requests for more, and I could never seem to make enough of it.

Serves 4-6

Preheat oven to 350° F

1-2 tablespoons oil, butter or margarine
4 chicken leg sections, (leg and attached thigh, although you can use breasts, legs and/or wings), cleaned and skinned, if you prefer
One 12-ounce jar of peach or apricot preserves
1 small bottle (1 ½-2 cups) Thousand Island dressing
1 envelope dry onion soup mix

1. Butter or oil the bottom of a 9x13-inch pan. Place the chicken into the pan, mix the remaining ingredients thoroughly together and pour over the chicken.
2. Bake for about 1 hour and 45 minutes or until a thick portion is pierced with a fork and the juices run clear.

Fried Chicken

I asked many southern friends to share a recipe for fried chicken to no avail, so I had to come up with my own. I wanted a recipe fit for a southern gentleman; crunchy, juicy and literally finger-lickin' good. According to all who have tasted this divine version, I did it. This chicken will have your kids licking all the goodness off of their fingers, your husband and/or friends kissing your cheek and all bellies served will be pleasantly full.

Serves 6-8

1 large skillet or a large electric skillet (if frying a large amount, use 2 large skillets)

3 pounds assorted chicken pieces, with or without skin
1 cup plus buttermilk
1½ cup flour
½ cup corn flour (yellow)
Salt and pepper to taste
¼ teaspoon minced garlic

½ teaspoon onion powder
2 teaspoons paprika
¼ teaspoon dried thyme or 1 teaspoon fresh, minced
¼ teaspoon dried sage or 1 teaspoon fresh, minced
⅛ teaspoon baking powder
Vegetable or corn oil for frying

1. Thoroughly wash the chicken under warm water, pat the pieces dry with paper towels and place them evenly into the bottom of a large shallow dish, pan or bowl. Pour the buttermilk over the chicken, cover and leave this to soak several hours in the refrigerator, or refrigerate overnight.
2. Place all dry ingredients into a paper or plastic bag. Drain the chicken, and add one piece at a time to the bag and shake, making sure to coat all sides well and evenly. Remove the chicken piece and place onto a piece of waxed paper. Continue until all chicken pieces are coated; discard any excess coating. Allow all pieces to sit for at least 10-12 minutes or until the coating dries. (This step is important because it helps the coating stick to the chicken while frying.)
3. While the coating is drying, pour approximately one inch of oil into the chosen pan and heat over medium to medium high heat (electric skillet set heat to 355-360° F).
4. Place the chicken into the pan, making sure that the pieces are not touching and that the pan is not overcrowded, and fry each side for 3-4 minutes. Reduce the heat to medium-medium low (electric skillet to 325° F), and cook the chicken in the oil, turning occasionally for another 30-40 minutes or until pierced and the juice runs clear. Smaller pieces such as legs and/or wings will take about 20-25 minutes. Place the fried chicken onto a plate or shallow bowl lined paper with towels for a minute or two and serve.

Variations:
• For a sweeter flavor, mix 2 tablespoons of honey or maple syrup into the buttermilk prior to soaking the chicken. Add 2 tablespoons brown sugar to the coating mix. You could also add ½ cup finely chopped pecans to the coating mix for a wonderful, nutty flavor.
• Boneless turkey breast or tenders can be used instead of chicken pieces.

Teriyaki Chicken Island Style

This fantastic recipe can be cooked on a grill or in a skillet and is perfect to serve when catering to family or friends. The divine splendor that this supplies to your palate will temporarily provide you with the impression that you have left the mainland and gone to a tropical island. Enjoy the trip; but don't forget your sandals and make sure to carry an extra fork so that you may share a few bites with all you meet during your imaginary journey!

Serves 3-4

1 pound skinless, boneless chicken breasts, washed and defatted
¾ cup teriyaki sauce
½ pineapple, peeled, cored and sliced with juice; put aside in a small bowl
  or substitute 15–16-ounce can sliced pineapple
1-2 tablespoons oil
1 teaspoon minced garlic
1 tablespoon minced onions, scallions or shallots
1 large or 2 small zucchinis, sliced
1½ cups chopped broccoli
3 cups cooked wild rice
⅔ plus cup chopped and toasted macadamia nuts

1. Mix the teriyaki sauce, reserved pineapple juice, onions and garlic in a large bowl. Add the chicken, cover the bowl and marinate in the refrigerator 6-8 hours or overnight.
2. Prepare the rice according to package directions and keep warm.
3. If cooking inside, steam, boil or microwave the broccoli and zucchini until crisp but tender, or place them onto a large sheet of foil, add 1-2 tablespoons of butter or margarine, wrap the foil tightly around the vegetables and place this package on the grill for about 20 minutes. Remove and mix into the cooked rice, or keep warm as a side dish.
4. If cooking inside, heat the oil over medium in a large skillet. Add the marinated chicken, and sprinkle with a little of the marinade. Turn the chicken over 2-3 times making sure to cook evenly, decrease the heat to low, add ¼ cup of marinade to the skillet, top each chicken piece with pineapple, cover and allow to simmer for 15-20 minutes or until the juices flow clear when a chicken piece is pierced. If grilling the chicken, brush generously with the marinade several times until the chicken has cooked through. Just before it has finished cooking, place a pineapple slice on top of each breast and brush with marinade and grill for another few minutes.
5. Heat the remaining teriyaki sauce and place in a bowl or several small bowls and use to dip the chicken into.
6. Remove all foods from heat source, divide rice evenly between serving plates, and top each mound of rice with the chicken and pineapple, sprinkled with the macadamia nuts.

Hint: To toast macadamia nuts, sprinkle them onto a cookie sheet, place in a preheated oven, set at 375-400° F for 1-2 minutes, no longer. Remove from the heat and cool.

Chicken Cordon Bleu My Way

The simplicity of this elegant dish is what makes it so special. Whenever I order a tempting entree at a restaurant and end up a little disappointed with the flavor, I often come back home determined to develop a better version. This is how I came up with the following recipe. A waiter may never serve this dish to you or yours in a white shirt and black bow tie; however, the taste will ensure a positive impression and have your guests and family coming back for more again and again.

Serves 3-4

Preheat oven to 350° F

1 pound boneless, skinless chicken breasts
8 ounces sliced ham
8 ounces shredded or sliced Gruyere or Swiss cheese
1 egg
1 plus cup buttermilk or milk
2 plus cups breadcrumbs
1 scant teaspoon garlic powder

½ teaspoon onion powder
1 tablespoon minced fresh parsley
A pinch of dill (optional)
¼ teaspoon each thyme and marjoram
¼ cup white wine
Salt and pepper to taste
2-3 tablespoons butter, margarine or oil

1. Wash and remove all fat from the chicken breasts; pound each with a meat tenderizer or mallet until flattened to about ¼-inch.
2. Place buttermilk and egg in a large shallow bowl and beat thoroughly.
3. Layer each breast with the ham and cheese, drizzle with wine, roll each up like a jellyroll and hold together with a toothpick. Place each roll into the buttermilk mix to soak for a few minutes. Turn once so that all sides are soaked in the liquid.
4. Place the breadcrumbs into a shallow bowl and mix in all the spices.
5. Grease a 9x13-inch pan with butter, margarine or pan spray and melt the butter in the pan or spread oil around in the pan.
6. Coat each chicken roll in the breadcrumbs and place in the prepared pan. Bake for 35-45 minutes or until the crust is golden and when a roll is pierced the juices run clear.   *OR*
   You could fry the rolls in a large skillet. Simply heat ¼ cup of oil in a pan over medium high heat, melt 4-5 tablespoons butter in the pan and when the butter begins to foam add the chicken rolls and fry until golden brown and crisp. Turn each roll often until done.
7. Serve hot, drizzled with Mornay Sauce (p. 339)

Variation:
Substitute spinach and sliced mushrooms for the ham and proceed as directed.

Country Casserole

The fantastic thing about casseroles is that they provide a delicious means for using leftovers and are not very time-consuming to prepare. Years ago at a large holiday gathering, there was so much leftover food, the host handed each guest a large plate or container full of leftovers as we departed. The next night when the dinner bell clanged in my stomach, I put the leftovers into a casserole dish, added a tad of this and that and cooked it all together. De-licious!

Serves 4-5

Preheat oven to 350° F

½ cup (1 stick) butter or margarine, divided into 3- and 5-tablespoon chunks
2 cups dried bread cubes
½ cup chopped onions
⅓ slightly rounded cup flour
2 cups light cream (heavy cream will work just as well and will supply a richer flavor)
1 cup milk
½ teaspoon sage
¼ teaspoon minced garlic
1½ plus cups frozen peas
2 cups cooked cubed ham
3 cups cooked chopped chicken or turkey
Salt and lemon pepper to taste

1. Melt 3 tablespoons butter in a medium saucepan over medium heat, add the bread cubes, stir to coat them with the melted butter and set aside.
2. In a larger saucepan, melt the 5 tablespoons of butter over medium heat, add the onions and sauté until tender. Whisk in the flour and cook a little more than a minute. Remove from the heat, stir in the cream, milk and spices, then return to the heat and stir constantly until this comes to a full rolling boil.
3. Immediately remove from the heat and stir in the peas and meats.
4 Grease a 2-quart casserole dish or 12x7-inch pan and pour this mixture into the pan.
5. Spread the top with the bread cubes and bake for 30-35 minutes or until the mixture is bubbly and the bread cubes are golden brown. Serve over pasta, potatoes or rice.

Variation:
Substitute the peas with chopped broccoli and/or asparagus.

Chicken Florentine à la Casserole

This is an outstanding dish to prepare, especially when in a hurry and/or unexpected company is coming over shortly. Imagine, you have just arrived home from work or ferrying the kids to and from activities. You check your messages and hear one from your husband informing you that a wealthy potential client is coming over for dinner. "Oh no!" is your first thought and as you look at the clock, you realize that you only have about an hour to put together an impressive meal. ARGH! No problem, all you need to do is follow this recipe; the client will sign on the dotted line before dessert is served.

Serves 6-8

Preheat oven to 375° F

3 pounds boneless, skinless chicken, cooked or boiled and chopped into bite-size pieces
18-20 ounces fresh spinach, washed and chopped, (two 10-ounce frozen bags works fine)
1 tablespoon butter, margarine or canola spread
¾ teaspoon minced garlic
Pinch of lemon basil or basil
Pinch of marjoram
1 tablespoon plus 1 teaspoon flour
⅓ cup light or heavy cream
3 tablespoons butter, margarine or canola spread
3 tablespoons plus 1 teaspoon flour
¾ cup light or heavy cream
¾ cup chicken broth
1 cup shredded Parmesan cheese
Sea salt and pepper to taste

1. Boil or microwave the spinach in water until dark green and thoroughly cooked, drain completely and pat with paper towels to remove most of the excess water.
2. Melt 1 tablespoon butter in a medium to large saucepan, mix in the spices. Over medium heat, whisk in the flour and ⅓ cup of cream. Stir constantly until this mixture bubbles and thickens, remove from heat.
3. Stir the cooked spinach into spiced cream mixture and pour it into a 2-quart casserole dish. Sprinkle the chopped chicken all over the top of the spinach mixture and put aside.
4. Make a roux by melting the remaining 3 tablespoons butter in a medium saucepan, whisk in the flour and continue to whisk until a paste forms. Add the remaining cream, broth, salt and pepper. Continue to stir over medium heat until thickened; pour over the chicken and spinach mixture. Sprinkle the top with Parmesan cheese and bake uncovered for 25-30 minutes. Serve hot over pasta of choice.

Sweet Poultry Kabobs

Sweet, tangy and positively delicious, these special kabobs are a must-have at all BBQs.

Serves 4-6

6 large skinless, boneless chicken or equivalent amount of turkey breast, washed and cut into 1-inch pieces
1 yellow pepper, chopped into 1–2-inch chunks
1 red pepper, chopped into 1–2-inch chunks
1 large yellow squash, chopped into 1–2-inch chunks
2 medium zucchinis, chopped into 1–2-inch chunks
2 large red or yellow onions or 1 bag of pearl onions, chop large onion into 1–2-inch chunks
6 ounces Portabello mushrooms caps, washed and chopped into 1–2-inch chunks
1 cup chopped pineapple pieces
1 cup honey
½ cup spicy mustard
3 tablespoons soy sauce or teriyaki sauce
1½ tablespoons cider vinegar
3 tablespoons corn starch
⅓ cup water

1. Preheat the grill to a moderate heat.
2. Prepare the sauce in a 2-quart sauce pan. Fill the pan with the honey, mustard, soy sauce and vinegar and heat at medium high until boiling.
3. In a small bowl, mix the cornstarch into the water until smooth; add to the heated ingredients and stir constantly until it boils. Continuing to stir and boil for 2 minutes or until it has thickened slightly. Remove from the heat and take out to the grill.
4. Alternating the poultry pieces and vegetables, thread onto six 12-inch skewers. Make sure to alternate the colors of the vegetables and poultry as you go for a pretty effect.
5. Brush all vegetables and poultry with the sauce, and place on the grill. Continue cooking and brushing with sauce occasionally, until the poultry is done and the vegetables are tender but crisp, about 20-25 minutes.

Cookie's Chicken BBQ

Cookie is one of the Lovely Ladies and I grew up often hearing how marvelous her Chicken BBQ was. I remembered how the Ladies would rave about it; so when I began this book I called and asked her to share. Living up to my reputation of being a pain in the fanny to these ladies, I called and emailed her often, bugging her to share the goodness. Finally, I received an email with this recipe attached. The next day, I made it and discovered why the Lovely Ladies had a reason to rave!

Serves 4-6

Preheat oven to 350° F

1 broiler or fryer chicken, washed thoroughly and cut up
¼ cup soy sauce
2 tablespoons vinegar
¾ cup ketchup
¾ cup water
½ cup brown sugar
1 onion, diced
Coarsely ground pepper to taste
1-2 minced garlic cloves

1. Place the chicken pieces into a baking dish.
2. Mix all the ingredients together in a bowl. Pour over chicken in pan.
3. Bake uncovered 1½ hours or until browned. I let it get very brown, as if it was on the barbecue.

Hints: This recipe can be doubled or tripled easily. This recipe can also be made on the grill, the same way it is in the oven, just place the grillproof pan on the grill, put the lid down and cook.

Chicken Parmigiana

A festive dish indeed! My version sways just a bit from the more traditional varieties served daily in various venues around the globe, but is just as good. For starters I do not bread the chicken, nor do I use a smooth tomato sauce, instead I smother the chicken with my Chunky Italian Sauce adding a diversity of tastes with each bite. Many who have had the opportunity to be presented with a plateful have responded with recipe requests and statements such as, "This one of the best Chicken Parmesans I've ever tasted!"

Serves 8-10

Preheat oven to 340-350° F

1 cup ricotta cheese
3 tablespoons Parmesan cheese
1 egg
1 tablespoon fresh diced parsley
Pinch of minced garlic
2-3 tablespoons butter or margarine
4-5 pounds skinless, boneless chicken breasts, washed and cleaned of fat
1¼ teaspoons Italian seasoning or a couple pinches each parsley, basil, oregano, marjoram, thyme and sage, mixed
    together in a small container
4-6 cups Chunky Italian Sauce (p. 199), Marinara Sauce (p. 198), or your favorite bottled Italian tomato sauce
1 teaspoon minced garlic
1 cup freshly grated Parmesan cheese
¼ cup grated Romano cheese (more can be used if you prefer)
12-16 ounces sliced Provolone and/or mozzarella cheese

1. In a small bowl, thoroughly mix together the ricotta, 3 tablespoons Parmesan, egg, parsley and pinch of minced garlic. Set aside.
2. Grease the bottom and sides of a 9x13-inch pan with butter or margarine. Place each chicken breast into the pan and sprinkle slightly with Italian seasoning.
3. Pour the sauce into a bowl and mix in a teaspoon of minced garlic. Then take a teaspoon of the ricotta mix, form it into a little ball, and very gently mix the ball into the sauce, making sure not to break it up. Repeat using all the ricotta. Pour the sauce over the chicken and sprinkle the top with Parmesan and Romano cheese.
4. Cover the pan with foil and bake for 45-55 minutes. Remove the foil, layer the cheese slices over the top and return to the oven until the cheese begins to brown.
5. Serve hot with spaghetti or any chosen pasta and a side salad.

Roast Turkey

Roasting a turkey is a long and tenacious process; there is much to do to prepare the bird for the oven.
However, all the time involved is worth the effort, for the flavor is superb. As the hours of temptation build up,
I long for my favorite part of the process, picking and tasting little bites just as it comes out of the oven.
For some reason, these little tidbits make the whole process worth it for me.

Plan ¾ pound of whole turkey per person when deciding what size to buy, or how many to invite for dinner.

Preheat oven to 325° F

DRESSING/STUFFING:
2 tablespoons melted butter, margarine or canola spread
1¼ chicken broth and/or unsweetened apple juice
4 cups dried bread cubes
1½ cups diced celery
1½ cups diced sweet yellow onions or pearl onions, sliced in half
1-1½ cups raisins, dark and golden, craisins and/or dried cherries
2 Granny Smith apples, peeled, cored and diced
¼ teaspoon paprika (optional)
¼ teaspoon each poultry seasoning, dill, celery seed, parsley and minced garlic
Sea salt and pepper to taste

TURKEY:
One 18–24-pound young turkey, preferably fresh; otherwise, completely thawed
2-3 tablespoons butter, margarine or canola spread
1-2 teaspoons minced garlic
½ teaspoon celery seed
¾ teaspoon basil
¾ teaspoons dry parsley
Dash of paprika (optional)
2 teaspoons honey, brown sugar or unsweetened apple juice (optional)

GRAVY:
2 tablespoons pan drippings
1 cup white wine or chicken broth
2-3 tablespoons flour or cornstarch

1. In a large bowl, mix all dressing ingredients together and set aside to soak for a few minutes.
2. To prepare the turkey, first remove the bag containing the neck and giblets from the cavity and rinse the inside and outside of the bird thoroughly with cool water. If you need to loosen the legs from the clamp, gently push down on

the legs and they will slip right out of it. Once washed, place the turkey on the roasting rack inside of the pan, fill the cavity with the prepared dressing and reset the legs in the clamp.

3. Mix together the butter, spices and honey, sugar or juice. Rub this all over the turkey; including the legs, wings and thighs. Salt and pepper the top and sides, fill the bottom of the pan with ½-inch of water and the turkey pieces previously removed from the cavity. Place the rack in the pan, the turkey on the rack, cover the pan with a loose foil tent and place the pan in the oven.

4. Baste the turkey about once every half hour or so. Remove the foil about 1 hour before the turkey has finished roasting, allowing the top to brown. You will know when the turkey has finished roasting when the thermometer pops up and/or reads 175-185° F. It will take approximately 5-7 hours for a large stuffed bird, 4-5 hours if not stuffed.

5. Remove the pan from the oven. Allow the bird to cool for a few minutes before removing it from the rack and placing it onto a plate to be carved. Spoon the dressing into an ovenproof bowl before carving, drizzle it with 2-3 tablespoons of the drippings and place it into the oven to keep warm. Remove the neck and gizzards from the pan and set aside to serve with the turkey.

6. Prepare the gravy. Remove about 2 tablespoons of the drippings from the pan and put into a large cup. Add 1 cup white wine or chicken broth and 2-3 tablespoons flour (or cornstarch) and whisk vigorously breaking up any lumps, then add this to the drippings in the pan and whisk continuously over medium heat until the gravy thickens and no lumps remain. Pour gravy into a gravy bowl, or keep warm in the roasting pan over low heat.

The Grand Bottled Turkey

Sit back and enjoy this Thanksgiving story and a surprisingly wonderful recipe. It may take a bit to explain, but I guarantee that this will be one of the juiciest, best flavored and likely the most expensive turkey that you'll ever indulge in.

It all began one snowy Thanksgiving morning. The day before, I had purchased a fresh young turkey with the intention of impressing my new boyfriend with a traditional turkey dinner. I prepared the turkey, just as listed on pages 236 and 237, only I did not add any water to the bottom of the pan. I basted the bird with the limited drippings and did everything properly, so I thought.

With over two feet of fresh snow on the ground and another two feet expected, the turkey in the oven, and hours to kill, we decided to take my four dogs out to play. We were having so much fun in the snow that I didn't realize how much time had passed. Suddenly, I remembered the turkey in the oven!

I ran into the house as fast as I could to baste my turkey before it dried out. But I was too late! There were no drippings to baste with, and this 22-pound bird was drying out with each passing minute. I was trying to think of what to do when I spotted a large unopened bottle of Grand Marnier. Instinct suggested that this exquisite orange liqueur might just rescue my bird.

I used a fork to poke holes all over the turkey, and then I poured ¾ of the bottle of Grand Marnier over it. I put the foil back on and left the liqueur to do its job, hoping it would rescue my turkey from the disgrace of dryness.

It worked! A while later my friend carved into a lusciously moist and tender bird. Juice was flowing out of each and every slice, the flavor was amazing and he never knew that our first Thanksgiving together was rescued by a bottle of Grand Marnier.

Anne's Homespun Turkey Skillet

Country spice and goodness all made in one pan; a home cooked meal doesn't get much better than this. This is a fine recipe for all who avoid red meat, but still want to enjoy a hearty meal. I have made this dish often since Anne shared it with me; one of my neighbors has requested the recipe because her husband loves it, as I am sure you will too.

Serves 3-4

2 tablespoons olive oil
1 pound ground turkey
1 cup chopped onion
3-5 chopped garlic cloves
One 28-ounce can whole tomatoes, undrained
One 12-ounce can corn kernels, drained
One 12-ounce can kidney beans, drained
1 cup uncooked elbow macaroni
1 tablespoon chili powder
1 teaspoon basil
Salt and pepper to taste
4 ounces shredded cheese
Sour cream

1. Heat a skillet over medium high or preheat an electric skillet to 425° F. Add the oil and meat, and stir frequently for 5-6 minutes. Stir in the salt and pepper.
2. Add the onions, garlic, tomatoes, corn, beans and macaroni to the meat and heat until it bubbles.
3. Lower the heat to medium or 350°F and continue cooking until the macaroni is tender, about 20 minutes, then stir in the chili powder and basil and heat through.
4. Serve on individual plates or bowl, sprinkle with cheese and a couple dollops of sour cream.

Anne's variations:
• This can also be served topped with a fried egg.
• Use buffalo or yak meat in place of turkey.

Country Chicken Pot Pie

*The comfort supplied by a pot pie is incomparable and this recipe is often described in one word, AWESOME!
I happen to have two recipes for pot pie; the first is made with leftovers, while the next one is a bit more time consuming,
but very, very tasty. So why not make both, on separate occasions, and let your loved ones determine which
they like the best? Both have been savored and requested by family, friends and customers for years.*

Serves 4-6

Preheat oven to 375° F

⅓ cup butter
6 tablespoons flour
2 cups canned or homemade chicken/turkey broth
1 cup heavy cream
salt and freshly ground pepper to taste
¾ cup frozen peas, thawed and drained
2-3 carrots, washed and sliced diagonally into 1/2-inch pieces
2-3 celery stalks, sliced diagonally into 1/2-inch pieces
12 small pearl onions, or 1 onion, diced
¼ teaspoon each dill, celery seed, thyme, minced garlic and nutmeg or cloves
1 cup fresh green beans, cleaned, ends pinched off and sliced
4 cups bite-size pieces of leftover cooked chicken/turkey
Two 9-inch Pie Crusts, prepackaged or Grandma's Pie Crust, double recipe (p. 297)

1. Thoroughly grease a deep dish pie pan with butter, margarine or pan spray and fit the pie crust into the pan.
2. Melt the butter in a saucepan and stir in the flour. Cook and stir this mixture for 2-3 minutes over medium heat or until it turns pasty and a light brown color. Gradually add the turkey broth, cream, pepper and salt to taste. Cook until thickened and smooth, about 6-7 minutes.
3. In the meantime, place the vegetables and onions into a bowl, cover completely with water and microwave this until the vegetables are tender but still crisp. Drain the water and add the vegetables to the saucepan. Stir this for a minute or two, add the chicken/turkey pieces and stir to coat.
4. Pour all into the prepared pie pan, place the pastry shell on top, fold and flute the edges to seal, poke holes all over the top and bake for 35-45 minutes or until pie shell is golden brown. Allow the pie to rest for 5 minutes before serving.

Nothing-To-It Pot Pie

This is a two-pot pie; one pot is used to prepare it, the other is used to bake it. I make this often because it is so splendidly simple to prepare. Additionally, the flavor from this country-style dinner pie will knock your socks off and hopefully get your kids to eat vegetables of various colors. I do not use potatoes in my pot pies; I think they add more starch than necessary. But if you must, add two peeled and diced potatoes when adding the celery and onions to the first pot.

Serves 4-6

1 plus pound skinless, boneless chicken/turkey breasts, washed with fat removed and cut into 1-inch pieces
2 tablespoons butter or margarine
3 carrots, washed and sliced into ¼-inch pieces
3 celery stalks, washed and sliced into ¼-inch pieces
1 small onion, diced
1 cup frozen peas, thawed and drained
1 cup corn kernels, fresh, canned or frozen, thawed and drained
1 cup chopped broccoli or cauliflower
¼ teaspoon each, dill, thyme, rosemary and nutmeg or cloves
½ teaspoon garlic powder
2 packets dry chicken or turkey gravy
Two 9-inch Pie Shells, prepackaged or Grandma's Pie Crust, double recipe (p. 297)

1. Place the chicken and butter into a large stockpot, cover with water and cook over medium high heat. Once this boils, skim the scum from the top of the water, lower the heat to medium, add the carrots and continue to cook for 20-30 minutes and then add the celery, broccoli and onions. Bring back to a boil, lower the heat to medium low and cook for 10-15 minutes or until the carrots can be pierced but are still crisp.
2. Preheat oven to 375° F, grease a deep dish pie pan with butter, margarine or pan spray and line it with one of the pie shells.
3. Decrease the heat to low and vigorously stir the dry gravy mixes and spices into the pot, breaking up any lumps as you stir. Add the peas and corn and simmer for a few minutes or until the gravy begins to thicken.
4. Once the gravy has thickened, pour into the prepared pie shell, cover with the remaining shell, fold and flute the edges and bake for 30-40 minutes or until the crust is golden brown.

Poor Man's Scampi

I came up with this unique, inexpensive recipe during my first year in college. Because I have always enjoyed playing with food, I often created alternatives to the unappealing food offered by the cafeteria. This recipe was developed in my dorm room one cool, rainy summer eve. All reveled in this homemade dish, and many actually asked for the recipe. By the way, every child that I have ever prepared this for just loved this, as I am sure yours will also.

Serves 2-4

1 plus pound salad shrimp
½ cup (1 stick) butter
3-4 scallions diced
1 lemon
1-2 garlic cloves, minced or 1 teaspoon garlic powder
1 cup (more or less) white wine
One 16-ounce package small shell pasta or macaroni, cooked according to package directions
1½ cups peas, frozen and thawed or 1 can, drained (optional)
Parmesan cheese for sprinkling

1. In a medium saucepan or skillet melt the butter over medium heat, squeeze in the juice from the lemon, add the wine, garlic and shrimp and heat until heated through.
2. Pour the cooked pasta into the shrimp mixture, stir to completely coat, heat through and serve in bowls with a sprinkling of Parmesan cheese.

Seafood Scampi

Sensationally spectacular!

Serves 8

4 pounds large raw shrimp, shelled deveined, and split open down the back (butterflied)
¾ cup (1½ sticks) butter (no substitutes)
¾ cup extra virgin olive oil
3 tablespoons fresh squeezed lemon juice
1/4 cup finely diced scallions, sweet onions or shallots
1 tablespoon minced garlic
3-4 tablespoons finely diced fresh parsley
½ cup white wine (optional)
Smidgen of cracked pepper to taste

1. Rinse the shrimp under cold water and pat dry with paper towels.
2. Melt the butter over medium high heat. Mix together the oil, lemon juice, garlic, scallions, wine and pepper in a bowl and add to the melted butter.
3. Decrease the heat to medium low; add the shrimp to the skillet, stirring to coat all sides; and simmer for about 5-8 minutes or until the shrimp have turned white, slightly curled and are firm to touch.
4. Heat a shallow bowl in the microwave, and using tongs, remove shrimp from the skillet and place them into the warmed bowl. Pour the sauce from the pan over the shrimp and garnish with the parsley.
5. Best served with angel hair pasta and a side salad.

Hint: If using frozen shrimp, wash them well under cool water and then pat off the excess water with paper towels.

Variation:
For a tangy and citrus flavor, substitute Grand Marnier or Cointreau Liqueur for the wine.

Crab Imperial

Absolutely, positively heavenly! My mother and I would occasionally go to a restaurant by the bay in S. New Jersey that made the best Crab imperial I had ever tasted. Late one afternoon, I began to crave a taste for this incredible dish, so Mom and I went to go there for dinner. As we arrived, all that remained of this restaurant were a lot of wooden planks and boards where the windows and doors once were. A large sign said it all; "Out of Business". Saddened by the loss of such a fine establishment, Mom wanted to go back home. With the scent of the sea surrounding me, my craving grew stronger, so I suggested that we stop at the fish market on the way back to the house. At the market, she bought a dinner to go, and I ordered some fresh crab meat, in addition to picking up a few necessary ingredients. I then made the following recipe based on the flavors in my memory. As I shivered with delight over my creation, Mom put her dinner in the refrigerator and we relished contently in a taste of heaven until it all disappeared.

Serves 3-4

2 tablespoons butter (no substitutes)
2 tablespoons flour
½ cup plus 1 tablespoon whole milk
2 egg yolks, well beaten
1-2 tablespoons finely diced green pepper
1 pimento, finely diced
1-2 drops Worcestershire sauce
1 drop Tabasco sauce
1 tablespoon fresh minced parsley
1 pound cooked crabmeat, preferably fresh, but frozen or canned will work fine

1. Over medium heat, melt the butter in a shallow sauce pan or in a medium skillet. Add the flour, mix thoroughly into a paste. Add the milk and continue stirring until thickened.
2. Add all remaining ingredients to the pan and stir constantly until heated through. Do not allow this mixture to boil, rather heat it slowly, but thoroughly. Turn on the broiler in your oven.
3. Pour into 3-4 individual casserole dishes, place the dishes under the preheated broiler for 2-3 minutes or until the tops are slightly browned and serve.

Variation:
Add 1 cut up cooked lobster tail to the other ingredients and cook as directed.

Shrimp Kabobs

One summer evening, on the way to see friends, I stopped at the store to pick up something for dinner as it was my turn to bring the food. I bought a little of this and that and we made these marvelous fruity kabobs on the grill that night.

Serves 3-4

1 plus cup teriyaki sauce
1 teaspoon minced garlic
Juice from ½ an orange
Juice from ½ a lemon
2-3 tablespoons finely diced scallions
Pinch of dry ginger
2 zucchinis, sliced into 1-2-inch pieces
2 small to medium Vidalia onions, cut into wedges
1½ navel oranges, peeled with sections separated
1 plus pound raw large shrimp, fresh or frozen, thawed, shelled, deveined, washed, and butterflied

1. Heat the grill to medium heat.
2. Make the teriyaki sauce by mixing the first 6 ingredients together in a bowl and set aside.
3. Thread the remaining ingredients onto 6-8 skewers, alternating the various ingredients.
4. Brush with teriyaki sauce, place each skewer on the grill, and continue to brush the kabobs with sauce and turning until the shrimp is cooked and the vegetables are tender and crisp, about 20-30 minutes.
5. Place the extra teriyaki sauce on the table for dipping and serve kabobs hot.

Variation:
Substitute chicken/turkey pieces, steak or pork pieces, large scallops or lobster meat for the shrimp.

Seafood Au Gratin

What can I say? This recipe combines some of my favorite foods, all served on one platter; oh yeah! This magnificent dish provides a luxurious flavor, fit for royalty and sure to please and impress all who have the tasty opportunity to bask in its glory.

Serves 4-6

½-pound raw medium shrimp, shelled, deveined, and split open down the back (butterflied)
½-¾ pound large scallops
2-3 lobster tails, cut into pieces (and claws if available)
2 cups crab meat, lump, claws, legs or canned and drained (whatever you can get)
¼ cup (½ stick) butter

1 teaspoon plus minced garlic
Pinch of dill
2 tablespoons fresh squeezed lemon juice
½ cup or so of white wine
One batch of Mom's Mashed potatoes (p. 5)
2 tablespoons minced fresh parsley for garnish
Mornay Sauce, recipe follows

1. Melt the butter over medium heat in a deep skillet. Add the wine, garlic, dill and juice and stir. Add the seafood, lower heat to medium low and stir occasionally until thoroughly cooked, about 15-20 minutes. Remove from heat, drain the liquid into a bowl and put aside.
2. Have the mashed potatoes previously made but still warm. Line a large deep dish serving plate with the potatoes; spread some up the sides of the plate, like a pie crust.
3. Preheat oven to 275-300° F. Layer the seafood over the potatoes, and drizzle with a smidgen of the reserved liquid. Cover with foil and place in the oven to warm while preparing the Mornay Sauce.

MORNAY SAUCE:
3 tablespoons butter
⅓ cup finely diced sweet yellow onions, scallions or shallots
1 large bay leaf
3 tablespoons flour

Sea salt and pepper to taste
3 cups milk
¾ cup shredded Gruyere or Swiss cheese
⅓ cup grated Parmesan cheese
2 egg yolks, well beaten

1. Melt the butter over medium heat in a large saucepan. Add the onion and sauté until tender, about 5-7 minutes. Add the flour and stir over medium for 3-4 minutes but do not allow the flour to brown. Gradually whisk in the milk, add the bay leaf, salt and pepper, stir occasionally and allow this mixture to thicken.
2. Remove the pan from the heat and let the sauce cool slightly. Gradually add the cheese and stir until melted.
3. Remove about 2 tablespoons of the sauce and mix it into the beaten egg yolks, then gently stir this back into the pan and cover to keep warm on top of the stove.
4. Remove the seafood platter from the oven, and drizzle lightly with the sauce. Pour the sauce into a gravy bowl and bring it to the table so that more sauce can be added to each plate.

Hint: Any combination of seafood can be used in this recipe.

Variation:
Newburg Sauce, (p. 338) may be used instead of the Mornay Sauce.

Elizabeth's Crab Cakes

*Elizabeth shares my passion for seafood, so when she made me this recipe, I found these cakes so good,
I instantly requested that she allow me to share it with my readers. There was no hesitation, for she smiled brightly
and immediately wrote it down while stating that this recipe is wonderfully easy, even her kids can make it. Neither of us
may be wealthy with coins and greenbacks, but our palates share a wealth of well-prepared foods, especially seafood.*

Makes 6 cakes

1 pound crabmeat (be sure all cartilage and shells are removed from crabmeat)
1 cup Italian-seasoned breadcrumbs
1 large egg (or 2 small)
¼ cup or so mayonnaise
1 teaspoon Worcestershire sauce
1 teaspoon dry mustard
½ teaspoon salt
¼ teaspoon pepper
Butter or oil for frying

1. In a bowl, mix together the breadcrumbs, egg, mayonnaise and seasonings. Add crabmeat and mix gently, but thoroughly. If mixture is too dry, add a little more mayo. Shape into 6 cakes.
2. Over medium heat, add just enough oil/butter to a frying pan to prevent sticking, place the cakes into the pan, and fry until browned; about 5 minutes on each side. Remove them from the pan, place onto a plate lined with paper towels for a few seconds to soak up any excess grease.
3. Serve with fresh lemon wedges and/or cocktail sauce.

Carolyn's Cucumber Salmon

Carolyn, my tanned island friend, shared this spectacular recipe with me years ago. She knows that I prefer salmon cool and made this one late afternoon while I was visiting. I knew that she could cook, but never knew how well and was highly impressed with this remarkably easy recipe. Much too good to not share, revel in the delightfully light flavors offered by this perfectly lovely dish.

Serves 2-3

Preheat oven to 350° F
Two 8-ounce salmon steaks
1 tablespoon butter
¼ teaspoon dill
½ teaspoon minced garlic
1 English cucumber, peeled
3 tablespoons mayonnaise
⅔ cup sour cream or plain yogurt
2 tablespoons fresh squeezed lemon juice
Sea salt, white pepper and a pinch of dill to taste

1. Place each salmon steak onto a piece of foil; spread each with a bit of butter, garlic and a sprinkling of dill. Wrap the foil around each piece, twist the edges together and bake for 40-45 minutes. Remove from the oven, drain the juice and allow to cool to room temperature, or refrigerate until cold.
2. Shred the cucumber in a food processor, remove from the processor and mix with all the remaining ingredients.
3. Serve salmon with dollops of the cucumber sauce, fresh fruit salad and a few rolls.

Cheesy Crab in Pastry

Decadence at its finest. This is a perfect dish to serve on special occasions or when entertaining a small group of guests. Additionally, I have found that if I am preparing this recipe for children and adults, many of the kids have a tendency to prefer Monterey Jack or marbled cheese over the rich, matured flavor of Brie. And, if you do not want to mess with the phyllo sheets, puff pastry works just as well.

Serves 4

¾ pound of fresh or canned lump crabmeat, drained and gently patted dry
1 large previously-cooked lobster tail, cut into bite-size pieces
2 scallions, thinly sliced, including part of the green stem
½ teaspoon minced garlic
pinch of dill (optional, a drop or 2 of hot sauce will also work)
20 sheets phyllo dough, divided into 2 stacks or 2 sheets of puff pastry sheets, thawed
¼ cup butter, melted for spreading onto the individual phyllo sheets
10 ounces Brie cheese, frozen removed from freezer and rind removed while still very cold
1 egg
1 tablespoon water

1. In a medium bowl, gently combine the crabmeat, scallion, garlic, pepper and dill or hot sauce.
2. Prepare the phyllo dough according to the package directions, making sure to spread a little melted butter on each sheet. Stack the sheets together, then cut the stacked layers into 4 equal squares. If using puff pastry, cut each sheet in half and roll each out into a square.
3. Cut the Brie in half width-wise, from the center across, so that you have 2 rounds, then cut each in half so that you have 4 equally sized pieces of Brie. Place each into the center of the prepared phyllo or puff pastry squares.
4. Mound the crabmeat mixture on top of each round of Brie and then fold the sheets/pastry over the top. Twist and pinch the edges to completely seal in the ingredients.
5. Mix the water into the egg, and brush all over the pastry. Place the triangles into an oven-proof pan and bake until golden about 20-30 minutes and serve hot with a side salad.

Variation:
Add a few slices of avocado around the pastry, prior to serving.

Fresh Trout

While on a camping adventure, a friend caught several trout and it was my job to cook them on a small grill over a fire, once he had cleaned and filleted them. So I added a pinch of this and a smidgen of that and we ate to our hearts' delight. Years passed, we went our separate ways and then one day out of the blue, he called for the recipe. Evidently, he had tried to reproduce the flavor, but was unable to, had just gotten married and wanted to impress his new wife when they went camping. So I shared it with him and a few days later his wife called thanking me, for she had never before eaten such tasty trout.

Serves 2-3

2-3 fresh trout, cleaned and filleted
½ cup (1 stick) butter or margarine
1-2 lemons
3-4 scallions diced or ¼ onion, diced
½ teaspoon minced garlic
1-2 pinches dill

1. Melt the butter in frying pan over medium heat or over a grill. Add the trout and cook until tender and done, flipping once.
2. Remove the trout from the frying pan and squeeze the juice from the lemons into the pan. Add the scallions, garlic and dill to the pan and stir until very hot. Let this mixture simmer a few minutes, place the trout onto serving plates, and smother with the sauce.

Variation:
Substitute trout with choice of: sole, flounder, swordfish, halibut, fresh tuna or blue fish and proceed as directed.

Patt's Fresh Tuna Steaks

*Patt's husband Pete is an avid fisherman who spends many weekends out on the ocean with friends,
fishing to their hearts' content. I have had the privilege to eat his fresh-caught endeavors on many occasions and honestly,
fish is never better than when prepared and served fresh off the boat. This divine recipe can be used with swordfish as well,
and the taste will entice you to make more than necessary because this does offer a remarkable fresh taste of the sea;
even when high up on a mountain with no sea in sight.*

Serves 4

Four 6-ounce tuna or swordfish steaks (preferably fresh)
2-3 tablespoons butter
1-2 teaspoons fresh grated ginger
¼ cup soy sauce
1 tablespoon toasted sesame seeds
1-2 teaspoons light molasses (do not use blackstrap molasses, it is too thick and pungent)

1. Thoroughly mix together the ginger, soy sauce, sesame seeds and molasses and rub it all over both sides of the fish.
2. Melt the butter in a large frying pan or skillet over medium to medium high heat. Add the steaks and sear them on both sides until cooked to your liking. It is recommended to serve pinkish in the center for best flavor.
3. Serve hot with potatoes and side salad.

Large Seafood Stuffed Shells

I found this recipe in my grandmother's magical tin box. I swear that this box holds secrets and magic for preparing some of the most sensational foods one could even begin to dream of eating, better yet prepare in their own kitchens. The newspaper page was amber, torn and faded, but this recipe smelled much too good in my imagination to pass up. As difficult as this recipe may appear, have no fear, for it is actually very simple to prepare.

Serves 6

12 jumbo-sized pasta shells, cooked according to package directions
3-4 tablespoons butter
1 medium onion, finely diced
½ pound cooked crabmeat (lump or canned and drained, with shells removed)
½ pound large shrimp, shelled and cleaned, steamed or poached
1 cup ricotta cheese
1 egg
½ teaspoon pepper
½ teaspoon minced garlic
1-2 tablespoons butter or margarine
½ cup half and half
1 cup chicken broth
Pinch of nutmeg (optional)
⅓ cup shredded Parmesan cheese
2 tablespoons grated Romano cheese

1. Grease a 2–3-quart casserole dish with butter, margarine or pan spray.
2. Melt 2 tablespoons butter in a skillet over medium heat. Add the onions and sauté until tender. Remove from the heat and cool.
3. Put the ricotta cheese into a large bowl. Gently stir the crabmeat and shrimp into the ricotta and then add the egg, pepper, garlic and onions and mix gently. Stuff each precooked pasta shell with this mixture with a spoon and place each into the prepared casserole dish.
4. Make a roux by melting the butter over low heat in a saucepan, add the flour and stir into a paste, warm for about 2 minutes. Whisk in the broth and half and half; let this simmer until thickened and then stir in the cheese.
5. Pour the sauce over the shells and bake for 20-30 minutes or until bubbly and slightly browned on top.

Spinach Manicotti

*A taste of Italy made fresh in your own kitchen; no need for airline tickets! Traditionally, this creamy,
rich dish is slathered with a tomato-based sauce, i.e., Marinara, Chunky Italian or your favorite bottled, but I have
a tendency to prefer this with creamy Alfredo or Herbed White Sauce. Whichever sauce used will only enhance
the magnificence of this lovely, dreamy Italian favorite.*

Serves 4-6

Preheat oven to 350° F

One 8-ounce package jumbo manicotti pasta shells
10-12 ounces fresh spinach, washed, dried with a paper towel and chopped into bite-size pieces,
    then cover in water and microwave until dark green and tender (9-12 minutes)
One 16-ounce container ricotta cheese
1½ cup shredded mozzarella cheese
¾ cup Parmesan cheese
1 extra large egg or 2 medium eggs
2-3 teaspoon minced fresh parsley
¼ teaspoon minced garlic
½ teaspoon onion powder
Sea salt and white pepper to taste
2-3 cups tomato sauce (Marinara Sauce (p. 198), Chunky Italian Sauce (p. 199)
Additional Parmesan and or mozzarella cheese for sprinkling on top

1. Cook the shells in boiling water until tender but not quite cooked. Drain the water, and rinse under warm water.
2. Thoroughly mix the ricotta, cooked spinach, cheeses, egg and spices. Use a spoon to stuff the shells with the filling.
    If you have an extra shell or two, place them into a freezer-safe baggie and freeze for another use.
3. Butter or oil a 9-inch square pan. (Do not use pan spray.) Place the shells in the pan, smother with choice of sauce,
    and bake for 25-35 minutes or until hot and tender and serve hot with some garlic bread and a side salad.

Hint: Substitute Alfredo Sauce (p. 340) or White Herbed Sauce (p. 340) for the tomato-based sauce.

Grandmom's Philly Chicken and Pasta

When I was young and my mother was in the hospital for a brief stay, I called my grandmother for a recipe to prepare for Dad. As she shared this with me, she added that this had always been one of his favorites growing up, but he hadn't tasted it in years. I called him at the hospital and asked him to stop at the store on his way home to pick up a precooked rotisserie chicken and some broccoli. Although a bit taken back by this request, he hesitantly agreed to give me this opportunity. Boy, did he shine when I brought the finished product to the table, for he recognized it immediately. At the end of the meal, he winked while praising my efforts and affectionately confirmed that his mother had taught me well.

Serves 4

8 ounces pasta, cooked according to package directions, drained and covered to keep warm
3 cups of chopped cooked chicken or turkey
2 cups chopped broccoli or cauliflower, steamed until tender
8-ounce package cream cheese, Neufchatel (low fat) works fine
½ cup plus 1 tablespoon milk (half and half for a richer flavor)
¼ cup shredded Swiss, Jarlsburg or Parmesan cheese
½ teaspoon onion powder
½ teaspoon garlic powder
Pinch of dill (optional)
1 teaspoon fresh minced basil or lemon basil (optional)
Sea salt and pepper to taste

1. Keep the chicken and broccoli hot by placing into a saucepan, cover and keep over low heat stirring occasionally to disperse the heat.
2. Combine the milk and cheese in a medium saucepan, set the temperature to medium low and stir continuously until melted and smooth. Add the cheese and spices and continue stirring until all ingredients are incorporated.
3. Divide the pasta between serving plates, top the pasta with the warmed chicken and broccoli and smother with the sauce.

Garlicky Angel Hair Pasta

So good, simple and satisfying, even the kids will love this one. An FYI for all who have claimed that they do not know how to cook or do not have the time; if you know how or have the time to turn on a stereo, TV or VCR, then you have time and know how to make this delightfully easy recipe.

Serves 4-6

One 16-ounce package of angel hair pasta
½ bulb of garlic, peel the outer layers but leave the last papery skin on the cloves or 1 tablespoon plus minced garlic
½ cup (1 stick) melted butter
¼ cup extra virgin olive oil
2-4 tablespoons shredded Parmesan cheese for sprinkling

1. Boil the pasta according to package directions; add the garlic cloves to the boiling water. When pasta is tender, drain over hot water, remove the cloves, pour the pasta into a large serving bowl and toss with butter and oil.
2. Squeeze each garlic clove from the skin into a bowl. Mash them and add to the pasta or simply toss in the minced garlic here.
3. Serve hot, sprinkled with Parmesan cheese on top.

Hint: More garlic can be added if this amount is not enough to soothe your desire.

Variation:
Add 1 pound of leftover chopped chicken, turkey, shrimp, scallops, lobster or crabmeat to the pasta when stirring it all together.

Zucchini Pasta

This is another of those easy recipes, illustrating that there are no true excuses for not cooking at home. It is also a vegetarian's delight and always sold out in minutes whenever I made this at my shop. The lucky recipients of this rich and flavorful dish will think you spent much more time in the kitchen, rather than the few minutes that it actually took to toss it together.

Serves 4-6

Preheat oven to 350° F

2-3 tablespoons butter, margarine or canola spread
2-3 large zucchinis
1 jar of your favorite tomato sauce or 4 cups Marinara Sauce (p. 198)
1 teaspoon or 2 minced garlic
8 ounces sliced provolone cheese
½ cup shredded mozzarella cheese (optional)
One 16-ounce package rotini pasta, cooked according to package directions, drained and kept warm

1. Spread the butter all over the bottom and sides of a 9x13-inch pan.
2. Slice the zucchinis into ¼-inch slices and layer in the bottom of the pan. Pour the sauce over the zucchini, mix the garlic into the sauce and bake for 25-30 minutes.
3. Cover the entire top with the cheeses and continue baking until cheese has melted and begins to brown.
4. Serve over the warm pasta.

Eggplant Parmigiana

Thick, hearty and amazing to taste! Many believe that good eggplant parmesan is difficult and time-consuming to prepare, when actually it is not as difficult to assemble as you may have thought. Make this one day and sit back and listen to the contented munching of your loved ones, for this will become a favorite in your home as it is in mine.

Serves 4-6

Preheat oven to 350° F

2 eggplants, sliced into ¼–⅓-inch slices
2-3 cups Italian seasoned bread crumbs, placed in a medium-sized bowl or a plate
1-2 eggs
1 plus cup milk
1 teaspoon garlic powder (optional)
8 cups tomato sauce, bottled or homemade Marinara Sauce (p. 198)
8 ounces sliced provolone or mozzarella cheese
4 ounces shredded mozzarella or provolone cheese
1 cup shredded Parmesan cheese

1. Grease a large pan with butter, margarine or pan spray.
2. In a medium bowl, beat the eggs with the milk and garlic powder. Dip each slice of eggplant into the milk mixture and then into the breadcrumbs; turn to coat and place slices into the prepared pan. Line the bottom of the pan with 1 layer of breaded eggplant slices, cover with a thin layer of sauce, then a few slices of cheese and then repeat with another layer of eggplant and so on, until all the eggplant is used.
3. Make sure that there are enough cheese slices left to cover the top, sprinkle the top with the Parmesan cheese and bake for 35-45 minutes. Serve over or accompanied with pasta.

Patt's Linguini and Clams

Growing up in Philadelphia, I learned early on to appreciate a variety of ethnic foods commonly found throughout the city. I always loved this little Italian restaurant that my dad would take me to, for they served the best non-tomato-based dishes I have yet to taste. Colorado has some fabulous restaurants, but the variety of ethnic foods is not quite as broad as that in Philly, especially up here on the mountain. So when Patt made this, I asked her to write it down so I could make it at home. Months went by and I got a craving, bought some frozen clams and to my delight it tasted just as wonderful as the dish I had first sampled in that little Italian restaurant and at Patt's home. You can use canned clams, but I advise using fresh or frozen cherrystone clams, to accentuate the full flavor of this pleasantly satisfying recipe.

Serves 4-5

Preheat oven to 275-300° F

1 pound linguini, cooked according to package directions, placed into a large ovenproof bowl. Cover with foil and place into a warm oven.
25-35 fresh or frozen cherrystone clams or about 1½-2 cups canned clams, do not drain
2 tablespoons clam juice (add only if using canned clams)
½ cup extra virgin olive oil
3 cloves garlic, finely diced
1-2 tablespoons freshly squeezed lemon juice
¼ cup plus 1 tablespoon sherry
3 tablespoon fresh diced parsley
Sea salt and pepper to taste
3 tablespoons butter

1. Steam the clams in a large pot until the shells open, remove the clams from shells. Chop the clams into pieces and pour the excess juice into a small bowl.
2. Heat the oil over medium heat in a medium saucepan, add the garlic and sauté for 4-5 minutes or until slightly browned. Add the clams, lemon juice, sherry, parsley, reserved juice and salt and pepper to the saucepan. Heat this mixture and stir for 3-4 minutes, add the butter and stir until melted.
3. Pour the hot clam mixture over the top of the linguini, either on a large plate or on individual serving.

Pasta Primavera

A colorful presentation; filled with some of your favorite, edible things, mixed into a plateful of pasta and drizzled with a sauce. The best part about this recipe is that you may use whatever diced or julienne vegetables, poultry, meats and/or seafood your taste buds desire, toss it into the pasta along with the sauce, and serve with a smile.

Serves 3-4

1 pound spaghetti, fettuccini, or linguine, cooked according to package directions and drained
3-4 tablespoons olive oil or butter
2 teaspoons minced garlic
2-3 teaspoons fresh minced parsley
1 tablespoon fresh minced basil or lemon basil
4 cups fresh vegetables, cooked chopped poultry, meat and/or seafood/fish

MOM'S SAUCE:
⅓ cup (¾ stick) butter
½ cup shredded Parmesan cheese
1 cup plus 1 tablespoon heavy cream
⅓ cup fresh chopped basil
1 tablespoon fresh squeezed lemon juice
¼-½ cup chicken broth or non fat milk (optional)
2 tablespoons combined grated Parmesan and Romano cheeses

1. Heat the oil/butter over medium in a large skillet. Add the garlic, parsley and basil; sauté for a minute or two and add the vegetables, poultry, meats and/or seafood and continue sautéing until the vegetables are still crisp but tender. Remove the pan from the heat and set aside.
2. Melt the butter in a large saucepan over medium heat, add the cheese, cream, basil and juice and stir over medium heat until thick. Do not boil. Add the pasta to the pan and toss to coat. If this is too thick for your liking, add small amounts of the broth/milk until the sauce reaches a consistency that you prefer.
3. Add ⅓-½ vegetables/meats to the pan and toss. Pour all into a serving bowl and top with remaining vegetables and/or meats.
4. Sprinkle extra cheese onto top of each serving.

Ann's Peppery Pasta with Tofu

A full-flavored vegan favorite that has been shared around the table with many. I have made this several times for friends who do not eat meat nor any other animal-based foods and they are thrilled with the spicy essence. I am so thankful that Ann has shared this with me because there has never been a drop left in the bowl and frequent recipe requests are now fulfilled. For all who choose to steer clear of animal-based foods, such as meats and cheeses, then you must have this recipe because it is positively wonderful!

Serves 4-6

2 tablespoons olive oil
1 large red pepper, seeded and diced
1 large green pepper, seeded and diced
6 garlic cloves chopped
¾ cup onion, diced
½ cup chopped fresh basil
¼-½ teaspoon red chili flakes (optional)
One 28-ounce can Italian plum tomatoes with juice
1-pound box of penne pasta, cooked according to package directions
8 ounces tofu, coarsely crumbled

1. Heat oil over medium high heat in a large heavy skillet or Dutch oven. Add peppers and garlic and sauté until the peppers have softened, about 4-5 minutes. Mix in the basil, then the tomatoes and simmer until the sauce is slightly reduced. Break up the tomatoes with the back of a spoon as you stir for another 5-7 minutes.
2. Add the freshly cooked pasta and toss to coat in the sauce, then add the tofu and toss to blend.
3. Serve immediately with a green salad.

Variation:
Substitute feta cheese for the tofu; still vegetarian, but no longer vegan.

Mary's Wild Rice

Lizanne first sampled this fragrant dish when her mother, Mary was preparing to entertain friends. Once having had a taste, she couldn't resist the temptation, but wasn't allowed back into the kitchen while her mother was cooking the meal. She anxiously waited outside the back door until the guests arrived. When her mother left the kitchen to greet her company, Lizanne sneaked back into the kitchen and helped herself to a large bowlful. To this day, her mother still does not know why there seemed to be less rice than what she had prepared!

Serves 4-6

One 16-ounce box wild rice
1 pound sausage
4-6 scallions, chopped
8 ounces sliced mushrooms
½ teaspoon minced fresh rosemary
1 small jar current jelly
Jelly jar full of Burgundy cooking wine

1. Cook rice according to package directions; fluff the rice with a fork.
2. While the rice is cooking, crumble and brown the sausage over medium in a frying pan. Add the mushrooms, lower the heat and sauté a few minutes, drain off grease and add the scallions.
3. In a saucepan, melt the jelly, fill the empty jar with the burgundy cooking wine and add to the melted jelly, heat over medium until warm.
4. Once the rice has finished cooking, add the sausage mix and rosemary and stir well. Put this mixture into a greased 2-quart casserole dish, preheat the oven to 275° F, then stir in ⅓ of the jelly mixing, cover and bake for 40-50 minutes.
5. Pour the remaining burgundy sauce over the rice when serving.

Hint: This can be used as a dressing/stuffing for poultry.

Elizabeth's Sixties Brown Rice

During the late 1960s, while living in her bus, Elizabeth and friends ate this groovy recipe almost daily. In her words this recipe is, "far out and goes with anything your heart desires as long as you have a good imagination." *She then added that they always stashed the free soy sauce packets that came their way, as that is what added to the special taste so fondly remembered.*

Serves 2-3

1 cup natural brown rice (do not use Minute Rice)
2 cups water
½ cup diced onion
1 cup chopped broccoli
1½ edamame (cooked and shelled soy beans)
2 tablespoons soy or tamari sauce
Smidgen of minced garlic
Butter to taste
Sea salt and pepper to taste

1. Rinse and drain rice, place it in a saucepan and add the water. Heat uncovered over medium high until the water boils. Cover and remove from heat and then allow to sit without lifting the lid for one hour.
2. Fluff the rice, stir in all remaining ingredients and serve.

Variations:
Substitute pea pods for the edamame.

Spanakopita

I am thankful for the fabulous variety of traditional and cultural foods that are now available globally, to be enjoyed by all. For all who prefer a pinch of diversity in their choice of foods, this incredibly marvelous and rich Greek spinach pie provides one with the delicious opportunity to taste the cuisine of a foreign country right in your own home. Do not be intimidated by trying something new or by the list of ingredients and the procedure, for when it comes down to it, this dish is actually pretty simple to prepare and sure to impress all to whom it is served.

Serves 4-5

Preheat oven to 300° F

¼ cup olive oil
½ cup finely diced onions
¼ cup finely diced scallions, including part of the green stems
2 pounds fresh spinach, washed, drained, stems removed and patted dry with paper towels
1 bunch (2 ounces) fresh dill, finely minced and measuring just over 2 tablespoons
¼ cup fresh chopped parsley
Pinch sea salt
Fresh cracked pepper to taste
Scant ½ cup milk or cream
8-10 ounces feta cheese, crumbled
4 eggs, lightly beaten
1 cup melted butter (no substitutes)
16 phyllo dough sheets, slightly thawed and stored covered in the refrigerator

1. Heat the oil in a large skillet over medium heat, add the onions and scallions and sauté about 6 minutes or until soft and tender. Stir the spinach into the onions and stir frequently for 5-7 minutes. Stir the dill, parsley and spice into the pan. Continue to stir constantly until most of the liquid has evaporated and the spinach has darkened in color. Remove the pan from the heat.
2. Pour the skillet vegetables into a large bowl, stir in the milk and allow this mixture to cool. Once cooled to room temperature (about 20 minutes), gently but thoroughly mix the beaten eggs and feta crumbles into the vegetables. Set aside.
3. Prepare a 12x7-inch pan by brushing the bottom and sides with some of the melted butter. Remove 8 phyllo sheets from the refrigerator. Keep them covered with a damp cloth while assembling the layers. Press one sheet into the bottom and up the sides of the prepared pan. Brush this sheet with melted butter, place another sheet on top and brush with melted butter. Continue this layering and buttering until the 8 sheets have been added to the pan.
4. Pour and evenly spread the spinach mixture on top of the phyllo sheets and then pull the remaining sheets out of the refrigerator and repeat the layering and buttering process with the remaining sheets on top of the spinach.
5. Bake for 60-75 minutes or until the phyllo sheets are crisp and slightly browned, cut into squares and serve hot with a fresh bowl of fruit.

Spaghetti Squash

An unusual squash that produces crunchy strands that look like spaghetti and melts in your mouth with any added sauce. This kind of squash is also wonderful served simply with melted butter, nutmeg and cheese of preference. I first tasted its unique flavor at my aunt's and was shocked to learn that it was a vegetable, not pasta. I instantly had to have the recipe, to which she said, "There is none, you just mix it with whatever you want and serve."

Serves 2-4, depending on size of squash

Preheat oven to 375°

1 spaghetti squash
1-2 tablespoons honey or brown sugar
Butter to taste
A sprinkling of cinnamon, nutmeg or ginger or a combination

1. Cut the squash in half lengthwise, remove the seeds and arrange them cut side down in a baking dish. Fill the dish with ¼-inch of water and bake for 25-35 minutes.
2. Turn the slices upright in the pan, add melted butter, honey and spice and bake an additional 30 minutes or until tender.
3. Remove the squash from its shell with a fork, place in a bowl and serve as is or top with your favorite pasta sauce.

Acorn Squash

*Before being introduced to this wonderful vegetable, I always thought that they were difficult to cook.
I soon learned differently and now I can smell this recipe each and every time I begin to think about it.
This excellent squash is usually served as an accompaniment to the main meal and pairs deliciously
with poultry, rice or a vegetarian meal. However, I have often had just this for dinner.*

Serves 2-4

Preheat oven to 375° F

2 acorn squashes, washed well
¼ cup (½ stick) butter or margarine
¼ cup brown sugar, maple sugar or 2 tablespoons maple syrup per squash or equivalent amount of sugar substitute
Pinch of sea salt
1 teaspoon cinnamon
¼ teaspoon nutmeg
⅓-½ cup chopped pecans or walnuts (optional)

1. Cut each squash in half lengthwise, remove seeds and membranes and place each half, cut side up, in a 9x9-inch greased baking pan. Dot each with butter and sprinkle with sugar or syrup and salt. Mix the cinnamon and nutmeg together and sprinkle across the squash, then sprinkle the nuts on top.
2. Bake for 30-40 minutes, then cover the pan with foil to prevent the top from browning too much and bake for 30 minutes more or until soft and tender. Serve hot.

Variation:
Dot the squash halves with butter or margarine. Mix together ½ cup fresh squeezed lemon juice, ⅔ cup raisins, ½ cup brown sugar or substitute and 3 cups unsweetened chunky applesauce, spread this all over the squash halves and bake accordingly.

Elizabeth's Roasted Winter Vegetables

Have you ever been in the mood for something warm and hearty, but not wanting heavy meats, poultry or seafood? When this feeling arrives, simply toss the following together, place it in the oven, allow all to roast until tender and indulge in the glory of quickly roasted, naturally sweet vegetables.

Serves 4

Preheat oven to 425° F

2 sweet potatoes, ends trimmed and sliced into ¼-inch rounds
3 small red onions, cut into ¾-inch slices
2 small turnips, cut in ¼-inch slices or smaller
5 large carrots, sliced in ¼-inch or smaller diagonal slices
3 winter squashes, edges trimmed, seeded and cut into ½-inch slices
3-4 red potatoes, sliced into ¼-inch slices
2 tablespoons olive oil
½ teaspoon sea salt
1½ teaspoon mixed minced fresh rosemary, thyme, sage and oregano

1. Combine all of the ingredients into a large bowl and toss to coat.
2. Arrange the vegetables in a single layer on a foil-lined cookie sheet.
3. Roast until soft on the inside, browned on the outside and tender, approximately 19-22 minutes. If you want, turn the vegetables over, halfway through cooking.
4. Sprinkle with salt and pepper and serve hot.

Lizanne's Mother's Ratatouille

Lizanne says that her mother was an excellent cook and would be overwhelmed with joy that I have asked her daughter to a share a few favorites to place in this book. Friends have commonly described this succulent blend of fresh vegetables as, "to die for," and one taste can temporarily take you from the mountains and fields to a luxury resort on the Mediterranean. In response to all who have asked for this recipe, here it is, in its full splendor.

Serves 6-8

½ cup olive oil
2 garlic cloves, minced
2 eggplants, cut into ½-inch cubes, equaling 12 cups
2 large zucchini, cut into ½-inch cubes, equaling 4 cups
3 large onions, coarsely chopped, equaling 3 cups
1 red pepper, chopped
1 yellow pepper, chopped
1 green pepper, chopped
2 teaspoons each of fresh basil and thyme, chopped
2 tablespoons fresh parsley, chopped
5 scallions, cut into ½-inch pieces, greens included
2 cups cherry tomatoes, quartered (or more if you like)
1½ tablespoons balsamic vinegar
Sea salt and fresh cracked pepper to taste
2-3 tablespoons combined Parmesan and Romano cheese, for sprinkling on top (optional)

1. In a large heavy skillet or Dutch oven, heat the oil over medium high heat, add the garlic, eggplant and zucchini and sauté until lightly browned. Reduce the heat, add the onions, peppers and herbs and stir. Cover and stir occasionally for 25-35 minutes.
2. Add the tomatoes, cover and cook an additional 20-30 minutes, stirring occasionally, until the vegetables are tender and the sauce has thickened slightly.
3. Remove the skillet from the heat, sprinkle the vegetables with balsamic vinegar, salt, pepper and cheese and then serve hot with warm fresh breads.

Vegetables Julienne

This is a fabulously quick meal that provides flavor, nourishment and sustenance at the end of the day, especially on those evenings when you don't feel like eating heartily, just something light and pleasing. This recipe also works great as a side dish and adds a touch of beautiful color to all dinner plates.

Serves 4

2 cups brown rice, cooked according to package directions (optional)
2-3 tablespoons oil
2 small zucchini, julienned (cut into small sticks)
2 carrots, julienned (cut into small sticks)
2 medium white turnips, julienned (cut into small sticks)
4 scallions, sliced thinly on the diagonal or 2 shallots, minced
1 cup chopped broccoli (optional)
¼ cup teriyaki sauce (more to taste)
1 teaspoon minced garlic
2 teaspoons fresh diced lemon basil or basil
2 teaspoons fresh minced parsley
Sea salt and pepper to taste

1. Heat the oil in a skillet over medium, add vegetables and seasonings, and sauté until crisp but tender.
2. Mix all into the rice and serve as a side to any main course.

Nancy's Potato Latkes

I always believed that my mother made great latkes, until Nancy shared this recipe. These are so good and much tastier than Mom's, but please, when you get to heaven and see my mother, do not tell her that I have said this; she may become insulted and temporarily stop sending rainbows my way.

Serves 4-6

4 pounds potatoes
1 zucchini
1 sweet potato
10 garlic cloves
2 yellow onions, peeled and cut into wedges
½ cup matzo meal
1 teaspoon baking powder
3 eggs
Salt and pepper to taste
Vegetable oil for frying

1. Shred the potatoes, zucchini, sweet potato, garlic, and onions together in a food processor.
2. Add the matzo meal, baking powder and eggs to the vegetables to form the latke mix.
3. Fill a large skillet about ¼-inch of oil and heat over medium high.
4. Take a handful of the latke mix and squeeze out any excess juice into a bowl or sink. Shape into a semi-flat round and place in frying pan. Repeat with the remaining mixture, but do not overcrowd the pan. You may need to add more oil to the pan.
5. Fry the latkes on each side until they are crisp and golden brown, remove from the pan and drain them for a second or two on a paper towel-lined plate and serve hot with applesauce, maple syrup, sour cream and/or ketchup.

Hint: This is a large batch. Store leftovers in the refrigerator or wrap tightly in foil, then place in a freezer-safe baggie and freeze.

Creamy Scalloped Potatoes with Broccoli

There are many prepackaged mixes for scalloped potatoes available on the grocer's shelves, but none of these can compare with the homemade flavor that comes from making your own. It may take a little bit longer, but the flavor of this creamy old-time favorite is so full of wealth that you may even impress yourself for a job well done.

Serves 4-6

Preheat oven to 375° F

5-6 cups thinly sliced potatoes
1½ cup chopped broccoli (optional)
2 cups plus 2 tablespoons milk
1½ cups heavy cream
2 garlic cloves, crushed or 1 teaspoon minced
1-2 tablespoons butter
Pinch of nutmeg (optional)
½-1 teaspoon parsley
¾ cup shredded Swiss or Gruyere cheese
Sea salt and white pepper to taste

1. In a large saucepan combine the potatoes, milk, cream, garlic, nutmeg, parsley, salt and pepper and over medium heat, bring this mixture to a boil. Stir constantly to prevent burning.
2. Grease a 9x9-inch pan well with butter, margarine or pan spray.
3. Remove the pan from the heat, gently stir in the broccoli and pour all into the prepared pan. Sprinkle the top with the cheese and bake for 60-75 minutes or until the potatoes are easily pierced and tender. Serve hot as a meal or side dish with a variety of foods.

Variation:
Add ¼ cup diced scallions or 2 thinly sliced shallots to the cream mixture.

Sweet Potato Casserole

For a change of pace from mashed potatoes, give this luscious potato casserole a try. So good it is, crunchy but soft with a smidgen of added sweetness; this dish is wonderful just as is or goes perfectly along side a roasted piece of pork or poultry.

Serves 4-6

Preheat oven to 375° F

3-4 sweet potatoes or yams, peeled, cooked and mashed
1 cup sugar
2 tablespoons vanilla or maple extract
½ cup plus 1 tablespoon evaporated milk
½ cup (1 stick) butter or margarine
1 cup brown sugar
¼ cup (½ stick) melted butter or margarine
¾ cup flour
1 cup finely chopped pecans

1. Combine the mashed sweet potatoes with one cup sugar, vanilla, evaporated and butter. Mix this thoroughly and then using a spatula, scrape all into a greased 3-quart casserole dish.
2. Combine the brown sugar, melted butter, flour and pecans and sprinkle all over the top of the potatoes and then bake for 30-40 minutes. Serve hot as a meal or side dish.

Variation:
Mix ½ cup golden raisins or fresh pineapple chunks into the potato mixture in combination with the other ingredients. If adding pineapple chunks, only use ¾ cup white sugar in the sweet potato mixture.

Carolyn's Pineapple Nut Slaw

Carolyn gets much pleasure in leaving messages on my answering machine, informing me that she is on her way to the sea for a day of diving off the coast of a Hawaiian island, her home. She shared this recipe, generously offering the pleasant flavors of the tropical islands. This recipe will make you dream about packing your bags and heading over to Hawaii on the first plane available. However, there is no need for such extremities, because all you need to do is put on your favorite sarong or shorts and sandals, light a strand of Flamingo lights, say Aloha *to your loved ones and then dive into a bowl of this lovely and fragrant salad.*

Serves 4-6

2 cups fresh chopped pineapple
1 head green cabbage, shredded
1 medium carrot, shredded
1 medium green pepper, julienned (cut in small sticks)
3 tablespoons red wine vinegar
3 tablespoons unsweetened pineapple juice (natural is best)
1-2 tablespoon honey
1-2 teaspoon canola oil
3-4 ounces crumbled gorgonzola cheese
¼-⅓ cup of chopped macadamia nuts

1. Gently toss the pineapple, cabbage, carrots and green peppers together in a medium bowl.
2. Whisk together the vinegar, juice, honey and oil and then pour this over the pineapple mixture and toss to coat. Cover and refrigerate for an hour.
3. Just before serving, sprinkle the top with the gorgonzola and chopped macadamia nuts.

Mom's Carrots and Raisins

A beautifully cool dish, perfect to serve as a side dish at a BBQ or picnic while still good and nutritional enough to serve as a light meal all by itself.

Serves 2-3

¼ cup canola or safflower oil or ¾ cup plain nonfat yogurt
2 tablespoons honey
1-2 tablespoons fresh squeezed lemon juice
½ teaspoon cinnamon
¼ teaspoon nutmeg
3 cups shredded carrots
⅔ cup raisins, dark and golden combined
¼ cup canned unsweetened crushed pineapple, drained

1. In a large bowl, stir the yogurt/oil, honey lemon juice cinnamon and nutmeg into a smooth dressing. Add carrots, raisins and pineapple to dressing and stir gently, but thoroughly, until combined.
2. Cover and chill for 15-30 minutes, drain the excess liquid that may have accumulated in the bottom of the bowl and serve as a side dish or light meal.

Sunshine Pie

A pound of patience, you must find

Mixed well with loving words, so kind

Drop in two pounds of helpful deeds

And thoughts of other people's needs.

A pack of smiles, to make the crust,

Then stir and bake it well you must.

And now, I ask that you may try,

The recipe of Sunshine Pie.

Anonymous

The Force of Enticement

This amazing force has been mentioned a couple times in the previous chapters but truly emerges in its full glory when baking, preparing and serving desserts. The power of this force is uncontrollably activated when our senses are awakened by the aroma and visual appeal of irresistible foods. It causes loss of all conscious control, which is forfeited to the mindless actions of a few fingers, a fork or spoon. These eating utensils magically develop a brain of their own. There is no control over their actions, for while our palates are salivating for a sample taste, these utensils somehow deliver it right into our mouths, before our minds have an opportunity to catch up with them.

How many of you have had the strength to turn your back on a hot chocolate chip cookie straight out of the oven? Or what about a batch of homemade pudding? Somehow the spoon just delivers a sample to your awaiting taste buds before you even know what is happening and then you look into the pot and find that half of it is gone. These actions are what I affectionately refer to as the Force of Enticement.

Shortbread Cookies, Page 277
Dark, Sweet Cherry-Filled Brownies, Page 285

Shortbread Cookies

The slightly sweet, buttery and rich flavors make these cookies a pleasant addition to any dessert table, although they can and have been eaten any time of day. I received this recipe eons ago, for this was kindly offered to me by a stranger, the grandson of a woman who resides in Scotland. Each and every bite just melts in your mouth; they have regularly been praised as some of the best cookies I have ever made.

Makes approximately 3 dozen cookies

Preheat oven to 325° F

2 cups (4 sticks) butter (no substitutes)
1 cup powdered sugar
4 cups plus 1 tablespoon flour
Sugar, cinnamon sugar, or other flavored sugar* to roll cookies in

1. Mix together the butter, sugar and flour until completely mixed and there are no crumbs remaining in the bottom of bowl.
2. Grease three cookie sheets.
3. Sprinkle sugar, cinnamon sugar, vanilla sugar*, maple sugar or colored sugar over the entire surface of a cutting board or countertop. *Do not use flour or powdered sugar!*
4. Roll out one third of the dough at a time onto the prepared surface and then cut out cookies with cookie cutters and place onto the prepared cookie sheets, sugar side up. Gather up leftover dough; add it to another portion of the remaining dough. Sprinkle and spread more sugar onto rolling surface and repeat rolling and cutting out cookies until all the dough is gone.
5. Bake 4-5 minutes (depending on the size) or until slightly brown around the edges.

Hints: Allow cookies to cool on the baking sheets for 10-15 minutes before tasting; if cookies are handled too soon they may fall apart. Do not store cookies in a plastic container, for they will get too soft. Store cookies in a can lined with waxed paper or simply wrap in plastic wrap.

*To make Vanilla Sugar, place 4 cups of sugar into a jar with a tight fitting lid, then slice 2 vanilla beans straight down the center of the bean and place into sugar. Seal the jar and put it into a cool, dry spot for at least 2 months before opening. Vanilla Sugar can be used in place of sugar in a wide variety of recipes.

Gemstones

These flavorful cookies got their name because they resemble little white rocks filled with colorful gemstones. Now this name does not imply that these are hard cookies, for they are neither soft nor hard, but they are delicious. When I took a bag full of samples to my "guinea pigs" at the local post office, I handed it to a gentleman behind the counter with instructions to share, as I needed all of their feedback. However, he never did share, instead he found these little gemstones so irresistible that he ate the whole bag by himself. This made it necessary for me to bake another batch, so that I could get the desired reviews, besides just that of an immensely satisfied "Cookie Monster."

Makes approximately 3 dozen cookies

Preheat oven to 350° F

8 ounces cream cheese
1 cup (2 sticks) butter or margarine
⅔ cup sugar
1 egg yolk
1 teaspoon vanilla
½ teaspoon baking powder
Pinch cream of tartar
2½ cups flour
Various preserves or 2 tablespoons chocolate chips

1. Cream together the butter, cream cheese, sugar and vanilla, then beat in the egg yolk.
2. Add all remaining ingredients but the preserves and/or chocolate chips and mix thoroughly or until all ingredients are incorporated.
3. Grease two cookies sheets with butter, margarine or pan spray.
4. Pinch approximately 2 teaspoons of dough per cookie and roll it into a ball in the palm of your hands. Using either your pinky finger or the end of a chopstick, put a little indentation into the center of each cookie, fill this with a tiny bit of preserves or a chocolate chip and bake the cookies for 10-13 minutes or until the edges just begin to golden. Allow to cool for a couple minutes and remove from the cookie sheets. Store in a baggie or plastic wrap-lined can with a tight-fitting lid.

Snickerdoodles

---

*Soft in the center, crunchy on the edge, these are one of, if not the most popular cookie, that I have ever baked.
The best part about this recipe is that it is adaptable to a wide variety of flavors. For instance, if you want to bake a batch
of Almond Cookies, all you need to do is add a smidgen of almond extract, roll the dough in white sugar and sprinkle a few
almonds on top. For Vanilla Cookies, simply roll the dough in vanilla sugar or make a batch of Nut Cookies by finely
chopping some nuts, mix them with a couple tablespoons of sugar, roll the dough in the nuts and bake accordingly.*

Makes approximately 3 dozen cookies

Preheat oven to 350° F

CINNAMON SUGAR MIXTURE:
¾ cup sugar
2-3 tablespoons cinnamon

Mix together and set aside in a small bowl.

COOKIES:
1 cup (2 sticks) butter
1 cup sugar
1½ tablespoons vanilla
1 egg
2 cups plus 1 tablespoon flour
1 teaspoon baking powder
¼ teaspoon baking soda
⅛ teaspoon cream of tartar

1. Cream together the butter, sugar, and vanilla, then add the remaining ingredients, ending with the egg. Thoroughly beat all the ingredients for 2 minutes on medium-high.
2. Grease two cookie sheets.
3. For smaller cookies, roll 1 tablespoon of dough into a ball with the palms of your hands. For larger cookie (4-5 inches), roll ⅓ cup of dough into a ball with the palms of your hands.
4. Roll each cookie in the cinnamon/sugar mixture, completely coating it, and place onto prepared cookie sheets. Slightly flatten each cookie with the palm of your hand.
5. Bake smaller cookies 7-10 minutes and larger cookies 10-12 minutes or until edges are lightly browned. If you prefer crunchier cookies, bake for 2-3 minutes longer, or until entire cookie is a light golden color.

Palmier Cookies

I truly believe that these must be the easiest and one of the most elegant cookies on earth. I used to make these with developmentally disabled kids, so I can honestly say that no one has any excuse not to make these deliciously fine little treats. Perfect to serve with after dinner tea or coffee; but please make a special effort to share a few among loved ones just before bed, as an offering of sweet dreams to last through the night.

Makes approximately 3 dozen cookies

Preheat oven to 400° F

1, 17 ounce package puff pastry sheets, thawed
¼ cup sugar
1½ teaspoons cinnamon
¼ cup (½ stick) butter, melted
Powdered sugar or powdered sugar mixed with a pinch of cocoa for sprinkling

1. Cut each pastry sheet in half lengthwise; keep the other sheet covered in the refrigerator until ready to use. Mix together the cinnamon and sugar.
2. Brush each half sheet with melted butter, and sprinkle with 1 tablespoon cinnamon sugar. Fold both edges of the sheet towards the center. Fold again so that the edges almost meet in the center and fold this over one more time.
3. Place this roll on a plate and put into the refrigerator for 15-20 minutes and repeat procedure with remaining pastry sheets.
4. Grease two cookie sheets with pan spray. Slice each pastry roll with a serrated knife into ¼-inch pieces, place them onto the prepared cookie sheets, brush with melted butter, sprinkle the tops with a little cinnamon sugar and bake for 20-25 minutes or until golden. Cool and then sprinkle with powdered sugar or cocoa powder if you like.

Rhonda's Chocolate Krinkles

Rhonda has come to my rescue more times than I can count; I thank her much for her generosity and smiles. One day while chatting over lunch, I told her of my disastrous adventures in trying to develop a good Chocolate Krinkle recipe and that I simply couldn't do it. She laughed as she told me that all I had to do was ask, because she had a really good one; by the time I got back home she had already sent it to me. These are so good. You can alter the taste just by adding a variety of different Hershey kisses on top; for example I like these with Caramel Kisses, but Rhonda prefers Peanut Butter Kisses.

Makes approximately 30 cookies

Preheat oven to 350° F

½ cup vegetable shortening
4 squares unsweetened chocolate, melted
2 cups sugar
4 eggs
2 teaspoons vanilla
2 cups plus 2 tablespoons flour
2 teaspoons baking powder
¼ teaspoon salt
½ cup powdered sugar
30-36 unwrapped Chocolate Kisses in various flavors (optional)

1. Grease two large cookie sheets.
2. Cream the first three ingredients together, add eggs one at a time and then add the vanilla.
3. Add the other ingredients to the chocolate mixture and mix thoroughly.
4. Pinch about 2 teaspoons of dough and roll it into balls with the palms of your hand and then roll each ball in powdered sugar and place onto the prepared cookie sheets.
5. Bake for 10-12 minutes and immediately upon removing from the oven, top each cookie with a Chocolate Kiss.

Hint: Mix a little cinnamon or cocoa into a portion of the powdered sugar for a variety of flavors.

Gingersnaps

♥

Crunchy but soft centered, spicy and low in fat, what more could one ask for from an everyday cookie; well except for the fact that it must also taste good? This recipe definitely does. I still make these for a few special customers with specific dietary needs as well as for those who can and usually do eat anything that they want. This remains a favorite around the winter holidays but is also requested frequently during the warmer months. The pleasing spicy flavor will be a welcome addition to all recipe collections.

Makes approximately 2 dozen cookies

CINNAMON SUGAR MIXTURE:
¾ cup sugar
2-3 tablespoons cinnamon

Mix together and set aside in a small bowl.

COOKIES:
½ cup (1 stick) margarine
½ cup canola or safflower oil
1 cup sugar
½ cup plus 1 teaspoon brown sugar
2 eggs or equivalent amount of liquid egg substitute
⅓ cup molasses
2½ cups flour
2 teaspoons baking soda
2 teaspoons each of ginger and cinnamon
½ teaspoon each of nutmeg and cloves
Additions if desired: raisins, golden and dark and/or dried cranberries, nuts, etc.

1. Mix together the margarine, oil and sugars. Add the eggs and molasses and mix thoroughly.
2. Add flour, baking soda, spices and optional addition to the sugar mixture and then mix all ingredients together thoroughly. This batter will be very moist.
3. Grease two cookie sheets.
4. Lightly flour the palms of your hands (optional), scoop up a tablespoon full of batter (or use a small ice cream scoop) and roll the dough into a ball with the palms of your floured hands.
5. Roll each cookie ball in the cinnamon sugar mixture, place onto the prepared cookie sheets, lightly flatten each cookie with the palm of your hand and bake 10-14 minutes, depending upon whether you want soft or crunchy cookies.

Variation:
Subsitiute 1 cup (2 sticks) butter for the margarine and canola oil.

Chocolate Chocolate Chip Ice Cream Sandwich Cookies

Customers asked if I could bake a double chocolate cookie and to their delight years ago, I came up with this recipe; since described as little, rich, squished brownies. Then a neighbor asked if I could make ice cream cookie sandwiches for his son's birthday. The birthday boy loved these chocolate cookies, so I made a batch of huge ones, took them to his house, pulled out their ice cream and made a few sandwiches. In response to this fun endeavor, the birthday boy thanked me with a hug as he happily stated, "These are the greatest sandwiches I've ever tasted!"

Makes approximately 6 large sandwiches

Preheat oven to 375° F

1 cup (2 sticks) butter
1 cup brown sugar
¾ cup sugar
⅔ cup cocoa
1 tablespoon vanilla
3 eggs
1 teaspoon baking soda
2½ cups plus 1 tablespoon flour
1½ cups chocolate chips
Additions if desired: 1 cup macadamia nuts, walnuts, pecans, peanuts, peanut butter chips, white chocolate chips, or dried fruit.

1. Cream together the butter, sugars and vanilla, add the cocoa to the butter mixture and mix thoroughly. Add the remaining ingredients and mix thoroughly.
2. Grease two cookie sheets.
3. Scoop approximately ⅓ cup of dough for each cookie and place each onto prepared cookie sheets. Slightly flatten each mound of dough with the palm of your hand and bake 10-13 minutes.
4. Allow the large cookies to cool. To assemble sandwiches place 1 scoop of ice cream onto 1 large cookie, let it sit for a minute to soften, then place another large cookie on top of the ice cream, squish down gently to spread the ice cream just a smidgen and enjoy with napkins in hand!

Variation:
For smaller cookies, bake 7-9 minutes. Use a small ice cream scoopful per cookie.

Chocolate Cream Cheese Brownies

*These are not your typical cream cheese swirl brownies; instead they are a bit richer and better tasting.
I tried developing a cream cheese swirl brownie, but either the brownie part was overcooked or the cream cheese swirl got
overcooked. Months ago, I was expected to bring a dessert to a friend's gathering, so I tried once again and ended up
pleasantly pleased with my endeavor. Granted, it took a couple trials after the party to get the chocolate base as soft as
I wanted, but when I did you can bet that I the heard the expression, "Ooooh la la, " playing happily on my taste buds!*

Makes 9-12 brownies

Preheat oven to 350° F

BROWNIE BASE:
4¼ ounces unsweetened chocolate
½ cup (1 stick) butter
Scant 2 cups sugar
4 eggs plus 1 egg yolk
1 tablespoon vanilla
1 cup plus 1 tablespoon flour

FILLING:
8 ounces cream cheese
2 tablespoons butter
1 egg
1 teaspoon vanilla
1 tablespoon cornstarch
One 14-ounce can sweetened condensed milk

TOPPING:
6 ounces semi sweet chocolate (1 cup chips)
½ cup heavy cream

1. Grease a 9x13-inch pan.
2. Melt the chocolate and ½ cup butter for 1-2 minutes in the microwave or until both have thoroughly melted. Then mix this with the eggs, egg yolk, vanilla and flour until thoroughly incorporated; pour into the prepared pan. Bake for 11-13 minutes.
3. While the brownies are in the oven, beat together the cream cheese, 2 tablespoons butter, vanilla and cornstarch until smooth and fluffy. Gradually pour the condensed milk into the cream cheese, then the egg; mix thoroughly.
4. Immediately upon removing the brownies from the oven, spread the cream cheese over them and return the pan to the oven for another 25-35 minutes while making the topping.
5. Combine the chocolate and cream in a sauce pan and over low heat, stir constantly until the chocolate has melted and the mixture thickens. Immediately upon removing the brownies from the oven the second time, pour and spread the chocolate cream all over the cream cheese filling. Allow to cool for 30 minutes, then refrigerate for at least 1 hour to allow the ganache topping to harden. Cut into 9-12 bars and serve.

Dark Sweet Cherry-Filled Brownies

Said to be "awesome", "incredible", "happiness in a bar", "the best I have ever tasted" *by many friends and customers.*

Makes 9-12 brownies

Preheat oven to 350 degrees F.

3 cups sugar
1½ cups (3 sticks) melted butter
2 teaspoons vanilla
1 teaspoon kirsch or 2 teaspoons maraschino cherry juice
6 large eggs, if using smaller eggs use 7 instead of 6
1 cup plus 1½ tablespoons European or Dutch Cocoa (You can use regular cocoa but these brownies will not be as
    dark or rich.)
2 cups flour
1 teaspoon baking soda powder
1 cup chocolate chips
1½ cups sweet, dark pitted cherries

1. Cream together the butter, sugar, eggs and vanilla for 3 minutes.
2. Add the cocoa to the butter mixture and thoroughly mix for 1 minute.
3. Add the flour, baking powder and chocolate chips to the mixture and thoroughly mix for 2 more minutes.
4. Gently fold the raspberries thoroughly into the batter.
5. Grease a 9x13 inch pan.
6. Pour batter into the prepared pan.
7. Bake 45-55 minutes or until inserted knife or toothpick comes out clean. (The center will fall just a tad.)

High Altitude Only: When *tripling* this recipe add an extra egg, but not when making a double batch.

Frozen Yogurt Tarts

♥

Have you ever walked past a dessert tray in a bakery or restaurant and dreamed about eating those lovely little tarts placed so temptingly right in the front and center of the tray? You know the ones, with the creamy filling and the shiny fruits on top that cause your hips to expand just from the thought of fulfilling your desire to taste that luscious creamy filling swirling around your palate. If this has happened to you, these dreamy little tarts should appease your appetite, but you can shed your guilt, as they are low in fat.

Makes 4

Preheat oven to 350° F

CRUST:
1½ plus 1 tablespoon flour
2 tablespoons sugar or sugar substitute
½ cup canola oil
2 tablespoon milk

FILLING:
1 quart frozen vanilla, chocolate or strawberry yogurt, slightly thawed
1 cup fresh fruits such as: strawberries, berries, kiwi, nectarines, plums, peaches, pineapple and/or sweet dark cherries, pitted

GLAZE TOPPING:
3 tablespoons sugar
2¼ teaspoons cornstarch
3 tablespoons lemon juice
1½ tablespoons orange juice
1½ tablespoons water

1. Grease four 4-inch round tart pans with pan spray.
2. Mix the first four ingredients together thoroughly, roll the dough out on a floured surface, cut into 4 rounded pieces, fit each into the prepared tart pans. Bake for 12-15 minutes or until golden brown.
3. Whip the frozen yogurt until smooth, fill each tart shell to about ¼-inch from the top with yogurt and smooth it down with a spatula so that the surface is flat. Design the tops with your choice of fruits. Place them into the freezer while making the glaze.
4. Combine the sugar, cornstarch, juices and water in a saucepan, heat over medium high until the mixture boils. Stir and boil for 1 minute or until the glaze appears clear.
5. Remove the tarts from the freezer, brush the glaze over the fruit and serve.

The Grand Milkshake for Adults Only

Imagine it is a hot, humid, summer evening; the kids are gone or at the local fair for several more hours, the adults have just finished dinner and are in the mood for something cool but extraordinary for dessert. It is just the two of you and a couple friends, so why not make this quick and quite delicious milkshake, literally for adults only? Then sit back and enjoy.

Serves 4

One ½ gallon (32 ounces) of light coffee ice cream
1⅓ cups milk (amount depends on how thick you like your shakes, it can be decreased)
⅓ cup Bailey's Irish Cream
⅓ cup Grand Marnier or Cointreau Liqueur
⅓ cup Amaretto
⅓ cup Kahlua
Couple splashes Tia Maria

This will take two separate batches for four adults, unless you have a very large blender, and then you can add everything at once.

1. Place half of each ingredient into a blender, beginning with the ice cream, blend at low speed until all ingredients are thick but thoroughly combined, and pour into two large glasses, place a straw into each and serve.
2. Repeat with remaining ingredients and enjoy one of the luxuries of being an adult.

Grandmom's Bread Pudding

Comforting and phenomenal in taste, what more could you ask for after a long day and a home-cooked meal? Growing up, the kids were forbidden to taste this amazingly soft-centered dessert. We were told that we had to wait a few more years, as this was only for adults. Decades later I found out why, when I found this recipe in my grandmother's bottomless tin box and noticed that this special dessert was made with whiskey. I then understood their reasoning but could wait no longer for a taste of this luscious comfort—once reserved for adults only.

Serves 4-6

Preheat oven to 350° F

PUDDING:
Six 8-inch long stale French breads or sub sandwich rolls, crumbled into pieces and crumbs.
4 cups milk
3 eggs
1½ cups sugar
2 tablespoons vanilla or 1 tablespoon vanilla and 1 tablespoon maple extract
1¼ cup dark and golden raisins, combined or you could use dried tart cherries

TOPPING:
½ cup (1 stick) butter
1 cup sugar
¼ cup plus 1 tablespoon whiskey
1 extra large egg

1. Place bread pieces and crumbs into a large bowl, pour the milk over the bread and allow to soak for 1 full hour.
2. Generously butter a 2-quart casserole dish.
3. In a separate bowl, beat the eggs into 1½ cups sugar, add the vanilla, mix and gently add the bread mixture and stir in the raisins until just combined.
4. Pour this mixture into the prepared dish and bake 45-55 minutes.
5. Begin to prepare the sauce as soon as you place the bread mixture in the oven. Using a double boiler, fill the bottom section with hot water and heat over medium high until boiling. Put the top section over the boiling water, melt the butter and add 1 cup sugar, continuing to stir until the sugar has dissolved and the mixture is very hot. Remove the pan from the heat and vigorously whisk in the egg. Continue whisking until this mixture has cooled to room temperature and then whisk in the whiskey.
6. Remove the pudding from the oven and turn on the oven broiler. Pour the sauce all over the pudding and then place on the lowest oven rack below the broiler. Broil the pudding until the sauce bubbles and has thickened, remove and serve immediately.

Variations:
Top the finished product with whipped cream, or serve with a bowl of ice cream. Substitute your favorite brandy for the whiskey, and add dried chopped apricots instead of raisins.

Great Grandmother's Cake Crumb Pudding

Once again I found magic in that old tin box, written on an old piece of tablet paper in my great-grandmother's script. The paper was darkened and the writing faded, but I saw the words "use old cake" so my curiosity was sparked. I soon realized that our ancestors used their imaginations and never wasted or threw out a crumb of food that could still be used. Instead, they used the leftovers to make additional comforts such as this pleasing pudding that is made from the crumbs of old cake. Since finding this recipe, rarely will I ever throw out my not-so-pretty cakes anymore, instead I just let them get crusty and crumbly and then make this scrumptiously easy treat.

Serves 4-6

Preheat oven to 350° F

6 tablespoons (¾ stick) butter
½ cup sugar
1 extra large egg or 2 medium eggs
½ cup buttermilk mixed with ½ teaspoon baking soda
⅔ cup raisins, dark and golden combined
½ cup pecans
½ cup Karo syrup or molasses
¼ cup flour
1 teaspoon cinnamon
2 cups old cake crumbs

1. Cream together the butter and sugar, then add the egg and stir until combined. Mix the baking soda into the buttermilk and let sit for 1-2 minutes.
2. Stir the buttermilk into the sugar mixture, add the raisins and nuts, stir and add the flour and spices. Mix and stir in the cake crumbs.
3. Grease a 2-quart casserole dish, pour the mixture into the dish, cover with the lid and bake for 15 minutes, then remove the lid and bake for an additional 15-18 minutes. Serve hot with milk or cream, or refrigerate until serving.

Variation:
Add 1-2 teaspoons maple extract for a different, wholesome flavor.

Cookie's Kugel

*For those who do not know what kugel is, it's a baked noodle pudding, customarily served on the Jewish Sabbath
or holidays. However, you do not need to be Jewish to indulge in its marvelous sweet flavor. Growing up, I had always
heard the Lovely Ladies talk about how Cookie makes the best kugel. So I asked her to share and she finally sent it to me.
I made a batch within the next couple days, and must say that the Ladies were right,
for Cookie's kugel is fantastic and definitely should be shared with all.*

Serves 8-10

Preheat oven to 350° F

8 ounces thin egg noodles, cooked and drained according to package directions
2 tablespoons corn flake crumbs
2 tablespoons sugar
6-7 large eggs
¾ cup sugar
1 pound small curd creamed cottage cheese
½ cup (1 stick) butter or margarine, melted
4 ounces cream cheese
1 cup sour cream

1. Grease a 9x13-inch Pyrex pan.
2. Mix the corn flake crumbs and sugar together and put aside.
3. Mix the remaining ingredients (except the noodles) until foamy, then add the noodles, stir, pour into the prepared
   pan and bake for 20-23 minutes.
4. Remove from the oven, sprinkle the crumbs on top of the pudding, place the pan back in the oven and bake for
   45-55 minutes.
5. Serve warm with sour cream and fresh berries.

Variation:
Add ½ cup raisins and 1 teaspoon cinnamon and serve with warmed maple syrup.

Hint: If freezing or serving later in the day, bake 20 minutes, cool and freeze. Before serving, thaw the kugel, then
sprinkle with the crumbs and bake for an additional 20-30 minutes, or until set.

Grandmom's Rice Pudding

This creamy, rich, phenomenal-tasting treat is one of my all time favorite desserts. I was so excited the day that I found this recipe written on an index card that I immediately preheated the oven, stirred the ingredients together and anxiously waited for the hours to pass until I could dive my fork right into the bowl. I called a friend over to sample this delight. She arrived just as I was taking it out of the oven. We decided to forfeit the serving bowls and helped ourselves right out of the casserole dish. After our satisfying frenzy, there was only a small serving left, so I gave it to her to take to her daughter so that she could share a taste of homemade goodness.

Serves 4-6

Preheat oven to 300° F

2 tablespoons butter
2 cups cream (only heavy cream will work)
2 cups milk
¼ cup sugar
½ cup uncooked white rice (preferably long-grain)
1-2 teaspoons vanilla
Pinch or 2 salt
1 teaspoon cinnamon
⅔ cups raisins, dark and/or golden

1. Generously grease a 2-quart casserole dish (with a matching lid) with the butter.
2. In a large bowl, thoroughly mix together all remaining ingredients. Pour the mixture into the prepared casserole dish, cover with the lid and bake for 60 minutes.
3. Remove the dish from the oven, stir the rice mixture and place back into the oven uncovered for 60-70 minutes or until all liquid is absorbed and the mixture jiggles slightly.
4. Serve hot or cover tightly with plastic wrap to prevent a skin from forming on the top.

Lizanne's Caramel Flan

A friend first tasted this dessert at a small Cuban café on Elizabeth Street in Key West. Lizanne immediately determined that this was a taste of heaven right there on the spot and decided that she would have to try to reproduce the magnificent flavor. Her recipe is so scrumptious that I did not need to come up with one of my own; she generously wrote this down to share while we were indulging ourselves with much too much of this wonderful dessert.

Serves 4

¾ cup sugar (for caramelizing)
8 large eggs
¾ cup sugar
1 quart (4 cups) milk
1 tablespoon vanilla
½ cup flaked or shredded coconut (optional)

1. Put the sugar into a skillet and cook over low heat, without stirring, until the sugar turns into a golden brown clear syrup.
2. Scrape the syrup into a 1½-quart round mold or casserole and rotate the pan until the entire inside is coated with a thin layer of caramelized sugar.
3. In a medium bowl beat the eggs while gradually adding the remaining sugar. Then beat in the milk and vanilla. Pour the mixture into the sugar-coated pan.
4. Fill a larger pan with 1 inch of warm water and put the pan with the egg mixture into the pan of water.
5. Bake the flan for 1 hour and 20 minutes; remove from the oven, cool to room temperature and then refrigerate for several hours.
6. Loosen the edges of the flan with the tip of a sharp knife, then turn the flan upside down and let it drop onto a platter, the caramel will run slightly down the sides of the flan onto the plate. Sprinkle the top and sides with coconut if desired.

Hint: This recipe can be made using 6-8 small Pyrex dishes, the instructions are not altered but the baking time is decreased by 20 minutes. This can also be served slightly warm.

Tapioca Apples

♥

After my grandmother passed away, my father sent me her gigantic walnut hutch. Somehow I was able to bribe the neighborhood boys (the power of chocolate chip cookies on kids is miraculous) to bring it upstairs. After they left with warm cookies in hand, I began opening the drawers and cabinets. I was thrilled when I found a few treasures inside: an ancient fan, some linens, knick-knacks and a couple of old books. One of these books was titled The Early American Cookbook, *by Hyla O'Connor, published in 1974. As I skimmed the pages, a familiar recipe caught my eye, and I specifically remembered her making something like this after I had my wisdom teeth extracted. Instinct told me that I just had to make this recipe, but if I remembered correctly, Grandmom added a pinch of something that was not listed in the ingredients. So I began to play and the following recipe was the delicious, comforting result.*

Serves 4-6

Preheat oven to 350° F

¼ cup pearl tapioca, (do not use Minute Tapioca)
2 cups water
¼ teaspoon salt
5 cooking apples (Granny Smith, Gala, Rome) peeled, cored and quartered
½ cup sugar
1 teaspoon cinnamon
⅔ cup dark and golden raisins, dried cherries or craisins (optional)

1. Soak the tapioca in the water for several hours or overnight in a bowl. When ready to use, pour this mixture into a saucepan and heat over medium for about 20-25 minutes or until the tapioca is transparent. Stir in the salt.
2. Mix sugar and cinnamon together. Place the apples into a 2-quart casserole dish, sprinkle them with the cinnamon sugar and raisins and then pour the tapioca mixture over the apples and bake for 45-55 minutes or until the apples are tender. Best served warm, but tastes just fine cool. Store any leftovers covered in the refrigerator.

Variation:
Substitute apples with pears, peaches and/or apricots.

Elizabeth's Favorite Vanilla Seashore Pudding

In her words, "Every summer while I was growing up, we spent 6-8 unforgettable weeks at the 'shore,' otherwise known as Ocean City, New Jersey. We always stayed in a rental house, (a half block from the beach and my beloved ocean) near a friends' house who were there for the whole season. Our friends had a maid who fixed us this wonderful pudding on days when it rained, so that we still had something to look forward to. Since we couldn't spend the day on our rafts or building sand castles as usual, we went into town to see a movie and came back to their house to enjoy the best pudding ever. We ate it warm, dribbled with chocolate syrup as a grand finale to the day's enjoyment! There were at least four of us eating like we were starving and the adults were lucky if they got any!"

Severs 3-4

½ cup sugar
3 tablespoons cornstarch
⅛ teaspoon salt
2 cups whole milk
2 egg yolks
2 tablespoons unsalted butter
1 teaspoon vanilla extract
Chocolate syrup optional

1. Whisk together the sugar, cornstarch, and salt in a saucepan.
2. Pour ¼ cup of the milk into the sugar mixture, stirring to form a smooth paste. Then whisk in the remaining milk and the egg yolks.
3. Cook the pudding mixture over low heat, stirring continuously with a wooden spoon until thickened, about 15 minutes. Do not allow it to boil! Remove from heat and stir in the butter and vanilla. Scrape the pudding into a bowl and serve or cover with plastic wrap, pressing it to the surface to make an airtight seal and prevent a "skin" from forming. Refrigerate until well chilled, about 1 hour.

Variations:

Banana Pudding

Add 1½ sliced bananas to the pudding or slice the same amount into serving bowls and top with the pudding. A pinch of nutmeg adds a bit of a different flavor as well.

Banana Cream Pie

Make the Vanilla Pudding recipe and bake a single Pie Crust (p. 297). Slice 3 bananas into ¼-inch slices over the bottom of the prepared crust bottom, cover the bananas with the pudding and then make Whipped Cream Topping.

Whipped Cream Topping

1 cup heavy cream
1-2 teaspoons vanilla
2 tablespoons sugar

1. In a mixing bowl beat all ingredients together until stiff peaks form and then spread the whipped cream topping over the filling. Swirl the cream around with a rubber spatula or the back of a spoon and refrigerate until serving.

Hint: It is best to spread the whipped cream topping on a pie or cake just before serving to prevent it from slightly separating in the refrigerator.

Cherry Pudding

Add 1-1½ cups pitted and finely chopped cherries plus 1 teaspoon of kirsch, cherry extract or 1 tablespoon of maraschino cherry juice to the pudding.

Berry Pudding

Add 1-1½ cups fresh berries and an extra teaspoon vanilla to the pudding.

Cecil's Date Pudding

Cecil, a charming gentleman, has also spent many of his days baking and serving his delicious creations. When we first met, I was delivering a few of my Baking at High Altitude books to his gift store in Grand Lake, Colorado. As his wife and I were talking, he informed me that he had also self-published his own cookbook, titled Home Cookin' Old and New Favorite Recipes, *published in 2001. When he handed me a copy, I immediately noticed that he included a recipe for date pudding, and inquired if I may use it in this book. He generously granted me permission with a big smile. When I got back home, I made his recipe; trust me when I say that this pudding is fabulous and must be shared.*

Serves 6

Preheat oven to 350° F

1½ cups chopped dates or figs
1 teaspoon baking soda
1 cup hot water
1 cup sugar
1 tablespoon butter
1 egg
½ teaspoon salt
1 cup flour
½ cup chopped nuts

1. Mix the dates, water and baking soda together.
2. Mix all remaining ingredients together and then stir them into the dates. Grease a 9x9-inch pan and pour mixed ingredients into the pan.
3. Bake the pudding for 30 minutes and serve.

Grandmom's Pie Crust

Flaky, full flavored and easily assembled or doubled, this recipe is a welcome addition in any household's recipe collection.

Makes 1–9-inch Pie Crust

1½ cups flour
½ teaspoon salt
2-3 tablespoons cold water
½ cup plus 1 tablespoon cold vegetable shortening

1. Sift together the flour and salt in a medium bowl.
2. With a pastry blender or two forks, cut the shortening into the flour/salt combination until little beads begin to form. Using a fork, work the water into the flour and shortening mixture until the dough begins to form into a ball. Do not overwork the dough.
3. Press the dough into a flat ball and roll out onto a floured surface. Turn the dough carefully over two or three times during the rolling process.
4. Once the dough is rolled out, gently lift and fit the dough into a 9 or 10-inch deep dish pie pan.
5. Trim off any excess dough and either flute the edge or press the edge with the tines of a fork to the side of the pan.

Variations:

DOUBLE PIE CRUST
Double the above recipe and divide the dough in half prior to rolling. Have top crust rolled out and ready to apply on top of the filling. Once placed on top of the filling tuck the edges of the top crust under the edge of the bottom crust, flute the edge, poke a few holes into the top crust so that the filling can breathe and bake a chosen pie as directed.

LATTICE TOPPED PIE
Follow the same directions as for a Double Pie Crust, only slice the top crust into 12 strips. Place 6 strips over the filling, then place the remaining strips in the opposite direction over the filling, in a woven pattern; fold the edges under the bottom edge and flute, then bake the pie according to given directions.

Low Fat Pie Crust ♥

1 cup plus 1 tablespoon flour
2 tablespoons canola oil
1 tablespoon skim milk

1. Mix all ingredients together and roll as you would for any other pie crust.

Chocolate Cream Pudding or Pie

Ok, yes, this pie is also listed in Baking at High Altitude; The Muffin Lady's Old Fashioned Recipes, *my first cookbook, but it is so good that I couldn't resist adding it to these pages as well. My favorite part about making this amazingly versatile pie is that it provides the exquisite opportunity to taste the outstanding filling while it is still hot (and at its finest in my opinion) and before it is poured into the pie shell to cool. Actually, when I came up with this recipe, I was on a mission to make homemade chocolate pudding and did not know that I had created a filling for a chocolate crème pie until a few hours later after it had cooled and could easily be sliced. However it doesn't matter how you choose to indulge in this recipe, for whether served cold or hot it is literally one of my finest creations. Enjoy!*

Serves 6

Preheat oven to 350° F

1 single pie crust recipe, baked (p. 297), or prepackaged pie shell

3¼ squares of unsweetened chocolate
¾ cup plus 2 tablespoons sugar
¼ cup plus 1 tablespoon cornstarch
3 egg yolks
2⅔ cups of milk
¼ cup heavy cream
1 tablespoon vanilla
2 tablespoons butter

1. Melt the chocolate in a small microwave-safe bowl and set aside.
2. In a medium saucepan, completely mix together the sugar and corn starch. Add the milk, vanilla and eggs to the sugar and mix with a rubber spatula, making sure all sugar is incorporated. Scrape the bowl for lingering sugar on the bottom.
3. Cook over medium high heat, stirring constantly to prevent burning. After about 7-10 minutes the mixture will begin to thicken. Just when it begins to boil, turn off the heat, remove the pan from the heat and continue stirring for 1 minute.
4. Immediately add the melted chocolate and the butter to the filling and thoroughly mix until fully incorporated. (Now, only if you want to, put a big spoon in and taste it; to me, this is the best part of making this pie.) Immediately cover the filling with a piece of plastic wrap to prevent a skin from forming and then allow to cool for 30 minutes.
5. After 30 minutes, remove the plastic wrap, stir the filling and pour it into the prepared pie crust. Cover the filling again with plastic wrap and refrigerate for at least 2½ hours prior to serving with the whipped cream topping.

Whipped Cream Topping

1 cup heavy whipping cream
1 teaspoon vanilla
2 tablespoon powdered sugar (optional)

1. In a mixing bowl beat the ingredients until stiff peaks form, spread the whipped cream topping over the filling and swirl the cream around with a rubber spatula or the back of a spoon. Sprinkle the topping with grated unsweetened chocolate or chocolate sprinkles.

Hint: Always put the whipped cream onto the pie just before serving, otherwise it may begin to separate.

Variations:

Banana Chocolate Cream Pie

Add 2-3 sliced bananas to the bottom of the crust prior to pouring in the filling and you've made a different but absolutely scrumptious pie.

Berry Chocolate Cream Pie

Sprinkle 1 tablespoon sugar into the berries, (any kind, or use sweet dark pitted cherries) and spread them into the bottom of the prepared pie crust. Pour the chocolate filling on top of the fruit. A few fresh berries on top of the whipped cream supplies a colorful effect.

Spiked Chocolate Cream Pie

Add ¼ cup of Grand Marnier to the filling when adding the chocolate, and add 3-4 tablespoons Bailey's Irish Cream to the Whipped Topping instead of the sugar and vanilla.

Cheddar Apple Pie

SUGAR
FREE

I know many of you have superb apple pie recipes, but this recipe has been said to be one of the best.
Enjoy this pie with a glass of milk, cup of coffee, tea or a warmed snifter of brandy. When served warm with
a scoop of ice cream and/or a drizzle of caramel sauce, rumor has it that this makes a perfectly delightful dessert.

Preheat oven to 375° F

1 double pie crust recipe (p. 297)

6½ cups (about 3¼ lbs) apples, peeled, cored and thinly sliced
½ cup sugar or equivalent amount of sugar substitute
1 tablespoon lemon juice
2 tablespoons flour
2 teaspoons cinnamon
½ teaspoon nutmeg
1 packed cup shredded cheddar cheese
2 tablespoons butter or margarine

1. Prepare the crusts, gently place the bottom crust into a 9-inch pie pan and trim the edge. Sprinkle ¼ cup cheese all over the bottom crust and then roll out the remaining crust and have ready to place on top of the apples.
2. Toss the apples with the lemon juice.
3. Stir together the dry ingredients.
4. Gently mix the dry ingredients, remaining cheese and the apples together to coat and then spoon or pour the apples onto the bottom crust. Dot the apples with slices of the butter.
5. Cover the apples with the remaining crust. Fold upper crust edge under the lower crust edge and flute the edge. Poke a few holes into the top crust with a fork. Sprinkle the top with 1-2 teaspoons cinnamon sugar.
6. Bake for 50-60 minutes. If the edges begin to brown too early, cover the edge of the pie with a piece of foil to prevent burning and continue baking.

Variations:

Apple Cranberry Pie

Omit the cheese, decrease the amount of apples by 1½ cups and add 1¼ cup fresh cranberries.

Maple Apple Pie

Omit the cheese and substitute ½ of the sugar with pure maple syrup mixed with ½ teaspoon maple extract and bake accordingly.

Dad's Favorite Apple Pear Oatmeal Crustless Pie

♥ SUGAR

Although it is best to make this lovely combination when the fruits are at their peak, I saw my mother make this often in the off season because my dad loved it. Unfortunately dad suffered from diabetes and had an unfulfilled sweet tooth. My mother would try this or that recipe, he would always taste them, praise them and then when she wasn't around he'd toss a good portion down the garbage disposal and later tell her he ate it. So when I saw him joyfully munching on this dessert and taking an extra bite out the pan, I knew that it had to be good and asked my mother to write it down. Since then, I have made it for many, with disease and without; all seem to savor it just as Dad did.

Serves 6

Preheat oven to 375° F

3 cups peeled, cored, and thinly sliced Granny Smith apples
4 pears, peeled, cored and thinly sliced
⅓ cup plus 1 tablespoon sugar or equivalent amount of sugar substitute
Juice and grated zest of 1 lemon
¼ teaspoon ground nutmeg
1 teaspoon cinnamon
1½ tablespoons cornstarch
1 cup all-purpose flour
½ cup old-fashioned rolled oats (not instant)
⅓ cup firmly packed light brown sugar or equivalent amount of sugar substitute
½ teaspoon ground cinnamon
½ cup (1 stick) very cold unsalted butter or margarine, cut into ¼-inch pieces
2-3 tablespoons butter, margarine or oil

1. Grease a 9-inch pie pan or a 9x9-inch square pan well with butter, margarine or pan spray. Place the pan onto a cookie sheet lined with foil.
2. Combine the apples and pears, ⅓ cup 1 tablespoon sugar, lemon juice and zest in a large mixing bowl. Mix well and then add the nutmeg, cinnamon and cornstarch to the fruit and mix thoroughly.
3. Pour the mixture into the prepared pan and bake for 30-35 minutes. While the pie is baking, cut the butter into the flour, oats, brown sugar, and cinnamon until it resembles small peas or coarse crumbs; refrigerate until use.
4. Remove from pie from oven and sprinkle the top with the oat mixture, place back into the oven and bake for another 30-35 minutes. If the topping begins to brown too much, loosely tuck a piece of foil around the pie. Bake until the center is bubbly and the top crumbs are golden brown.

Peach Pecan Pie

In the words of a few of my 'guinea pigs,' "This pie is the best of the best!"

Preheat oven to 350° F

1 double pie crust recipe (p. 297)

6 cups fresh, pitted, skinned and sliced peaches or 3 cans sliced light peaches, drained
⅔ cup plus 1 tablespoon chopped pecans
½ cup sugar
2 tablespoons brown sugar
2½ tablespoons tapioca
1 tablespoon lemon juice
1½ teaspoons cinnamon
½ teaspoon nutmeg
3 tablespoons butter
1 tablespoon milk
1 teaspoon sugar

1. Prepare the pie crusts and gently place one into a 9-inch pie pan; have the top crust rolled and ready to apply. If using a lattice top crust, precut the strips and have them ready to apply on top of the filling.
2. Toss together the peaches, ⅔ cup pecans, sugars, tapioca, juice and spices and pour into the prepared pie crust, then dot the fruit with slices of butter.
3. Gently place top crust onto the filling and flute the edge. With your fingers or a pastry brush, brush the crust with a tablespoon of milk or water, sprinkle a teaspoon of sugar and the remaining tablespoon of pecans on top, poke a few holes around the crust and bake for about 1 hour or until juices begin to bubble and crust is golden.

Blueberry Pie

❤ **SUGAR** ~~FREE~~

What can I say about a pie that is as appealing and enticing as a pie can be, is full of anti-oxidants and vitamins and has been requested over and over again for many years? I guess I could say that this pie is somewhat healthier than a candy bar or prepackaged dessert, or I could say that each person who tastes a piece raves about it to all they meet, or I could advise that this magnificent pie should be in everyone's recipe collection. I think I pretty much said it all!

Preheat oven to 375 degrees F.

1 double pie crust recipe (p. 297)

6 cups of fresh blueberries, or two 12-ounce packages frozen blueberries
⅔ cup sugar or sugar substitute
2½ tablespoons tapioca
½ teaspoon cinnamon
1 tablespoon lemon juice
3 tablespoons butter, margarine or canola spread
1 tablespoon milk

1. Prepare the pie crusts and gently place one into a 9-inch pie pan, and have the top crust rolled and ready to apply. If using a lattice top, precut the strips, and have them ready to apply on top of the filling.
2. Toss together the blueberries, tapioca, cinnamon and lemon juice and pour the berries into the pie crust. Dot the top of the fruit with slices of the butter.
3. Gently place the top or lattice strips crust onto the berries, flute the edge and brush the crust with a tablespoon of milk or water, using your fingers or a pastry brush. Sprinkle a teaspoon of sugar on top of the crust and poke holes into the crust with a fork.
4. Bake for about 45-50 minutes or until juices begin to bubble. If the pie's edge begins to brown, cover the edge with a piece of foil and continue baking. Allow to cool for 30 plus minutes prior to serving.

Variations:
Raspberry, blackberries, huckleberries or what ever berry your heart desires can be used with or instead of the blueberries in this pie.

Mine and Elizabeth's Favorite Cheese Pie

Do the members of your household have a variety of tastes? No problem, for diverse tastes can be catered to with this dreamy treat. Elizabeth and I are as close as sisters, but we sure argue over how to best prepare this favorite recipe, generously shared by her mother. She claims that the following is best without cherries, while I will say that this is best with cherries. So for purposes of resolving this difference of opinion, I came up with a remarkable solution; I add cherries to half of the pie, and leave the opposite side empty prior to spreading the topping and we are each as happy as can be.

Preheat oven to 350° F

12 graham crackers
¼ cup (½ stick) butter
12 ounces cream cheese
2 eggs, beaten
¾ cup sugar
2 teaspoons vanilla
1 teaspoons lemon juice
1 cup sour cream
3 tablespoons sugar
1 teaspoon vanilla
½ teaspoon lemon juice
1½ cups fresh, pitted cherries (optional or ¾ cup cherries placed on ½ of the pie)

1. Roll out the crackers until fine and crumbly and set aside 1 tablespoon for the topping. Mix crushed crackers with melted butter and pat into a 9-inch pie pan.
2. Beat together the cream cheese, eggs, sugar, vanilla and juice until smooth and fluffy, pour this into the prepared crust and bake for just 15 minutes while preparing the topping.
3. Thoroughly mix together the sour cream, sugar, vanilla and juice until smooth and creamy.
4. Remove the pie from the oven and let cool for 5 minutes. Sprinkle the crumb topping on to the hot filling, gently place the cherries all over (or on one half of) the filling, spread on the topping, place back into the oven and bake for an additional 10-15 minutes. Allow the pie to set in the refrigerator for at least 5 hours before serving.

Apple Pandowdy

A few months ago I met a wonderful man who specifically requested that I bake him some Apple Pandowdy, something that I had never heard of before. I soon learned that it is a type of plain (dowdy) fruit cobbler (also called duffs, grunts or slumps depending on one's country of origin), baked in a pan. I came up with this recipe and was thrilled that something so plain and easy could taste so remarkably good. When I took him a plateful, he beamed at first sight, then gave me a hug of thanks and grabbed a fork. This made my day for he was as happy as could be and ate the whole plateful with requests for more.

Serves 6

Preheat oven to 350° F

1¼ cups (2½ sticks) butter
⅔ cup sugar
1 egg
1 cup plus 1 tablespoon milk
2⅔ cups flour
1 tablespoon baking powder
4 cups peeled, cored and sliced apples (or pears, peaches or plums)
⅓ cup brown sugar
2 teaspoons cinnamon
½ teaspoon nutmeg

1. Grease a 9x9-inch pan.
2. Combine flour and baking powder and put aside. Mix the brown sugar, cinnamon and nutmeg and put aside.
3. Place the sliced apples in the prepared pan and sprinkle with the brown sugar mixture.
4. Cream the butter and sugar until fluffy, mix in the egg, and add the flour in parts, alternating with milk, and mix thoroughly between each addition. Spread batter evenly over apples and bake for about 50 minutes or until golden brown.

Hint: You can serve it right out of the pan, or invert it onto a serving plate like an upside-down cake; warm or at room temperature. Top with whipped cream or ice cream if desired.

Fried Bananas

For a change of pace, why not make a batch of these fabulous treats, and then watch them disappear right before your eyes? Although not necessary, the splendor of this lovely treat is enhanced with a drizzle of chocolate or caramel sauce. And the best part is, you can also use this same dough to prepare Fried Apples, Peaches or Pears, so make a variety and please everyone's tastes.

Serves 4-8

4 large semi-green bananas, peeled and cut in half lengthwise
1 cup plus 1 tablespoon flour
1 cup water
2½ teaspoons sugar
1 teaspoon cinnamon
¼ teaspoon nutmeg
Oil for frying
Chocolate or Caramel Sauce (p. 343) (optional)

1. Mix the flour, sugar, cinnamon and nutmeg into a large bowl, make a well in the center, pour in the water and whisk until just combined, leaving a few lumps of flour. Let this sit for 25-30 minutes.
2. Fill a deep skillet ⅓ full of oil and heat until hot. You will know when it is hot enough by sprinkling a couple drops of water into the oil; if it immediately sizzles the oil is ready.
3. Dip and coat each banana in the flour mixture and let any excess batter drip back into the bowl. Using a pair of tongs, place each banana into the hot oil and allow it to fry for 2-3 minutes or until golden, and immediately remove and place onto a paper towel-lined plate.
4. Serve hot with choice of sauces (pp. 343-344) and/or with a scoop of frozen yogurt or ice cream.

Rich Pound Cake

As often as I had tried to make a good pound cake up here on the mountain, it always sank in the center, no matter how many adjustments I made. Then I asked a friend and local pastry chef what I was doing wrong. God bless him, for he said that for a good pound cake, the ingredients must be mixed a little at a time and at a very slow speed, but added that pound cake has a tendency to rapidly dry out up here as a result of the low humidity. I dislike dry baked goods and refuse to serve or sell any, so I had to alter my recipe, ensuring that the cake would be nice and moist. Little did I know when I began, I was producing a remarkably richer, more pleasing cake than initially intended!

Preheat oven to 325° F

1½ cups (3 sticks) butter
8 ounce cream cheese
2¾ cups plus 2 tablespoons sugar
2 teaspoons vanilla
1 teaspoon almond extract
6 large eggs (do not use medium, only large or extra large)
3¼ cup flour

1. Thoroughly cream together the butter, cream cheese and sugar until light and fluffy.
2. While butter mix is blending, sift the flour once and then remeasure the sifted flour into 3¼ cups.
3. Begin to slowly add the flour and eggs by first adding ½ cup of the flour, mixing it thoroughly into the butter mixture, then adding 1 egg and thoroughly mixing it in before adding more flour. Continue to add the flour and eggs this way, slowly allowing each addition to thoroughly incorporate into the batter before adding another.
4. Continue to slowly mix these ingredients for another minute while you grease a 10-inch bundt pan with butter or pan spray and a dusting of flour to prevent sticking.
5. Spread the batter evenly into the prepared pan and bake for 1 hour and 15-25 minutes or until an inserted knife or toothpick comes out clean. Let the cake cool in the pan for 5 minutes, invert onto a plate, cool for a few minutes or longer and serve as is or with fresh sliced fruit, a drizzling of chocolate sauce or a dollop of ice cream.

Butter Cream Filled Coffeecake
(The Cake of Edible Sin)

This luscious cake offers a taste of the purest of edible sins in my opinion. Sinful was the word that came to mind when I delivered the first exquisite bite to my palate. A streusel topping of nutty crunch, and a rich, buttery filling added to the center, puts this delicious cake right at the top of any list of desired desserts. Positively perfect to serve after a fine meal with a cup of coffee or tea; I have yet to meet someone who will turn away from a slice of this sensationally, enticing treat.

STREUSEL TOPPING:
½ cup (1 stick) butter
1 cup plus 1 tablespoon flour
1⅓ cup brown sugar
1½ teaspoons cinnamon
⅔ cup chopped walnuts, pecans or raisins (preferably golden raisins)

CAKE:
2 cups plus 3 tablespoons flour
¾ teaspoon baking powder
1 teaspoon baking soda
Pinch of salt
¾ cup (1½ sticks) butter
1 cup sugar
3 eggs
1½-2 teaspoons vanilla
1⅓ cup sour cream

FILLING:
⅓ cup plus 1 tablespoon flour
1⅓ cups plus 2 teaspoons milk
1 cup (2 sticks) butter
1⅓ cups sugar
1½ teaspoons vanilla

Preheat oven to 325° F

1. With a pastry blender or whip of an electric mixer, cut ½ cup of butter into 1 cup plus flour, brown sugar and cinnamon until crumbly (you will want fine small crumbs, not large ones); then stir in the nuts or raisins and put aside in a separate bowl.
2. Cream ¾ cup butter, slowly add the sugar; cream until light and fluffy. Adding 1 egg at a time and incorporate it into the butter before adding another, then slowly mix in the eggs and then the vanilla.

3. Sift the flour, baking powder, soda and salt once onto a large piece of waxed paper. Gradually add the flour to the butter mixture, alternating with the sour cream. (It is best to begin and end with the flour.)

4. Mix the batter thoroughly at slow speed while you grease a 9x13-inch pan with butter or pan spray and dust the pan lightly with flour. You could also line the bottom and sides of the pan with a very large piece of waxed paper, making sure that the paper overlaps the sides of the pan and is extremely smooth along the bottom and sides of the pan; then grease and flour the paper.

5. Spread the batter into the prepared pan and sprinkle the top with the crumbs previously put aside. Bake for 45-55 minutes or until an inserted knife or toothpick comes out clean.

6. Allow the cake to cool for 10 minutes and very gently invert the pan onto a large plate; gently thump the bottom of the pan, allowing the cake to loosen from the sides and bottom and easily slide out onto the plate. Gently invert onto another large plate so that the streusel topping is right side up. Let this sit for 3-4 minutes and then loosely cover in plastic wrap and cool completely. If you have lined the pan with waxed paper, allow the cake to cool for 15 minutes and then very gently lift it out of the pan, cool for a few minutes and then lightly cover with plastic wrap.

7. Once the cake has cooled, begin to prepare the butter cream filling. Mix 1/3 plus cup flour and milk into a saucepan and heat over low, stirring constantly until it is very thick and the consistency of a frosting, remove from the heat and cool.

8. Cream the remaining butter and sugar until fluffy, add the thickened milk, beat until light and fluffy. Blend in the vanilla.

9. Remove the plastic wrap from the cake, slice the cake in half horizontally with a large serrated knife and as gingerly as you can (to prevent breaking), put the top half onto a large piece of waxed paper.

10. Spread the butter cream all over the bottom layer, top the cream with the streusel layer of the cake by simply sliding it off of the waxed paper and onto the filling and serve or cover tightly.

Hint: Refrigerate in areas of high humidity.

Mom's Cherry Oat Cake

♥ SUGAR

When I walked into my parents' home one day, I noticed this fragrant cake cooling. It was still hot and I knew from experience that I had better not touch it, but it looked so good with all those cherries that the temptation was hard to resist. Just as I was opening a drawer to grab a fork, I heard the motherly words, "Don't you dare, this cake is for your father," coming from behind me. As I turned to plead my case, Mom reminded me that this was their anniversary, company was coming over, the cake was for dessert and that I would be better off disappearing for the evening. I dismally replaced the fork and walked away. Later that evening I found one piece of leftover cake sitting on the counter with a note in Dad's handwriting saying, "Randi's piece."

TOPPING:
2 tablespoons flour
¼ cup oats
2 tablespoons brown sugar
¼ teaspoon mace, nutmeg or cinnamon
1 tablespoon cold margarine or canola spread
⅓ cup sliced almonds (optional, Mom did not use)

CHERRIES:
1¼ cups pitted tart or sweet dark cherries
2 tablespoons minute tapioca

CAKE:
3 eggs or equivalent amount of liquid egg substitute or 4 egg whites
3 tablespoons canola oil
8 ounce container cherry yogurt, the kind with fruit on the bottom, not premixed
½ cup sugar or equivalent amount of sugar substitute
1½ teaspoon vanilla
½ teaspoon almond extract (optional)
1⅔ cups flour
1 cup oats
2 teaspoons baking powder
½ teaspoon baking soda

Preheat oven to 350° F

1. Grease a 9-inch heart-shaped, removable bottom pan with margarine or pan spray, then dust the bottom and sides lightly with flour. (A 9x9-inch square pan can be used instead of the heart-shaped pan.)
2. Pit the cherries over a bowl, so that you do not lose any juice. Mix the tapioca into the cherries, cover the bowl and allow this to soak for 10-15 minutes or until thickened slightly.
3. In a medium bowl, use a pastry blender or 2 knives to blend the 2 tablespoons of flour and brown sugar, ¼ cup of oats, the cold margarine and spice until crumbly. Gently toss in the almond slices and put aside.

4. In a mixing bowl, mix together the eggs, oil, yogurt, vanilla and almond extract.
5. Combine the oats, flour, baking powder and baking soda in a large bowl, gradually add to the yogurt mixture and mix at slow speed or with a fork until moist. (Do not mix the batter too hard as it may cause the cake to collapse.)
6. Spread half of the batter into the bottom of the prepared pan, dollop half of the cherries all over this layer, then spread the remaining batter over the cherries, dollop the top with remaining cherries and sprinkle the reserved crumbs all over the top. Bake the cake for 45-55 minutes or until an inserted knife or toothpick comes out clean. Allow to cool in the pan covered with plastic wrap until serving.

Variation:
Substitute blueberries, diced peaches or apples for cherries and add 2 tablespoons lemon juice to the berries or apples when soaking with the tapioca, then bake accordingly.

Julie's Mother's Apple Cake

♥

I met Julie at a culinary conference where she was representing the company India Tree, a purveyor of various sugars, spices and fine foods from around the globe. As we got to talking, we soon found that we had much in common, including the fact that her mother is a fine cook, as was mine. I specifically requested this kind of cake and a few days later I received the recipe by e-mail. I didn't wait a day or two; I immediately mixed the ingredients and anxiously waited for a taste. Was I ever pleased, for this cake is wonderful and just like my mother's, if not better!

5-6 baking apples, peeled, cored and diced into small chunks
2 tablespoons fresh squeezed lemon juice
½ cup brown sugar
2 teaspoons cinnamon
3 eggs or equivalent amount of liquid egg substitute
½ cup canola oil
1 teaspoon vanilla
¼ cup orange juice
1⅔ cups flour, sifted once
1 tablespoon baking powder
¾ cup brown sugar
1 teaspoon salt
2-3 tablespoons warmed honey

1. Grease a round, high-sided pan, such as a bundt or fancy shaped cake pan with a minimum of 3-inch sides. Dust the pan with flour after greasing.
2. In a medium bowl, mix the lemon juice into the apples. Combine ½ cup brown sugar and the cinnamon and sprinkle over the apples. Put aside.
3. Thoroughly mix together the eggs, oil, vanilla and juice, stir in the flour, baking powder, brown sugar and salt and mix all ingredients until thoroughly incorporated. The batter will be thick.
4. Spread half the batter into the prepared pan, sprinkle this layer with half of the apples, then spread the remaining batter over the apples and top this layer with the remaining apples. Bake for 60-70 minutes or until an inserted knife or toothpick comes out clean.
5. Allow the cake to rest in the pan for 5 minutes, invert it onto a large plate, drizzle with warmed honey and serve, or allow to cool slightly and cover, to be served later in the day drizzled with warm honey.

Old Fashioned German Kuchen

Great effort was applied to developing this old time favorite, to no avail. I tried many different recipes,
all shared from friends and neighbors, but the kuchen never turned out as I had previously seen or tasted.
Then I decided to combine a few different recipes, a little bit from this one, a cup from that one
and finally developed a marvelous tasting, fruity German-type coffeecake, Kuchen.

Makes 2 coffeecakes

2 packages of dry yeast or 2 yeast cakes
1 tablespoon sugar
½ cup warm water
⅓ cup shortening, melted
½ cup sugar
2 eggs
3¾ cups plus 2 tablespoons flour
½ cup plus 1 tablespoon warm milk
1 cup plus 1 tablespoon flour
½ cup brown sugar
½ cup sugar
¼ cup butter or shortening
1 tablespoon vanilla
6 peaches or 7 plums, skinned, pitted and cut in half or two 16-ounce cans light peach or plums halves, drained.
1¼-1½ cups dark sweet cherries, pitted

1. Dissolve the yeast with 1 tablespoon sugar in the ½ cup of water until bubbly, about 5 minutes.
2. Mix together the melted shortening, sugar and eggs, then gradually add 2 cups of flour and yeast and mix. Add enough remaining flour and mix until a soft dough forms, remove the dough from the bowl and knead on a floured surface until smooth and elastic. Place the dough into a greased bowl, cover and allow to rise in a warm place until doubled in bulk.
3. Mix the additional flour, both sugars, butter, and vanilla until crumbly and put aside.
4. Once the dough has doubled, preheat oven to 375° F, grease two 9-inch round pans with butter or pan spray, divide the dough in half and fit each half into the prepared pans. Sprinkle dough with the crumbs, place the peaches on top of the crumbs in one pan and the cherries on top in the second pan.
5. Bake for 25-35 minutes or until an inserted knife or toothpick comes out clean.

Variation:
Omit the cherries and make one Kuchen with peaches and the other with plums.

Pineapple Upside-Down Cake

So many are fearful of making this magnificent dessert, thinking that it will collapse, over-rise and be dry or that all of the sensational topping will bubble out and over the sides of the pan, causing a mess. You are not alone; I too was a bit fearful, but temptation got the best of me and I conquered my fear just for a taste of this amazingly awesome tasting dessert. In the words of a teenager, this cake is "Fresh." I am not quite sure what that means, but I know it has to mean something good, for as little as she is, she ate a huge piece.

Preheat oven to 350° F

(This cake is best made in a 10-inch diameter seasoned cast iron skillet.)

TOPPING:
½ ripe pineapple, peeled, cored and sliced into 1/2-inch pieces
¾ cup (1½ sticks) plus 2 tablespoons butter
¾ cup plus 1 tablespoon brown sugar
12-16 pecans

CAKE:
2 cups plus 2 tablespoons flour, sifted once
1 teaspoon baking soda
1 teaspoon baking powder
1 cup sugar
2 eggs
1 cup plus 1½ tablespoons buttermilk
2 teaspoons vanilla
1 tablespoon rum (preferably dark)
4 dark sweet cherries, pitted and cut in half

1. Place ¼ cup butter into the skillet or baking pan and heat over medium heat. Stir in the brown sugar, increase the heat to medium high and cook until bubbly, about 2-3 minutes.
2. Place the pineapple slices into the pan in a circular pattern and continue to cook for 2 more minutes or until the sugar darkens to amber. Turn the slices, remove the pan from the heat and carefully fill the spaces between the pineapples with the pecans.
3. Combine the flour with the baking powder and baking soda and put aside.
4. Cream together the remaining butter and sugar until fluffy, add the eggs one at a time just until all ingredients are incorporated. At a slow speed, mix in the flour in 3-4 batches, alternating with the buttermilk until just combined. Slowly stir in the vanilla and rum.
5. Spoon the cake batter into the fruit-filled pan and bake for 35-45 minutes or until golden and an inserted knife or toothpick comes out clean.
6. Allow the cake to cool for 3-5 minutes then run a sharp knife along the edge of the pan. Place a large plate or cake plate tightly to the pan surface, working quickly and holding the plate securely to the pan, invert the pan onto the plate and gently lift the pan from the cake. (If any pineapples stick to the pan bottom, carefully remove and place in appropriate place.) Fill each pineapple center with a fresh cherry half.

Great-Grandmother's Carrot Cake

This delightfully moist and full-flavored cake, has generously been baked, eaten, shared and savored for generations. I feel very fortunate that I found this recipe, originally titled Mom's Carrot Cake, in that bottomless tin box of my grandmother's. It is now my honor to pass this golden recipe on to you so that it may continue to be shared with today's and future generations.

Preheat oven to 350° F

2 cups plus 2 tablespoons flour
2 teaspoons baking soda
2 cups sugar
3 eggs
¾ cup canola oil or sunflower oil
¾ cup buttermilk
One 20-ounce can crushed pineapple (drain the juice into a bowl and reserve for icing)
3 cups grated carrots
Additions if desired: 1 cup raisins (dark and/or golden) and or chopped walnuts

1. Thoroughly mix all ingredients together, except the reserved pineapple juice.
2. Grease a 9x13-inch or two 8-inch round pans (if you prefer a layer cake) with butter, margarine or pan spray. Pour the batter into the prepared pan(s).
3. Bake 40-50 minutes or until an inserted knife comes out clean. Cover the cake with plastic wrap after 5-8 minutes and then allow it to cool completely before frosting
4. Spread Cream Cheese Icing on top of the cake, refrigerate and serve.

CREAM CHEESE FROSTING:
8 ounces cream cheese
½ cup (1 stick) butter
3¼-3½ cups powdered sugar
2 tablespoons reserved pineapple juice

1. Mix the ingredients together and spread on and between the layers of the cooled cake and refrigerate for at least an hour before serving.

Variation:
Maple Icing also goes well with this cake; omit the pineapple juice, and add 2 teaspoons maple extract to the cream cheese icing.

Pumpkin Cake

♥

Perfectly divine any time of year, especially around the winter holidays. Made with an extra dose of spice, this beautiful cake is sure to become a favorite and guaranteed to fill your home with the fragrance of homemade love.

Preheat oven to 350° F

Scant 2 cups sugar
1 cup canola or safflower oil
4 large plus 1 small egg or equivalent amount of liquid egg substitute
2 cups plus 2 tablespoons flour
2 teaspoons baking soda
1 teaspoon baking powder
1 tablespoon cinnamon
1 teaspoon ginger
¼ teaspoon nutmeg
¼ teaspoon cloves
2 cups canned pumpkin
¾ cup golden raisins or chopped pecans (optional)

1. Grease two 9-inch round pans with pan spray and then lightly dust each with flour.
2. Cream together the sugar, oil and eggs in a large mixing bowl.
3. Sift the flour, baking soda and powder into the egg mixture, mix thoroughly while adding the pumpkin and spice. Mix until all ingredients are thoroughly incorporated. Pour batter into prepared pans and bake for 35-45 minutes or until an inserted knife or toothpick comes out clean. Cool 5 minutes, remove from the pan, cool for another 5 minutes, wrap each layer in plastic wrap and cool completely prior to spreading the Cream Cheese Frosting.

CREAM CHEESE FROSTING:
¼ cup butter or margarine
8 ounces cream cheese, (Neufchatel works fine)
3¼ cups powdered sugar
1 tablespoon vanilla
½ cup chopped pecans (optional)

1. Mix frosting ingredients thoroughly together. Remove the plastic wrap from each layer of cake, brush away any lingering crumbs and place one layer onto a plate. Cover this layer with frosting, put the second layer on top of the bottom layer and continue to cover the cake with the frosting. Sprinkle the top with chopped pecans, if desired.

"Oh My God" Chocolate Cake

You may think you have died and gone to heaven after eating a slice of this cake. I came up with the concept for this cake long before I came up with the recipe. I wanted an unusually special cake that would be welcomed, remembered and prepared for years to come. I also wanted a cake that was not served in restaurants, truly distinguishing it from others. It took me a few trials and a couple of tasty errors, but the final product sent me to heaven, where I said hello to my family and then boarded a cloud back to earth so that I may share this extraordinary recipe with you.

Step 1

THE CAKE:

Preheat oven to 350° F

3 cups plus 2 tablespoons flour
1 cup cocoa
2⅓ teaspoons baking soda
⅓ teaspoon baking powder
5 eggs
2½ plus 1 tablespoon cups sugar
1½ tablespoon vanilla
1½ cups plus 1 tablespoon mayonnaise
2 cups water

1. In a medium bowl, combine the flour, cocoa, baking soda and baking powder together and put aside.
2. Beat the eggs, sugar, vanilla and mayonnaise at medium speed for 3-4 minutes.
3. Add the flour mixture in parts to the egg mixture, alternating with the water. Thoroughly mix all the ingredients together.
4. Grease three 9-inch round cake pans and dust each with flour.
5. Pour the batter into the prepared pans and bake 25-30 minutes. Use a toothpick or knife inserted in middle to see if cake is done. One or two crumbs should stick to the knife or toothpick. Allow individual layers to cool for 3-4 minutes, remove from pans, cool for a few minutes, wrap each layer in plastic wrap and prepare the chocolate filling, fruit filling, ganache and icing.

Step 2

CHOCOLATE FILLING:
The filling needs to be prepared the same day that this cake is served.

2 tablespoons butter
2 squares unsweetened chocolate
½ cup sugar
1 teaspoon vanilla
One 5-ounce can evaporated milk

continued on next page

1. In a double boiler, melt the chocolate and butter.
2. After the chocolate and butter have melted, add the sugar, evaporated milk and the vanilla. Stir constantly over medium heat until mixture thickens; approximately ½ hour.
3. Remove the icing from the heat, cool for a couple of minutes and while still warm, pour and spread the filling on only the top of one cake layer, place a second layer of cake on top, spread more filling on top of this layer, then top with the third layer of cake but leave its top plain. Cool completely before adding the fruit filling and ganache. (You may have some extra filling; store it in the refrigerator for another use.) You may want to store the cake in a large plastic cake container with a tight fitting lid, or gently cover with plastic wrap until ready to add the filling.

Step 3
FRUIT FILLING:
The filling needs to be prepared the same day that this cake is served.

2 cups strawberries, sliced into ½-inch slices or sweet dark cherries, pitted
8 ounces cream cheese
3 tablespoons sugar
2-3 tablespoons heavy cream
2 teaspoons vanilla

1. Thoroughly mix the cream cheese and cream together. Gently mix in the fruit until fruit is evenly distributed. Do not beat the creamed mixture when adding the fruit.
2. Using a 6-inch-long metal cannoli tube, insert the tube into the cake layers from top to bottom in eight places, then remove the tube, leaving open holes around the cake (holes should be placed about 1½-2 inches from the outer edge and evenly spaced). Fit a pastry bag with a circular piping attachment, fill the bag with the fruit filling and pipe the filling into each hole. Make sure that you do not overfill the hole, as you want the filling to stay a smidgen below the cake surface.

Hint: You may want to stick toothpicks into the side of the cake indicating where each filled hole is so to help with slicing later. I then put a strawberry or cherry on top of the icing above the toothpick and remove the toothpick. This way I know that I must slice the cake to either side of each piece of fruit.

Step 4
GANACHE:

¾ cup finely chopped bittersweet chocolate or semi sweet chocolate chips
¾ cup heavy cream

1. In a small saucepan, heat the cream over medium high until it just begins to boil. Remove from heat and immediately stir the chocolate into the hot cream. Allow to sit for a minute and then stir until the chocolate has thoroughly melted and completely mixed into the cream. Stir occasionally while allowing the mixture to cool for 20-30 minutes, or until a thin ribbon drips from a rubber spatula and the mixture is still slightly warm. Very slowly pour and gently spread the ganache over the cooled cake. Allow it to cool and harden completely before spreading the icing (step 5 below) onto the cake.

Step 5
WHIPPED CREAM CHEESE FROSTING:

16 ounces cream cheese
1 cup (2 sticks) butter
4 cups powdered sugar
1 teaspoon vanilla
½ cup whipping cream
2 cups whole strawberries or cherries, stems removed
1 tablespoon finely grated semi-sweet or bittersweet chocolate

1. Cream together the butter and cream cheese, scraping the sides of the mixing bowl frequently; mix in the sugar and vanilla. Beat in the whipping cream until the frosting has thickened and reaches a smooth spreadable consistency. Generously spread the icing over the cake, being careful not to push in the protruding toothpicks. Place a piece of fruit on the top of the cake above each toothpick, remove the toothpicks, smooth over the icing and then place the remaining fruit in a circular design towards the center of the cake. Sprinkle the grated chocolate over the top of the cake and strawberries, and refrigerate until serving.

Hints: If by some chance you have some leftover pieces, store them covered in the refrigerator. This icing also pairs deliciously when this cake is made as a sheet cake or a simple chocolate layer cake, such as for birthdays.

Annie's Favorite Butter Cream Layer Cake

Annie, a beautiful young lady and neighbor, has a favorite cake—Butter Cream Layer Cake. When her mother asked if I could make one for her birthday, my immediate response was, "Sure, just give me a day or two to figure out the recipe." This recipe is the result of Annie's request: I hope that you enjoy it as much as she does.

Preheat oven to 350° F

1 cup (2 sticks) butter
2 cups sugar
1 tablespoon vanilla
4-5 eggs (depends on egg size)
2¾ cups plus 1 tablespoon flour
1 tablespoon baking powder
1 cup plus 1½ tablespoon milk

1. Grease two or three 9-inch round pans (number of pans depends whether you want thin or thick cake layers) with butter, margarine or pan spray, and lightly dust with flour.
2. In a mixing bowl, cream the butter, sugar and vanilla at medium high speed for 1 minute. Add the eggs one at a time, making sure that each egg is thoroughly incorporated into the batter before adding another.
3. Add the dry ingredients in two parts at low speed, alternating with the milk. Mix until ingredients are just combined. Do not overmix the batter as it may cause the cake to collapse.
4. Pour the batter into the prepared pans and bake for 30-40 minutes or until an inserted knife or toothpick comes out clean. Cool for 10 minutes, remove the cakes from the pans, allow to sit for another 3-4 minutes, wrap each in plastic wrap, and allow to completely cool prior to applying the frosting.

BUTTER CREAM FROSTING:
¾ cup butter
2¼ cups powdered sugar
3 tablespoons milk
1 teaspoon vanilla

1. Mix ingredients together thoroughly. Remove the plastic wrap from each layer, brush away any lingering crumbs and place one layer onto a plate. Cover this layer with frosting, put the second layer on top of the bottom layer and continue to spread the cake with the frosting. Sprinkle the top with rainbow sprinkles if you'd like.

Variation:
Substitute Rich Chocolate Cream Frosting (next page).

Rich Chocolate Cream Frosting

1 cup (2 sticks) plus 2 tablespoons butter
6 tablespoons (¾ stick) margarine
3 tablespoons dark corn syrup
1½ tablespoons vanilla
6 cups sifted powdered sugar
1 cup cocoa
Pinch of salt
½ cup heavy cream

1. Beat the butter and margarine together for 3 minutes, add the corn syrup and vanilla and continue to beat this mixture until thoroughly combined. While this is mixing, sift together the powdered sugar, cocoa and salt.
2. Reduce the speed to low and in 2-3 parts add the sugar to the butter mixture, mixing each part in thoroughly before adding the next part.
3. Continue mixing at low speed as you gradually add the cream to the frosting, then increase the speed and continue to mix until the frosting is smooth and silky. Frost the awaiting cake. If the frosting is too thick to your liking add up to an additional tablespoon of cream.

German Chocolate Cake

Many customers specifically requested a recipe for this exquisite cake, but I had none to share so I frantically searched that tin box of my grandmother's and found a piece of newspaper, dated 1957 with this recipe on it. As I read the article, I soon learned that this wonderful cake was not of German descent, but that a woman in Dallas, Texas developed the recipe almost 50 years ago, using German's Chocolate. The article indicated that any chocolate cake recipe can be used for the cake and that it is the creamy, sweet, pecan and coconut icing that distinguishes this special cake from all others. Fortunately my grandmother must have been thinking as she read, for she wrote her own cake recipe on the back of this paper and the rest is history.

Preheat oven to 350° F

1 cup (2 sticks) butter
1½ cups sugar
¾ cup brown sugar
7 extra large eggs (use only extra large eggs or the cake may be a tad dry)
9 ounces bittersweet chocolate
   or 1 cup chocolate chips (6 ounces) and 3 squares (3 ounces) unsweetened chocolate, melted
1 tablespoon vanilla
3¼ cups flour, sifted once and remeasured
1 tablespoon baking powder
½ teaspoon baking soda
½ teaspoon salt
2⅓ cups milk

1. Grease three 9-inch cake pans with butter or pan spray and dust each with flour.
2. Cream the butter and sugars for about 5 minutes, or until light and fluffy. Add the eggs one at time, beating each into the batter for 1-2 minutes before adding another. Beat the melted chocolate and vanilla thoroughly into the egg mixture.
3. Add the baking soda, salt and baking powder to the sifted flour. With a rubber spatula, not a mixer. fold in the dry ingredients in 4-5 parts, alternating with the milk. Make sure that each addition is thoroughly incorporated into the batter before adding the next.
4. Pour batter evenly between the three pans and bake for 25-35 minutes or until an inserted knife or toothpick comes out clean. Remove the cake from pans, cool for a few minutes and wrap each in plastic wrap, then prepare the icing.

COCONUT PECAN FROSTING:
6 egg yolks
2 cups sugar
1 cup cream
1 cup milk
½ cup (1 stick) butter
1 tablespoon vanilla

5 cups coconut
2 plus cups chopped pecans

1. Beat the egg yolks and sugar until light yellow and slightly thickened, then beat the milk and cream into the eggs.
2. Pour this mixture into a medium saucepan, add the butter and heat over medium, stirring continuously until the mixture has thickened and has a light golden tone. Remove pan from heat, stir in the vanilla, pecans and coconut and allow to cool for 20-30 minutes before spreading between each layer and on top of the cake.

Hint: The frosting does not cover the sides of the cake, if you want the sides frosted, either use the Rich Chocolate Cream Frosting (p. 321), or increase this recipe by one third. The cake recipe makes a fabulous chocolate cake for any style cake, whether you prefer a layer cake, a sheet cake or cupcakes and can be iced according to personal preference.

Cheesecake

One of the finest recipes I could ever share! Savor each and every moment of the irresistible richness provided from this sensational delight.

Preheat oven to 325° F

¾-1 cup graham cracker crumbs, plain or with 1 teaspoon cinnamon mixed in.
4 pounds (64 ounces) cream cheese
2 cups sugar
8 eggs
1 tablespoon vanilla
2 teaspoons fresh squeezed lemon juice
2 cups fresh strawberries, blueberries, raspberries or pitted sweet dark cherries, for topping (optional)

1. Generously butter a 10-12-inch round spring form pan. Sprinkle the graham cracker crumbs all over the bottom of the pan. I usually cover the outside bottom of the pan tightly with foil to keep anything from oozing through.
2. Thoroughly beat together the cream cheese and sugar, then add the eggs one at a time, making sure each egg is incorporated into the cream cheese before adding the next. Add the juice and vanilla and continue beating until this mixture is smooth and creamy. Pour into the prepared pan.
3. Partially fill a larger pan with hot water, put the filled cake pan into the water and place both onto the middle shelf of the oven. (The hot water in the larger pan should be a little higher than halfway up the sides of the cheesecake pan.)
4. Bake for 90 minutes or longer. You will know it has finished baking when the edges are firm and the center just slightly jiggles. Gently remove the cake from the pan of water and place it onto a counter to cool for 30 minutes then refrigerate at least 4 hours prior to serving.
5. When ready to serve, place fresh fruits on the top in a circular design, slice and serve.

The Lovely Ladies' Favorite Apple Brie Cups

SUGAR

Ah, a treat to truly give thanks for! I first made these amazing treats just before the winter holidays, and everyone who got a taste stated that they were to die for. Months later, while visiting back east, I made these for the Lovely Ladies one evening while the men were attending a basketball game. The immediate response between the oohs and aahs was that I must write the recipe down right then and there or I would be disowned forever after. My first thought was something like na na no boo boo; and then I laughed with them as I recited the ingredients. Each of their mouths dropped open when they heard just how easy the elegant assembly of these treats really is.

Makes 12

Preheat oven to 375° F

1 package of puff pastry sheets, thawed and cut into 12 squares (6 squares per sheet)
6-7 large Granny Smith or Gala apples, peeled, cored and thinly sliced (Granny Smith if diabetic)
2 tablespoons lemon juice
¼ cup sugar or equivalent amount of sugar substitute
¼ cup brown sugar or equivalent amount of sugar substitute
1 teaspoon cinnamon
Pinch nutmeg
14-16 ounces Brie, rind removed and cut into 12 sections/slices

1. Mix the apples with lemon juice, both sugars, the cinnamon and nutmeg, until well coated.
2. Grease 12 large muffin pan sections and fit each pastry square into a section. Fill each evenly with apples and bake for 40-45 minutes or until you see bubbling juice.
3. Remove the pans from the oven and immediately top each pastry with a slice of brie. Place the pan back into the oven for 1-2 minutes or until the brie just begins to melt. Remove from oven, cool for 1-2 minutes, remove each pastry from the pan and serve.

Variation:
½ cup raisins or chopped walnuts or pecans can be added to the apple mixture.

Cream Cheese Puffs

It really doesn't get much easier or more impressive than these little sweets. I am often amazed at just how easy these lovely little puffs are to make. Anything this tasty should take hours to prepare, instead of just a few minutes.

Makes approximately 36-42 puffs

Preheat oven to 375° F

1 package puff pastry sheets, thawed
12 ounces cream cheese
¼ cup plus 1 tablespoon sugar
2 teaspoon vanilla
1 extra large egg
Fresh berries and/or pitted cherries

1. Grease 36-42 mini-muffin pan sections.
2. Slice the puff pastry sheets into 1½-inch squares; stretch and pull each square and fit into the prepared muffin sections.
3. Beat together the cream cheese, sugar, vanilla and egg until smooth and creamy. Fill each pastry section with 1-2 teaspoons of cream cheese mixture and bake for 15-18 minutes. The crust should be golden, but the filling should not be golden or brown.
4. Immediately place a berry or cherry on top of each puff, remove from the pan and cool completely before serving, or store in the refrigerator until serving.

Chocolate Fondue

Absolutely fabulous! Once again I have saved the best for last. Although this recipe was developed over 75 years ago by my aunt's aunt as an icing for her sister's chocolate cake, I have used it more often as chocolate fondue. The first time I tried this as fondue for a friend's birthday party, I made a double batch and before the quests arrived, she, her kids and I ate the entire pan. The Force of Enticement took complete control of the four of us; her kids just kept dunking fruit and she and I kept filling our spoons and delivering this outstanding smooth, creamy, rich and warm chocolate straight into our mouths. We swore that if we died at that moment, at least we would die with a bright smile planted on our faces.

Serves 6-10

6 tablespoons (¾ stick) butter
6 squares unsweetened chocolate
1½ cup sugar
1 tablespoon vanilla
One 15-ounce can evaporated milk
Various berries, sliced fruits or small cubes of cake.

1. In a double boiler, melt the chocolate and butter.
2. Stir the sugar, evaporated milk and vanilla into the melted chocolate mixture. Stir continuously over medium heat until it thickens, approximately ½ hour.
3. Remove from heat and serve or pour into a fondue pot and keep warm while serving with fruits and cake cubes.

Hint: Although best served fresh, this can also be stored in the refrigerator and heated by placing the container into a pot of boiling water. Once it begins to melt, stir until fully melted and smooth.

Happiness is not so much in having as sharing.

We make a living by what we get,

but we make a life by what we give.

Norman MacEwan

The Accessories of Foods

~ All flavored butters need to be refrigerated.
~ Make sure all butter, margarine and/or cream cheese is softened at room temperature before adding.
~ Salad Dressings are to be served cool, unless indicated otherwise, and most sauces are to be served warm.
~ Many of the following recipes will remain fresh for 2 days to 1 week, if refrigerated.
Make sure to store in a jar or container with a tight fitting lid.

According to my older Oxford Dictionary and Thesaurus, one of the definitions for the word accessory reads: "additional or extra thing." Therefore, I can only surmise that the flavored butters, syrups, gravies and various other sauces used on, over and around the broad diversity of edible delights that we indulge ourselves in, are accessories. These additional items are what make these pleasant dishes so phenomenally sensational to our palates. I mean, imagine Eggs Benedict without the hollandaise sauce. It would be just an egg and a piece of meat; good to taste but relatively boring until that rich creamy sauce is drizzled on top, turning it into something to be savored with pure delight. Or what about a plain old bowlful of pasta with no sauce; pretty boring, right?

Some foods need accessories to brighten them up, just like a plain skirt needs a pair of fancy shoes, and possibly a smart jacket to brighten it up, for a more pleasing effect. Think about it, when it comes down to it, the accessories used are what makes the difference between, *"Okay,"* and, *"Mmmmm, this is soooo good."*

Clockwise from top:
Dad's Favorite Blueberry Syrup, Page 331
Quick Blueberry Butter, Page 333
Hot Cinnamon Butter, Page 333
Maple Honey Butter, Page 332
Herbed White Sauce, Page 340

Homemade Syrups

These are those marvelous little accessories that add a final and appetizing touch to a wide range of recipes found on these pages, as well as many of your own. Have you ever grabbed a bottle of syrup or honey only to find that the contents have hardened and/or crystallized and are unusable? Now, you can make your own and impress all you serve.

Pecan Syrup

Makes approximately 1½ cups

2 cups sugar
1 cup water
1 teaspoon vanilla or maple extract
¼ cup (½ stick) butter
½ cup chopped pecans

1. Boil water and sugar until sugar is dissolved. Add pecans. Reduce heat and simmer for 5 minutes.
2. Add maple extract and butter and thoroughly mix into the pecan mixture.

Dad's Favorite Blueberry Syrup

Makes approximately 2 cups

½ cup sugar
¼ cup water
¼ cup light corn syrup
1 tablespoon cornstarch
2 teaspoon lemon juice
2 cup blueberries, raspberries, strawberries, blackberries, pitted dark red cherries, sliced peaches or plums

1. Combine sugar and cornstarch in 1-quart casserole or saucepan. Add the water, syrup and juice, stir in blueberries and microwave; or cook over medium high heat and stir continuously for about 5 minutes or until thickened. For a thicker sauce, add an additional teaspoon of cornstarch.

Maple Syrup (if you don't have the real stuff)

Makes approximately 1 cup

1 cup brown sugar
¾ cup water
1-2 teaspoon maple extract

1. Mix sugar and water in saucepan. Bring mixture to a boil; simmer for 15 minutes. (Don't let it boil again)
2. Add maple flavoring; chill.

Brown Sugar Syrup

Makes approximately 1¼ cups

1 cup plus 2 tablespoons water
2 plus cups packed dark brown sugar

1. Bring the water to a boil, sprinkle in the sugar, breaking up any lumps as you go, turn down the heat to low medium and allow to simmer for 5-6 minutes or until mixture thickens slightly. Add a couple tablespoons butter for a richer appeal.

Quick and Easy Fruit Syrup

¼ cup of your favorite jam or preserves, per serving
1 tablespoon butter per ¼ cup of preserves

1. Melt the jam and butter in a dish in the microwave for a few seconds; mix and pour over the delight. If still too thick, add an additional tablespoon of warm water to the melted preserves.

Flavored Butters

I find it amazing how the simple addition of a flavored butter can turn an everyday piece of bread, muffin or biscuit into one of subliminal ecstasy. Refrigerate most flavored butters until one hour before serving, allowing time to soften to room temperature.

Real Butter

My first experience making butter dates back to when I was a little girl in 3rd grade, and a Girl Scout. We had all been requested to bring in a clean jar with tight fitting lid and a few marbles each. At the next meeting, all the little girls proceeded to pour this thick milk into our jars, toss in the marbles, tightly close the lids and for the next hour or so, we just shook and shook those jars, laughed and shook some more. When the liquid solidified, we were allowed to remove the lids from our jars and spread some of the sweetest butter I had ever tasted onto saltine crackers.

Tip: When the kids get a little rambunctious and need something to occupy their time during a rainy day, go for this recipe. You will not need to supervise very much, just make sure that the lid is tight and enjoy the results.

1 glass or plastic jar, with a tight fitting lid
3 marbles, washed
1-3 cups heavy whipping cream or double cream
Pinch to 1 teaspoon salt

1. Shake the cream in the jar until it solidifies, carefully remove the marbles and refrigerate.

Variation:
Way back in the olden days, many frontier women would add a tiny bit of carrot juice to their butter. The juice would add a pinch of color to the butter; hence making the butter look attractive on the table. If you choose to do this, only add about 1 teaspoon of carrot juice per 8 ounces cream or the juice may affect the taste.

Honey Butter

½ cup(1 stick) butter
½ cup honey or less if you prefer

1. Mix thoroughly together and refrigerate.

Variation:
Add ¼-⅓ cup toasted finely chopped pecans, walnuts or almonds, or add 1 teaspoon cinnamon and ¼ teaspoon nutmeg to any combination of the above.

Maple Honey Butter

½ cup (1 stick) butter
¼ cup honey
¼ cup pure maple syrup or 1-1½ teaspoons maple extract
½ teaspoon cinnamon

1. Mix all thoroughly together and refrigerate.

Variation:
Add ⅓ cup toasted finely chopped pecans

Lemon Butter

½ cup (1 stick) butter
1 tablespoon fresh grated lemon zest

1. Mix together in a mixer and refrigerate.

Variation:
Add 1 tablespoon lemon curd for more lemon flavor.

Orange Butter

½ cup (1 stick) butter
1 tablespoon fresh-grated orange zest
1 tablespoon orange marmalade
Couple snips of fresh orange balsam, enhances the
    orange flavor

1. Blend together in a mixer and refrigerate.

Sweet Cinnamon Butter

1 cup (2 sticks) butter
⅓ cup brown sugar
⅓ cup honey
¾ teaspoon cinnamon

1. Mix all ingredients together and refrigerate.

Hot Cinnamon Butter

½ cup (1 stick) butter
1 heaping tablespoon red hot candies

1. Melt the Red Hots in the microwave. Beat the melted Red
   Hots into the butter until fully incorporated; refrigerate.

Quick Blueberry Butter

1 cup fresh blueberries
½ teaspoon vanilla
1-2 teaspoons powdered sugar (optional)
½ cup (1 stick) butter

1. Blend together in a mixer and refrigerate.
   Or
   If you prefer a smoother butter, puree the blueberries
   in a food processor, add the vanilla, then mix this into
   the butter. This also works with cherries or strawberries, but not raspberries or blackberries—they contain
   too many seeds.

Quick Peach Butter

1 large peach, peeled, pitted and diced
½ cup (1 stick) butter
¼ teaspoon nutmeg

1. Blend together in a mixer and refrigerate.

Salad Dressings

Some prefer to use a few lemon wedges to moisten leafy salads; many more prefer to use a seasoned prepared dressing. Please find a few favorites listed below; they are easy to prepare and enhance the taste of an enormous variety of mixed leafy greens, vegetables, pasta, meats, nuts, seeds and fruits.

Kathleen's Salad Dressing

Makes approximately 2 cups

1 cup mayonnaise
1 cup sour cream or yogurt
Juice from 1 lemon
1½ teaspoons Worcestershire sauce
½ teaspoon dry mustard
2 teaspoons fresh finely chopped dill

1. Mix all ingredients in a bowl, cover and chill until serving.

Oriental Salad Dressing

Makes approximately 1 cup

3 tablespoons vinegar
3 tablespoons sugar
¼ teaspoon salt
2 tablespoons pineapple juice
1 tablespoon soy sauce
1 teaspoon black pepper
¾ cup oil (can reduce to ½ cup)
2 tablespoons sesame seeds (optional)
1-1½ teaspoons Chinese 5-Spice seasoning. (Usually contains, star anise, fennel, cloves, cinnamon and Szechwan pepper, although some blends have ginger and cardamom added for a Chinese 7-spice powder, which also works well.)

1. Mix all ingredients together, serve or refrigerate for later use.

Mom's Yogurt Dressing

Makes approximately 1½ cups

½ cup vegetable oil
2 tablespoons white wine vinegar
1 cup plain yogurt
3 tablespoons red chili sauce or ketchup
   (if using ketchup, add a couple drops of hot sauce)
2 teaspoons finely minced onion
2 teaspoon fresh finely minced parsley
½ teaspoon dry mustard
¼ teaspoon pepper
Pinch of sea salt

1. Beat all ingredients with a wire whisk until blended. If too thick for your liking, add a few tablespoons water and whisk to blend. Refrigerate for at least 2 hours before serving.

Blue Cheese Dressing

Makes approximately 2½ cups

1 cup sour cream or yogurt
1 cup mayonnaise
4 scallions, finely minced
¼ cup fresh squeezed lemon juice
1 cup blue cheese crumbles
½ teaspoon pepper

1. Thoroughly mix and refrigerate for several hours before serving for best flavor

Mom's Ranch Dressing

Makes approximately 2 cups

1 cup mayonnaise
1 cup buttermilk
½ teaspoon sea salt (optional)
½ teaspoon pepper, white or black
¼ teaspoon celery seed
1 teaspoon minced garlic or 1 teaspoon garlic powder
1 teaspoon onion powder or 2 teaspoons finely diced scallions (white bulb only)
2 teaspoons parsley
1 teaspoon chives
1 plus teaspoon dill

1. Thoroughly mix all ingredients and refrigerate for at least 2 hours before using to allow flavors to blend.

Variations:
• Add bacon crumbles and 1-2 tablespoons Parmesan cheese.
• Add ½ cup of your favorite Pico De Gallo sauce or ½ teaspoon cayenne pepper and a couple drops of hot sauce.
• Add one peeled, seeded and pureed cucumber.

Patt's Cucumber Ranch Dressing

Makes approximately 2 cups

1 cup mayonnaise
1 cup buttermilk
1 English cucumber, peeled and pureed
2 teaspoons fresh minced parsley
2 teaspoons celery seed
2 tablespoons finely diced scallions
1 teaspoon minced garlic
¼ teaspoon paprika
¼ teaspoon onion powder
2 pinches of cayenne pepper or a couple drops of hot sauce

Black pepper to taste
Pinch of salt (optional)

1. Combine all the ingredients and blend well. Make sure to refrigerate for 2 hours before serving for best flavor.

Variation:
Add ½ cup blue cheese crumbles

Spicy Seafood Salad Dressing

Makes approximately 2 cups

1½ cups mayonnaise
¼ cup chili sauce
3 tablespoons finely minced green onions (include some green tops)
2 tablespoons finely minced green pepper
1-2 tablespoons fresh lemon juice
1½ teaspoons Worcestershire sauce
¼ teaspoon hot sauce

1. Whisk together all ingredients in a large bowl and gently toss in to the salad.

Mom's Thousand Island Dressing

Makes approximately 1 cup

1 cup mayonnaise
⅔ cup ketchup or red chili sauce (can be combined)
2 tablespoons finely minced green pepper
2 tablespoons finely minced onions or scallions
2 tablespoons sweet pickle relish or finely diced kosher pickles
1 teaspoon fresh finely-diced parsley and or basil
2 teaspoons Tabasco or Worcestershire sauce

1. Mix all ingredients and refrigerate until serving.

continued on next page

Russian Dressing

Makes approximately 1½-2 cups

1 cup vegetable oil, mayonnaise or yogurt
½ cup ketchup
1 tablespoons sugar or sugar substitute
2 to 3 tablespoons fresh squeezed lemon juice
1 tablespoon red wine vinegar
½ teaspoon salt
½ teaspoon paprika
1½ teaspoons celery seed
1 teaspoon minced garlic
1 tablespoon Worcestershire sauce
¼ cup grated onion

1. Mix all ingredients together and refrigerate for at least 2 hours prior to serving.

French Dressing

Makes approximately 2 cups

1 cup vegetable oil
½ cup red or white wine vinegar
   (tarragon vinegar will also work well)
¼ cup ketchup
1 teaspoon celery seed
½ teaspoon dry mustard (optional)
1-2 tablespoons fresh squeezed lemon juice
1 teaspoon onion powder
Dash of paprika to taste

1. Mix thoroughly in a tight-lidded jar or container and refrigerate for 2-3 hours before serving.

Italian Dressing

Makes approximately 2 cups

1½ cups virgin olive oil
¼ cup white wine vinegar
¼ cup fresh squeezed lemon juice
1-2 garlic cloves finely minced garlic cloves
3 tablespoons finely minced onions or scallions

1-2 tablespoons sugar or sugar substitute
2 teaspoons Worcestershire sauce
1 teaspoon dry mustard
½ teaspoon paprika
½ teaspoon fresh thyme
½ teaspoon fresh basil
½ teaspoon oregano
½ teaspoon marjoram
½ teaspoon chervil

1. Mix thoroughly in a tight-lidded jar or container and refrigerate for at least 2-3 hours before shaking vigorously and serving.

Hot Bacon Dressing

Makes approximately 1¼ cups

4 strips bacon, cut into small pieces
1 tablespoon flour
1 beaten egg
⅓ cup sugar
¼ cup cider vinegar
¾ cup water
½ teaspoon salt (optional)

1. Brown the bacon pieces in saucepan over medium heat, add the flour and stir until smooth.
2. Mix the egg and sugar together, then beat in the vinegar, water and salt and mix this to the bacon. Continue to cook and stir until the mixture has thickened. Serve warm.

Oil and Vinegar Dressing (for Pasta Salad)

Makes approximately 1¼ cups

½ cup red wine vinegar
1 teaspoon pepper
¾ cup olive oil
2-3 teaspoons oregano
½ teaspoon basil

1. Mix together and stir into the cooked pasta before adding meats and vegetables.

Balsamic Vinaigrette Dressing

Makes approximately 1 cup

⅔ cup olive or walnut oil
⅓ cup balsamic vinegar
2 teaspoons minced garlic
Salt and pepper to taste

1. Thoroughly mix all ingredients and refrigerate for a minimum of 2 hours to blend flavors before using.

Raspberry Vinaigrette Dressing

Makes approximately 2 cups

⅔ cup seedless raspberry jam
⅔ cup raspberry vinegar
1 cup vegetable or walnut oil
1½ teaspoons poppy seeds (optional)

1. Mix all ingredients in a blender or food processor until thoroughly combined, and refrigerate until serving.

Honey Lemon Dressing

Makes approximately 1 cup

¾ cup canola, safflower, walnut, peanut or sunflower oil
3 tablespoons fresh squeezed lemon juice
¼ cup clover honey
¼ teaspoon each: basil, garlic powder, onion powder, thyme, salt, pepper, chives and chervil

1. Blend all ingredients thoroughly, pour into a tightly covered jar or container and refrigerate for a minimum of 2 hours.

Poppy Seed Dressing

Makes approximately 1¾ cups

1 cup vegetable oil
⅔ cup white wine vinegar
2 tablespoons water
1 small onion finely diced
1 teaspoon dry mustard
⅓ cup sugar or honey
1-2 tablespoons poppy seeds

1. Whisk all ingredients thoroughly together, place into a tightly fitted jar or container and refrigerate. Shake vigorously before serving.

Dill Dressing

Makes approximately 2 cups

1⅓ cups vegetable oil
½ cup red wine vinegar
1-2 tablespoons sugar, honey or sugar substitute
1 teaspoon dried dill or 1 tablespoon finely minced fresh dill (fresh tastes better)
1-2 pinches curry powder
Salt and pepper to taste

1. Place all the ingredients into a saucepan, heat and stir about 5 minutes. Remove from heat and refrigerate until cool and ready to serve. Refrigerate any leftovers in a tightly fitted jar or container. Shake vigorously before serving.

Garlic Dressing

Makes approximately 2 cups

1 cup walnut, peanut or safflower
1 cup olive oil
¼ cup white wine vinegar
3-4 cloves garlic, crushed
3 tablespoons Worcestershire sauce

1. Combine the oils and garlic in a bowl, cover and allow to sit for 24+ hours. Strain the oils through a sieve and discard the garlic. Whisk in the remaining ingredients and store in a tightly covered jar or container in the refrigerator; shake vigorously before serving.

The Magic of a Sauce

Sure, baked chicken is satisfying as is, but try it smothered in a creamy herb sauce and you've got quite a savory meal. Have you ever eaten a piece of beef that seemed a bit dry? Well, the gravy is as far away as the closest stove. Although I have included a few of these recipes previously, paired with other dishes, they are listed here again for your convenience. In addition, I have a few more up my sleeve that I would like to share. You, too, may prepare such dishes as broccoli smothered in a cheesy sauce, or pasta spiced with chili and sun-dried tomatoes, to name a few. Use your taste buds as your guide and explore the yummy ideas of your imagination. Picture it, taste it, and create it.

Basic White Sauce

Makes approximately 1 cup

A white sauce is the base of many delectable sauces and dishes. Once you make this sauce, a whole world of spices, herbs and flavorings can be added, turning a plain every-day dish into a luscious offering of tastes and flavors.

2 tablespoons of butter
2 tablespoons flour
¼ teaspoon salt
1 cup milk

1. Melt the butter in a saucepan over medium heat. When it begins to bubble, stir in the flour and salt and mix into a paste. Continue stirring while gradually adding the milk. Stir and heat until the mixture has thickened and is smooth, then gently add your choice of spices, herbs and flavorings.

Hints: For a thinner sauce, decrease butter and flour by 1 tablespoon each. For a thicker sauce, increase butter and flour by 1 tablespoon each

Hollandaise Sauce

Makes approximately 1 cup

3 large egg yolks
2 tablespoons fresh squeezed lemon juice
A pinch each salt and white pepper

A couple drops of hot sauce or Worcestershire sauce (personal preference)
1 tablespoon water
1 cup (2 sticks) clarified butter, melted, no substitutes (To clarify butter, melt and strain it through a cheese cloth or very fine sieve into a measuring cup.)

1. Using a double boiler, fill the bottom section with 2 inches of warm water. Heat the water to a gentle simmer, not a full boil, put the top section on, and let it warm for a few seconds. Whisk in the egg yolks, juice, hot sauce or Worcestershire sauce, spices and water and continue to whisk until all ingredients are incorporated. It is very important to keep stirring, making sure that the eggs do not begin to cook and solidify.
2. Gradually add the melted butter, 1 tablespoon at a time, and continue whisking until all butter is used. If very thick, whisk in an additional tablespoon of water or cream. Once thickened, remove from the heat and cover to keep warm until the foods are prepared and ready to be served. (If the sauce cools too much, reheat this top pan over very low heat, stirring constantly until warmed. If it begins to separate, whisk an egg yolk in a separate bowl or cup and then whisk into the sauce.)

Newburg Sauce

Makes approximately 1¼ cups

½ cup butter
⅓ cup flour
¾ cup water and/or broth

1 cup milk

2 beaten egg yolks

2 tablespoons sherry

Pinch paprika

1. Melt the butter in a saucepan over medium heat. Whisk the flour and salt into the butter until smooth and pasty.
2. Mix together the water, milk and egg yolks and gradually stir into the flour mixture. Continue stirring until the mixture has thickened, and serve.

Cheese Sauce 1

Makes approximately 3 cups

⅓ cup canola or vegetable oil

3 tablespoons flour

3 cups warmed milk

4 ounces shredded cheddar, Colby or American cheese

Salt and pepper to taste

1. In a medium saucepan, mix the oil and flour together until thick and no lumps remain. Heat over medium heat; add the cheese and milk while stirring continuously. Stir until the sauce begins to thicken, allow sauce to simmer for 1-2 more minutes, stir in the spices and pour over individual servings of the desired dish.

Cheese Sauce 2

Makes approximately 2 cups

1-2 tablespoons butter or margarine

½ cup finely diced onion

½ teaspoon minced garlic or a garlic clove, crushed

2 tablespoons flour

2 tablespoons butter

2 cups plus 1 tablespoon warm milk

1 packed cup of cheddar, marbled, Monterey Jack or Colby cheese

2 tablespoons white wine

½ teaspoon dry mustard

Couple drops hot sauce

1. Sauté the onion and garlic in butter over medium heat until soft and tender, about 5 minutes.
2. Make a roux by melting the butter into a sauce pan, stirring in the flour to make a paste and cooking for about 2 minutes.
3. Add the warm milk, stir constantly until thickened and then add in all remaining ingredients, including the sautéed onions. Serve warm over pasta, potatoes various meats, poultry or vegetables.

Mornay Sauce

Makes Approximately 2½ cups

3 tablespoons butter

⅓ cup finely diced sweet yellow onions, scallions or shallots

1 large bay leaf

3 tablespoons flour

Sea salt and pepper to taste

3 cups milk

¾ cup shredded Gruyere or Swiss cheese

⅓ cup grated Parmesan cheese

2 egg yolks, well beaten

1. Melt the butter over medium heat in a large saucepan. Add the onion and sauté until tender, about 5-7 minutes. Add the flour and stir over medium for 3-4 minutes but do not allow the flour to brown. Gradually whisk in the milk, add the bay leaf, salt and pepper, stir occasionally and allow this mixture to thicken.
2. Remove the pan from the heat and let the sauce cool slightly. Gradually add the cheese and stir until melted.
3. Remove about 2 tablespoons of the sauce and mix into the beaten egg yolks, and then gently stir this back into the pan and cover to keep warm on top of the stove.

continued on next page

Carolyn's Cucumber Sauce

Makes approximately 1¾ cups

1 English cucumber, peeled
3 tablespoons mayonnaise
⅔ cup sour cream or plain yogurt
2 tablespoons fresh squeezed lemon juice
Sea salt, white pepper and a pinch of dill to taste

1. Shred the cucumber in a food processor, remove from the processor and mix with all the remaining ingredients.

Alfredo Sauce

Makes approximately 3 cups

6 tablespoons butter
2 cups heavy cream
¼ teaspoon nutmeg
½ cup shredded Parmesan cheese
½ cup grated Romano cheese
1 egg yolk
Sea salt and white pepper to taste
2-3 extra tablespoons grated Parmesan cheese to sprinkle on top (optional)

1. Over medium heat, melt the butter in a saucepan and then stir in the cream, the cheese and spices. Continue to stir until the cheese has melted; mix in the egg yolk. Stir and simmer for 4-6 minutes and serve over pasta, potatoes and/or vegetables.

White Herbed Sauce

Makes approximately 2 cups

¼ cup (½ stick) butter
1½ cups heavy cream
2 pinches nutmeg
Pinch of sea salt
1 cup finely diced fresh herbs: parsley, basil, chives and chervil
¼ cup shredded Parmesan or Swiss cheese
Couple drops of hot sauce

1. Over medium heat, stir the butter, cream, nutmeg and salt into a medium saucepan. Allow this to heat but not boil, until slightly reduced, about 15 minutes.
2. Vigorously whisk in the remaining ingredients, stir and simmer until the cheese has melted, about 5-6 minutes, taste and adjust seasoning if necessary. Serve over chicken/turkey, seafood or pasta.

Country Gravy

Makes approximately 2½ cups

½ pound of pork sausage
¼ cup sausage drippings (mixed with melted butter if necessary to make ¼ cup)
4 tablespoons flour
2 cups milk
Salt and pepper to taste
Couple drops hot sauce (optional)

1. Brown the sausage in a frying pan until a few small chunks remain and the rest is crumbly. Drain ¼ cup of the excess fat/grease into a heat proof cup. Pour the grease into a small/medium saucepan while leaving the cooked sausage in the frying pan for now.
2. Add the flour to the saucepan, heat the pan over medium and stir the flour into the grease, making a paste. Remove the pan from the heat and stir in the milk, return the pan to the heat and continue stirring until it begins to thicken. Add the sausage and spices, and then stir until hot and thick.
3. Serve by immediately pouring the gravy over the biscuits.

Homemade Gravy

Makes approximately 3-4 cups

3 tablespoons of beef or poultry fat/juice/dripping taken from the bottom of the roasting pan
3 tablespoons butter or margarine
3-4 tablespoons flour
1 teaspoon minced garlic (optional)
3-4 cups of juice or broth

1. Melt the butter over medium heat in a saucepan, mix in the flour to make a paste and cook for 2-3 minutes, until slightly browned. Whisk in the fat/drippings until combined then whisk in remaining ingredients, stirring constantly until thickened and hot.

Hint: For thicker gravies, add a smidgen more flour, for thinner gravy add a small amount more broth.

Mom's Primavera Sauce

Makes approximately 2 cups

⅓ cup (¾ stick) butter
½ cup shredded Parmesan cheese
1 cup plus 1 tablespoon heavy cream
⅓ cup fresh chopped basil
1 tablespoon fresh-squeezed lemon juice
¼-½ cup chicken broth or non fat milk (optional)
2 tablespoons combined grated Parmesan and
   Romano cheeses

1. Melt the butter in a large saucepan over medium heat, add the cheese, cream, basil and lemon juice and stir over medium heat until thick. Do not boil. If this is too thick for your liking, add small amounts of the broth/milk until the sauce reaches a consistency that you prefer. Serve over pasta with vegetables. See Pasta Primavera (p. 259)

Ann's Sun-Dried Tomato Chili Sauce

Makes approximately 1 cup

¼ cup dried red peppers, crushed
½ cup sun dried tomatoes halves, dried
4 ounces canned black olives, chopped
2 tablespoons dry basil
2 tablespoons dried parsley
1 teaspoon marjoram
3 garlic cloves, minced
½ cup olive oil
2 teaspoons fresh cracked pepper

1. Soak the tomatoes in boiling water until soft, and then cut them into strips with a very sharp knife or scissors.
2. Combine all remaining ingredients with the softened strips of tomatoes, refrigerate for several hours or overnight in a covered bowl and serve over cooked pasta, sprinkled with a tad of Parmesan cheese.

Philadelphia Cream Cheese Sauce

Makes approximately 1¼ cups

8-ounce package cream cheese
½ cup plus 1 tablespoon milk (for a richer flavor,
   use half and half)
¼ cup shredded Swiss cheese or Parmesan cheese
½ teaspoon onion powder
½ teaspoon garlic powder
Pinch of dill (optional)
Sea salt and pepper to taste

1. Combine the milk and cream cheese in a medium saucepan, set the temperature to medium low and stir constantly until melted and smooth. Add the cheese and spices and continue stirring until all ingredients are incorporated.

Variation:
Add 1 tablespoon finely minced fresh lemon basil or basil

Quick Homemade Salsa

Makes about 1 cup

1 large tomato, diced
6-7 leaves of fresh cilantro, finely chopped
1 jalapeno, diced or one 4-ounce can diced jalapenos
2-3 tablespoons diced onion
½ teaspoon minced garlic
½ teaspoon oregano
1 teaspoon hot sauce
Pinch of cumin

1. Mix all ingredients together and put in a bowl for immediate use or refrigerate for later use.

Green Chili Sauce

Makes approximately 3-4 cups

1 pound of pork (roast, butt or shoulder), cut into ½-inch chunks, fat removed
½ pound chorizo or ground sausage (optional)
3-4 large tomatoes, diced
1-2 garlic cloves, minced (1 heaping teaspoon)
½ teaspoon cumin
1-2 teaspoons dried cilantro
8 ounces of fresh green chilies, seeded and finely diced, or an 8-ounce can of diced chilies
¼-½ teaspoon oregano
Couple drops of hot sauce (optional)

1. In a large skillet, brown the meats, add the remaining ingredients, cover the pan, and allow to simmer over medium low heat about 40-50 minutes or until the tomatoes are tender.
2. Store leftovers tightly sealed in the refrigerator.

Guacamole 1

Makes approximately 1½ cups

4 avocados
1 tablespoon lemon juice
1 garlic clove, crushed
1 tomato, diced
¼ cup finely chopped onion
¼-½ teaspoon minced garlic
¼ teaspoon ground cumin
3 drops hot pepper sauce

1. Peel, pit, gently mash and mix the avocados together with all remaining ingredients. Do not puree this mixture; you will want a few small chunks of avocado remaining in the guacamole.
2. Store any leftovers in a container covered with plastic wrap and then sealed with a lid and refrigerated. Stir before serving to dissolve the darkish green color that may develop.

Guacamole 2

Makes approximately 4 cups

5-6 avocados
2 tablespoons cream cheese, chopped into small chunks
1 teaspoon Worcestershire sauce
¼ plus cup salsa, jarred is fine
3 tablespoons sliced black olives
1 tablespoon diced jalapenos
Couple drops of hot sauce to taste

1. Peel, pit, gently mash and mix together the avocados with all remaining ingredients. Do not puree this mixture; you will want a few small chunks of avocado remaining in the guacamole.
2. Store any leftovers in a container covered with plastic wrap and then sealed with a lid and refrigerated. Stir before serving to dissolve the darkish green color that may develop.

A Few Choice Dessert Sauces

To be poured over cakes, ice creams, fruits or whatever your imagination can conceive.

Chocolate Sauce 1

Makes approximately 1 cup

2 squares unsweetened chocolate
2 tablespoons butter
⅔ cup sugar
½ cup evaporated milk
1 teaspoon vanilla
¼ cup sherry, kirsch or Amaretto (optional)

1. Melt the butter and chocolate together in a saucepan over low-medium heat. Stir in the sugar and milk. Continue stirring until the sugar has dissolved and this mixture begins to thicken, and add the vanilla and liqueurs, if using. Stir until combined and serve warm.

Chocolate Sauce 2

Makes approximately 1¼ cups

1 cup cream
8 ounces bittersweet chocolate, finely chopped or grated
2-3 ounces Bailey's Irish Cream, Grand Marnier, Frangelica or Kahlua (optional)

1. Heat the cream to a boil in a small saucepan over medium high heat. Remove the pan from the heat and stir in the chocolate. Allow this to sit for a minute or two, then stir it until smooth and creamy and stir in the liqueur. Serve hot or store covered in the refrigerator.

Hint: Reheat by placing the container in a pot of very warm water, allow it to sit and warm for a few minutes and stir.

Caramel Sauce

Makes approximately 2½ cups

½ cup (1 stick) butter
1⅓ cup brown sugar
½ cup corn syrup
⅔ cup cream
1 tablespoon honey
1 teaspoon vanilla

1. Combine all ingredients but vanilla in a saucepan and heat over medium heat, stirring constantly to prevent burning. Once this mixture has thickened, remove from the heat and stir in the vanilla until smooth. Serve hot or cool, cover and store in the refrigerator.

Variation:
4 ounces of finely grated semi-sweet chocolate can be added and stirred in with the vanilla after removing the mixture from the heat.

Hint: Reheat in a pan of hot water and stir until smooth.

Butterscotch Sauce

Makes approximately 2 cups

1⅓ cups brown sugar
¾ cup light corn syrup
½ cup butter
2 tablespoons water
½ cup heavy cream

1. Mix together the sugar, corn syrup, butter and water in a saucepan and heat over medium. Stirring constantly,

continued on next page

bring this mixture to a boil, let it boil for a bit, but no more than 2 minutes. Remove from the heat, cool for a few minutes and then stir in the cream. Serve or store covered in the refrigerator. Reheat before using for best flavor.

Berry Sauce

Makes approximately 4 cups

2½-3 cups fresh berries
One 16-ounce bag of same or mixed frozen berries, thawed but not drained
¾ cup sugar
1 tablespoon fresh-squeezed lemon juice

1. Combine all ingredients in a saucepan and heat over medium heat until the mixture begins to simmer.
2. Lower the heat to low, stirring frequently until the sauce thickens.
3. Once the mixture has thickened, remove the pan from the heat, and pour into a bowl through a fine sieve to remove any seeds, cool and serve.

Fresh Lemon Sauce

Makes approximately 1½ cups

1 beaten egg
1 scant cup sugar
⅓ cup fresh-squeezed lemon juice
2 teaspoons lemon curd
Fresh-grated zest of 1 lemon
1-2 tablespoons butter

1. Over low heat, mix together the egg, sugar, juice and zest in a saucepan and stir constantly until thickened. Stir in the butter until melted and serve over cakes, puddings, fresh fruits and/or ice cream.

Strawberry Sauce

Makes approximately 1½ cups

1 quart fresh strawberries, stems removed and sliced ½-inch thick
⅓ cup water
1½-2 tablespoons cold water
1 tablespoon cornstarch
½ cup sugar
1 tablespoon vanilla

1. Put ⅓ cup water and the sugar into a sauce pan and bring to a boil over medium high heat. Allow this to boil for 5-6 minutes.
2. Mix the cornstarch into the remaining water and stir until completely dissolved. Slowly whisk this into the boiling water. Bring this mixture back to a boil and boil for 2-3 more minutes.
3. Remove the pan from the heat and gently fold the strawberries and vanilla into the syrup. Refrigerate the syrup until it cools, for up to 3 days.

To share

a part of oneself with another,

is the greatest gift

of all!

The Gourmet Mash for the Elder Horse

Have you ever wondered how you were going to continue feeding your horse of many years, once he or she got older? Their teeth begin falling out and thus they cannot continue to chew and digest the hay and grasses that they contently grazed upon throughout the years. Several years ago, I almost lost my buddy, my son of over 25 years, my horse Pal. While he was in the hospital it was discovered that age had taken most of his back teeth, thus, he was unable to chew adequately; so his diet, previously supplied by Mother Nature, had to be adjusted. I soon learned adequate foods to feed him were readily available as processed grains and pellets made of the same ingredients grown naturally in pastures and fields. So I developed the following recipe for his nutritional benefit. He has enjoyed it for several years, and often welcomes the opportunity to share it with his local friends—the deer; who help themselves to this lovely mash in his bucket on a daily basis. Evidently foods really are for sharing; no matter what age, species or flavor is served!

To be made twice a day, for breakfast and dinner.

EQUIPMENT:
Two 2 gallon buckets
1 large spatula or spoon to mix

MASH:
8-9 cups Middling Wheat Bran
2 cups whole oats
16-17 cups Equine Senior
4-6 cups Alfalfa pellets (6 cups in winter, 4 in spring and early fall, 2-3 cups in the summer)
1 tablespoon Sand Clear (to help pass the foods through)
1 scoop/tablespoon Corta-Flex, in the morning only (to help with the aches and pains of age)
¼ cup sugar
2-3 teaspoons salt
Warm water in cold months, cool water in warm months.
1-2 peppermints per meal

1. In one bucket, place the bran and oats, Sand Clear, Corta-Flex, sugar and salt. Mix this thoroughly together with water. Fill the bucket with water to just below the top rim.
2. In the other bucket, place the Equine Senior and Alfalfa Pellets and fill this bucket with water to just below the rim. (No need to mix this combination.)
3. Unwrap and feed the peppermints prior to pouring the mash into the feeding bucket.
4. Pour both buckets into the feeding bowl/bucket and watch the food disappear.

Variation:
For a treat on special occasions, such as birthdays and holidays you can mix a jar of organic baby food carrots or make your own pure carrot juice, (about ¼-½ cup) and mix it into the mash.

Substitutions and Equivalents

One of the most important sections of any recipe book is the Substitution section. How many times have you grabbed for an ingredient halfway through mixing a recipe and discovered you are out of it or do not have it? This has happened to me more times then I can count. The following is a list of substitutions and measuring equivalents that can be used in the recipes found among the previous pages, unless specified otherwise.

WHEN RECIPE CALLS FOR:	YOU CAN USE:
1 cup flour:	¾ cup plus 2 tablespoons whole wheat flour, or for a wheatless product use ¾ cup plus 2 tablespoons buckwheat flour mixed with 2 tablespoons quinoa flour
1 cup sugar:	1 cup of a sugar substitute such as Twin or Splenda When measuring, measure the substitute just below the cup line.
1 pound box powdered sugar:	3 ½ to 3 ¾ cups powdered sugar
1 tablespoon cornstarch:	2 tablespoons flour for thickening purposes
1 teaspoon baking powder:	½ teaspoon cream of tarter and ¼ teaspoon baking soda, for leavening purposes
2 ½ tablespoons tapioca:	Only use minute tapioca in these recipes. This is equivalent to 5 tablespoons pearl tapioca soaked in water or 2½ tablespoon flour
½ cup butter or margarine:	½ cup is equivalent to 8 tablespoons, 1 stick or a ¼ pound of butter or margarine. Unless specified otherwise one can be used in place of the other.
½ cup melted margarine:	Unless specified to use margarine only, ¼ cup of canola oil and ¼ cup melted margarine can be used instead of a ½ cup melted margarine. For reducing fat and cholesterol. This does not apply to butter
1 cup canola oil:	1 cup sunflower or safflower oil. Do not use corn oil, or any other kind of vegetable oil, olive oil or peanut oil.
1 cup milk:	½ cup evaporated milk mixed with ½ cup water

1 cup buttermilk:	1 tablespoon vinegar and enough milk to fill a cup or 2 tablespoons lemon juice and enough milk to fill a cup, or a cup of plain yogurt.
1 cup sour cream:	1 cup plain yogurt or 1 tablespoon lemon juice and enough evaporated milk to fill 1 cup
eggs:	Equivalent amount of liquid egg substitute; check the container for equal amount. 1 extra-large egg is equivalent to 2 medium eggs.
1 teaspoon lemon zest:	Zest is the grated rind of the lemon. 1 lemon rind will grate to equal 1 teaspoon. 1 lemon, when fully squeezed, will give you just shy of 2 tablespoons of lemon juice, ½ teaspoon of lemon extract is also equivalent to 1 teaspoon of lemon zest.
1 teaspoon or more of vanilla:	Only use pure vanilla extract or 1 teaspoon of Kahlua Liqueur.
1 square unsweetened chocolate:	3 tablespoons cocoa mixed with 1 tablespoon butter.
6 cups peeled and sliced peaches:	9-10 large peaches or 4 cans of sliced peaches drained of juice.
2 cups sliced fresh rhubarb:	1 pound fresh rhubarb
1 cup shredded cheese:	4-5 ounces of grated cheese
1 cup chopped walnuts and pecans:	Walnuts and pecans can be used interchangeably. 1 cup chopped is equivalent to about 5 ounces of pecans or about 6 ounces of walnuts.

The Alligator Pear

Let me tell you about The Alligator Pear. Oh boy is he good too.

He doesn't walk or talk but is fervent about pleasing.

And his dress can be decadent or plain, it is a matter of personal feasting.

He has a tendency to grow in warm moist areas, but is neither animal,
reptile nor amphibian!

He comes in only one color, but varies according to meridian.

He is round but long; skinny but fat; and even has a seed on the inside of his hat.

Do you know the Alligator pear, for he is found everywhere?

More than likely he hides in the grocery all dressed in green.

When you find him fully preened, please call him by his formal name,
his fame, his motto,

The Avocado.

Cooking Language Conversions found in this book

AMERICAN	BRITISH
Avocado	Alligator Pear
Canadian Bacon	Back Bacon
Sausage	Bangers
Beets	Beetroot
Blueberry	Bilberry
Sweet Cookie or Cracker	Biscuit
Beef Stock/broth	Brown Stock
Corned Beef	Bully Beef or pressed ham
French Fries	Chips
Chocolate Sprinkles	Chocolate Vermicelli
Meatballs	Faggots or Collops
Cilantro	Coriander Leaves
Corn	Maize and Sweetcorn
Corn Starch	Corn Flour
Romaine Lettuce	Cos
Zucchini	Courgette
Heavy Cream/Cream	Double cream
Light cream/Half and Half	Single cream
Potato Chips	Crisps
Brown sugar	Demerara
Drippings	Fat from roasted meats
Cupcake	Fairy

AMERICAN	BRITISH
Spatula	Fish Slice
Cornmeal	Maize Flour
Green Beans	French Beans
Ham	Gammon
Gingersnap	Gingernut
Corn syrup	Golden Syrup
Waxed Paper	Greaseproof Paper
Green Pepper	Bell Pepper
Red Pepper	Capsicum
Powdered Sugar	Icing Sugar
Pie Pan	Pie Dish
Seeds	Pips
Cooked Oatmeal	Porridge
Small Shrimp	Prawns
Dessert	Pudding
Sirloin	Rump Steak
Sweet Sherry	Sack
Seeded	Stoned
Golden Raisins	Sultanas
Pie	Tart
Molasses	Treacle
Tuna Fish	Tunny
Chicken or Fish Stock/Broth	White Stock
Wholewheat Flour	Wholemeal Flour

U.S. to Metric Conversions

OVEN TEMPERATURES

Fahrenheit	Celsius	Gas	
250° F	121° C	1	Low heat
325° F	162° C	3	Moderate heat
350° F	180° C	4	Moderate heat
375° F	191° C	5	Higher heat
400° F	205° C	6	High Heat
425° F	210° C	7	HOT
450° F	220° C	8	Very HOT

Basic Measurement Conversions - All measurements supplied have been rounded to the nearest 10th.

VOLUMES

U.S. measurement	Metric	Imperial
1 Tablespoon	15 ml	½ fl oz
2 Tablespoons	30 ml	1 fl oz
¼ cup (4 Tbls)	59 ml	2 fl oz
⅓ cup (6 Tbls)	79 ml	3 fl oz
½ cup (8 Tbls)	118 ml	4 fl oz
¾ cup (12 Tbls)	175 ml	6 fl oz
1 cup (16 Tbls)	237 ml	8 fl oz
1¼ cup	296 ml	10 fl oz
1⅓ cup	316 ml	11 fl oz
1½ cup	355 ml	12 fl oz
1¾ cup	415 ml	14 fl oz
2 cups (1 pint)	473 ml	16 fl oz
3 cups	710 ml	24 fl oz
4 cups (1 quart)	1000 ml (1 liter)	32 fl oz

Weights - All measurements supplied have been rounded to the nearest 10th.

WEIGHTS OF OUNCES TO GRAMS

Ounces	Grams	Ounces	Grams
¼ oz	7 grams	9 ounces	250 grams
½ ounce	15 grams	10 ounces	300 grams
1 ounce	28 grams	11 ounces	325 grams
2 ounces	57 grams	12 ounces	352 grams
3 ounces	85 grams	13 ounces	377 grams
4 ounces	113 grams	16 ounces	
5 ounces	142 grams	(1 pound) (1 liter)	454 grams
6 ounces	170 grams	24 ounces	750 grams
7 ounces	200 grams	32 ounces	900 grams
8 ounces	227 grams	35 ounces	1 kilogram

1 LB. Butter/Margarine

½ stick, ¼ cup, 2 oz.	56 grams
1 stick, ½ cup, 4 oz.	113 grams
2 sticks, 1 cup, 8 oz.	227 grams
4 sticks, 2 cups, 16 oz.	454 grams

Cream Cheese

1 block, 8 oz	226 grams
2 blocks, 1 pound or 32 ounces	454 grams

Yeast

1 dry package	1 tablespoon or 4 grams

ABBREVIATIONS
tbls: Tablespoon
ml: Milliliter
fl: Fluid Ounce
lb: Pound
oz: Ounces

TIPS AND HINTS
- When measuring flours, these measurements are based on all-purpose flours, not pre-sifted or self rising. Therefore, if a recipe calls for sifted flour, measure the all-purpose flour, sift it and then re-measure it.
- When using low gluten flours (not gluten free, just low in gluten) in higher elevations, add an additional 1.5-2 tablespoons of flour per cup, in addition to adding an extra egg white to the recipe.
- Self-raising flour contains 1½ teaspoons baking powder and ½ teaspoon salt per each cup of flour. Please adjust the baking powder accordingly; although, my suggestion is to avoid using self-rising flour in higher elevations, if possible.
- My suggestion is to avoid using self-rising flour in higher elevations if possible.
- FYI: US whole wheat flour is interchangeable with UK wholemeal flour.
- When these recipes indicate ½ cup milk, water or juice, use 4 ounces or a little more than 110 grams.

When converting these recipes to metric or imperial measurements, I have found the following formulas to be helpful and as close to accurate as possible per such measurement conversions.

Cups to milliliters:	multiply cups by 236.5
Cups to liters:	multiply cups by 0.236
Teaspoons to milliliters:	multiply teaspoons by 4.93
Tablespoons to milliliters:	multiply tablespoons by 15
Ounces to grams:	multiply ounces by 28.35
Grams to ounces:	multiply grams by 28.35
Fluid ounces to milliliters:	multiply ounces by 29.57
Milliliters to fluid ounces:	divide milliliters by 29.57

$\mathcal{I}ndex$

SUGAR *Sugar Free*

♥ *Low Fat and/or Low Cholesterol*

continued on next page

continued on next page

continued on next page

Notes